TIME BOMB

TIME BOMB

GRANT McKEE
AND
ROS FRANEY

With a Foreword by
Ludovic Kennedy

BLOOMSBURY

First published in Great Britain 1988
Copyright © 1988 by Grant McKee and Ros Franey

Bloomsbury Publishing Limited, 2 Soho Square,
London W1V 5DE

ISBN 0-7475-0099-1

Typeset by Rapid Communications Ltd, London WC1
Printed by Richard Clay Ltd, Bungay, Suffolk

Picture Credits

Terry Fincher page 4 bottom
Press Association page 1 top right, page 6 bottom left,
page 12 bottom right
Southern News Service page 4 top, page 12 top left
Universal Pictorial Press & Agency Limited page 12 bottom left

CONTENTS

FOREWORD

In the autumn of 1975 three young Irishmen and a teenage English girl were sentenced to life imprisonment for having planted in two Guildford public houses bombs which had subsequently exploded with horrific damage and loss of limb and life. The only evidence against the accused were 'confessions' which, the police said, they had made voluntarily. Their own accounts of how the confessions were obtained read rather differently. One of the accused, Gerry Conlon, after relating how the police spent several sessions calling him a fucking, murdering Irish bastard, squeezing his testicles, hitting him in the kidneys and slapping his face, said this:

> I was crying and frightened. Simmons said if I didn't make a statement, he would ring Belfast first thing in the morning and I would never see my mother or sister again. The last of my resistance shattered when he said this. I was crying and shaking uncontrollably. I said my family hadn't done anything. I fell apart. Simmons said what happened to my family was up to me. I said I would make a statement like they wanted, but it wouldn't be true as I really didn't do it...
>
> I started to write the statement, but as I hadn't done the bombing I didn't know what to write. [The police then fetched a statement made by another suspect, Paul Hill, and suggested he follow that.] I wrote a statement from what I read on Hill's. I just wanted to get it over. I didn't care any more. I was tired, frightened, and to tell the truth I was beginning to believe I had maybe done the fucking bombing. I just couldn't take it any more. It seemed easier to do what they wanted.

'Mum,' he wrote home later, 'we were fitted up something rotten.'

And this is what the teenage girl, Carole Richardson, said, after also alleging police brutality:

> The statements which I wrote were virtually dictated to me and I wrote down what they said and suggested to me. When I wrote out my statement, I did not know what to write. Longhurst asked me questions and made suggestions and would indicate that I write down what he said. I was forced to go along with what was happening because I was terrified of them and of what further treatment I would get if I continued to deny my involvement.

It has been my experience, in more than 30 years of studying miscarriages of criminal justice, that guilty people asserting innocence (which, contrary to popular belief, few do) express themselves differently from innocent people asserting innocence; and I would say that the two statements quoted above bear all the hallmarks of the innocent. The alternative — that the statements were made by hardened, professional killers from one of what the IRA calls its active service units — is in my view simply not credible.

Grant McKee and Ros Franey are not the first to be concerned about the convictions of the Guildford Four. Two of our most distinguished former judges, Lord Scarman and Lord Devlin, as well as the Cardinal Archbishop of Westminster, Basil Hume, have expressed doubts about the verdicts. Mr Alastair Logan, the defendants' dedicated solicitor, is totally convinced of their innocence. So is Mr Robert Kee, who wrote an earlier book on the case, *Trial and Error*. So are Lord Fitt and several MPs. So are Mr Brendan Dowd and Mr Joseph O'Connell of the IRA, two of the gang who actually planted the bombs, who admitted it while serving life sentences for other IRA activities and who say that the four convicted had nothing to do with it (or them) whatever. O'Connell was one of those captured after the siege of Balcombe Street, and, at the end of his own trial, angered that he had not also been prosecuted for the Guildford bombings (as he should have been), made this statement: 'We have instructed our lawyers to draw the attention of the court to the fact that four totally innocent people are serving massive sentences for three bombings, two in Guildford, one in Woolwich. The Director of Public Prosecutions was made aware of these submissions and has chosen to do nothing.' (Had he prosecuted, of course, the innocence of the Guildford Four might have been made plain.)

It was understandable, if not forgivable, that the Guildford police, aware of the sense of public outrage and anger brought about by the bombings, and under great pressure to find the perpetrators, should have deluded themselves into believing the guilt of the Guildford Four. It was less understandable that the four should have been convicted solely on the evidence of the disputed confessions (had the events taken place in Scotland, where corroboration of incriminating evidence is required, it is unlikely the four would have ever come to trial). What was unforgivable was the conduct of the Appeal Court judges, led by Lord Justice Roskill, when convened to hear Dowd's and O'Connell's evidence: first, in assessing it themselves, instead of sending the whole case back to a jury who could have considered it and the 'confessions' evidence together (a decision that greatly disturbed Lord Devlin); and, secondly, in the light of what Dowd and O'Connell had to say, in refusing to quash the convictions.

The ingenuity that Roskill displayed in explaining away the IRA men's meticulous evidence as to how they had planted the Guildford bombs was quite breathtaking. Although there was not a scrap of evidence to show that the IRA men had ever been in contact with any of the Guildford Four, Roskill came to the conclusion that this was a case of the IRA supporting the IRA, and with all the assurance of the truly blind declared that the Dowd/O'Connell evidence was 'a cunning and skilful attempt to deceive the court by putting forward false evidence'. He could find nothing to say by way of rebuttal of Dowd's statement that he had seen two old men with shopping-bags in one pub where he had planted a bomb, a truth known only to the police and not mentioned in any of the statements of the Guildford Four. Roskill dismissed the evidence of a scientist who said that the technical evidence of the Guildford bombings was in all respects similar to that of other bombings committed by the Balcombe Street gang, and referred to it contemptuously as 'allegedly scientific evidence of a Mr Yallop'. He said of the very sound alibi evidence for Carole Richardson given by her friends Frank Johnson (who also claimed to have been roughed up by the police) and Lisa Astin that it 'bore all the hallmarks of concoction'. He made a meal out of one or two minor inaccuracies in the evidence of Dowd, given some two years after the bombing (the make and colour of a hired car etc.), while blandly ignoring what the authors claim as 153 discrepancies and contradictions in the statements of the Guildford Four. And he finally concluded that while one or two of the IRA men might have been at Guildford, there was no evidence to show that the Guildford Four had not been there too.

Inevitably one has to ask, 'Why did Roskill and his colleagues, all intelligent, experienced men, allow common sense to desert them?' The answer is what it has always been, a deep reluctance on behalf of the judiciary to have to admit to major miscarriages of justice, especially where the verdicts rest on police evidence. It was, in my view, for the same reason that the Lord Chief Justice and two other judges recently dismissed the appeal of the six men convicted of the Birmingham pub bombings that occurred at about the same time; for as Lord Denning said in one of the hearings in which the six applied for legal aid:

> If the six men fail, it will mean that much time and money will have been expended by many people for no good purpose. If the six men win, it will mean that the police were guilty of perjury, that they were

> guilty of violence and threats, that the confessions were
> involuntary and were improperly admitted in evidence and
> that the convictions were erroneous. That would mean
> the Home Secretary would either have to recommend
> they be pardoned or he would have to remit the case
> to the Court of Appeal. *This is such an appalling
> vista that every sensible person in the land would
> say: it cannot be right that these actions go any
> further.*[1]

If that does not mean that it is better for convicted men who
may be innocent to rot in prison rather than allow the possibility
of police perjury, it is difficult to know what it does mean. So in
some cases the innocent can find themselves in double jeopardy:
where the police, deluding themselves into believing that a
suspect is guilty, corrupt themselves by taking unlawful steps to
ensure his conviction; and where Appeal Court judges, deluding
themselves into believing the police are incorruptible, declare
convictions to be safe and satisfactory which quite clearly are not.

In my experience, cases that go on demanding to be heard
years after all official hearings and appeals have been exhausted
are cases about innocent people. Guilty men do not have the
conviction or the motivation or indeed the acting skills to sustain
protestations of innocence for any length of time. It took 18
years for authority to admit that Oscar Slater had been wrongly
convicted and imprisoned, 16 years before Timothy Evans was
granted a posthumous free pardon, seven years before Patrick
Meehan was cleared of murder and another five before he was
granted £50,000 compensation.

The Guildford Four have now been in prison for 14 years.
Carole Richardson, 17 when she was arrested, is now 31 and
must soon despair of ever having children. Paul Hill claims that
his papers are marked 'Never to be released'. The only man
now who can bring about the release and rehabilitation of these
wretched people is the Home Secretary, who so far has shown

1 My italics.

as marked a reluctance as the judges to set the record straight. Let us hope, for the sake not only of the Guildford Four but of the much tarnished reputation of British criminal justice generally, that this new and convincing book on the case will persuade him and his advisers to have a change both of heart and of mind.

Ludovic Kennedy
July 1988

CHRONOLOGY

1973
November   Armstrong arrives London, settles Kilburn.

1974
July 20   Body of murdered British ex-soldier Brian Shaw discovered, Belfast.

early August   Dowd and O'Connell arrive London via Heathrow to set up IRA London Active Service Unit (ASU).

August 3   Gerry Conlon arrives England with girlfriend Eileen McCann.

23   Hill arrives England with sister Elizabeth and girlfriend Gina Clarke.

September 20   Hill and Conlon move to Hope House Catholic hostel, Kilburn.

21   Three members London ASU recce Guildford pubs.

29   Police search Armstrong and Richardson's squat, Linstead Street, Kilburn, for drugs.

October 5   Five members London ASU place time bombs in two Guildford pubs, the Horse and Groom and the Seven Stars: five killed.

6   150 detectives drafted into Guildford. Surrey Bomb Squad formed.

9   London ASU kidnaps Basil Dalton.

10   Duggan and Butler join London ASU.

11   London ASU bombs Victory Club and Army and Navy Club.

18   London ASU ties up two policemen, Semley Place car-park.

19   Conlon leaves Hope House hostel. Returns Belfast. Hill moves in with aunt and uncle, Anne and Frank

London ASU throws two bombs, Talbot Arms.

early December Hugh Doherty joins London ASU.

December 1 Squatters living with Armstrong at Algernon Road, Kilburn raid chemist's shop for drugs. Armstrong starts three-day drug-taking bout.

2 Guiseppe Conlon travels to England.
Gerry Conlon makes first admissions on Guildford.

3 Anne and Paddy Maguire, their children, Guiseppe Conlon and all at 43 Third Avenue, Harlesden arrested.
Richardson and Armstrong arrested. Paul Colman arrested.

4 Gerry Conlon sees solicitor and is charged with murder at Guildford.
Armstrong makes first admissions on Guildford.

5 Richardson makes first incriminating statement.

7 Richardson, Armstrong, Anne Maguire, Brian Anderson, Paul Colman and John McGuinness charged with murder.

9 IRA cease-fire talks, Feakle, County Clare.

11 Richardson and Armstrong see solicitors for first time.
House of Commons debates capital punishment.
London ASU bombs Naval and Military and Cavalry clubs.

14 London ASU shoot-out at Churchill Hotel.

17 London ASU bombs three telephone exchanges.

19 London ASU leaves bomb outside Selfridge's.

20 London ASU leaves bomb at Aldershot railway station.

21 London ASU bombs Harrods and the King's Arms, Warminster.

22 London ASU attempts assassination of Edward Heath.

23 Police discover IRA safe house, Southampton.

1975

January 19   London ASU shoot-out at Carlton Tower and Portman hotels.

23   London ASU bombs Woodford pumping station.

27   London ASU plants seven time bombs around London. Marks end of 'Phase One' of its campaign.

February 3   Sean Mullin acquitted of conspiracy to cause explosions, Guildford. Charges dropped against Anderson, McGuinness and Colman.

9   Provisional IRA announces cease-fire.

24   Murder charge against Anne Maguire dropped.

25   PC Stephen Tibble shot dead.

March 17   Committal opens, Guildford Four, Guildford.

20   Committal opens, Maguire Seven, Guildford.

April 15   Hill charged with Shaw murder, Belfast.

June 23   Hill convicted of murdering Shaw, Belfast.

July 10   Dowd and members of the Northern ASU arrested, Manchester.

August 27   Beginning of London ASU's 'Phase Two' bombings: time bomb at the Caterham Arms, Caterham, Surrey.

September 16   Guildford trial opens, Old Bailey.

October 17   Court of Appeal quashes convictions of four youths sentenced (largely on confession evidence) for murdering Maxwell Confait.

22   Armstrong, Conlon, Hill and Richardson convicted on confession evidence of murder, Guildford and Woolwich.

December 6   O'Connell, Duggan, Doherty and Butler hold Mr and Mrs Matthews hostage, Balcombe Street, London NW1.

12   Balcombe Street siege ends. London ASU members arrested.

1976

January 27   Maguire Seven trial opens, Old Bailey.

March 4   Maguire Seven found guilty of possession of nitroglycerine.

May 11   Dowd and members of the Northern ASU convicted.

October/   Alastair Logan and James Still interview Balcombe
November   Street men and Dowd in prison.

1977

January 24   Trial of Balcombe Street men opens, Old Bailey.

February 7   Balcombe Street men convicted.

July 20   Maguires' appeal opens, Old Bailey.

29   Maguires' appeal rejected.

October 10   Guildford appeal opens, Old Bailey.

28   Guildford appeal rejected.

1980

January 23   Guiseppe Conlon dies.

July 18   Cooper and McMahon released from prison after intervention of Lord Devlin and Ludovic Kennedy.

August 4   Guiseppe Conlon's case debated, House of Commons.

1983

December 20 Home Office rejects submissions on Dr Caddy's misgivings about the TLC test and other matters.

1984

March 6   'Aunt Annie's Bomb Factory' (*First Tuesday*, ITV) transmitted.

1985

February 22 Anne Maguire released from prison — last of the Maguire Seven to be set free.

May 13   Channel 4 shows RTE programme on the Maguire case.

17   Debate on the Maguire case, House of Lords.

1986

April 30   On behalf of the Home Office, independent psychiatrist and psychologist MacKeith and Gudjonsson interview Carole Richardson, Styal Prison.

July 1   'The Guildford Time Bomb' (*First Tuesday*, ITV) transmitted.

2   Home Secretary announces internal review of the Guildford case.

October 13 *Trial and Error* by Robert Kee published. Cardinal Hume, Lord Devlin and Lord Scarman write to *The Times* following publication.

1987

January 20 Home Secretary refers Birmingham Six case to Court of Appeal but announces neither Guildford nor Maguire case is to be remitted.

March 3   'A Case That Won't Go Away' (*First Tuesday*, ITV) transmitted.

4   Home Secretary agrees to examine new evidence in Guildford case.

July 23   Cardinal Hume leads delegation to Douglas Hurd; it includes former Home Secretaries Roy Jenkins and Merlyn Rees, and Law Lords Lord Devlin and Lord Scarman.

August 14   Home Secretary announces investigation into Guildford case by Avon and Somerset Police.

1988

January 28   Birmingham Six appeal rejected.

February 16 London ASU member William Quinn convicted of Tibble murder, Old Bailey.

April 14   Birmingham Six refused leave of appeal to the House of Lords.

PRINCIPAL CHARACTERS

Pte Caroline Slater, WRAC
Pte Ann Hamilton, WRAC
Guardsman William Forsyth, Scots Guards
Guardsman John Hunter, Scots Guards
Paul Craig
} Killed by bomb, Horse and Groom, Guildford, October 5 1974

Alan Horsley, barman
Gunner Richard Dunne, Royal Artillery
} Killed by bomb, King's Arms, Woolwich, November 7 1974

Hugh Doherty

Joseph O'Connell
Eddie Butler
Harry Duggan
} Members of IRA London Active Service Unit captured at Balcombe Street

Admitted bombing Guildford and Woolwich

Brendan Dowd
Sean Kinsella
Paul Norney
Stephen Nordone
Noel Gibson
} Members of Northern Active Service Unit captured in Manchester

Marion Coyle
Marlene Coyle
Eddie Gallagher
Joseph Gilhooley
Margaret McKearney
Kieran McMorrow
William Quinn
} Other IRA personnel allegedly on active service in England, 1974-75

Ronnie McCartney
'Walsh' (a pseudonym)
} Claimed to be the 'Belfast Boys'

Brian Keenan — Director of operations for mainland bombings, 1974

Daithi O'Conaill — Chief of Staff, IRA, 1974

Patrick Armstrong (Paddy)
Gerard Conlon (Gerry)
Paul Michael Hill
Carole Richardson
} Convicted of the Guildford and Woolwich bombings, 1975: the Guildford Four

Anne Maguire
Patrick Maguire (Paddy) — Her husband
Vincent Maguire
'Young Patrick' } Their sons
Patrick Joseph Conlon (Guiseppe) — Father of Gerard
Sean Smyth — Anne Maguire's brother
Patrick O'Neill — Maguire family friend
} Convicted of possession of nitroglycerine, 1976: the Maguire Seven

Paul Colman — Arrested at Algernon Road

Brian Anderson
John McGuinness
Sean Mullin — Arrested at Rondu Road
Robert Carlisle
Alastair Cully
} Charged with Guildford Four but charges dropped for lack of evidence

Not charged

Elizabeth Hill (Lily) — Paul Hill's mother
Anne Keenan
Theresa Smalley } Lily Hill's sisters
Frank Keenan
Errol Smalley } Their husbands
Elizabeth Hill — Paul's sister
Patrick Hill — Paul's brother
Eugenia Clarke (Gina) — Paul's girlfriend, 1974

Eileen Armstrong — Patrick Armstrong's mother

Anne Richardson — Carole Richardson's mother
Alan Docherty — Carole's stepfather

Sarah Conlon	Guiseppe's wife; Gerry's mother; Paddy Maguire's sister
Ann McKernan	Gerry's sister
Joe McKernan	Ann's husband
Hugh Maguire	Gerry's uncle
Kathleen Maguire (Kitty)	His wife
Sean Tully	Friend of Hugh Maguire
Fr Vincent McKinley	Canon of St Patrick's Procathedral and parish priest to the Conlons and the Armstrongs
Fr Denis Faul	Former mediator between Republican prisoners and the authorities. Campaigned to reopen the Guildford and Maguire cases
Peter Matthews	Chief Constable of Surrey, 1974
ACC Christopher Rowe	In charge of the Guildford investigation
DCS Walter (Wally) Simmons	Head of Surrey CID

Det. Sgt Anthony Jermey
Det. Supt Ronald Underwood
DCI Brian Richardson
DI Tim Blake
DCI Lionel Grundy
DC Peter Lewis
Det. Sgt John Donaldson   } Surrey detectives principally involved in interrogation of the Guildford Four, Anne Maguire and alibi witnesses
DC Vernon Attwell
DI Graham Powell
DCI Alan Longhurst
DC Martin Wise
WPC Anita Mills
DCI Thomas Style

Dr Kasimir Antoni Makos	Police doctor called to Carole Richardson in custody. Reported her first 'confession'
WPC Lesley Croxson	Accompanied him
Commander Bob Huntley	Head of the Metropolitan Police Bomb Squad, 1974

Chief Supt Jim Nevill	(Later Commander)	Involved in
Det. Supt Peter Imbert	(Later Metropolitan Police Commissioner, 1987-)	interrogations of Guildford Four, Maguires and
DCI David Munday	Metropolitan Police Bomb Squad	Balcombe Street ASU

DCS Albert James Cunningham, RUC		Investigating Shaw murder. Took Hill's statement. Questioned Conlon on arrest
DC John McCaul, RUC		

Sir John Donaldson	(Later Lord Donaldson, Master of the Rolls)	Guildford and Maguire trial judge
Mr Justice Cantley		Dowd and Balcombe Street trial judge
Lord Eustace Roskill		Leading appeal judge, Guildford and Maguire cases
Sir Michael Havers QC, MP	(Later Attorney General and Lord Chancellor, 1987)	Leading counsel for the prosecution, Guildford, Maguire and Balcombe Street trials and Guildford and Maguire appeals

Michael Hill QC	Junior Crown counsel, Guildford
Arthur Mildon QC	Leading counsel for Hill
John Leonard QC	Leading counsel for Armstrong
Eric Myers QC	Leading counsel for Richardson
Lord Wigoder QC	Leading counsel for Conlon
John Mathew QC	Leading counsel for the Crown, Balcombe Street trial
Ian Macdonald	Leading counsel for Joseph O'Connell, Balcombe Street trial
Ted Jones	Conlon family's first solicitor, Belfast
David Walsh	Solicitor's clerk dealing with Conlon's case (trial)

Brian Rose-Smith	Conlon's solicitor (appeal)
Gareth Peirce	Conlon's solicitor, 1987-
John Avey	Solicitor's clerk dealing with Richardson's case (trial and appeal)
David Melton	Solicitor's clerk dealing with Hill's case (trial and appeal)
Michael Fisher	Hill's solicitor, 1987-
Alastair Logan	Armstrong's solicitor, 1974- . Solicitor for Hill and Conlon, 1977-87. Solicitor for Richardson, 1985-

Robert Burns
Jimmy Cooper
Helen Jean Kettles } Witnesses chiefly relied on for 'courting couple', Horse and Groom
Jonathan Cook
Paul Lynskey
Julie Spooner

Simon Moodie	Doorman at South Bank Polytechnic	Saw Richardson arrive at the concert
William 'Mitch' Mitchell Ray Laidlaw	Members of Jack the Lad rock band	

Brian McLoughlin	Fellow squatter of Armstrong and Richardson	Prosecution witness

Fr Carolan Fr Ryan	Priests at Hope House hostel, Kilburn

Tom and Jacqueline Walker Thomas Leniston	Fellow squatters of Armstrong and Richardson	Armstrong's alibi witnesses

Francis Johnson (Frank) Elizabeth Astin (Lisa)	Friends of Carole Richardson	Richardson's alibi witnesses

Kathleen Crosbie	Gina Clarke's sister	Hill's Guildford alibi

Leslie Hutton Arthur Jones	Horse and Groom customers	The 'two old men' described by Dowd

John and Sheila Matthews	Tenants of 22B Balcombe Street, London NW1	Taken hostage by London ASU
James Still	Retired Superintendent, Metropolitan Police	Interviewed Balcombe Street men and Dowd for Guildford appeal
Brian Shaw	British ex-soldier, murdered in Belfast, 1974	
Martin Skillen	Friend of Hill. Shot in Belfast, 1974	
Hector Young	Acquitted of Shaw's murder	
Martin Monaghan	Convicted of conspiracy, Shaw case	
Douglas Higgs ⎫ Donald Lidstone ⎬	Principal scientific officers, Royal Arsenal Research and Development Establishment (RARDE). Crucial witnesses in Maguire and Balcombe Street trials	
John Yallop ⎫⎪⎪ Dr Brian Caddy ⎬	Former principal scientific officer, RARDE Strathclyde University	Disagreed with Higgs on TLC test (Maguire case)
Yvonne Fox ⎫ Malcolm Crosbie ⎬ Maura Kelly	Alibi witnesses for Hill Alibi witness for Richardson	Not heard in court
Professor Lionel Haward Barrie Irving Dr James MacKeith ⎫ Dr Gisli Gudjonsson ⎬	Surrey University (Later Director, Police Foundation) Royal Bethlem and Maudsley hospitals	Experts on confession evidence, concerned with the Guildford case
David Howell	MP for Guildford	
Douglas Hurd	Home Secretary, 1985-	
David Mellor	Parliamentary Under-Secretary of State, Home Office, 1983-86. Minister of State, Home Office, 1986-87	

Sir John Biggs-Davison	MP for Epping Forest	Politicians who
Lord Fitt	Former MP for West Belfast	campaigned to reopen the
Christopher Price	Former MP for Lewisham West	Guildford and Maguire cases
Roy Jenkins	Home Secretary, 1974-76	
Merlyn Rees	Secretary of State, Northern Ireland, 1974. Home Secretary 1976-79	Some of the public figures now calling for review of the
Cardinal Hume	Archbishop of Westminster	cases
Lord Devlin Lord Scarman	Law Lords	

NOTE

On August 14 1987 Douglas Hurd, the Home Secretary, announced that Avon and Somerset Police would conduct an inquiry into the Guildford and Woolwich bombings. The inquiry was officially concluded at the end of March 1988. Douglas Hurd told the House of Commons on July 21 1988 that he would be examining its findings during the summer parliamentary recess. This book records the history of the case.

INTRODUCTION

There is neither justice nor security in wrongful convictions. For the bereaved and the still suffering victims of the IRA bombings in Guildford and Woolwich in the autumn of 1974, it is harrowing that the matter can still not be laid to rest. But there is unfinished business. Our contention is that there has been a dreadful miscarriage of justice and that four innocent people are serving life sentences; that seven more innocent people were wrongfully imprisoned in an associated case; and that while some of the true perpetrators are behind bars, three guilty people remain at large.

We do not know the identities of the three missing bombers and nothing in the text should be construed as suggesting that we do. What is known and is recorded is that there are a number of people living in the Irish Republic who are still wanted by the police — on claims of fingerprint and other evidence — as terrorists who were operating in Britain during the time under review and who, for various reasons, have never been extradited.

At the heart of the trial of the four young people known as the Guildford Four lie serious allegations of impropriety against officers of Surrey Police. These were made under oath and attested to in open court and have been widely reported. It is stated categorically here and in the relevant chapters that the allegations were uniformly and absolutely denied by the officers concerned; that no supporting evidence was produced to uphold the allegations; and that the jury wholly rejected all the allegations. We do not now rely on those claims of impropriety in making the case that the confessions of the Guildford Four were false.

In our contention that there has been a miscarriage of justice we trust that we have omitted nothing that is inconvenient to that contention; that this is a 'warts and all' account. This book is not an apologia for anyone who thinks that an English public house is a legitimate bombing target. The authors have no connection with or sympathy for the IRA or the resort to violence for political ends in Northern Ireland. At the outset we invited the present Chief Constable of Surrey to tell us of anything, inadmissible or otherwise, that might cause us to see the case in a different light. Nothing was proffered. The official position of Surrey Police on the whole affair remains that the matter was properly put before judge and jury. Today, as in 1974, the sole evidence against the Guildford Four consists of their uncorroborated confessions to the police.

Our sources have been official wherever possible: court transcripts, sworn statements and affidavits, lawyers' records. The fullest newspaper reports of the relevant trials are to be found in the *Surrey Daily Advertiser* and the *Guardian*. We have kindly been granted much access to personal correspondence and to unattributable briefings from senior police officers and intelligence sources. Where information comes solely from an unattributable source this is indicated. There is no invented dialogue.

There are numerous debts of acknowledgement and gratitude. We record particularly our thanks to Barry Cox and John Shirley for access to their unpublished work on the Balcombe Street Active Service Unit and their exclusive information on the culminating siege. Other journalists such as Gavin Esler, David McKittrick and Chris Mullin first recognized the importance of the case. Tom McGurk brought the story to Yorkshire Television via Jonathan Dimbleby. Invaluable help has followed from Peter Chippindale, David Frost, Mary Holland, Robert Kee, Ludovic Kennedy, Anne McHardy, Olivia O'Leary and Bob Woffinden. Gareth Peirce, in particular, has given generously of her expertise. At Yorkshire Television John Willis has been an inspiration for four years. We also wish to thank Ronan Bennett, Sir John Biggs-Davison, Dr Brian Caddy, Sister Sarah Clarke, Irene Cockroft, Lord Devlin, Father Denis Faul, John Fairley,

Michael Fisher, Professor Lionel Haward, Cardinal Basil Hume, Barrie Irving, Father Vincent McKinley, Peter Newby, Frank Pocklington, Christopher Price, Merlyn Rees, Brian Rose-Smith and Father Paddy Victory. Our thanks also to others in England and Ireland, whom we have undertaken not to name. Penny Phillips, David Reynolds and Alan Wherry at Bloomsbury have been patient and supportive and so too, more personally, have been Jamie Lane, Jill Turton, Geoffrey Winter and our families.

Alastair Logan, Guildford solicitor, is the rock upon which everything has been built. He still practises in Guildford, where he originally took the case by chance, and has worked on unpaid — and to some opprobrium — for more than a decade. When the Guildford Four are released his commitment will be fully recognized. But for his conscience, tenacity and sacrifice their case would be long forgotten. We thank him for his trust.

Equally, we thank and pay tribute to all those at the heart of the case — relatives, friends and witnesses — who have had the courage and integrity to endure throughout 14 years: they will be vindicated too. In particular, the loyalty of Lisa Astin and Frank Johnson has been a profound example to us.

Our gratitude to those cited does not imply that any of them necessarily shares in our interpretations or conclusions, much less in any mistakes we may have made.

We dedicate the book to Patrick Armstrong, Gerard Conlon, Paul Hill and Carole Richardson.

Grant McKee
Ros Franey
August 1 1988

1
A FUNERAL IN COUNTY CLARE

'This is something deep in their hearts; inherent in their blood. I tell them what is right but I cannot force them on to that path. I pray to God that it will end.'

Father Michael Keating, parish priest, Feakle, County Clare

By rights, Father Keating should have officiated at Harry Duggan's funeral. Harry was a local boy, approaching his 21st birthday.

It was the autumn of 1973 and Harry Duggan senior was the first to be told of his son's death. Details were sketchy but it seemed there had been some sort of explosion across the border; a Provo bomb had detonated prematurely; Harry had been involved; Harry was dead. In security-force shorthand it had been an 'own goal'.

There were no lengthy death notices in the Republican prints, no Irish tricolour draped over the coffin, no tattered volley of small-arms fire by an honour guard of hooded paramilitaries. The funeral was so private that neither Father Keating nor Harry senior or Bridget Duggan was invited. An unmarked grave appeared overnight in Feakle cemetery, and it was accepted locally that Duggan had died on active IRA service; that the burial had been kept secret to deprive the British of a small propaganda victory and to preserve the morale of other volunteers.

It was an IRA tactic that dated back as far as 1921 when the Black-and-Tans had dug up three unmarked IRA graves in a field in Limerick and reburied the bodies; even after death the struggle continued. Secret funerals were thought to be used by all sides in the present 'Troubles': Protestant paramilitaries occasionally buried their dead covertly to minimize their casualties; there was a strong Republican suspicion that the British Army attributed some deaths to training accidents in Germany for the same reason; and now the Provos were at it again.

This time, however, the IRA played a variation on the old trick. They put it about on the streets of Bogside and West Belfast that a Southern volunteer called Harry Duggan had been killed. The secret burial became public knowledge in Republican communities and, as intended by the Provisionals, the rumour was taken out of the ghettos by touts, the informers who plagued IRA security, and passed on to the security forces. Gradually the rumour became accepted fact, and no one yet bothered to disinter the fresh mound in Feakle cemetery.

There had been an explosion, and some young Provo had been blown to unrecognizable bits on top of his own bomb — but it was not Harry Duggan. Volunteer Harry Duggan was alive and well and ready to go on active service again, this time as Michael Wilson. The Army Council was putting together a crack team for a job on the British mainland, and they would have been delighted to know that Duggan's 'death' was registered on the list of subversives held at the Harcourt Square headquarters of C3 in Dublin. The Irish Republic's counter-terrorist agency regularly contacted the Metropolitan Police in London with the names of likely young Republicans known to be 'missing from home' for unusually long periods of time.

One day that same autumn George DeMeo, a 40-year-old Sicilian arms-supplier from Yonkers, New York, parked his Cadillac and walked into the B and B gunshop in Winston, North Carolina — a routine call. DeMeo was connected to the powerful Mafia family of Colombo. He had twice successfully fought off charges of illegally running weapons to anti-Castro forces, Haitian revolutionaries and rebels in Chad. With the agreement of Howard Bruton, the owner of the B and B,

DeMeo bought a consignment of guns under a series of names of dead and fictitious persons and drove the load back to New York.

Using a bill of lading under the name of Standard Tools Inc., with the address of a garage of a middle-aged couple in New York's Bronx, DeMeo shipped the arms in containers to Northern Ireland and the Irish Republic, along with ammunition stolen from the US Marine Corps base at Camp Lejeune, North Carolina. Both the US Customs and the New York dockers had been sufficiently infiltrated by Republican sympathizers for the containers to pass unopened.

The system was so apparently foolproof that DeMeo did not bother with the precaution of removing the serial numbers of the weapons. Among the 1973 assignment were Armalite AR180 rifles, ideal for this sort of shipment as each weighed only seven pounds and could be broken down into four parts and concealed easily among machinery spare parts. A conversion kit, easily obtainable from an American gunshop, turned a civilian issue Armalite into a fully automatic military M16 with a muzzle velocity of 3,250 feet per second, powerful enough to penetrate the flak jacket of a British Army soldier. George DeMeo would not have known it, but Armalite number SP 12641 was bound for Harry Duggan.

The raw material for bombs in 1973 came from closer to home — from Irish Industrial Explosives Ltd in the small town of Enfield, on the border of County Meath and County Kildare, 20 miles west of Dublin. Here was the main supply point for quarrying explosives both north and south of the border. There was security, of course. All the gelignite was colour-coded and quantified according to the quarry of destination, and consignments sent to Northern Ireland were escorted by the Royal Ulster Constabulary. Nevertheless, workers simply carried gelignite out in their lunch-boxes. Three short sticks of solidified nitroglycerine could fit into a trouser pocket or the false bottom of a briefcase and, in the days before vapour-detectors at airports, could be carried safely into England. Eversoft Frangex was the IRA's preferred variety.

The man who brought together the volunteer, the Armalite and the explosives was one of the least known but most important Provisionals of the 1970s — Brian Keenan, at 32 an IRA 'General', the Dublin-based quartermaster of the entire Provo effort. Keenan had been born and brought up in South Derry. In West Belfast he had become a highly successful quartermaster for the Belfast Brigade, earning a reputation as cool and intelligent; an astute planner. It had been a key posting. When violence flared in Belfast in 1969, the IRA could boast only a dozen rifles in the city. Keenan was instrumental in changing that and is credited with establishing the IRA's productive Libyan arms link with Colonel Qaddafi.

Keenan had come comparatively late to prominence in the IRA. In the 1960s he had moved to England and worked as a television repair man in the Midlands around Northampton, collecting a minor theft conviction for breaking into a cigarette machine in Luton (on which he left his fingerprints). His electronic expertise got him a job on the Grundig production line in Belfast. It is not known when he joined the IRA, but he quickly established himself as a trade-union activist and when internment was introduced in 1971 Keenan soon left Belfast for the South. The socialism demanded by the IRA *Green Book* of rules was wishful thinking in the case of most volunteers from the North, but not with Brian Keenan, a fully-fledged Marxist. He described the IRA's campaign as 'the most important anti-capitalist struggle in Europe'. By the time of his eventual arrest in 1979, he had risen to become Deputy Chief of Staff and was so highly valued by the Army Council that they — unsuccessfully — attempted to spring him from Brixton Prison by helicopter.

In 1973 Keenan was entrusted with a new role by Dublin command — that of Director of Operations for mainland bombing and, in particular, with forming the Provisional IRA's next London Active Service Unit. It was going to bomb Britain as Britain had never been bombed before, and it was not to repeat the mistakes of the Price Sisters fiasco earlier that year when several members of a bombing team, including Marion and Dolours Price, had been arrested at Heathrow awaiting take-off for Ireland just as three car bombs were primed to explode in central London. To have the bombers attempting to leave Britain on the day of the bombings, albeit before the bombs were due to explode, had been incompetent planning. The sealing of ports and airports was always the first reaction to any suspected terrorist activity on the mainland.

Keenan's plan was to put together a team with the patience and skill to integrate themselves fully into living in London full-time like secret agents behind enemy lines; not a one-off hit-and-run team but an undercover unit who could sustain a long-term bombing campaign and survive long spells of inactivity. Except in dire emergencies, they would have no contact with the established Irish Republican movement in London — a prime target for Special Branch monitoring. They would operate on their own initiative as far as possible to minimize contact with Dublin and the risk of being uncovered by informers. They would select their own targets and times, working to a predetermined strategy of hitting military, establishment and economic institutions. Details of fresh targets, as well as supplies and funds, would be brought into England by couriers. Keenan dispatched a former British paratrooper, Peter McMullen, for the initial military reconnaissance.

The men chosen for the Active Service Unit would have to have minimal 'form' and would come preferably from the South, from the Republic — so many young men in Belfast and Londonderry were routinely picked up and 'screened' by the security forces regarding their and their friends' movements that volunteers from the North represented an unacceptable risk. Besides, the Dublin commanders who were still running the IRA in 1973 were not impressed by the general calibre of volunteers offered up by the North as illustrated by the Price Sisters fiasco. This also suited the Belfast commanders. They doubted the wisdom of running another mainland campaign and had no desire to offer up their best volunteers for a Dublin plan when they were stretched to the limit by internment and the courts. In 1973 and 1974 the authorities had charged 2,700 people from the North with terrorist offences. Nevertheless, the preference for using men from the South was not exclusive; Keenan himself was a Northerner.

He wanted men of commando quality and his trawl concentrated on the south-west triangle of counties Clare, Limerick and Kerry where the IRA's roots ran back to the beginning of the century. In his view, the most reliable men came from families with an unbroken tradition of Republican action and sympathy; men with cross-border experience who were unknown to the British security forces. A shortlist of 20 was drawn up and vetted by the Army Council. Initial training was borrowed from the British Army. The men were dropped in open countryside and instructed to survive by living rough for three days. A more selective explosives course followed.

The principal members of the Active Service Unit put together by Keenan all had experience in laying mines and placing bombs across the border in the 'bandit country' of South Armagh. Each agreed to an undercover assignment in London, with an option of pulling out after three months.

They were the 'late' Harry Duggan, now 21, of Feakle, County Clare; Martin Joseph O'Connell, 21, of Kilkee, County Clare; Edward Butler, 24, of Castleconnell, County Limerick; Brendan Dowd (sometimes known as O'Dowd), 24, of Tralee, County Kerry; and Hugh Doherty, 22, originally from the Irish-Catholic estate of Toryglen in Glasgow but brought up principally in County Donegal. A sixth man cannot be named definitively. They became the hard core of the London ASU, but there were more to be added to their number. Two young and trusted women were lined up as the main couriers. A middle-class Dublin woman known only as Graine, Grainne or 'Cirainne' was appointed co-ordinator. They would operate a classical cell structure. As few people as possible, even in the highest echelons of the IRA, would know who they were. They were destined to become the most devastatingly successful team the IRA has ever assembled.

Harry Duggan typified the gang in the apparent sublime innocence of his home background: his upbringing with two brothers and a sister in a stone farmworker's cottage in the backwoods of County Clare, and an unremarkable school career in the two-room Bodyke National School, near Feakle. He was good at sport and carpentry; remembered in his village as quiet, law-abiding and baby-faced. Duggan followed his father as an apprentice in the Scariff Chipboard kitchen furniture factory in Ennis, proving competent enough to have his period of apprenticeship cut from five years to three. He was also reputed to be rather lazy, with a penchant for sleeping in as long as possible and an ability to make people laugh. He was athletically built, six feet tall and liked to wear his dark hair long.

Sometimes he shared a flat with Joseph O'Connell in Lower Market Street in the county town of Ennis. He knew Eddie Butler too. Sometimes he sold *An Phoblacht*, the Sinn Fein newspaper, in the local bars — not a remarkable sight in those parts. He applied to emigrate to Canada but was turned down. Then he went on a trip to Dublin and was never seen at home again. His mother, Bridget, who had separated from Harry Duggan senior, had not seen him since 1970.

The transition from country boy to effective terrorist was fast. There are unsubstantiated reports of his involvement in cross-border raids and sniping at the British Army, but one exploit soon after his manufactured 'death' marked him down as being of the required calibre for Brian Keenan's ASU. He was one of the team who pulled off one of the world's most lucrative robberies.

On April 26 1974 four armed men and a woman rang the front doorbell of Russborough House in Blessington, County Wicklow, the stately home of 71-year-old Sir Alfred Beit, heir to a South African gold and diamond fortune, a former Conservative MP and, more famously, the owner of one of the world's most valuable private art collections. The IRA gang burst into the hall and within five minutes had rounded up the Beits and the five members of staff, dragged them into the library at gunpoint and tied them up with nylon stockings. Sir Alfred was accused of being a 'capitalist pig' and of 'exploiting workers' and was struck on the side of the head with the butt of a revolver. Lady Beit was bound hand and foot and left in the cellar. No one had a chance to press the alarm that linked Russborough House to the local Naas police station.

The gang forced staff to explain the alarm system, deactivated it and proceeded to cut 19 Old Master paintings from their frames with a screwdriver. They included three Rubens, two Gainsboroughs, a Goya, a Vermeer and a Velasquez. Within a further five minutes the gang had escaped, in a silver-grey Ford Cortina. The paintings, valued at between £8,000,000 and £10,000,000, were obviously impossible to sell, and three days later came a written ransom demand for £500,000 and for the return of the Price sisters and two of their colleagues from English prisons — where they were on hunger strike — to Northern Ireland.

The demand was ignored, and 10 days after the robbery the haul was recovered at a rented cottage in Glandore, County Cork. With it, caught red-handed, was Dr Bridget Rose Dugdale, the 32-year-old daughter of a millionaire English landowner. She was already wanted by the Manchester police for suspected arms-smuggling into Northern Ireland and by the RUC for the extraordinary bombing attempt on Strabane police station when milk-churns packed with explosives had been dropped (missing their target) from a hijacked helicopter.

Another member of the Beit robbery gang had spent the night in the cottage at Glandore and had left just before the gardai arrived. Dr Dugdale was duly convicted of handling the stolen paintings, but the name of Harry Duggan was never associated with the crime. He next proved his mettle under pressure when he was holed up with another IRA man in an abandoned house at Charleston, County Mayo and, surrounded by police, shot his way out. He left behind his fingerprints but they were not identified until years later.

A young country carpenter had turned into a fearless guerrilla. Harry Duggan went to war against the British with a sense of injustice partly instinctive and partly inculcated. He had found an escape from rural privation and an exciting identity which merged rapidly into a fanatical adventure. The laughing, baby-faced boy was destined to be described by one of his later hostages as a 'cold-blooded psychopath'.

Such a transition is enigmatic to a British mentality. Perhaps Father Keating understood it best as a matter of heart and blood. At any rate, Harry Duggan was now set on an irreversible course of multiple killings that could lead only and surely to a lifetime in a British prison, a sacrifice for the cause. He must have known it and embraced it. His colleagues were much the same.

Joseph O'Connell's parents were County Clare farmers and the family lived in a little blue and white bungalow outside Kilkee, overlooking the Atlantic near the mouth of the River Shannon. The area is a stronghold of Gaelic-speaking inhabitants and old-guard IRA sympathizers. Joseph was a good all-round pupil at Querrin Vocational School in County Clare, a skilful footballer and a ready learner. He had no difficulty in getting a job as a radio operator and electronics trainee at Marconi in Cork.

Joe was invariably well dressed, of medium height and build; his face was markedly thin and sharp. He is remembered locally for his quiet, almost shy manner combined with a thoughtful intelligence and ready wit. Active Republicanism was well established in the family. His younger brother Michael served a year in prison for possessing explosives and for IRA membership. Joe O'Connell remained a practising Catholic, and at one stage was thought to have a vocation for the priesthood. He was widely-read, totally committed and clearly had leadership potential. Already he was a training officer in the Republic, but for the

London mission, under the assumed identity of John O'Brien, he was the explosives expert.

Eddie Butler, one of four brothers from Castleconnell, a prized salmon-fishing haunt on the east bank of the Shannon, was the only one with a criminal record. As a youth, he had been caught daubing anti-British and pro-Republican graffiti on the roads near his home in County Limerick. He was never chased up to pay the fine. Butler settled down after that — there were bigger jobs to be done — and joined the Provisionals in 1972. He was tough and burly, but his physical presence went with a country wariness: he was not given to Republican tirades or any form of flashiness. The last man the IRA would expect to crack under police interrogation, he was, however, frightened of flying. Butler enjoyed going to the cinema and watching football. He was the dependable back-up man, whose job would regularly entail providing covering fire with a Sten-gun on the Unit's missions.

Hugh Doherty, born in Glasgow, was ostensibly the odd man out, but his Irish roots stood out as much as his red hair and beard. His family, like many others, had migrated from the Irish Republic to Scotland to look for work shortly after the Second World War. They had ended up on the dingy council estate of Crossbank Road, Toryglen, in Glasgow, in conditions almost as sectarian as those of a Northern Ireland city. Every year the Dohertys spent their holidays in their home fishing village of Carrickart, County Donegal, in the narrow north-western spit of the Republic — less than 30 miles from Londonderry and 'The Troubles'. Doherty eventually settled there with his elder brother, leaving behind another brother and five sisters. Donegal is correctly reputed to be a frontline recruiting ground for the Provisionals. Doherty was the altar-boy who left school at 15; who became an itinerant building-site labourer, twice in London — including a spell as a joiner for Cubitt's on the Plumstead flyover, Woolwich — and also in Dublin; who was, according to Brian Keenan, who recognized a fellow ideologue, 'a very deep friend'; who became a Provo volunteer. He would return to Glasgow to pick up stolen bank books and a driving licence that would provide one of his aliases: Don Joseph Kelly.

The acknowledged first boss of the Unit was Brendan Dowd: 'Big Bren', an imposing six-footer. He was the nerveless leader-by-example. He was brought up the youngest of a family of seven brothers and seven sisters (six of whom died) in a small-holder's cottage at Raheeny, near the riverside town of Tralee on the Dingle Peninsula, home of the famous 'Rose of Tralee' beauty contest. His father, a retired forestry worker, was a member of Sinn Fein and his mother was equally committed. Unswerving family loyalty to 'the cause' and to 'the boys' was enjoyed by all the members of the Unit.

There was plenty of Republican reading matter in the cottage and Dowd was a voracious reader as a youngster, especially fascinated by geography, but his academic career was short-lived. En route to enlisting with the Provisionals he became a crane-driver and motor mechanic, a line of work that led him to travel frequently to England. His expertise with vehicles would later be adapted to serve an additional skill — stealing cars — but his principal job was to establish the London Active Service Unit and, once that was operating effectively, to set up further ASUs elsewhere on the mainland. He would first become John O'Shea and then Dennis Power, postgraduate student.

Dowd and O'Connell were the first to arrive on the mainland, crossing from Shannon to Heathrow in early August 1974. If anyone wanted to know their business, the prearranged cover story was simply that they were country Irishmen looking for work. Once in London, they headed for Fulham, where there were enough Irish residents not to make them conspicuous but not so many as to constitute an obvious community like that in Kilburn, where Irish gregariousness and police interest could put them at risk. They rented a twin bed-sit flat at 21 Waldemar Avenue, close to the junction of Fulham Road and Fulham Palace Road. A third, unnamed man joined them shortly after. The £10 weekly rent was paid with scrupulous punctuality. They were polite to the neighbours but never stopped to encourage conversations on the doorstep or in the hallway. They left and returned at regular hours as if going to work. They were seen to be smartly but casually dressed. The first of a succession of 'safe houses' was thus quietly established.

2
ON ACTIVE SERVICE

'I would like to say as I am going before my God, as I am condemned to death, I am innocent, and later I am sure it will all come out that I had neither hand, act nor part in it. That is all I have to say.'

Peter Barnes, sentenced at the Old Bailey to hang as an accessory to the IRA bombing campaign in England, 1939

The IRA rationale for bombing Britain is, of course, rooted in history; history that long pre-dates the formation of the IRA.

In 1867 a group of Fenians planted a bomb at Clerkenwell Prison in London in an unsuccessful attempt to spring a colleague. It killed 12 people and moved Ireland to the top of the British political agenda of the day, thus giving birth to the Republican notion that one bomb in Britain is worth 100 bombs in Belfast. Both the truth and the fallacy of the argument hold good today.

A bomb on 'England's sod' has always commanded overwhelmingly greater press and public reaction than any explosion in Ireland, either north or south of the border. The corollary has also been vehement anti-Irish emotion, with stiff anti-terrorist legislation and a redoubled political will set against concessions in the face of violence. British politicians understand their electorate well enough to know that there have never been votes in being seen to bow to terrorism. Historically, the IRA has won nothing of political substance from its various bombing campaigns, unless it believes that the death and destruction caused have been worth it for keeping the issue of Republicanism alive and for the winning of internal propaganda victories. It has done signally little to persuade the British public of the merits of the cause — and much to alienate them from it.

Nevertheless, the IRA has, at irregular intervals, brought the war to Britain. In 1936 Sean Russell, a member of the IRA's Army Council, announced to the *Daily Mirror*: 'Then, over in England, where we shall also take the offensive, we have another secret Army of Irishmen who meet quietly, for drill and target practice. We have also quantities of ammunition and other war material in England. Our Air Force may be small, but it is reasonably efficient. When hostilities start we shall certainly send planes to bomb England... '

The surreal notion of an IRA air force fostered the rumour that supporters in New York were going to sponsor a transatlantic bomber to blitz the House of Commons before crash-landing in France because the plane would not have enough fuel to fly back across the Atlantic. Nothing transpired of these grandiose plans, but in 1939 a sustained conventional campaign was mounted.

A 12-man team dispersed to Glasgow, Liverpool, Manchester, Birmingham and London. An ultimatum calling for British withdrawal from Ireland was sent to the British Government (and, for good measure, to Hitler and Mussolini). It went unanswered, and between January and August there followed 127 attacks and six fatalities, five from a single explosion in Coventry. The targets were railway termini, broadcasting and military installations, letter-boxes and telephone-boxes and gas and electricity stations. Young women volunteers released tear-gas in crowded cinemas.

Sixty-six people were convicted, and Frank Richards and Peter Barnes were sent to the scaffold for their parts in the Coventry explosion. Barnes's part was his being found with a receipt for a flour-bag and suitcases used subsequently in the bombing. He had no proven part in the making or placing of the bomb and was nowhere near Coventry when it went off.

The political repercussions were swift on both sides of the Irish Sea. De Valera, the Irish Premier, denounced the bombings;

the IRA was outlawed and the Offences Against the State
Act, allowing detention without trial, was passed. In Britain,
Parliament enacted the Prevention of Violence (Temporary
Provisions) Bill, giving police the right to hold suspects for five
days without warrant or charge and empowering the Home
Secretary to expel and prohibit suspects from the country. The
bombing campaign petered out in 1940, to be supplanted by
Hitler's blitz.

Apart from perpetrating some maverick attempts to raid
weapons stores in the 1950s and 1960s, the IRA did not re-
emerge in Britain until well into the current era of violence. In
1972 the Official IRA bombed the military garrison at Aldershot
in a claimed reprisal for the Catholic deaths on Londonderry's
Bloody Sunday. The bomb killed a Roman Catholic chaplain,
five cleaning-women and a gardener — a catastrophic outcome
which prompted the Officials to order a cease-fire for an indefi-
nite period.

By now the Provisional IRA had taken over the military
side of the campaign, considering the Officials to have reneged
on the true principles of 32-county Republicanism and to have
failed to defend the Belfast Catholic ghettos against the waves
of Protestant attacks in 1969. The split was formalized in 1970,
and the Provisionals' first mainland bombings followed in 1972
with the Price sisters' car bombs in Whitehall and the Old Bailey.
Further bombs were defused outside Scotland Yard and the
headquarters of the British Forces Broadcasting Services. There
was one death and 180 injuries as a result of the explosions.

Later in 1972 came the event that initiated a sustained
campaign — the disastrously brief summer cease-fire, negoti-
ated directly between the British Conservative Government
and the most powerful figures in the Provisional IRA in the first
such direct talks since those between Michael Collins and Lloyd
George.

Sean MacStiofain, Daithi O'Conaill, Seamus Twomey, Martin
McGuinness and Gerry Adams, who between them held down
all the key posts in the Provisionals' command structure, found

themselves on board an RAF Andover bound for England. On arrival they were driven to one of London's most exclusive addresses, Cheyne Walk in Chelsea, where luminaries as various (and as wealthy) as Mick Jagger and John Paul Getty junior have lived. Number 93 was the home of Paul Channon MP, a millionaire Guinness heir and a junior Minister in the Northern Ireland Office. The Secretary of State for Northern Ireland, William Whitelaw, invited the Provos to list their grievances.

By the end of this extraordinary meeting the two sides had hammered out a fragile cease-fire, which lasted two days and was ended by a fracas — provoked by the IRA — on the Lenadoon estate in West Belfast with troops firing rubber bullets into a Catholic crowd. But, according to the IRA delegation in Chelsea, Whitelaw had made a throwaway remark that revealed an attitude of cold expediency towards 'The Troubles'. 'We can accept the casualties,' Whitelaw is claimed to have said. 'We probably lose as many soldiers in accidents in Germany.' More than one member of the delegation is supposed to have determined in that instant to bomb Britain to test the theory of an acceptable rate of casualties.

In 1973 and 1974 a number of one-off attacks took place: 40 schoolchildren were injured and a woman killed by a blast at the Tower of London (the standing instruction to avoid 'innocent' victims has been interpreted loosely throughout the history of the mainland campaigns). Peter McMullen, the defecting paratrooper, had meanwhile linked up with 'English Joe' Gilhooley, from Moss Side in Manchester, who had settled in Dublin, adopted Irish citizenship and become another of Brian Keenan's chosen bombers. The two men coolly walked through the front gates of Claro Barracks in Yorkshire, a base of the Royal Engineers, and planted a time bomb which injured a woman canteen worker.

These bombings coincided with a spate of mainland letter-bomb attacks, involving another man whom Keenan would attach to the London Active Service Unit — William Joseph Quinn. Quinn was the second son of Juanita Gonzales and Jim

Quinn, and had been born and brought up in the Irish-American district of Sunset in San Francisco — an American citizen. Juanita, a school clerk, was Mexican; Jim, a car mechanic, was Irish; both were then non-political Catholics. They divorced when William was four years old and he went to live with his mother. He appeared a model child, serving as an altar-boy at Holy Name Church and working on a morning newspaper round before school. His school career was unremarkable; he is recalled only for his talent as an athlete and for his earnest, soft-spoken nature. He dropped out of High School at 11th grade in his last year, in 1967, but subsequently earned an 'equivalency' degree. These were heady times in California, and in San Francisco in particular, but William Quinn was not to be seen on the Berkeley campus demonstrating against the Vietnam War or taking wing with the first LSD generation in Haight-Ashbury. Instead, he was rediscovering his Irish roots. He immersed himself in Irish history and politics; after his day-shift as a clerk with the US Mail he taught himself Gaelic and attended Irish-dancing evening classes.

By 1970 what Quinn saw on the television news from Belfast and Londonderry spurred him into active Republicanism. He had always avoided the romantic Irish nationalist bars of the Mission and Richmond districts, where the walls were festooned with IRA ephemera and posters but the clientele's bravery was measured according to the intake of imported Guinness. Instead, he and another man, Seamus Gibney, co-founded the San Francisco chapter of the Irish Northern Aid Committee, ostensibly a fund-raising body for the families of imprisoned Republicans in Northern Ireland, but better known as Noraid, the transparent front for Provisional gun-running. In 1971 he quit his job with the US Mail and left for Ireland: 'I saw it as the struggle that had lasted for 100 years being resumed again.'

Seamus Gibney tried to talk him out of it: 'I was with him the night before he left. He was too valuable in the work he was doing here but he had made his mind up. He was going and that was that.' Quinn's mother had no idea what his fund-raising work involved; his father did not even know he had left the United States.

Details of Quinn's first two years in Ireland are obscure. He lived in County Sligo and Dublin, where his Noraid connections brought him into contact with Brian Keenan. The letter bombs of 1974 were his induction into active service for the Provisional IRA. Quinn's fingerprints were on devices sent to three of the numerous 'establishment' British mainland targets — one to Judge John Hazzard, who lost a finger, at his home in Haxted, Surrey; one to the newspaper magnate Sir Max Aitken, at the *Daily Express* offices in Fleet Street, where a security guard lost two fingers handling it; and one to Bishop Gerard Tickle, at his London home, a bomb that failed to detonate. Brian Keenan was now ready to attach Quinn to the mainland Active Service Unit.

Frightening as the flurry of letter-bomb attacks was, it was the M62 coach bomb that proved that the Provisionals were now able to place highly proficient bombers in England. During the height of the February 1974 General Election campaign, reconnaissance had established from where and when troop-carrying coaches left a Manchester bus depot for Catterick Camp in Yorkshire. As the soldiers' belongings were loaded into the luggage hold, a time bomb was slipped in alongside. High on the Pennines between Huddersfield and Bradford it ripped the coach apart, killing two children, their mother and nine soldiers. The two main perpetrators got away. Judith Ward, a flat-mate in their safe house, was sentenced to 30 years' imprisonment for her role in the attack.

All this was a grim foretaste of the campaign to be waged by the new Active Service Unit now setting up in Fulham in August 1974. Brendan Dowd, the leader, and Joe O'Connell, the explosives expert, began to list their targets, make their first discreet reconnaissances and assemble their lethal equipment.

From the beginning it was apparent that they intended to bomb and shoot their way through as much of the British legal, political and military establishment as possible. They obtained the *Army List*, the *Civil Service Year Book*, *Who's Who*, *Whitaker's Almanack* and lists of senior policemen, stipendiary magistrates and high sheriffs. From *The Times* they clipped the full list of Parliamentary candidates and the names of mourners at the memorial service for Sir Philip Waldron, former Commissioner of the Metropolitan Police.

There was a list they marked 'Historical and Cultural' which noted the locations of HMS *Discovery*, the National Army Museum, the Royal Exchange, Madame Tussaud's and the Tate Gallery. They put down instructions for finding the public gallery entrance at the Stock Exchange and the address of the Prison Department of the Home Office. Also on the list was the name of a café in Maidstone frequented by soldiers.

They cut out a photograph of Lord Harlech. They wrote down the names of three MPs: Airey Neave, who as Secretary of State for Northern Ireland was later assassinated by the Irish National Liberation Army in a car-bomb attack at the Palace of Westminster; Reginald Maudling, a former Home Secretary; and the former Prime Minister, Edward Heath. Alongside Heath's name was written 'Blue Rover JMX 815N'.

The list was later expanded to include 58 MPs, largely irrespective of political party, and 30 judges. O'Connell took the judges' names from pulp magazines such as *True Stories* and added English judges who had sentenced Irish Republicans: 'Melford Stevenson — he sentenced some of us here, didn't he?' There were wholly inexplicable names such as the actor Sir Ralph Richardson.

Potential targets ranged from Fortnum and Mason, Cartier, Harley Street and various streets in Knightsbridge to the International Telephone Exchange, a major telex exchange for City dealers, Walthamstow reservoir and Hackney Downs pumping station. O'Connell made a sketch plan of the environs of New Scotland Yard.

They accumulated railway timetables, a set of Liverpool and London telephone directories — stolen from post offices and libraries — and enough maps to fill a British Airways holdall:

street maps of London, Liverpool, Bristol and Bath and the Medway towns and bigger motoring atlases of Great Britain. Their reading matter was often austere *Freedom: The Wolfe Tone Way, Technology of Repression: Lessons from Ireland* and *The Anarchist's Cook Book*, which did at least promise in its foreword to provide a witty guide to bomb manufacture. Fiction ranged from *All Quiet on the Western Front* to paperback Westerns such as *Badge of a Gunfighter* and *The Loneliness of the Gun*, and thrillers — *Red File for Callan* and *Underwater Saboteur*. O'Connell made a point of taking a daily newspaper.

Harry Duggan, the youngest, and Eddie Butler, perhaps the toughest, arrived on October 10 to take a second bed-sit on the top floor of the same Waldemar Avenue house. Social life was necessarily Spartan. The team drank occasionally and sparingly at the Durrell Arms round the corner in Fulham Road. Hugh Doherty, who arrived in late 1974, joined an Irish social club in Camden Town — a dangerous move by the Unit's rigorous standards. The only evidence of incipient sexuality was Harry Duggan's visit to a Soho strip club (enabling him to confirm to his colleagues that the management did not search the clientele) and a spoof reply to a *Time Out* 'Lonely Hearts' advertisement, filled out by the rest on behalf of Doherty but never posted.

The female couriers began their runs from Dublin — once every two months — usually carry fresh targeting suggestions and £1,000 in cash for living expenses. The route used for guns, ammunition and explosives is less clear. In 1974 the Provisionals had supporters installed in ferries and airlines and among baggage-handling staff at points of entry to Britain. There were stories of explosives being smuggled in the door panels of cars, but the most common method was still by fishing-boat, with secret landings on the Lancashire coast, or in containers through the port of Liverpool. In Fulham, the gelignite was wrapped in sawdust and wood shavings, placed in suitcases or under floorboards and intermittently turned to prevent 'weeping' and the onset of 'NG head', the searing headache caused by proximity to exposed nitroglycerine.

The Unit also did their own shopping. Coach bolts — 'Belfast confetti' — for inclusion in anti-personnel shrapnel bombs were picked up at hardware stores. (O'Connell rejected nails for such devices because they were known to melt in explosions of the ferocity he was planning.) For use in delayed-detonation devices — time bombs — Smith's alarm clocks were bought in quantity at branches of Comet and Woolworth.

3
PREPARATIONS FOR A BOMBING

'I was in charge of the operation.'

Brendan Dowd, October 26 1976

The car was a Ford Escort. Dowd signed his name clearly: 'Martin Moffitt'. The woman from Swan National checked his driving licence and added the time and date: 17.30, September 21 1974. She signed her own name, 'Liz', with a small circle over the 'i'. Dowd needed no instruction about the car; he was used to Escorts. He swung out into the Saturday traffic and headed west from Victoria back to Fulham. It would be useful for Joe O'Connell to come on the recce to Guildford tonight. Joe was good, but inexperienced in England, having arrived from Dublin only a month before. He needed to learn what to look for: the kind of pub; the clientele; the safest places to plant a bomb; discretion in matters such as parking. Besides, it was instructive for Joe to be a tourist in the British Home Counties, a far cry from County Clare. They would all three go, Dowd decided; two bombs, two pubs — one to enter each, and Joe to observe.

They had been given the names of several pubs in Guildford. That Saturday evening, the three men parked in a side-street and went in search of the first. The Star, they had been told, was a soldiers' pub, but when they found it there were no soldiers. They left at once and wandered round the centre of town until they found a second pub with 'star' in the name: the Seven Stars. Perhaps their informant had got it wrong. They entered the bar and could see at once that although it was fairly empty, the clientele were soldiers all right. They had a drink and looked around them. Across to one side of the pub there was a disco, but they didn't go into it, deciding instead to leave for an hour and return once it had filled up.

They turned left into the alley outside the Seven Stars and found themselves in North Street. Across the road and up the hill a short distance was the Horse and Groom. Glancing around from the doorway, Dowd took in a collection of tables set in alcoves to the left and a bar to the right; a juke-box; dim lighting. The place was already crowded with soldiers; the three stood near the bar and had a drink. Dowd made a mental note that it would be necessary to arrive here early to ensure getting a seat; otherwise there would be a problem. A bomb could perhaps be planted under one of the round tables, but it wasn't possible in this crowd to examine the options in detail. They would have to come back on a quieter night. Dowd was a meticulous planner.

Returning to the Seven Stars they found that the disco was now packed with people. Most of them were soldiers; it was the haircuts that gave them away. Again the three Irishmen stood at the bar and watched the drinkers and the dancers. These were the right pubs, military pubs, Dowd thought. There would be no warning.

O'Connell didn't go on the second reconnaissance, which occurred one night the following week. The other two got home at about 11 o'clock and talked it over with him. Dowd said the best place for the Horse and Groom bomb was under a bench seat in one of the alcoves. In the Seven Stars they would leave it in the disco.

At 2.30 p.m. on Friday October 4, 'Martin Moffitt' presented himself once more at the Swan National office next to Victoria Coach Station. This time he hired a white Hillman Avenger, RAE 211M, arranging to keep it over the weekend (though in the event he retained it for almost a week, until the following Thursday).

The bombs were made at the flat in Waldemar Avenue, Fulham, the next morning; there were six pounds of explosive — 12 sticks of gelignite, Frangex — in each. Dowd and O'Connell made the two bombs. The third man made the timers, using

Smith's Combat pocket-watches. O'Connell explained later how this was done: first he removed the glass of the watch and snipped off the second-hand, leaving nothing but a stump. At the 10-o'clock position he stuck a piece of tape on to the glass of the watch and made a hole towards the centre so that the hour-hand would pass underneath it, across the hole. Then he replaced the glass on to the watch mechanism. Removing an inch of plastic coating from a piece of wire, he doubled the end back and inserted it through the hole he had made in the glass. (Dowd added that if he or any of the others had been making the timer, they would have used a drawing-pin for this; it was more accurate.) He then taped the wire in place. Then 10-o'clock position was chosen as a safety precaution — in the event of the hour-hand's loosening and slipping downward, the bomb would not detonate before time. 'Real time' would be ignored in the setting: a bomb primed at six to explode at nine would be set three hours before the 10-o'clock position, at seven. The other end of the wire was connected to a four-and-a-half-volt bell battery with two terminals, via an electrical detonator which was inserted into the centre of the sticks of gelignite. As the hour-hand touched the wire, the circuit would be completed and the bomb would explode.[1]

Towards the end of the afternoon, the team was ready to set out. The bombs were to be carried into the pubs by two young women who now arrived from North London. Each carried two bags of similar design: one bag to convey the bomb into the pub while the other, hidden under her coat, would be produced afterwards so that she appeared to carry out what she had brought in. They were ladies' handbags, about 12 inches long and seven inches deep; one pair were imitation-leather shoulder-bags with a flap and a fastener (one brown, the other black); the second pair were identical to each other, dark cloth with wooden handles which closed together. The five young people climbed into the Avenger and headed south for the A3. Dowd, as usual, was

[1] Part of O'Connell's description has deliberately been omitted here.

driving. He had dressed unobtrusively, in a grey flecked sports jacket and black trousers, and was clean-shaven, with his dark hair cut fairly short. He was to forget what the women were wearing: the important thing was not to attract attention.

In Guildford, he parked the car in a multi-storey car-park tucked into a hollow behind the shops and flanked on one side by a cliff. He entered at ground level and made his way up to the top, knowing there to be a pedestrian exit to the town centre over a bridge from the uppermost storey. It was not yet dusk when they arrived, though rain-clouds reflected a fading, greyish light over the city. They sat in the car-park, set the hour-hand on each of the two watches and attached the wire of the timer to the battery and the detonator. The bombs were placed into the two handbags with the battery and the watch packed on top.

They discussed who should enter which pub. Dowd sent O'Connell with one of the women and the third man into the Seven Stars; then he and the second woman set out for the Horse and Groom.

It was still early when they entered the bar. Dowd was pleased with his timing: the Irish couple could mingle unobserved with the gathering crowd, but there were still empty seats in the dim recesses of the bar. Dowd ordered lager. They sat on a bench seat in an alcove, with their backs against the gable-end wall, and surveyed their fellow customers. Many of them were Saturday-afternoon shoppers waiting for buses home, Dowd guessed; he had noted the bus stop outside the pub door. A few WRAC recruits started to arrive and, as time passed, an increasing number of young soldiers. Dowd's choice was possibly more clever and more deadly than he knew. With the cheapest beer in town, the Horse and Groom was a favourite among young recruits from Army bases at Pirbright and Aldershot. After an initial month confined to barracks, a Saturday night at the Horse and Groom or the Seven Stars disco was often the first taste of freedom for those servicemen and women, many of whom were no more than 17 years old.

The woman with Dowd slipped her handbag under the seat. They sat over it for long enough to have three drinks. There wasn't a great deal to say. Witnesses saw them kiss each other; police were later to call them the 'courting couple'. Dowd estimated their time in the pub at an hour or more.

O'Connell and the others were quicker. They had planned to leave their bomb under a table in the disco, but the only suitable table was occupied, so instead they found seats in a corner of the bar, to the left of the door as they went in. O'Connell sat on a chair, the other two on a bench seat facing him — the woman to his left, the man to his right. She put her bag on the floor and the man pushed it with his foot under the bench on which they were sitting. Her second handbag she left on the table. The man stood up to buy drinks and put some records on the juke-box; it was rather too quiet in the bar for his liking. O'Connell noticed the barman watching them closely. Some Guardsmen came and sat beside them. One asked them a question about the time of buses to Aldershot.

After two drinks, the three left the pub and walked back to the car-park. It was still not dark and they could see from a distance that Dowd had not yet returned to the car. It was 15 minutes before he and his companion reappeared. As he drove out of the car-park Dowd made the only slip of the evening — a wrong turning which led them in circles around the city's one-way system and held up their departure. But they had allowed plenty of time. They reached Fulham, by O'Connell's estimation, at about 8.15, and had a drink at their local, the Durrell Arms on Fulham Road. As the time drew towards nine o'clock, the hour they had set for the detonation of the Guildford time bombs, they left the pub. Dowd and O'Connell drove the women home. They switched on the car radio to listen for the news.

4
EXPLOSION

'You do appreciate that in the manufacture of devices there is something known as *modus operandi*; that you can see between devices which are made by the same man, subtle techniques of assembly which show up time after time...'

Donald Lidstone, forensic scientist, Old Bailey,
February 1977

There was no warning.

The hour-hand on the Smith's Combat pocket-watch approached 8.50 p.m. and touched the bare wire in the timing device. The nitroglycerine-based explosive erupted from the bag beneath the bench seat in an alcove of the Horse and Groom in Guildford.

It exploded with pulverizing force. A phenomenon known as gas-wash hurled the tiniest particles — dust, grit, scraps of paper — from the point of detonation at a rate of two feet per millisecond to scour surrounding surfaces with the combined effects of a sand blaster and a shot-gun.

Those who heard it described the sound as a 'dull thud', a 'large woomph', a 'buzzing' and a 'muffled roar'. There was a dazzling flash of blue light, then blackness as everyone in the pub was engulfed by a wave of intense heat.

A passing motor cyclist was blown off his machine. A WPC in a passing Panda car radioed, 'Priority! Priority!' Special Constable Malcolm Keith stumbled into the Horse and Groom. He shone his torch on to a pile of people bleeding in a hole in the floor. He swung one woman to safety and grabbed at someone's leg. It came away in his hand and he let it go. He felt 'stunned and sick'. The wooden floor was subsiding into the cellar.

Rob King, a reporter on the *Surrey Daily Advertiser*, who was working late in his office 100 yards away, wrote: 'There was a vivid blue flash from North Street coupled with a large explosion which lit up the street... On the corner I nearly stepped on the outstretched body of a young man. He was covered in blood and being helped by a couple who were shouting... When I got round the corner it was horrific. People were running, shouting and screaming. Many of them were young girls and many were clutching bleeding heads. There was blood everywhere. The entire front of the Horse and Groom was blown out — there was rubble everywhere, glass, bricks, timber. People were scrabbling among the debris trying to pull people out of the mess. It was panic and chaos. Everything was happening, all so quickly. Everyone seemed covered in blood. I couldn't tell who were the injured and who were the rescuers. It was noise — screaming, shouting, girls crying and sirens wailing. "Bastards, the bastards" came from everywhere.'

Another reporter, Maureen Carter, encountered a man crying about his friend, 'He had a face. Now he doesn't have a face to recognize.' Another soldier was crying, 'I was just out for a good night. Just me and some squaddies. I was in the toilet and the door blew into me. I'd just picked up a young girl who's just joined the Army. She's lost her bloody leg.'

Robert Burns was in hospital for five weeks. He had been sitting in the alcove with a family party celebrating his daughter Carol's 19th birthday. Also in the party was Paul Craig, a plasterer from Hertfordshire, who was due to celebrate his 23rd birthday the following day. Paul and Carol had swapped seats just before 8.50 p.m.

There were five, instantaneous deaths from massive blast injuries: WRAC Private Caroline Jean Slater, 18, of Cannock, Staffordshire and WRAC Private Ann Ray Higgins Murray Hamilton, 19, of Crewe, who were both training at the Queen Elizabeth Barracks in Guildford; Guardsman William McKenzie

Forsyth, 18, and Guardsman John Crawford Hunter, 17, boy-hood friends from the same street in Barrhead, Renfrewshire, who had signed up with the Scots Guards three weeks earlier and were stationed at Pirbright; and civilian Paul Craig, the family friend who had swapped seats with Carol Burns seconds before the bomb went off.

The four young recruits had been sitting around a table in the alcove, two on stools and two on the bench seat. Caroline Slater had been sitting directly on top of the bomb. Particles of zinc from the battery of the bomb's timing mechanism were recovered from her body. Police photographs taken of the bodies do not bear description.

There were 57 injuries, major and minor. Those closest to the bomb suffered variously lost limbs, severe burns and cuts, fractures, burst ear-drums and lifelong facial scarring. People were blown over the bar counter, thrown through windows and blasted out of the front door into the street.

Private Jimmy Cooper described the moment from his hospital bed: 'We were sitting in the corner furthest away from the bar door with four or five Scots Guards and three from the Household Cavalry at our table. Before it happened I was talking to two Scots lassies from the WRAC. I had just leaned forward to get up to buy my round when there was a bang. I must have gone straight through the window because I was lying outside with my hair and clothes on fire. Some people tore off my jacket and shirt to save me from serious burns. My two mates were killed outright and another was critically injured.'

The front wall of the pub on North Street was all but blown out. This was actually fortunate, for if it had withstood the blast, much more of the explosive force would have been channelled back into the crowded bar and caused more casualties. As it was, the disintegrating floor absorbed much of the eruption. Had it not been for the recent insertion of steel supports into the brick pillars in the bar, the single-storey section of the building would probably have collapsed. Inside, furniture was reduced to matchwood. Outside, shop windows up and down North Street were shattered.

There were stories of narrow escapes: Brian Tancock, a part-time barman, had cried off that day; 70-year-old Mary Chadwick, who collected and washed glasses on Saturday nights, had been due in the Horse and Groom at 8.30 p.m. but was late; and her son John, the chief barman, had taken his mid-evening break and was drinking in a neighbouring pub, from where he heard the explosion. The Salvation Army *War Cry* seller should have been in the Horse and Groom but had been delayed by a telephone call.

The first 999 call from a member of the public was logged at Guildford Ambulance Depot at 8.50 p.m. A minute later the town's emergency planning was activated by Police Headquarters Control and, in an impressive response, five ambulances and a fire-engine were at the scene inside seven minutes. In all, 17 ambulances, including four military vehicles, were involved in the rescue operation. More doctors were summoned from a concert performance in the Civic Hall.

Ironically, the Horse and Groom was frequented by a number from Guildford's small Irish community. A police story later circulated that one of them, a well-known town drunkard, was found still standing impassively at the bar with his beer-mug full of plaster. He was in profound shock. Nobody, however, spotted another victim, Jim Tydeman. His glass had shattered in his hand. He simply walked over the rubble, staggered 100 yards down North Street and turned left into Swan Lane where, still deafened and dazed, he entered the Seven Stars and ordered another pint of bitter.

The disco in the Seven Stars was so loud that nobody heard the bomb go off at the Horse and Groom, but within quarter of an hour, talk at the bar of an explosion at the pub round the corner prompted the Seven Stars' manager, Owen O'Brien, to go and see for himself. His first reaction to the mass of police cars and ambulances was to give the order to his disc jockey Tim Cummin to shut down the disco. Then he took a second, closer look at the wreckage in North Street and hurried back to evacuate his pub.

Before he could call time he had to break up a scuffle in the bar. A Scottish merchant seaman who had been in the Horse and Groom had come into the Seven Stars calling for Irishmen. A local man of Irish descent had responded and a punch was thrown. The bombing had immediately been attributed — correctly — to the IRA.

As fast as the 200 customers could be ushered out, Owen O'Brien and his bar staff, including an Army sergeant, searched behind the bars, in the disco room, underneath tables, chairs and benches and in the toilets. They found nothing. At 9.25, just after the last customer had left, a blast ripped the Seven Stars apart.

'All I remember is a bloody great bang which hit me from behind,' recalled Tim Cummin, the DJ, who was helping Owen O'Brien in the search. 'I remember lying in a pile of debris surrounded by dust. I struggled to my feet and somehow got to the door.'

Mr O'Brien, his face and hands severely cut, also staggered out, before losing consciousness. His wife Dorothy rescued their two young children — aged six and four — uninjured from an upstairs bedroom, along with the family's pet poodle.

Remarkably, nobody was killed. Although the explosion had been as powerful as the one at the Horse and Groom, the wall nearest to the Seven Stars bomb and the concrete floor had both held up, and this had resulted in even greater internal wreckage. Had the evacuation not been ordered, the death toll at the Seven Stars might well have exceeded the five at the Horse and Groom. As it was, eight people were injured: the six bar staff still searching inside, Christine Coulter — the last customer to leave — and a passer-by in Swan Lane. The pub's brewery, Ind Coope, rewarded Owen O'Brien for his decisive action with an all-expenses-paid holiday. There was more wreckage in the narrow street outside. In a nearby pet shop the glass fish tanks shattered, leaving the goldfish to die on the shop floor.

The police now evacuated all other pubs in the town centre. Routes out of town were sealed off. Local military establishments were put on alert. A search was made of the grounds of Princess Anne's then home at the Royal Military Academy, Sandhurst.

Throughout the night, blue flashing police lights lit up North Street and Swan Lane. Blood donors arrived at the Royal Surrey Hospital, where amputations and other emergency operations continued all night. By 8.00 a.m., as the rest of Britain woke up to Sunday-morning news of the latest IRA horror, the bodies of the dead were being taken to Chertsey mortuary.

Shock and outrage swept through the country and beyond. The Queen, the Prime Minister and the Pope sent messages of sympathy and condemnation. The Home Secretary, Roy Jenkins, rescheduled his election campaigning to fly to Surrey. In the company of Peter Matthews, the Chief Constable of Surrey, and Commander Bob Huntley, head of the Metropolitan Police Bomb Squad, he donned a safety helmet to inspect the interior of the Horse and Groom, and emerged to tell the waiting press corps: 'My first reaction is one of sympathy and horror for all concerned at another of these senseless incidents. I've just come here on a brief visit to see the position and to make sure that every support is being given to the police, as indeed it is.' Mr Jenkins visited the injured and spoke with Surrey Police before briefing the Prime Minister.

Many Conservative politicians were quick to call for the restoration of capital punishment, among them a former Solicitor General, who in later Conservative governments would rise to become Attorney General and Lord Chancellor, the brilliant criminal barrister and QC Sir Michael Havers.

5
WOMBLE
SPACEMAN
INVADERS

'It all seems so embarrassing to think that's how we used to live then.'

Carole Richardson, HM Prison Styal, 1987

The occupants of 14 Linstead Street, NW6 were rarely any trouble in the morning. By 11.30 on Saturday October 5 nobody was stirring in the Victorian terraced house. As usual, the old blanket that served as a curtain hung limply from a piece of string, partially blotting the daylight from the downstairs front room. In 1974 a bunch of squatters was rarely any trouble to the neighbours in the morning.

Linstead Street, just east of Kilburn High Road, was run down and off the beaten track. There was little in the strongly Irish and black quarter of Kilburn to attract property speculators, and although the area would eventually be developed into one of neat, low-rise housing, it was now prime squatting territory. Not that these squatters were making any political gesture: they simply wanted a cheap place, the cheapest going, and if they got flung out — too bad. Empty houses were plentiful in NW6 and someone would soon open up another one nearby. They were changing squats almost monthly that autumn.

Paddy Armstrong and Carole Richardson had the front room downstairs. Scattered round the rest of the house were Tom and Jacko Walker, Vintie, Patrick Rayne, Lenno, Pearce, John Brown and Maggie Carrass. Others came and went. There was a deranged kitten — not destined to live long since some wit had thought it clever to slip LSD into its food — and there was Leb, Carole's recently adopted stray mongrel, part Labrador and part retriever, named after Lebanese Gold hashish. Kilburn was a predictable haunt for the young men, who, mostly Irish from Dublin and Belfast, were now well away from parental restraints and thoroughly enjoying the big city. The girls were mostly local, equally glad to be off the leash and making up fast for what in many cases had been repressive and unhappy home lives.

Behind the makeshift curtain on the ground floor lay the previous night's debris: the ashes of an orange-crate in the fireplace; stolen red workmen's lamps; the candles that they burned when they were tripping on LSD; and the remains of food, most of which had been lifted from the supermarket by Paddy. Many of the clothes strewn around the bare floor were also stolen and, as usual, no one had bothered to clear up the evidence of the previous night's dope-smoking. The hash, wrapped in silver foil, lay in full view and a number of incriminating roach-ends littered the ashtrays. The ashtrays themselves had been removed by Carole from nearby pubs.

The room's only furniture consisted of grubby mattresses laid out side by side on the floor. There were no sheets. Inside three sleeping-bags were Lisa Astin, 16, a regular visitor to the squat; her friend Carole Richardson, 17; and, curled beside her, Paddy Armstrong, Carole's 24-year-old lover from Belfast. Brian McLoughlin, who sometimes stayed in the front room, had not come back last night. A few tattered pop posters adorned the walls but the main decoration was the graffiti Lisa had written when she was stoned: 'Don't Get Out Of Your Head Get Into It', 'This Is The You Know?', 'Sugar And Spice All Things Nice, Speed And Smack Know Way'. There were drawings in attempted psychedelic style of butterflies and mushrooms and, biggest of all, a great beady eye which stared down with the accompanying warning: 'You Are Being Watched'. Lisa was 'into eyes' that year. The most probable watchers would have been the local Drug Squad — most of the squatters would be done for possession of drugs at some time or other — but Big Brother had little to fear from the Linstead Street household. They might have been a persistent drain on the local shopkeepers. They might have been living out their mothers' worst imaginings. They might have been a nuisance to their neighbours, occasionally rolling home late at night and noisily drunk. But not even the most appalled would have marked them down as plausible enemies of the State.

Predictably, they had all got stoned again the night before, but for them it had been a comparatively mild evening. On most Fridays Carole's idea of a good time was to drop acid and take the tube to the Aldwych for the all-nighter at the Lyceum Ballroom. It was a measure of her confidence with drugs that with her head streaming with LSD she could embrace a packed crowd of 2,000, some of the loudest music in London and a light-show dedicated to hallucinatory special effects and emerge at dawn, without ever having a bad trip.

But on this Friday they had settled for another regular haunt, the Windsor Castle on Harrow Road. Aspiring rock bands such as Randy, Fog and the Michigan Flyers played free of charge to the customers. Carole openly smoked a couple of joints, mindless of the bar staff, much less of the Harrow Road police station 200 yards down the road. Back at home after closing time, they gathered upstairs around Tom Walker's record-player. There was Pink Floyd, David Bowie and the current favourite, Eric Clapton's *461 Ocean Boulevard*. There was more dope and everyone crashed out at around 2.00 a.m.

Carole and Lisa were the first to emerge, shortly before midday. There was a semblance of routine in the household chores and Saturday — or every alternate Saturday — was launderette day. Fat chance that Paddy would volunteer to do the washing. His Saturdays were mapped out according to more traditional male imperatives: a number of lunch-time pints at the Old Bell or The Cock, where there was usually some cannabis circulating, and then an afternoon at the bookie's. For Paddy, the Kilburn drug scene was the most exciting aspect of London after life in Belfast.

Carole Richardson was his first and only girlfriend in London. They had first met briefly in a squat in West End Lane in July and had got together properly at a birthday party in Linstead Street on September 6. They were both tripping. Since then they had slept with each other on most nights although they rarely spent their days together. She was attractive: she had long brown hair, usually centre-parted, with a touch of red in it, and a strong, handsome face, with clear, sometimes mischievous eyes, and she was five feet seven inches tall — a good-looking girl. Paddy would never have let on, but he had tasted only a fraction of her experience with sex and drugs when he was 17.

Carole gathered up the dirty clothes as Paddy slept blithely on. He was already getting chubby in the face and the gut. That was the beer. He certainly didn't eat properly. He had immature sideburns and a long straggle of lank, fair hair which Carole thought he could wash more often. She looked on him fondly, as gentle and wise, a great soft thing. She called him Piggy: 'Silly Piggy'. The relationship was one month old and they were already talking precipitately of marriage. She didn't mind taking his clothes around the corner to the Hemstal Road launderette.

The laundry load was an hour's worth of washing and spin-drying, so while Lisa stayed to supervise, Carole would usually dash off to catch her mother at her regular Saturday hairdresser's appointment on Cricklewood Broadway. She was close to her mother and took care to keep in touch, but relations with her stepfather, Alan Docherty, were downright impossible. It had all come to a head in July with a series of increasingly ugly rows about stopping out all night. Carole and her friend Patsy Melody used the old teenagers' trick of each telling her mother she was spending the night at the other's house and gambling on neither mother's checking up. But then Carole met up with the squatting fraternity and a Scottish boy called Johnny Theed. She disappeared into his King's Cross squat for a drug binge which lasted three nights. She still hadn't returned to the family home in Iverson Road, West Hampstead when, one afternoon as she was sitting in the Copper Spoon snack bar on Kilburn High Road waiting for Johnny, Docherty passed by and spotted her through the window.

There was a screaming, stand-up row; slaps were exchanged and there was a parting ultimatum from Docherty: 'If you're not home in five minutes, don't bother coming back at all.' Carole did return home, but only to pick up some clothes. This time she left for good.

Docherty was not strictly Carole's stepfather in 1974, although that was what she called him. He had been living with her mother for four years, ever since they moved out of Carole's maternal grandparents' small flat in Dunster Gardens, Kilburn. The rows at Iverson Road had got progressively worse: rows about truancy; about her friends; about staying out late; about her under-age drinking; and particularly about her drinking in the Memphis Belle. By Kilburn standards the Memphis was not an especially Irish pub, but Docherty, a non-practising Catholic from County Wicklow who detested the IRA and its apologists, reckoned it was a haunt of Republican sympathizers. As for Carole's real father, she had never seen him and never knew his name.

Carole's mother was a meek soul who shrank from taking sides during the rows, and so mother and daughter now held unofficial meetings away from the house, at the hairdresser's or at the Regent Street Polytechnic where Mrs Ann Richardson had an office job. She despaired of her only daughter. What on earth was going on with Carole? The girl was running wild, out of control. Everything had gone so well until Carole was 13. Hadn't they been perfectly happy living in Dunster Gardens with her grandparents? Grandpa was Secretary of the Kilburn Evangelical Church, Grandma was the Sunday-school teacher and Carole used to go along every Sunday. She had seemed to like it.

Maybe it was the change of schools. She had been doing well enough in the junior school at Brondesbury Road, but then she started playing truant from Carlton Vale School for Girls. Some-one from Education Welfare came round to see Mrs Richardson about it once, but she never quite appreciated how often Carole was bunking off — it was almost every day. Carole didn't like the school; she didn't like the lessons; she didn't like the teachers and she didn't like the other pupils. She was bored, and bored as only an unhappy adolescent can be. It was no different when she transferred to Aylestone Middle School in Willesden. In fact, it got worse.

Bunking off school meant long, aimless wanderings around London and an early grounding in shop-lifting. It was on one of these expeditions that Carole, then 11, found herself in Hyde Park watching a group of horses and riders and trailed them back to Lilo Bloom's Riding School in Grosvenor Crescent Mews, Belgravia. There was always room for willing girls to muck out, and soon Carole was allowed to ride out with the others, too. A long attachment to horses began, holding out the promise of eventual work and a place to live away from the deteriorating atmosphere at home.

But soon there were competing interests. At 13 Carole discovered two drugs that suited her: cannabis and alcohol. They relieved her insecurities and gave her confidence in company. By the time she reached Linstead Street she had tried a comprehensive range of illegal drugs: cannabis (routinely), LSD (frequently), morphine, cocaine and various amphetamines. No surface damage was done. Carole was young, robust and not physically addicted to any of them, but she was probably psychologically addicted to drugs in general, to the idea of them, to getting outside herself.

The shop-lifting graduated into theft and then break-ins with a young, local gang. At 14 she got caught for a fumbled breaking-and-entering attempt at a Kilburn boutique. She was not arrested at the scene, but somebody grassed and she admitted it. Willesden Juvenile Court put her under a one-year supervision order but it was apathetically carried out and no sort of deterrent. In the same month, on July 19, at the end of the 1972 summer term, Carole officially finished with an education system that she had left in spirit and in practice long before. She sailed out into the world with a criminal record, her thoroughly mixed-up adolescence in full flood, and without a single CSE to her name. It was her 15th birthday.

There was the formality of the annual summer holiday at her aunt's in Newcastle, Carole's birthplace, before she could start living her own life. Her first job, as a sales assistant at Mindel's handbag and fancy-goods store on Edgware Road, ended abruptly when they found out about the supervision order. But with a reference from Lilo Bloom, she answered an advertisement in *Horse and Hound* for a live-in job as a groom at Malthouse Farm Stables near Chipping Norton, Oxfordshire. Within two months she was homesick and back in London. This set a pattern which was to bounce her between the distinctive attractions of working with horses in the countryside and the familiar, grimy streets of Kilburn.

Carole took 14 jobs during the next two years, none lasting more than a few weeks. She balked at the discipline of employment, and few of her employers shared her notions of time-keeping and absenteeism. She was sacked as an office junior (twice), as a postal clerk, as a Sainsbury's shop assistant and as a hotel chamber-maid. She walked out on as many jobs again. Some she was given and never turned up for. A local firm of solicitors, Beech and Beech in Cricklewood, gave her three spells of work as an office junior, but it was only horses that provided satisfaction. Giving her profession as groom, she worked the stables circuit; from Oxfordshire to North Devon, back to London and then around Newmarket. There was one spell with the Peter Robinson racing organization, one of the top-flight thoroughbred stables in the country, but she lasted no longer there.

Her most improbable job application was to the Women's Royal Army Corps. It was Patsy Melody's idea and they applied together. Carole thought the WRAC would provide better money and conditions for working with horses than she could hope for in the notoriously low-paid jobs in most commercial riding stables. In April 1974 she was interviewed at the WRAC barracks in Aldershot. She was duly rejected as 'unsuitable for service', undoubtedly a sound judgement from the point of view of both parties.

The hippy uniform fitted rather better. Work was a tedious, irregular necessity for scraping together money for drugs and concerts. Nothing got saved and pay-day was a good day to quit; Carole was simply not too bothered about money. Only once in those rootless two years did she claim benefit, and that was for a fortnight's sickness. The best way to spend time was to get stoned with Paddy and Lisa and some good music such as Pink Floyd, Van Morrison, Tamla Motown, Carole King or — her personal favourite — Loudon Wainwright III. She signed her letters 'Peace and Love', burned incense in the squat and took to wearing cheesecloth and lace-up sandals. The dope-induced humour shared by Lisa and Carole was typified by a set of passport-style shots they took of themselves in an instant-photo booth that October and gave to Paddy Armstrong. On the back of one Lisa wrote, 'You don't know me but I am me. From Me. Because I am what I am. That is Me.' Carole inscribed another, 'From The Womble Spaceman Invaders with love xxx'.

On October 5 1974 Carole Richardson felt as free as she had ever been. She was living for the moment; there was Paddy to dote on; and she was leading a lifestyle outside the system with a bunch of crazy friends, a lifestyle that even with its criminal edges seemed justifiable fun.

Carole and Lisa brought the washing back to Linstead Street. Paddy was out, doubtless at the pub, so they set off again — this time to Primrose Hill, attempting as usual to get half-price fares on the 31 bus. Lisa stood a better chance than Carole, being smaller and nine months younger. Lisa was impressed by Carole and imitated faithfully her bravado with drugs. Her home life was a similar mess — a father who had died before she was a year old, a mother she didn't get on with and an estranged stepfather whom she hated and feared. Lisa persistently ran away from home until she was placed under a care order by the local authority. She was now supposed to be staying at a hostel in Agamemnon Road, Kilburn, but she was allowed to come and go much as she pleased and she spent most nights on the floor at Linstead Street.

The girls were inseparable that autumn although they had met only two months earlier, in the Memphis Belle. It was at Lisa's 16th birthday party that Paddy and Carole had struck up their relationship. Lisa called Paddy 'Big Bruvver' and he called her 'Little Sister'. Sometimes Lisa felt rather the little sister to Carole, too, but that didn't really matter. They had been getting on very well recently, meeting up almost every day at the Kilburn Snack Bar, getting stoned and seeing bands. Today they had the prospect of a whole afternoon together and a concert in the evening.

There was a five-minute walk from the bus stop in Adelaide Road to England's Lane and the ABC bakery where Lisa's friend Maura Kelly worked. The girls hung around chatting for a while, then left Maura with the other two assistants and went window-shopping. One shop they went into sold all the hippy paraphernalia of the day — candles and joss-sticks and wickerwork. They bought — or stole — two 45p wooden dolls and went back to the bakery for coffee in the back room.

It must have been past 3.00 p.m. by then, because the manageress always used to collect the bulk of the takings by 3.00 p.m. on Saturdays and she had already been and gone. Carole and Lisa gave Maura one of the wooden dolls. In return, Maura lent Lisa £2 and gave Carole a blue bean-bag doll. Maura wanted to get in touch with her boyfriend and spent some time trying — fruitlessly — to obtain his mother's telephone number through directory enquiries. Then there was the business of the big chocolate cake. Strictly, the shop could not close early unless all the cakes had been sold, and since no one had bought the chocolate cake it would have to be sent back. What a waste, the girls agreed. They stayed on for a couple more coffees and then Maura undid the till and took it into the back of the shop for another of the assistants to cash up the late takings. Then she got her coat, and the three girls left together between 4.15 and 4.30 p.m.

Maura suggested they all go to see *The Exorcist*, which was on its last night at the Hampstead Classic. Carole would have liked to go, but she and Lisa had been promised two free tickets for a rock concert at the South Bank Polytechnic, so they turned down the offer and said goodbye to Maura at the Adelaide Road bus stop. Since there was no hot water at the squat, they got off the bus at Swiss Cottage to have a shower at the swimming-baths — but discovered to their annoyance that Saturday was men only. It was past 5.00 p.m. by the time they reached Linstead Street again.

At home they washed and changed. Paddy was back and, to the amusement of those who witnessed it, he agreed to dog-sit with Leb for the evening. Carole put on a cheesecloth shirt and denim top and borrowed Lisa's ankle-length wrap-around check Madras cotton skirt. It was a mild evening for early October so she stayed barefoot as she had been all day. Her sandals were broken and the only other shoes she possessed were hard-wearing suede lace-ups which she thought looked ridiculous with a long skirt. She put Maura's bean-bag doll in a red shoulder-bag which had an apple motif and a red and white plaited strap and they headed south of the river for the Charlie Chaplin pub at Elephant and Castle. They stopped for something to eat at a snack bar on the way to Kilburn Park tube station, from where it was a straight run to Elephant and Castle, the last stop on the Bakerloo Line. They boarded the tube without buying tickets in order to claim at the other end, as they habitually did, that they had travelled only a couple of stops.

The Charlie Chaplin was modern and functional, wholly in tune with the soulless landscape of Elephant and Castle, but it was a convenient landmark, perched directly alongside the shopping centre and the great roundabout — somewhere they should all be able to find. It was here — at Carole's suggestion —

that they were to meet Frank Johnson, who was their passport to the concert.

Carole had introduced herself to Frank Johnson one night in the Memphis Belle because, with her Newcastle origins, she had noticed his Geordie accent. Frank floated between Newcastle, Kilburn and Brixton. He seemed to know everybody. The girls thought him a bit weird — but in an affectionate sense. His troubled eyes blinked out through thick spectacles, belied by an amiable wit and a fount of unfocused knowledge which bubbled irrepressibly from him at all times. Frank had been a trainee teacher, had been thrown out of college after being convicted of possession of LSD and had led a nomadic life ever since, collecting and dispensing mysticism, fringe science and medicine, and cannabis. The concert had been his idea. He knew the band — Jack the Lad — and had secured free backstage passes for Carole and Lisa. The two girls had never heard of Jack the Lad but were impressed by the fact that two of them had split from the well-known Newcastle folk-rock group Lindisfarne, whose *Fog on the Tyne* album had been a bestseller the previous year. There were two other bands, Phoenix and, topping the bill, Stackridge. Complimentary tickets were not to be sneezed at.

One of Frank's traits was an old-fashioned punctiliousness about keeping an appointment. He had taken care to make an early start from the squat in Brixton where he was staying and had already been sitting in the almost empty bar for some time. Carole and Lisa, their confusion in the maze of underground passages at the tube station compounded by the effect of the joints they had smoked before leaving Kilburn and *en route*, finally stumbled up out of the correct exit and into the pub.

Carole, who had borrowed some money from her mother, bought a round: Guinness for Frank, cider for Lisa and a lager and lime for herself. She changed a 50p piece at the bar to play a few rounds on the electronic video game with Frank. It was the sort where each player controlled a moving vertical 'bat' to block the oncoming horizontal 'ball'. It might have been electronic soccer or tennis. The principle and format were almost identical. After about 25 minutes they set off for the Poly, briefly getting lost again on the pedestrian underpass to Newington Causeway, then threading their way through quiet back streets towards Borough Road. They looked in at pubs on the way to see if any of Frank's friends from the band were already drinking. Because it was Saturday night in a commercial area, some of the pubs did not open at all, while others opened later than usual. There was no sign of the band. The walk took about 10 minutes.

It was, therefore, sometime after 7.30 p.m. when Frank and the two girls went up the steps of the South Bank Polytechnic entrance. Maybe because Carole and Lisa were barefoot on an autumn night; maybe because a complimentary ticket made the doorman take a more careful look at them than at the hordes of young students pouring in; but in any case — quite remarkably — this doorman, Simon Moodie, who was a Polytechnic accommodation officer, was to recall and identify Carole and Lisa arriving at '7.30 p.m... No, between 7.45 and 8.00 p.m.'

Up another flight of steps Frank found the two people he was looking for. Ray Laidlaw and William 'Mitch' Mitchell of Jack the Lad were hanging around at the ticket desk outside the Entertainments Hall. They were expecting Frank, because he had recently telephoned Mitchell asking if he could put a couple of friends on his complimentary ticket. Mitchell and Laidlaw, like the doorman, remembered the barefoot girls, remembered thinking they looked stoned. Mitchell was 'more or less sure' the time was now between 7.40 and 8.00 p.m. Laidlaw put the meeting at 'about 7.45 p.m.', allowing a small margin of error either way. They had been frustrated by a delayed sound-check by Stackridge and had abandoned their own in favour of a drink.

Frank and the two girls joined four of the band for an expedition to the George in St Peter's Street round the corner from the Polytechnic. Phil Murray, one of the band, noticed Carole's bean-bag doll which Maura had given her that afternoon. She stood her round again and bought 60 Kensitas from a cigarette machine. They sat on the bench by the dart-board, and as the drink flowed Carole and Lisa lost their shyness. They borrowed cards from the bar and then progressed into play-acting, with imaginary games they called 'darts without darts' and 'dominoes without dominoes', laughing their way through several rounds until Simon Cowe, the one member of the band who had remained behind at the Polytechnic, arrived to remind them that they were due on stage at 9.15 p.m.

Everyone returned to the concert hall. It had been raining, so Frank gave the barefoot Lisa a piggy-back. When one of the band tried the same with Carole, they ended up in a chaotic heap in a puddle. With the extended complimentary ticket assured, Carole and Lisa had their wrists rubber-stamped in ink to confirm their free entry.

Jack the Lad reached the stage more or less on time and played their one-hour set. There was a small party afterwards in the band's dressing-room with a crate of Guinness. The two girls looked rather too young for Frank, thought Ray Laidlaw. Mitch Mitchell's brother-in-law Terry, on holiday from Canada and fortuitously in London for the concert, took impromptu photographs of the party. Marijuana was passed around. Carole took speed as well. She was certainly high now.

Sometime after 11.00 p.m. the party broke up as Polytechnic officers hustled them all out. Frank and the girls stopped for fish and chips on their way back to the complex at Elephant and Castle before splitting up. Frank went back to his squat in Brixton and the girls caught a late tube back to Kilburn. Paddy was in and asleep. Carole and Lisa wriggled into their sleeping-bags next to him. Lisa felt her feet. They were cold now but she didn't care. It had been a happy and carefree day. In due course, Carole Richardson would write down the substance of it in her brown diary — Saturday October 5 1974.

6
THE HUNT BEGINS

'It was not the work of a scatterbrain.'

Peter Matthews, Chief Constable of Surrey

On Sunday October 6, the morning after the Guildford explosions, a massive police effort to catch the bomber or bombers was already under way. One hundred and fifty detectives were drafted into Guildford from all over Surrey and installed in Guildford's brand-new police station, a gaunt nine-storey block of concrete and glass which had been recently opened by the Queen. The nerve-centre of the investigation was the first floor, calmly referred to as 'the incident room' by the man put in charge of the hunt, Surrey's second most senior officer. Christopher Rowe.

Rowe, a 57-year-old Lancastrian, had been Assistant Chief Constable of Surrey for three years. He had joined the Metropolitan Police in 1936 and spent 28 years as a detective. In 1939 he had been a London bobby on the beat as the IRA perpetrated their first mainland campaign. During the Second World War he had been an RAF Officer Navigator, and now sported a trim moustache of the type favoured by many ex-RAF officers. He was President of Guildford Rotary Club and liked to go up to Twickenham for the rugby internationals. His tall stature and military demeanour were offset by a slight stoop and a penchant for wearing trousers that were too short. He was acknowledged as a first-rate administrator but there was some surprise that he had been chosen to head the inquiry. He was effectively now a desk man. Detective Chief Superintendent Walter 'Wally' Simmons, the head of Surrey CID, who might have expected to get the job, was made Rowe's assistant. Simmons was more of a policeman's policeman, solidly built, shrewd and properly proud of his clear-up rate of murders for Surrey Constabulary.

Both men shared the determination of their Chief Constable, Peter Matthews, that Surrey Police could handle this inquiry — the biggest in its history. Even as the Metropolitan Police Bomb Squad headed for Guildford, the Surrey Bomb Squad was formed.

Rowe, who had heard the news of the bombings at a dinner party, arrived at the scene at 1.30 a.m., but nothing promising emerged overnight. No one had claimed responsibility, but there was an overwhelmingly prevalent assumption among the police that they were dealing with an IRA atrocity. The road-blocks had thrown up nothing useful. The bombers had got clean away.

There were three major lines of inquiry. First, intelligence information had to be culled from anyone who knew anything about terrorists in general and about the Provisional IRA in particular: the Metropolitan Police Bomb Squad, Special Branch, the Army, MI5 and MI6 (both then active in Northern Ireland), the Garda Siochana and informants on both sides of the Irish Sea. It was necessary to establish who was known or suspected to be currently operational and who was capable of organizing what looked immediately like an expert time-bombing.

Forensic scientists from the Royal Armament Research and Development Establishment (RARDE), based at Woolwich Arsenal, took away 20 dustbins of debris from the wrecked pubs in order to establish the type of bomb and links with other bombs, and to sift for other clues. This was the Surrey Bomb Squad's second line of inquiry.

Their third was to locate the 380 customers of the two public houses: some of them must have seen the bombers in the pubs at the time they were placing the bombs. If every legitimate customer could be traced, interviewed and eliminated, those described but unaccounted for ought, in theory, to include the bombers. Rowe hoped that telling and corroborating descriptions would emerge.

The painstaking, methodical trawl began. Surrey Police made numerous appeals for everyone who had been in either pub or its vicinity at any time on the evening of Saturday October 5 to come forward. The preponderance of Army recruits in the pubs made their task easier, but many knew their colleagues only by sight or by Christian name. Everyone to be interviewed was also photographed. A table of five-minute periods was drawn up and the established location of every customer throughout the evening was logged. Each was asked to describe everyone he or she had seen, whether friend or stranger. Each was invited to estimate the timings and movements of all other people seen, from opening time to the moment of the explosion.

Every detail was recorded on a card, cross-referenced and indexed. Every customer was interviewed and reinterviewed as the picture emerged. Christopher Rowe wanted nothing less than a chart of identified people and positions for every moment of the night in both pubs. Every hunch and suspicion of unusual behaviour was followed up.

On Monday October 7 two sketches of girls in flared trousers were released to the press. They had been seen running between the two pubs and 'may have been responsible', said the police. Within 24 hours the girls were produced by their parents and eliminated from the inquiry.

At the same press conference three further descriptions were issued which appeared more promising. A tall dark man had been seen in the Seven Stars at 8.40 p.m. on Saturday night — 45 minutes before the explosion — carrying a brown paper bag, folded at the top, which appeared to contain something bulky like a box. The man was described as 30 to 35 years old, five feet six inches to five feet eight inches tall, of slim build with a thin face.

Christopher Rowe was also looking for two more young women, one blonde and one brunette, from the Horse and Groom. They had been seen chatting up soldiers just 10 minutes before the first blast, had been moving between the two pubs and, according to Rowe, who was chairing the press conferences, 'were obviously spying out the land and appeared to have waited until the maximum number of young people were in them'.

Identikit impressions were issued later the same day along with descriptions. The blonde was said to have long hair, possibly dyed, to have been heavily made up and to be aged about 26 and five feet six inches tall. The brunette also had long, straight hair, had a round face and was aged about 22 and five feet eight inches tall. Journalists were told that Army officers were sure that the two women were not WRACs but, intriguingly, that the police had not ruled out the possibility of their being ex-WRACs. The police did not disclose what had inspired the hunch, but a fresh appeal was launched for all WRACs who knew colleagues or former colleagues to be Irish sympathizers to come forward immediately.

Rowe's enthusiasm for this lead was swiftly dispelled when the two women were almost immediately identified as victims: Isabella Price had been seriously injured and Ann Hamilton had been killed outright. The unfortunate error was not made public at the time and the Identikits were discreetly withdrawn, although not before they were published in *Police Review*, a fact that casts doubt on the official explanation that the embarrassing episode was the work of an over-enthusiastic journalist.

But there was a second, deeper significance in the release of the Identikits which raises early questions about the procedures of Surrey Police. The impressions hardly resembled at all the two women victims, but the blonde Identikit was uncannily similar, if not identical, to an Identikit issued by the Metropolitan Police Bomb Squad to the Press Association 12 months previously. It had been issued as a description of an Irish woman wanted in connection with IRA bombings — Marlene Coyle.

If Surrey Police were making any progress with intelligence contacts and looking for a woman suspect then Marlene Coyle must have been at the top of the list. Only three years earlier Coyle had been a WRAC recruit based near Guildford. Her hair was said to be dyed blonde. All British police stations were currently on the alert for her and her companion Kieran McMorrow, a former Irish Guardsman who had trained at nearby Pirbright; indeed, they were the two most wanted IRA terrorists thought then to be at large on the British mainland.

At the time of the Guildford bombings the trial was being held of Judith Ward for the IRA military coach bomb attack on the M62 in Yorkshire. McMorrow and Coyle's names were being freely touted by the press as the principal culprits. They looked like prime candidates for the Guildford bombs. None of the eye-witness statements had mentioned anything about ex-WRAC women in the Horse and Groom. This had been introduced by the police.

Thus, in issuing an Identikit of Marlene Coyle in place of someone else, Surrey Police had been forcing the pace. They could quite legitimately have announced that they were looking for Coyle anyway, but their hastily placing her in the Horse and Groom at a particular time, and promptly having their leap in detection disproved by the embarrassing twist that the woman they implied was Coyle was actually a victim, meant that they had permanently to withdraw an Identikit of someone who remained a plausible suspect for the bombings.

At the General Election on November 10 Harold Wilson's Labour Government was returned with an increased majority. Roy Jenkins was reappointed Home Secretary. Strong hints were trailed through the Parliamentary lobby system that the Home Secretary was examining a range of legislative measures granting special powers to combat the IRA. Locally and nationally, the pressure on the police to catch the bombers was intense, and the manpower on the Surrey Bomb Squad was stepped up from 150 to 200. The Regional Crime Squad, based at Weybridge, independently travelled to Aldershot to interview recruits who had been drinking in the two Guildford pubs.

The atmosphere in Guildford remained edgy and sometimes unpleasant. The police reported minor clashes between the town's small Irish community and other locals, although the worst predictions of confrontation were not realized. Two publicans reacted by banning soldiers from their bars, one acknowledging directly the fear of a repeat bombing, the other simply saying he was fed up with the soldiers' rowdy behaviour and bad language. Hand baggage was banned in one pub, while frisking became routine in others. One publican erected wire netting inside his windows to break the flight of any bomb that might be thrown into his pub — but failed in his attempt to get the brewery to finance his protection plan. Reg Messer, President of the Guildford branch of the Royal British Legion Club, announced to those who cared to listen, 'If our members could get their hands on some of these people they would be in real trouble.'

The Licensed Victuallers' Association announced a £1,000 reward for information leading to the conviction of the bombers. The Lord Mayor of Guildford's Appeal Fund moved towards its eventual total of £20,000. Several young recruits who had been caught in the explosions were invalided out of the Army, crippled for life. The five young victims were buried privately in their home towns.

Guildford further endured a minor plague of hoaxers. Pubs, restaurants, cinemas and even the children's session at a swimming-pool were tiresomely interrupted for thorough searches. No chances were being taken. A police cordon was posted around Guildford police station. The top floor housed a number of policemen's families in flats and the wives had their shopping methodically searched every day as they returned to their unsettling homes.

The first telephone call claiming responsibility was made to the local newsdesk of Yorkshire Television. An educated voice, speaking from a telephone box, announced that the bombings had been the joint work of the International Marxists and the IRA. The call had been delayed, it was explained, until the bombers were in the clear. No code was given.

More details emerged about the potential suspect for the Seven Stars bombing. He became known as the 'man in black' for his three-quarter-length black coat which several witnesses now recalled. He was now thought to have gone to the toilets with his bag before returning to sit at a table. He was further remembered for being unshaven to the extent of having a 'five-o'clock shadow'. He also wore plain lace-up shoes and dark trousers which were tight at the ankles. It was thought he wore spectacles 'from time to time'. Some witnesses had spoken of his carrying a plastic holdall. The first findings of the forensic scientists at Woolwich suggested that the bomb had been in a 'plastic-type holdall with a zip-fastener'.

Then Surrey Police revealed that they were co-operating with Wiltshire Police in the hunt for a gunman of a similar description who had attempted to murder Lieutenant-Colonel Richard Pinder at the front door of his home in Tidworth, Hampshire. The police were alternately circumspect and tantalized by the 'man in black'. 'This man may be completely innocent. We must talk to him,' Christopher Rowe told a meeting of the daily press conference. Elsewhere he was quoted as saying, 'The information we have pieced together of this man is without doubt the best so far.' But gradually police interest in the elusive 'man in black' waned and finally disappeared. He was never traced and never publicly removed from the list of those wanted for interview.

It was proving difficult to place all the customers of the Seven Stars. The disco had begun at 8.00 p.m. and there had been so much activity in subdued lighting that it was hard to be sure of people's movements. The picture of events at the Horse and Groom, however, was beginning to become clear. Another suspect, a woman of between 40 and 45 seen outside the Horse and Groom immediately after the explosion, was located after the issue of a photofit and eliminated from suspicion. For the most part, the work was what Christopher Rowe called the 'long hard slog'. Surrey Police were to take 4,000 statements and 600 photographs, interview 6,000 people and initiate 2,000 further factual inquiries, at a cost of £1,500,000 for 20,000 hours of overtime. Much of this concentrated on the time-charts of customers in the two pubs.

But it seemed to have paid off. On Friday October 26 the ITV programme *Police Five* transmitted an interview with Detective Chief Superintendent Wally Simmons, dramatically set in the still ruined interior of the Horse and Groom. Simmons revealed that the police had narrowed down the suspects for the Horse and Groom bomb to a couple seen sitting in an alcove where the bomb was believed to have been planted. He stressed that these were the only two people at the Horse and Groom at the relevant time who had not been eliminated from the inquiry: 'They are strongly suspected of being responsible for planting the bomb in the first public house.'

Simmons was further able to issue photofit impressions of the couple, accompanied by what were described as full descriptions from independent witnesses: 'The man is described as aged between 20 and 30, five feet 10 inches to six feet tall, of thin build with dark brown hair reaching the collar. His hair is thinning on top, straight, covering the ears, and not very well kept. He has a sallow complexion, a long face with sunken cheeks highlighting the cheek bones, a prominent nose, long upper lip, and is clean shaven but with a "five-o'clock shadow". He has dark, narrow eyes and dark eyebrows, and was dressed in dark clothing.

'The woman is believed to be in her early twenties, between five feet two inches and five feet four inches tall, and of a slim build with dirty blonde or light-brown shoulder-length hair parted in the middle and hanging down both sides of the face. She has a dimple in each cheek, and was wearing big brown patent-leather platform shoes.'

An unnamed police spokesman announced, perhaps optimistically, 'Every time *Police Five* has come to Guildford they have helped to clinch a solution.' More than 100 telephone calls were logged over the weekend 'giving some very valuable information. This is now being followed up but it will probably be some time before we see the results.'

Three weeks had now passed since the explosions. There were two faces to go on, but faces without identities. No one was mentioning names, but the girl with the dirty blonde hair still bore several similarities to the withdrawn photofit of Marlene Coyle. Coyle's official description was of a woman in her early twenties, five feet two inches tall, with blonde, shoulder-length hair, centre-parted.

Neither could people fail to notice that the Guildford bombings seemed to have signalled the start of a grim new wave of IRA terrorist attacks in London and the Home Counties. That Brendan Dowd and Joseph O'Connell's London Active Service Unit was now operational was apparent from the fingerprint and ballistic evidence they left behind them and from their later signed admissions to the police.

On October 9, four days after the Guildford bombings, Dowd, O'Connell and another member of the Unit kidnapped Basil Dalton, an East Kent bus inspector, at the National Car Park in Semley Place just off Buckingham Palace Road in Belgravia. They locked him in the boot of his Ford Corsair and set off on an abortive bombing mission to Faraday House, the international telephone exchange in the City. All three left fingerprints on the car, which they abandoned in Victoria, telephoning the police for Dalton to be released.

Two days later, on October 11, short-fuse hand-thrown bombs exploded within 10 minutes of each other at two West End clubs. At 10.30 p.m. a device containing two pounds of gelignite was thrown through a basement window into the empty billiard room at the Victory, an ex-servicemen's club in Seymour Street, Marble Arch. Then, less than a mile away, an identical bomb was thrown into the ground-floor smoking-room and bar at the Army and Navy Club in St James's Square. An American naval commander, dozing in an armchair, laconically remarked, 'That was a hell of a way to be woken up!' Remarkably, the only injury in the two shattered establishments was to a resident of the Victory Club who was cut by flying glass. Commander Bob Huntley of the Metropolitan Police Bomb Squad was able to give an instant assessment at the scene of the Victory Club explosion to the effect that he thought it was not connected with the Guildford bombings. Both bombs contained the bolts and nuts that were to be a gruesome trademark of the London Active Service Unit's work. No one has been charged with these explosions.

On October 18, Dowd and O'Connell, this time alone, carried out another hijacking at the Semley Place car-park. The risk inherent in returning to the scene of their former crime was underlined when two policemen disturbed them as they were testing stolen car keys on a Ford Cortina. Dowd drew a .45 Star automatic. PC Neal Nicholls escaped but PC Michael Lloyd was trapped. O'Connell took his warrant card and Dowd stole his watch before they tied him up and left him in the car-park. As they escaped, Dowd dumped his grey jacket in a dustbin for fear that his description was already being circulated.

On October 22 another bomb exploded in St James's, this time at Brooks's club, within 400 yards of the Army and Navy Club. It was thrown into an empty dining-room but the distinctive shrapnel of flying bolts severely injured the legs of two members of the kitchen staff. Edward Heath, the Conservative Opposition leader, was dining nearby in Pratt's Club and came to inspect the damage. The possibility that he had been a target was ruled out when he revealed that he had decided to dine there only 15 minutes prior to his meal. The police announced that a Ford Cortina had been seen driving away from the scene.

Then, shortly before midnight on October 24, a five-pound time bomb exploded outside a cottage in the grounds of Harrow School, until recently occupied by the head of the school's Combined Cadet Force. This was the first of the current wave to be accompanied by a warning. At 11.30 p.m. a man with an Irish accent had telephoned the Press Association from a coin-box, using the agreed, secret code of the IRA: 'There is a bomb at Harrow School, Harrow. There is a warning this time, but if nothing is done, there won't be any more. If you don't move the kids, they will be OK.' The instructions were relayed to the school and, although the bomb exploded before the police could arrive, no one was hurt.

All the targets had purported military or establishment connections. None involved fatalities, but the IRA unquestionably had in place a well-supplied active service unit of some skill and urgency.

Bomb-warning posters sprang up throughout the capital advising people to look out for suspicious packages. People began checking underneath their cars before setting out for work. It would be an exaggeration to make comparisons to a wartime blitz, but it was the beginning of the most sustained peacetime bombing campaign that London has ever experienced — before or since — and it was to last for 13 months, involving more than 50 major terrorist offences.

On October 24 Judith Ward gave evidence in her own defence at the M62 coach-bomb trial at Wakefield Crown Court. For the first time in the trial she showed emotion, weeping in the witness-box. She suddenly claimed that the statements she had made to the police in custody were rubbish; that she had made them because she was exhausted and frightened for her safety and that of her family. In particular she claimed she had lied to the police because she was afraid of two people she had called the Hardys but whose real names were Kieran McMorrow and Marlene Coyle. She admitted having told Coyle where the soldiers' coach left Manchester for Catterick Camp in Yorkshire, but claimed she had not realized that the information was to be used for a sinister purpose. Police, meanwhile, had been briefing the press that they believed it was McMorrow who had planted the bomb in the boot of the coach.

On the night of October 24 the Press Association received a telephone call from a 'well-spoken and rational' man who claimed to represent an extreme left-wing organization called Red Flag 74 which, he said, was responsible for the Guildford and London bombings, while disclaiming the Harrow School bomb: 'We have been formed only a matter of a few weeks. We are militant left wing and we intend pushing the country by force to the left.'

On the same day Scotland Yard found the grey Ford Cortina that had been seen at the Brooks's club explosion. It had been abandoned in a Chelsea street and carried false number-plates.

By the end of October Guildford was gradually returning to normal. The baggage checks were dropping off, the pubs were filling up again on Saturday nights and the police press conferences were no longer daily. Police were refining the descriptions of the missing man and woman from the Horse and Groom, but while Christopher Rowe kept up a perky front to the press, there was a tired edge to his voice: 'I think we're making progress but nothing to get really excited about at the moment. We've still got a long way to go; we've got a lot of hard work to do and we still want a lot of help from the public.' Either Rowe was keeping something very close to his chest or the investigation was going nowhere.

The first month's aftermath of the Guildford pub bombings had two poignant postscripts. Paratrooper George Fleming and Jan Oliver, a WRAC recruit, who had met for the first time as they stood by the juke-box in the Horse and Groom just before the bomb went off, announced their engagement to be married.

And 17-year-old Evelyn Stokes returned home to Cranleigh in Surrey, ending seven days of worry for her parents. She had been on a dazed 'walkabout' in London and could remember nothing of what she had done. Her father attributed her having been missing for a week to 'amnesiac shock' due to her being in the Horse and Groom at the time of the explosion. Evelyn and her mother proffered an additional explanation: although having been wholly cleared of any involvement in the bombing, she was in trauma as a result of the effects of a 10-hour interrogation by Surrey Police.

7
THE KING'S ARMS, WOOLWICH

'We decided of the pubs it was the best — the amount of soldiers in it — a definite target.'

Joseph O'Connell

Among the many places where the repercussions of the Guildford time bombs were felt was Woolwich police station, for prominent in its area of responsibility lay one of the biggest military establishments in London, the home of the Royal Artillery. The handsome barracks façade, over 1,000 feet long, looks out over Barrack Field and Woolwich Common on a hill above the south bank of the Thames. Here, the regiment was formed in 1714, though gunnery and the manufacture of ordnance had been carried on at Woolwich long before. Here too in 1741, the Royal Military Academy for the training of artillery and engineering officers was established.

As well as being a historic base of the British Army, in 1974 Woolwich had Royal Artillery regiments serving in a pertinent, modern battle zone — Northern Ireland. Throughout the year the barracks housed between 700 and 1,000 soldiers. It was an obvious target for the IRA and it was this thought that in mid-October prompted Woolwich police to call a meeting of local publicans.

Gerry Nash paid close attention to the police briefing. As landlord of the King's Arms he kept the pub nearest to the Royal Artillery Barracks entrance and his clientele was overwhelmingly military. Even though the base had banned privates from drinking there, Mr Nash's pub still attracted many cadets, WRACs and non-commissioned officers, especially on Thursday which was pay-day at the barracks. On his return he put up signs at the front and back doors which said simply: 'No one is allowed to take parcels inside.'

Almost to the day, the occupants of Flat 7, 21 Waldemar Avenue, Fulham had simultaneously reached the same conclusions about the potential of the King's Arms as 'a legitimate military target' and were aware of the risk of trying to place a time bomb inside without being spotted. Yet despite the mounting vigilance near all military establishments, Brendan Dowd and Joseph O'Connell decided the Active Service Unit would bomb the King's Arms. This is O'Connell's account:

Me and Dowd went to Woolwich intending to do intelligence on pubs near the Army camp. When we got to Woolwich we looked into three or four pubs along Artillery Road [Place] near the Army camp. We just looked in. There wasn't many soldiers in any. When we got to the pub nearest the barracks, the King's Arms, just as we were coming up to it a group of soldiers left, some in battle dress, some in civilian clothes. We knew by the hair and the walk they were soldiers.

We went in the bar for a drink — a lot of people in the bar, about 20 altogether, at least 15 soldiers. One of us got the drinks. I was just inside the door near a juke-box. Just on the right were a few playing darts. On the left were mostly soldiers sitting round tables. Benches along the wall. Had our drink watching them. The soldiers were watchful as well, you could see they knew we were strangers in the pub. Had another drink and left. There about 40 minutes. Outside, Brendan [Dowd] had a look in a lounge separate from the bar we had been in — a quick look — only a few couples there. Left the pub area. We decided of the pubs it was the best — the amount of soldiers in it — a definite target.

Back to London to 21 Waldemar Avenue, Fulham where I was lodging. On the next time to Woolwich, Brendan wanted to drive to see how easy it was to get away, we went by car. Just the two of us — just a few nights after the Guildford bombing — Dowd was driving. Didn't go in, drove straight to the pub, turned left into Frances Street. I found out the name later. He drove right past the pub to the end of the street. He said it was ideal to get away from.

Next time, about a week before the bombing, I went again with Dowd by train to Woolwich Arsenal — walked to King's Arms. At this time it was decided the bomb would be thrown into the pub so we didn't go in. We felt after Guildford there was no chance of planting a bomb. We intended a closer look at the windows of the pub on the Frances Street side of it. There was a bar window through which we could throw it. Walked past the pub and on the main-road side was a small car-park — not many cars in it, pretty dark. That side, there was a bigger window where you could look straight into the bar. I got the impression the bar was at a lower level than the car-park. Might have been because the window was so big and the ledge was only two feet from the ground. Decided couldn't do it from that side because of our getaway from Frances Street. To do it from the car-park would have meant stopping in the main road and then going past into Frances Street otherwise we would have to turn. That would have meant crossing a busy main road, so it was decided to be the Frances Street side but kept it in mind for checking who was in.

Did no more that evening except to follow a group of soldiers down to another pub near the river. It had a disco. Most inside were not soldiers. Left it at that and returned to Fulham. That was the last night we went there before the bombing...

November 6th we made the bomb in Waldemar Avenue. We used bolts we had got beforehand — Brendan bought them. They were three inches long with round heads. In the flat we had the explosives — gelignite sticks, eight ounces each. Brendan made it with help from Harry and Eddie [Duggan and Butler]. He used 12 to 14 sticks, six or seven pounds of explosives, taped together in a bundle, a sheet of plastic, placed bolts and nuts on it, put bundle of explosive on it and just rolled it over so nuts and bolts were spaced round explosive, then taped round the whole lot. I made detonator and fuse — that is, I attached fuse to detonator, black safety fuse — fuse about two and a quarter inches long, about seven seconds to burn out. When ready made hole in one stick in centre and inserted detonator leaving fuse sticking up and taped it securely so it wouldn't fall out. Taped one match — safety — to the fuse before insertion in bomb. It was then complete.

We decided who should get a car and it was decided Brendan and Harry who went out about seven o'clock. Me and Eddie arranged to meet in a pub in Sloane Square, a pub by the side of the tube station and theatre. I think it is tube, theatre, pub in that order. We went in, got a drink and sat down. We had the bomb in a duffel bag — not sure who. Well, after nine o'clock when Brendan, I think, came in we finished our drink and followed him out. The car was nearby, turned right outside pub. At the corner, crossed King's Road into Sedding Street which I can see on page 74 of *A-Z* de luxe edition. It was a white Corsair four-door. I got in front with Brendan who drove. Eddie and Harry in the back. It was mentioned they had problems in getting the car. Parked in Frances Street about 30 yards from the pub.

One of us got out — Brendan or I. I think Brendan. He checked the pub, looked through the car-park window, came back and said, 'Not many in it,' meaning soldiers. Shortly after I got out and did the same thing. Not many soldiers in it. Then decided to call it off. We thought we were too late getting there and decided to come back the following night and get there earlier. Drove back to London. I think we brought the car back across the river and abandoned it. Not sure how we got back — probably tube and bus.

Next day, I think it was a Wednesday or Thursday but it was a mid-week night we followed the same procedure except that Brendan and Harry left earlier. Eddie and myself

went to the Sloane Square pub. At about nine o'clock
Brendan and Harry came in and ordered drink. I think they
sat down on their own. When finished we followed them out.
Car in same area. It was a Cortina four-door, dark-coloured.
I knew it was a Cortina. It was in pretty good shape. I sat in
front. Brendan drove as on the previous night. I had the bomb
in front in a duffel bag on both occasions.

Just before Frances Street Eddie got out to look in the pub.
He must have been on the near side-street. We drove into
Frances Street, parked beyond a lorry. Lorry faced towards
pub, our car faced opposite direction. Back of the lorry was
open. A man sat in it. I think he was about 60, well towards
the driving-cab. He must have had some sort of stove by
which he was sitting. The lorry was lit inside.

When we parked the engine was switched off as well as the
lights. Other cars were parked without lights further along.
Eddie came back from the pub, got in the back and said,
'Good crowd in pub.' Just on left we saw an entry. I think
there was a house on the left. The entry was in darkness. It
looked like a hallway, no door on the front. An empty house,
I think, led to the back. We decided we should check it for
access via the back of the pub to the car-park which would
have meant we could throw the bomb from the car-park. I
got out and went to the entry, dark, lots of rubbish in sacks
on the floor. When I got to the back I found a wall about six
feet. Back-yard wall, I thought, so I decided that the entry
was useless, came back to the footpath, walked to the pub
car-park and looked through window — bar pretty packed
— back to the car and sat in. The bomb I had left in the car.
Decided to do it from Frances Street.

One should watch the man in the back of the lorry. He
appeared to be watching us. Other two go to the pub. I took
the bomb with me. Harry and Eddie got out. Eddie stayed
near the lorry to watch the man. Harry and I went to the
window. I was just in front. When I got there I stood beside
the window, lit the fuse by scraping a matchbox match on the

fuse, held it for a second to see it was alight and threw it at the window. I threw it very hard and I think it went well into the pub. Turned and raced back towards the car. It exploded as we were just past the lounge window before we reached the car. Jumped into the car.

Brendan had already started the engine and the car was driven off casually so that no one would notice it. As we drove off, on the footpath opposite I saw a woman running towards the pub, perhaps about 30 or 40 years. As we drove off, on our left was another pub. A lot of people came out, looking towards the blast but we didn't appear to be noticed. When we drove off the car lights were not on, I believe, to avoid our number-plate showing. They were switched on about the time we passed the second pub.

At the bottom of Frances Street we turned left and headed back towards the city, the centre of London. We must have driven two or three miles; then a lot of police cars were going towards the bombing, so we decided we had better abandon the car in case the number had been taken. I don't know the district but we overtook a bus and shortly after parked the car in a street off the left, up a steep hill, about 100 yards, turned left and parked in that street. There were old flats, about three storeys, in that street. Got out of car. Harry and I went off first. Brendan and Eddie came after us. Brendan, I think, locked the car before he left it. Went back to the main road, turned right to the bus stop and caught a bus we had just previously overtaken. Harry and myself got on the bottom, Eddie and Brendan went up to the top deck. I bought tickets for two. I think I asked for centre of London. At Elephant and Castle — I knew it — Harry and I got off because the bus was travelling very slowly. We got a tube to Putney Bridge or Parsons Green — not sure. Brendan and Eddie, I think, stayed on the bus.

I think me and Harry got in first, Brendan and Eddie about the same time. We listened to the radio as soon as we got in

and heard the report of the incident. We also read a good few
newspapers the next day.

There was plenty to read. The bomb had exploded at 10.17 p.m.
on Thursday November 7 and devastated the King's Arms. Two
men had been killed, a barman and a soldier. Twenty-six people,
including three servicemen and two WRACs, had been injured in
the blast.

Eyewitnesses spoke of pools of blood among the bits of
wrecked furniture. One witness who had been in the saloon
bar said he had heard the sound of breaking glass before the
explosion in the public bar next door: 'There was a deafening
crash and a blinding flash as the bomb went off.'

Miss Phyllis Barnett, a newsagent who lived three doors away
from the King's Arms said, 'There was a terrific thump and the
whole house shook. I went down to the pub at once to see what
had happened. I touched one man on the back of his coat to get
him to help me and my hand was covered with blood. He didn't
seem to know he was hurt.'

Another neighbour, Michael Hulse, described the scene as
'like a battlefield. I was watching television when it went off.
The windows shook and rattled. It sounded like a 25-pounder
cannon going off. I went outside and there were about a dozen
bodies lying in the road.'

A soldier who had been inside the King's Arms at the
time of the blast escaped uninjured. He wandered the nearby
streets in total shock before returning to the scene. Then he
refused offers of medical aid and just stood sipping a cup of tea,
smoking a cigarette with a shaking hand and gazing dumbly at
the shattered bar.

The blast had blown out all the ground-floor windows and
their frames on both sides of the building. The four approaches
to the crossroads at which the King's Arms stood were strewn
with shards of glass. As soon as the explosion was heard at the
Royal Artillery Barracks, an alarm was sounded and a roll-call
taken. The injured were laid out on the ground to await the

arrival of ambulances, and eight off-duty surgeons were called to the Brook General Hospital, Shooter's Hill, where all four operating theatres were soon in use. The injuries included broken bones and chest and stomach wounds. It was at Brook Hospital that Alan Horsley, a sales clerk and the part-time barman working in the public bar, died during the night. The dead soldier was later named as Gunner Richard Copeland Sloane Dunne.

Back in the devastated pub, twisted metal bolts were found embedded in furniture and bar struts; they had been built into the bomb to maximize personal injury. By midnight soldiers in combat uniform were setting up road-blocks and patrols in the vicinity.

Soon after, Detective Chief Superintendent Jim Nevill and Commander Robert Huntley of the Bomb Squad arrived. Huntley said that two women and a man had been seen getting away in a car. He did not rule out a link with the Guildford bombings. About the same time a man telephoned the *Daily Mail* and said, 'This is Red Flag 74. We claim responsibility for the Woolwich bomb.' The call was discounted by Scotland Yard and Red Flag 74 was not heard from again.

A week after the King's Arms bomb, the man who everyone assumed was ultimately responsible took part in a filmed interview with the much respected Irish journalist Mary Holland, which was transmitted on London Weekend Television's *Weekend World*. The man was David O'Connell — who preferred to style himself Daithi O'Conaill — the current Chief of Staff of the Provisional IRA. He had no apology to offer the British public:

O'Conaill: 'Over 12 months ago the IRA stated that they would strike at British military personnel when and wherever they deemed necessary.'

Holland: 'Even if it means killing children, even if it means killing civilians?'

O'Conaill: 'They warned civilians not to frequent places where military personnel are known to have established

haunts. It is basic. We have brought that point home in a Six
County situation. It is now registering in England... We have
clearly stated — military, judicial, political and economic
targets are within our brief at this point in time... As regards
military targets, there are no warnings, there will be no
warnings. We said last week in a statement that the British
Government and the British people must realize that because
of the terrible war they wage in Ireland they will suffer the
consequences.'

Holland: 'Will you escalate that campaign?'

O'Conaill: 'We will.'

The interview was shot in disconcerting close-up. At times
O'Connell's fierce blue eyes looked past his interviewer and
addressed themselves directly to the British Sunday lunch-time
audience.

Scotland Yard, meanwhile, was piecing together better details
of the Woolwich bombing. Nothing was exciting enough in itself
to warrant inclusion in newspaper reports, but a picture was
emerging.

Two Fords, reported stolen, were now found. Frederick
Haines had last seen his off-white Ford Corsair in Cresswell
Gardens, South Kensington on Wednesday November 6. It
was discovered undamaged two days later in Aylesford Street,
Pimlico, just north of the Thames.

Anne Simpson had last seen her maroon Ford Cortina in Ifield
Road, Fulham, at 6 p.m. on Thursday October 7. It was not found
until November 25, having been parked inconspicuously — and
locked — in Heald Street, New Cross. Heald Street is just over
three miles from Woolwich. To get to it, it is necessary to turn
left shortly after a bus stop on New Cross High Road, go up a
hill for 100 yards and turn left again. There is a view to a small
block of flats. Ms Simpson was pleased to get her car back. She
went to Deptford Police Station with a friend to collect it.

'The officer on duty questioned me about the vehicle at some
length. The officer, my friend and myself then went out into the

yard at the police station and joking reference was made to the fact that there might still be a bomb in the car, as I understood that that was what the police had suspected it had been stolen for. I therefore insisted that the car be searched in the presence of the policeman. It was during this search that the boot of the motor car was opened and we saw an Army-type green-coloured hat in the boot... washed out and floppy and grubby... This hat had most certainly not been in the boot of the car when I last saw the car and did not belong to me. My friend tried it on and said it was not hers and so, I think, did the policeman who said it wasn't his either. The policeman threw it into the boot of the car and I remember thinking that I would rather that he had kept it. I think it was put into the garbage as soon as I got home.'

The police were also being helped by a number of eyewitnesses with sharp recall who were good at distinguishing makes of Ford saloons. A consensus was emerging that the getaway car had contained three or four men, that it was a dark-coloured Cortina and had driven off initially without lights. The man who would later be shown to be the most hawk-eyed of all was Mr William Fairs of Frances Street. Roused by the explosion he had gone out on to his balcony: 'It was a Mark II Cortina, red or maroon, driven quite fast with no lights,' he told police. 'The Cortina flashed its main lights at the junction and went off.'

For now, these details of the getaway car would stay in police files.

8
NEWSFLASH

'We've just heard that a bomb has gone off at a public house at Woolwich in South-East London. It's at the King's Arms at Woolwich. Scotland Yard say there have been casualties.'

ITN *News at Ten*, November 7 1974

The hastily written ITN news report interrupted the running order of *News at Ten* at 10.26 p.m., nine minutes after the explosion. Twelve miles away from Woolwich, it was watched by Frank and Anne Keenan in their council flat at 91C Brecknock Road, Kentish Town, North London. It was just the kind of news they hated, having left Belfast in 1967 and stayed away in fear of and disgust at 'The Troubles'. They had no idea that, through the young nephew who sat watching television with them, the Woolwich bomb was to have a direct and stressful effect upon their lives.

Their nephew was Paul Michael Hill. He was a good-looking young man, with delicate features and wavy, light-brown hair, worn shoulder-length in the fashion of the time. Born on August 13 1954, the son of Anne's sister Elizabeth ('Lily') Hill, he was now 20. Lily, Anne and a third sister, Theresa, had all married Protestants, but while Anne and Theresa had moved to London, Lily had stayed in West Belfast. Her husband served in the Royal Navy and was at home only intermittently; Paul, the eldest of five children, was christened by a Catholic priest and grew up largely at his grandparents' near the Falls Road, the present and historic crucible of the IRA in Northern Ireland. Their home was in Cairns Street, one of the back-to-back Victorian terraced houses built for the city's linen and textile workers. Paul was educated at five Roman Catholic schools, the last of which — St

Peter's Secondary Intermediate in Britton's Parade, Whiterock — he left in 1969 when he was 15. He retained great affection for his grandparents and always regarded their house as his home, despite going back to live with his brothers and sisters after his mother moved from a cramped council house in Turf Lodge to a roomier one in nearby New Barnsley on the other side of the Springfield Road. Both were rock-solid West Belfast Catholic estates.

From the time he left school, however, periods at home were interspersed with lengthy visits to London. He had first gone there for two weeks' holiday in 1967. In 1969 he spent five months living with the Keenans, working as a van boy for an Islington flour mill. Between November 1971 and July 1972 he sold shoes at Bata International in Oxford Street and again stayed with the Keenans, who were always happy to give him a home. This time he was back in Belfast for only two months before returning to London in October. He stayed throughout the following year (1973) and worked on building-sites, one of which, Robert Hart's in Camden Town, also employed his uncle Frank. On his fifth visit, in the summer of 1974, Paul took another job at Robert Hart's.

Paul came to London because there was no work to be had at home. These were turbulent times in West Belfast and 'The Troubles' were at their bloodiest. The split between the Official and the Provisional wings of the IRA had developed into murderous gang warfare. With internment and the juryless Diplock courts fully operational and arrests at record levels, there was an unprecedented turnover of both leaders and volunteers in the Belfast Brigade of the IRA. Peace and political initiatives were foundering. Sometimes it looked like civil war; most of the time it looked like anarchy. And Paul Hill was involved.

'Sure I was involved,' Hill conceded in 1985. 'I'm not denying that. We were in a transition period where people were going from the battalion structure to the cell structure. There were only four of us left in D Company.'

Senior Provisional IRA sources have always denied that Hill was a member, while allowing that there was so much chaos in the organization in Belfast at that time that his membership might well simply not have been formally recognized. Certainly, some of those active in the IRA on the streets of Belfast in 1974 do remember him. He had no more of a criminal record than a juvenile conviction for theft for which he had served a period of probation, but he was known to the Army and the RUC and was suspected of minor IRA involvement while not being taken seriously as a major threat. An Army file noted that on one occasion, in October 1971, after being lifted by troops and spending three days in Palace Barracks and a day in Crumlin Road gaol before being freed without charge, Hill, with the Catholic pressure group the Association of Legal Justice, had filed a complaint against RUC officer Harry Taylor. He remembers a BBC television crew filming as he and a friend made their statements; the two programmes, which were about internment, were shown on *24 Hours* on October 21 and November 16. In June 1974, in the company of his schoolfriend Gerry Conlon, he was picked up and held for four hours. Hill's grandfather was with them at the time but was not arrested. Lily Hill recalls the weals on her son's body where he told her he had been beaten with a lavatory brush. There were no charges against Hill or Conlon; their families accepted the incident as part of the day-to-day harassment of young Catholics by the Army and the RUC which had become integral to Belfast life. Hill was arrested on other occasions but he was never interned and never charged with any offence.

Whether or not Hill was himself in D Company of the Provisionals, one close friend certainly was — as a string of notices placed by the IRA in the 'Deaths' column of *Republican News* was shortly to testify. Martin Skillen of Norglen Gardens, Turf Lodge, was a year older than Paul. He stayed in Belfast, finding work as a bricklayer, and it may have been through Skillen that Hill became involved in the single event that links him indisputably to the Provisional IRA.

On July 20 1974, a foot patrol found the body of a former British soldier, Brian Shaw, in a derelict building in a street off the Lower Falls. He had been shot twice in the head at close range. The Provisional IRA promptly claimed responsibility, saying that Shaw had been executed as an Army spy. The Army denounced the claim as 'utter rubbish'.

Shaw came from Nottinghamshire. He had completed three tours of duty in Northern Ireland with the 1st Battalion of the Royal Greenjackets, had bought himself out of the Army in May 1974 and on July 6, just two weeks before his death, had married a Protestant girl, Maureen Ashwood. He had settled in Carncaver Road, East Belfast, with his wife's parents and had taken a job as a driver for a soft-drinks firm.

Two weeks after his wedding, Shaw went into Belfast city centre to pay for his wedding flowers and ran into an acquaintance, Hector Young. Young was a loner, a native of West Belfast yet known by few in that close-knit community. Like Shaw he had been a soldier, but had been discharged from the Royal Engineers in 1960 for breaking and entering. Young and Shaw had several drinks at Mooney's in the city centre and went on to the Unicorn. According to Young, it was Shaw who then suggested they go for a drink in the Falls Road. Young says he remonstrated with him, but Shaw insisted he could look after himself and accordingly they took a black taxi for the short ride to the Glengeen Bar. This was a most extraordinary place for Shaw to go drinking, for the (now defunct) Glengeen with its live Irish music and Republican atmosphere was in the heart of the Divis Flats, at that time one of the most notorious IRA strongholds anywhere in West Belfast. Its dangers would have been self-evident to a former member of the Royal Greenjackets whose task it then was to patrol the Lower Falls. The fact that Young and Shaw went there by taxi suggested a deliberate purpose, yet the idea that Young could have forced or lured Shaw to the Glengeen was discounted by the Belfast court that absolved Young of any involvement in Shaw's subsequent death.

The Divis was, as ever, alive with talk of spies. A week before, two 15-year-old girls had been denounced as Army informers by the Provisionals. Their heads had been shaved and they had been left tied to the railings of nearby Dunville Park with placards proclaiming them to be 'self-confessed touts'. The two girls were supposed to have confessed to the Provisionals that they had been passing information to Shaw while riding up and down in the lifts of the Divis Flats.

Young later told how he and Shaw had about four pints at the Glengeen. A girl sitting at the same table commented on Shaw's English accent. Young's statement for the court described what happened next. 'Shaw had a short haircut and spoke and looked like a soldier. I don't recall anyone saying that Shaw was a soldier; I certainly did not say it, and I don't know whether Shaw told the girls or not. We were... both quite drunk. At one stage I went to the toilet and was there for some time. I don't know what transpired while I was away. After I came back, I noted that there was a group of young men in a corner watching us. I didn't mention this to Shaw. After a while, two men came in. They were in their early twenties. They did not speak. They went to Shaw and each took an arm and led him out. They did not speak and Shaw did not speak. I did not see Shaw again.'

If Shaw was to be interrogated, the Divis was not the place to do it. The balconies were regularly patrolled and the whole complex was kept under constant surveillance from the Army observation post on top of the Divis Tower. It was necessary to smuggle Shaw off the estate. The two young men who led him from the bar were, allegedly, Martin Skillen and Paul Hill. In a statement that Hill was later to sign, he told police that when they got outside, Skillen produced a gun from the waistband of his trousers and told Shaw to get into a car, which Skillen then drove to a house in Linden Street. Here, Shaw was questioned while Hill listened outside the door. According to Hill, Shaw told his interrogators he was now a 'plain-clothes soldier' stationed in Albert Street Mill, but that he wanted to work for the IRA; this was his explanation for having come to the Glengeen.

Notes taken at the interview were passed to a girl whom Hill accompanied to a house in Waterford Street, waiting outside for 15 minutes and then walking with her back to the house, where the interrogation was now reaching its conclusion. When Hill saw Shaw again, he said, he looked frightened and there were bruises on his face. Shaw was bundled into the car once more with Hill and two other men, one of whom had the gun Hill had seen earlier on Skillen (in court, the Army said it was a .45 Webley). He was taken to a derelict house in Arundel Street and shot in the head by the man with the gun.

The IRA have always claimed that incriminating papers were found on Shaw, together with one of the telephone numbers issued by the security forces to those wishing to pass information. He must undoubtedly have given them some cause for suspicion; Young, picked up and interrogated a week later by the IRA, was released — frightened but unharmed — when no similar evidence was found on him. The IRA's claim that Shaw was working as an undercover agent appears to have been founded partly on his alleged admission that he was 'operating' the two Divis girls whose touting activities had been exposed the previous week and that it was in order to investigate their sudden silence that he had braved the Glengeen. The IRA also say that a 9-mm Browning automatic pistol was found on him, of a type that was not then standard issue except to Army personnel working under cover (as the IRA may well have known). The Army's denial that Shaw was a spy or working with the Special Air Service included a denial that the SAS was active in Northern Ireland at all. This, at any rate, was untrue. But ultimately it is immaterial whether Shaw was a spy or simply a fool: Hill was an accomplice to his murder.

Two weeks after Shaw's death, during an internecine shoot-out between the Provisionals and the Official IRA, Skillen was shot by an Army patrol hidden in the derelict Clonard Picture House. A soldier saw him produce an Armalite rifle from under his coat and allegedly raise it to fire, whereupon the soldier himself fired two shots, hitting Skillen with the second. He fell at the corner of Sevastopol Street and the Falls Road; a girl recovered the Armalite and made off with it. Skillen died later that night, August 3, on the way to hospital.

Hill was still in bed the next morning when his mother came back from McAvoy's shop with the news. He was shocked and upset — for the two had been close. He was also angry: this killing further strengthened the hand of his mother, his girlfriend, Gina Clarke, and his sister Elizabeth, who had all been nagging at him to leave Belfast.

Hill learned where the Armalite had been hidden; it was in a place that in his opinion put others at risk. He moved it. But it was not this, he insists, that was to get him into trouble. Shortly afterwards, he left the Pound Loney club, where he had been drinking, to go to a late-night shop in Lady Street. While he was inside, he heard a single round fired, which he thought was from an Armalite. 'Because no one else was doing anything in that area I knew someone was using it without authority. I went to the dump, which was in a person's house. I took the Armalite from among other weapons there; from the smell I could tell it had recently been fired. I went to another house and asked the person would it be OK to leave it there and they said "yes". I went back to the dump and met some Fianna boys and I wanted them to scout for me. It was about 11.30 p.m. I took the weapon and went to the second house and along the way I met an Army foot patrol. Shots were exchanged. I fired first but I didn't hit anyone. Then I ran away. I ran down Leeson Street. I put the Armalite between a parked car and the kerb. The two Fianna boys witnessed it. I ran away then but I was challenged by two people I believe were soldiers, hiding in the derelict buildings. I had a lentil-soup packet in my pocket, full of Armalite rounds. The soldiers ran after me... I dropped the soup packet down a grating. Then I ran and dodged into a house and through to the back and smashed a window of another house at the back... ' Whether Hill twice moved an Armalite, or whether the chase and exchange of shots in fact occurred on the night of Skillen's death, is open to question.

Hill escaped from the security forces, but it now seemed he had fallen foul of the IRA, who believed he had misappropriated the Armalite. Hill disputes this, saying he reported the matter to the correct authority the next day, but his home was later visited by the Provisionals. If it was the missing gun they were after, Hill should have needed no further encouragement to leave town. Misappropriation of a weapon was regarded as a serious offence, meriting a knee-capping at best, or even a 'head job' — execution.

Hill certainly seems to have offended against the IRA code. Ronnie McCartney, an IRA member arrested in 1975, says he knew the IRA were looking for him. He recognized Hill in Southampton and sent back for instructions as to what should be done with him. Father Denis Faul, a strongly Republican priest who later fell out with the Provisionals over his acting as an intermediary between the British Government and the hunger strikers, in the 1970s officiated at Sunday mass for Republican prisoners in the H blocks of Long Kesh (The Maze) Prison. He quotes Billy McKee, the senior Provisional in the prison, as saying that the IRA were hunting for Hill. 'He wasn't too popular with the IRA for some reason or other. He must have transgressed some of their rules of conduct.' This reflects a view widely held in Belfast. Hill himself, in one statement to his solicitor, cited as a reason for his confessing to the Guildford bombing the fact that 'They also said that if I did not co-operate I would be taken back to Belfast,' suggesting a fear of reprisals by the IRA. One suggestion was that he was wanted for touting — the most serious offence in the IRA lexicon. But Republicans who associated with Hill at the time deny this, attributing his reputation of 'unreliability' to lesser — albeit serious and punishable — crimes such as misappropriation of arms. When Hill did return to Belfast the following year to await trial for the murder of Shaw, there is evidence he mixed with other Republican prisoners in Crumlin Road gaol, which would not have been safe for him to do had he been thought to be a tout. His Belfast solicitor knows of no threat to his safety.

This catalogue of Hill's involvement with the IRA is open to various interpretations. It could be argued that every customer in the Glengeen Bar was a party to Shaw's death. Nobody told the security forces that a man was being abducted. The Provisional writ runs so strongly in such circumstances that it would have been unthinkable for anyone to have done so. For some there would have been fear of reprisals; among others there would have been widespread support for the IRA action. In 1974 in the Lower Falls, to be a 'good citizen' according to a British concept of policing was an untenable position. The young man who did not go along with the Provisionals in such circumstances would be fighting a lone and foolhardy battle. But this does not alter the fact that Hill had taken part in illegal activities. At the very least, on his own admission, he was a member of Fianna, the IRA youth movement — a fact he deliberately withheld from his parents. Beyond that, he has variously admitted to membership of D Company (and, for what it is worth, the statements made to police by Martin Monaghan, one of his co-accused in the Shaw case, bear this out), to being an accessory to Shaw's murder and to shooting at a soldier. Elsewhere, on the other hand, he has denied all involvement. Paul Hill — his motivation and the truth about his exploits — remains a mystery. He seems to have enjoyed the thrill of involvement in Belfast, but how much of it was genuine and how much wishful thinking is unclear. To take pot-shots at an Army patrol from an exposed position appears suicidal and may be implausible, but if Hill was a serious IRA operative it was grossly irresponsible as well. There were few Armalites in circulation among the Provisionals in West Belfast and they were to be used with discretion. Here was a young man, possibly a fantasist, caught up on the fringes of the IRA; but in the evidence of his known, or alleged, activities in Belfast there was nothing to suggest he had the calibre for frontline operations on the mainland.

Whatever he was up to that summer of 1974, he was walking a dangerous line between the IRA and the security forces. After the incident with the Armalite he seems finally to have recognized this. Partly in submission to his mother, who had now had the security forces enquiring about him as well as the IRA, partly in response to his girlfriend's threats that if he refused to go with her she would set out for England alone, Paul Hill finally left Belfast with Gina Clarke and his sister Elizabeth on August 22. Paul's grandfather gave them the money for the trip. Paul was happy enough to go. His relationship with Gina, whom he had met in 1972, had deepened of late and they were planning to save up and get married. Shortly, Gina would become pregnant with Paul's child.

They sailed on the overnight ferry and docked at Heysham, Lancashire, at six the following morning, giving the address of Hill's other aunt in London, Theresa Smalley, to the Special Branch at immigration control. After a night at Theresa's, Gina — or Eugenia as she was fully called — went down to her sister's in Southampton, and Paul joined her as soon as she had checked that the family had no objection. They stayed together at 2 Stainer Close, Sholing, until September 20, Paul signing on in his correct name at the Labour Exchange in Southampton. He found a job as a street-sweeper while Gina worked in a card shop.

It was in Southampton that Paul met his old schoolfriend Gerry Conlon again. Gina saw him first — from the top deck of a bus in Shirley High Street — and the following week they bumped into each other at the King's Arms, Shirley. Paul was with Gina and Gerry with his girlfriend, Eileen McCann. They saw each other fairly regularly after that, though Gina was not overjoyed by the association. In her opinion, Paul and Gerry drank too much; it did not augur well for the wedding savings. Her disapproval of Conlon seems to have been matched by Eileen McCann's disapproval of Hill. When the two men decided on impulse to quit Southampton for London, they went without their girlfriends. They left on September 20.

After spending a night with Gerry's uncle Hugh Maguire in Maida Vale, the two presented themselves at the Irish Centre and were given a letter to take to Hope House (since renamed Conway House), a hostel in Quex Road, Kilburn. Father Carolan was the warden in charge of the dormitories.

'I vividly remember the night Paul Hill and Gerry Conlon came to the hostel,' he recalled later. 'It was raining. They were wet and looked miserable. They had no money... I did not want to take them in but they were so miserable-looking I had pity on them and took them in. They filled in cards. I gave them beds in one of the four-bed rooms, just next to my own room.'

Hope House specialized in providing shelter for a steady stream of young Catholic men from Ireland. The priests who ran it were alive to accusations of its harbouring members of the IRA and took elaborate steps to avoid doing so. 'My Church authorities asked me to be very vigilant,' says Father Carolan. 'We obtained as much information [as possible] about each person that we took in, even if it meant ringing their priest at home. I felt at the time that Conlon and Hill had told me the truth. They certainly did not look like young men who had come over to do an IRA job.'

Father Carolan's position as the Irish representative on the Camden Race Relations Board brought him into contact with a senior policeman from Hampstead. Father Carolan asked him to send uniformed police to the hostel from time to time, but was told that the police were already getting all the information they needed. 'We always suspected the police had a man planted in the hostel. When I suspected a young man, he left. Another one I asked was he a police informant, he too left without telling us. The police were regularly in and out of the hostel...

'Paul Hill stayed for some weeks. He always needed money to get to work — which I gave him. I got to know him very well. On the morning he left the hostel [October 19], he came to thank me for being so good to him. I can still see him going out the door with his case. That evening when the men returned from work their lockers had been raided and there were items missing. We knew Paul Hill had done it.'

In the pubs of Kilburn, to which Hill sometimes accompanied Gerry Conlon, they renewed several acquaintances from West Belfast. Conlon ran into Patrick Armstrong outside a bookie's

and introduced him to Hill. All three had been to the same
school, but Armstrong was three years older than Conlon
and never more than a casual friend either in Belfast or in
London. Conlon thought Armstrong looked very down-at-heel,
and when he visited one of the squats where Paddy was living he
considered it too Spartan for his own taste. Armstrong and Hill
did not remember each other at all from Belfast. With Carole
Richardson, the link was even more tenuous. Conlon met her
once or twice. But although she came to know Hill by sight, and
he became aware of her existence as Armstrong's girlfriend,
they were not even to meet before Hill implicated her in his
statements to police.

If the three young men from Belfast ran into one another
they would all have a drink together. On one such occasion —
it was at the Old Bell pub in Kilburn High Road — Hill says he
told Conlon and Armstrong what had happened to Brian Shaw,
changing some of the details for the sake of security. On another, he and Conlon ran into Armstrong in the Memphis Belle,
and Paddy invited them to his birthday party which was to be
held that night, September 28, at 15 Rondu Road, Cricklewood.
Conlon accepted the invitation — he remembers it as the night
he first met Carole Richardson and Lisa Astin — but recalls
that Paul did not: 'I believe that was because there was to be
cannabis-smoking at the party.'

Hill did not share Conlon's enthusiasm for drugs, and neither
of them appears to have had any time for the Kilburn squatting
scene. When newspaper reports later portrayed Hill as a dope-
smoking layabout he considered himself thoroughly insulted,
writing angrily to his brother Patrick, 'I never lived in a fucking
squat!! I've never been in one!!' He was lucky to have family to
whom he could turn instead, and on leaving Hope House he went
back, as on previous trips to England, to live with his uncle and
aunt, Frank and Anne Keenan, in Brecknock Road.

On September 23 he had started work once more with
his uncle at Robert Hart's. He now adopted the routine of
staying from Monday to Friday at the Keenans' and travelling

down to Southampton to spend weekends with Gina. He would phone her regularly either from a phone-box at the junction of Brecknock Road and Camden Road or from Kentish Town tube station some seven minutes' walk away. Frank and Anne, who had cut themselves off from all aspects of 'The Troubles', knew nothing of Paul's recent past in Belfast. They saw him as a friendly, generous young man who was a great help with their own young son, Francis. Paul and Frank were good work-mates, too; they shared their tea-breaks and lunch-breaks.

On Thursday November 7 they left for work at 7.30 a.m. as usual and spent all day at the site, a block of GLC flats which they were refurbishing, between Arlington Road and Camden High Street. At 5.00 p.m. they caught the bus together back up to Brecknock Road. Anne was making tea when they arrived. Frank went to the bathroom to wash and Paul sat watching television waiting for his turn. A friend of Anne's came round to the flat — Yvonne Fox, with whom Anne had worked at the Easiphit shoe shop. There had been a row at work over childcare arrangements and the two women had handed in their notice. Now they were to start a new job together in the canteen at the North London Polytechnic in Kentish Town; Monday November 11 would be their first day and Yvonne had dropped in to talk about it. The date was a special one for her because it was also her eldest daughter's birthday. She stayed on to watch television with the family: *Six Million Dollar Man*, *Mastermind* and *Monty Python's Flying Circus*.

In the middle of the evening Paul went out to call Gina. The Keenans and Yvonne Fox say he was gone for 20 minutes, 30 at the most. Paul recalls going first to the end of Brecknock Road, where the phone was occupied, and then, after waiting awhile, retracing his steps and turning down Leighton Road. He made the call from Kentish Town tube station. His money ran out and he had to get change from the ticket kiosk. In the end, Gina phoned him back.

Yvonne Fox remembers that Paul returned long before she left for her home five minutes away in Leighton Road — and that must have been after 10.15 because she missed the newsflash about the bomb at the King's Arms, Woolwich. There were just nine minutes between the explosion and the newsflash at 10.26. Yvonne's husband, Norman, told her about it when she got home.

Back in Brecknock Road, the Keenans prepared for bed. It had been an ordinary day, but the news of the Woolwich bomb stayed with them. As ever, the evidence that such acts of violence could follow them to London provoked in both a sense of dread.

9
THE HUNT
CONTINUES

'We must hunt these maniacs down.'

David Howell MP (Conservative) Guildford

The Woolwich explosion was the sixth of the autumn, and it left behind no decisive clues for the bomb squads of the Metropolitan Police and the Surrey Constabulary. Weeks were passing, bombs were still exploding and public frustration was growing. The pressure on the two bomb squads to find the culprits intensified with every outrage. Christopher Rowe's team were still methodically plotting the moves of the 380 customers of the two bombed Guildford pubs, while attempting to sharpen the descriptions of the seemingly all-important 'courting couple' in the Horse and Groom.

The fact was that the various descriptions on which the Crown were to rely at the trial seriously contradicted one another. Privates Jonathan Cook and Paul Lynskey agreed they had been watching the couple, waiting for them to leave, so as to take their seats and chat up the girls sitting nearby. Questioned shortly after the explosion they could remember nothing about the 'courting couple', but two weeks later, when the police interviewed them a second time, their memories had cleared. Cook now recalled a man aged 20 to 23, about five feet 10 inches tall, with dark, slightly wavy, collar-length, well-groomed hair and long sideburns to an inch below the ear. The girl was aged 18 to 20, of average build, with light, dirtyish-blonde hair, centre-parted. On the other hand, a third witness, WRAC Julie Spooner, described the man as aged 30, thin, over six feet tall, with dark, straight, collar-length, unkempt hair, thinning on top.

She said he had a sallow complexion, sunken cheeks, a long face with a big gap between nose and mouth, a prominent nose and dark slits of eyes and was unshaven but not bearded. According to her, the girl had warm brown, auburn hair and smiled a good deal.

The witnesses seemed to be describing completely different people. Much of Cook's description now resembled that issued by police of Kieran McMorrow and Marlene Coyle, their early suspects. Whatever the origin of the disparities, the police had a problem on their hands over the appearance of the 'courting couple'.

It was at this point that they hit on the notion of commissioning an artist's impression that would reconcile the contradictions. Much was made of the fact that the artist, Roy Reynolds, was a great-grand-nephew of the illustrious portrait painter Sir Joshua Reynolds, and that three years previously he had helped Surrey CID to unravel the mystery of an unidentified woman whose dismembered body had been found on a golf course at Leatherhead. He worked on the new images over three days, speaking to witnesses from the pub and building up a mental picture which he then sketched and refined. 'I had to do anything I could to help get those b---s who are blowing people up,' he said. The pictures appeared on November 20 and on being shown to Mr Burns, one of the victims still in hospital, seemed to produce an instant effect. Although unable to speak, 'he became very excited and nodded that that was them', a senior police official told the *Surrey Daily Advertiser*. Beyond this, the portraits apparently yielded little, although Surrey Police long held considerable faith in them.

No public attention was paid to a small news item in the Irish press, too routine to warrant any headlines: the standard 12-month sentence handed out for IRA membership. No one then realized it, but in early November the original mastermind of the mainland campaign was put behind bars. Brian Keenan, the Provisionals' Director of Operations, served eight months in Portlaoise Prison before he was released.

Meanwhile, the catalogue of bombings and acts of terrorism grew unabated. On November 11, four days after the Woolwich explosion, Joseph O'Connell and unidentified members of his team shot Allan Quartermaine, a wealthy London insurance broker, as his chauffeur-driven car waited at traffic-lights in the evening rush hour in King's Road, Chelsea. He died a week later. No one knows why he was shot. The police speculated that it was a case of mistaken identity. O'Connell, without elaborating, said it had been done on orders from Dublin. The linear scoring and striation marks on the bullets from the murder weapon, a .357 Astra Magnum automatic pistol, matched those made by an Astra Magnum later found in the Active Service Unit's possession. The killing appeared on the original indictment against O'Connell's team but the charges were ultimately dropped.

On November 25 O'Connell and members of his team posted without warning one-pound pocket-watch time bombs in three London GPO pillar-boxes — an echo of the IRA London campaign in 1939. The first bomb went off at 5.50 p.m. in Caledonian Road, King's Cross, injuring two passers-by. Ten minutes later central London was thrown into chaos as another pillar-box erupted in Piccadilly Circus. Sixteen members of the public were hit by flying fragments of cast iron. The third pillar-box bomb, which injured two more people, exploded outside Victoria Station at 6.50 p.m. An adjoining *Evening Standard* billboard announced: 'London Alert For IRA Bombs'. The entertainer Max Bygraves emerged from the Victoria Palace Theatre to declare, 'I lived through the blitz but this really frightened me.' Despite O'Connell's subsequent admissions, no charges were laid; a strange pattern was developing.

But it was two explosions four days earlier in Birmingham that made the public and political clamour for new legislation against the IRA irresistible. Two massive pub bombs in the city centre, the culmination of a separate IRA campaign in the Midlands, killed 21 people and injured 150 more — the biggest mass murder in British criminal history. On November 27 the Home Secretary, Roy Jenkins, introduced the Prevention of Terrorism (Temporary Provisions) Bill containing, in his own words, 'Draconian measures unprecedented in peacetime'. He was concerned both that the new law should stem the terrorist offensive, without appearing to make concessions to the IRA and, equally, to defuse the growing calls for the restoration of capital punishment.

The Bill authorized the issue of exclusion orders against people suspected of involvement in terrorism and promised the police extensive powers to arrest and detain suspected terrorists for up to 48 hours — and for up to seven days on the authority of the Home Secretary. 'These measures involve some infringement of civil liberties,' Roy Jenkins told the House of Commons. 'We will use them as selectively as we can, but I do not pretend that they will not occasionally inconvenience, perhaps more than inconvenience, a few people who may not deserve it.'

Almost inevitably, his speech coincided with another bombing by the London Active Service Unit, a mile and a half away from the Palace of Westminster. At 8.30 p.m. a two-ounce time bomb exploded in a pillar-box near an Army museum in Tite Street, Chelsea. However, there was also a frightening new development: 20 minutes later, a second and much more powerful bomb detonated from behind a hedge four feet away, blowing everyone within a 50-yard radius off their feet. The 20 injured included an explosives officer, six policemen and two ambulancemen. The 'come-on' bomb had arrived in England. Eddie Butler of the London ASU later explained the rationale:

'They were just small gelignite bombs with a pocket-watch arming mechanism. We did the Tite Street, Chelsea. There was a bomb in the post-box and one with an activating device in the railings behind it. I put the one in the pillar-box itself. Someone else put the one behind the wall. The intention was not to catch the law; it was to catch the Bomb Squad. Our lot don't exactly have orders to kill anyone on the Bomb Squad but they are your targets. For shooting and bombing it doesn't really matter as long as you're dead, eh?' Despite

Butler's admission, no one has been convicted of the Tite Street bombing.

During the following two days Roy Jenkins's Prevention of Terrorism Bill received an unopposed second reading and became law after a 17-hour all-night sitting, its passage through the Lords being completed in just five minutes at 9.00 a.m. on November 29. Its 'temporary provisions' remain on the statute book and were made permanent by the Conservative Government in 1988. The effects of the new law could be seen immediately at air- and seaports, where rigorous checks were instituted upon anyone travelling to or from Ireland. Six exclusion orders were instantly signed against suspected Irish terrorists.

But still the London onslaught showed no sign of respite. On November 30 Brendan Dowd, Joseph O'Connell and an unidentified man drove a stolen Ford Cortina to the Talbot Arms in Little Chester Street, Belgravia — 'a class area', according to O'Connell. It was 10.00 p.m.; there were 70 customers inside the pub and a singsong was in progress around the piano. Two short-fuse six-pound bombs were hurled at the ornate window. The landlord, Peter Sams, saw one device land on the floor. It failed to explode but, before anyone could react, the second device, which had rebounded from the window framework on to the pavement, exploded injuring five customers inside. For the police, the unexploded bomb was the best breakthrough in the campaign so far, providing a wealth of clues about the perpetrators of the series of throw-bomb attacks in the capital. The package was wrapped in one-inch matt black PVC tape. It contained 18 engineering bolts and 18 matching hexagonal nuts, weighing a total of three pounds, and two pounds of high explosive labelled 'Irish Industrial Limited Eversoft Frangex'. Dowd and O'Connell's fingerprints were on the tape. However, no charges were subsequently laid against them for the bombing.

It was during these frantic days that the Surrey Bomb Squad were moving towards their first arrest. Paul Michael Hill was destined to be the first person detained under the Prevention of Terrorism Act and the first charged with the Guildford bombings. The London *Evening Standard* declared that the breakthrough came thanks to the 'consummate thoroughness that is in the best traditions of classical British CID work'. However, the truth behind the trail to Paul Hill, then and now, is so garbled that the definitive explanations of the present Home Secretary, Surrey Police and Commander Bob Huntley, head of the Metropolitan Police Bomb Squad in 1974, are utterly contradictory.

During and after the eventual Guildford bomb trial, Surrey Police gave background briefings to court reporters and crime correspondents at a series of meetings in a public house near the Old Bailey. The unwritten understanding in these affairs is that the successful police force gets a good write-up and the journalist gets something of the inside story. It is all unattributable. The meetings stimulated a number of articles — typified by the *Surrey Daily Advertiser*'s 'How We Caught The Bombers'. However, far from pointing to 'consummate thoroughness', the press was more pragmatic. The *Daily Mail*, for example, ascribed the capture of Paul Hill in Southampton to 'an amazing stroke of luck'.

This was the version given by the *Mail*: the two photofit pictures of the dead and injured women in the Horse and Groom (supposedly distributed by an over-enthusiastic journalist), which had been hastily withdrawn when the police realized their embarrassing mistake, had none the less been circulated to Northern Ireland. A sergeant in Army intelligence is alleged to have recognized one of the women's photofits not as a woman at all but as Paul Hill. Enquiries in Belfast produced the information that Paul Hill had gone to England and was staying with Gina Clarke's sister in Stainer Close, Southampton. The address was out of date, since the couple had moved on to stay with Gina's brother in Aldermoor Avenue, Coxford, but the trail quickly led to the right house. When the eyewitnesses from the Horse and Groom were reinterviewed, they were adamant that the woman they had described could not have in fact been a man with long hair. It had, in any case, been a pointless exercise to ask them in that the intelligence officer had reacted to photofits supposedly based on the descriptions of two innocent victims. The final irony was that at no stage of the trial did the police claim that Paul Hill had ever set foot inside the Horse and Groom pub.

The *Daily Mail*, the *Daily Express* and the *Daily Telegraph* all printed similar stories, and all published the supposedly crucial impression alongside Hill's photograph — except that each newspaper likened Hill to a different woman. The *Express* compared him to the 'astonishing sketch' by Roy Reynolds (which the Crown, at the trial, had said was Carole Richardson); the *Mail* to the 'telling photofit' of the girl with dark, swept-back hair; and the *Telegraph* to the blonde victim whose Identikit was uncannily similar to the Metropolitan Police's 1973 photofit for Marlene Coyle.

The Times printed an entirely different story, namely that Detective Chief Inspector Brian Richardson of Surrey Police had gone to Belfast and handed £350 in 'used one-pound notes' in a 'dimly-lit public house' to an informer. This man told DCI Richardson that he had heard that Hill 'was becoming something of a folk hero and his name was the toast of many parties in Republican public houses and clubs' for his part in the Guildford bombing.

The contemporary version of Surrey Police, as told to the authors, is more prosaic: the lead on Hill did come from a military intelligence officer, but he had not been shown any photofits. When the Reynolds sketches were eventually sent out to Belfast, the officer who knew Hill retorted that the man looked nothing like him — if anything, the woman looked more like him than the man did. No Surrey officers went to Belfast before Hill's arrest, so the colourful tale of the used one-pound notes and the dimly-lit pub was a fantasy. The Southampton address had come via military intelligence and a sum of money was later paid to the source who had first produced Hill's name. No lucky identification, no consummate detective work; just a simple, still anonymous and still unverifiable tip.

This account contradicts that given by Commander Bob Huntley in his 1977 autobiography, *Bomb Squad: My War Against the Terrorists*: 'Mistaken identity, and a determined Army investigator, combined to trap the team of terrorists... Two witnesses described a blonde girl who went into the Horse and Groom in Guildford and left minutes later; when a photofit picture was issued by Surrey Police, the girl came forward to explain she had gone in to use the lavatory. Then a security man, based in Northern Ireland, saw the picture and was convinced the pub visitor was long-haired Paul Hill... He started to look for Hill in Belfast, and heard that he had been sent to England on bombing missions. However, he found the address of Hill's sister in Birmingham. This he telephoned to the Surrey Police, but they drew a blank. Undaunted, the investigator came to Guildford, called at Surrey Police headquarters, and promised to return with Hill's address within 48 hours. He was soon back with the name of a road he believed was in Southampton. It wasn't, but a search for streets with similar names led police, on November 29, to a flat where Hill was living with a girlfriend.' The book illustrates Hill and the photofit of the blonde victim who resembled Marlene Coyle, with the caption: 'A determined Army investigator led police to Paul Hill because he believed the photofit was of the girlish-looking Hill.'

The most extraordinary explanation, however, came from the Home Secretary, Douglas Hurd, in a written memorandum to the Houses of Parliament in January 1987. While he omits to comment on how Hill came to be arrested, he claims: 'The security forces in Northern Ireland had received information from as early as August 29 1974 suggesting that Hill had gone to England to carry out bombings.' The date cited is a week after Hill sailed for the mainland with his girlfriend. But what this alleged intelligence implies is that in the ensuing three months the security forces knew all along that Hill was a prime candidate for the unprecedented and undetected wave of bombings. Yet throughout those three months, Hill was living, working and signing on openly in his real name. He was living in the Quex Road hostel where the priest in charge liaised regularly with the police about his residents. Not once was Hill picked up or questioned or apparently even kept under surveillance while the press, politicians, public and police were all desperate for a breakthrough in the hunt for the bombers. The Home Secretary's account is either nonsensical or it illustrates an appalling and costly collapse in basic police competence. It is also curious that this damning intelligence, unveiled for the first time in an unverifiable way 12 years after the event, played no part in the Crown case at the trial or at the appeal. However, it will be seen that there were many simple errors in the Home Secretary's 1987 memorandum.

The police in 1974, meanwhile, were steadily moving towards Hill. Enquiries in Belfast, they said, also led them to Hill's 17-year-old sister, Elizabeth, who found herself under arrest in the Midlands. Once again this appears to have happened more as a result of luck for the police than by virtue of judgement. On November 21 Elizabeth Hill had gone to Coventry with a girl friend to take part in the commemorative march for James McDade, an IRA man killed the week before by his own bomb. Police moved in after trouble with the National Front and Elizabeth's friend was one of many people arrested. Elizabeth went to the police station to enquire after her, gave her own name and was instructed to wait. A few minutes later, she recalls, she was told she was under arrest for the Guildford bombings: 'I just started laughing. They picked me up by the elbows and carried me away.'

It was while she was in custody that the Birmingham pub bombs exploded. She was held for several days, first in Coventry and then in Guildford. By her account, she was stripped, interrogated, taunted with helping her brother to plant bombs and eventually — dishevelled, unwashed and badly in need of a sanitary towel — put on an identity parade. Out of three witnesses, none picked her out and she was finally taken back to Birmingham and released.

When she reached her aunt Theresa Smalley's in London, Elizabeth learned that the Smalleys had been questioned by the Special Branch. Anne and Frank Keenan, too, had had a visit from police enquiring, according to the Keenans, after Patrick 'Benny' Hill and Peter 'Butch' Masterson, a friend of Patrick's. 'Benny' was a nickname used for both Patrick and Paul Hill by contemporaries, but within the family only for Patrick, and the Keenans have always been adamant that the police further specified Patrick by using his Christian name as well. Paul Hill was actually in the Keenans' flat at the time. The police went away but, clearly, they were closing in on the whole family. Other relatives in England and Belfast, including Paul's mother, were raided. When Paul telephoned Theresa's that night, Elizabeth told him of her own arrest and warned him to leave Southampton. Paul said that was impossible since he had no money. Paul Hill now knew that the police hunting the bombers were systematically working their way through his family towards him. Inexplicably, if he was a guilty man, he stayed put.

10
FIRST ARREST

'We lifted the man and he sang.'

DCS Wally Simmons, quoted in the *Daily Mail*,
December 5 1974

Two police cars and a police van crept down Aldermoor Avenue
and stopped outside number 29. Before those inside knew what
was happening, police had the house surrounded. Leaving time
for two of his colleagues — Richardson and Fitchett — to go
through the front door, Detective Sergeant Anthony Jermey
slipped round to the back and let himself in. He found most
of the occupants in the sitting-room: two women, a 10-year-old
girl and a young man reading *The Sun*.

'Name?' Jermey asked the man.

'Paul Hill.'

Jermey bundled Hill into the hallway, where they met
Detective Chief Inspector Richardson coming out of the kitchen.
'This is Hill,' Jermey told him. And to Hill: 'We're arresting you
on suspicion of causing explosions.'

'You're kidding!' Paul said. 'Is it that serious?'

Police searched the house and searched Hill. A forensic officer
swabbed his hands for traces of explosive. He could see they had
a photograph.

'What are you arresting me for?' he asked.

'The Guildford offence.'

Someone came downstairs with Hill's suitcase and carried it
out to the car. Hill was taken out after it. It was 11.15 a.m. on
Thursday November 28.

At Shirley police station, where he was held for three and a
half hours before being taken to Guildford, Hill says two police

officers came into his cell carrying revolvers, loaded the guns in front of him and, holding up the bullets, said that if he tried to make a run for it he would get one of them. In the car going to Guildford, they asked him the way.

'I don't know,' said Hill.

'You're a wide monkey,' one of the officers replied.

At Guildford police station, Hill alleges, Jermey grabbed him by the hair to hustle him down to the cells and said, 'You've had your hair dyed, you murdering bastard,' pushing his face against the cell door when they arrived. Jermey was to deny this. They took scrapings from under his nails and brought Detective Superintendent Ronald Underwood to see him.

'You're trying to put Guildford on me?' Hill asked when tackled about it, to which the police are said to have replied, 'We're not trying to put it on you. It is on you and your chick.'

Underwood said he had a file on Hill from Northern Ireland and asked him what he knew about the Guildford bombs.

'The soldiers' pubs,' said Hill.

'That's right. What d'you know about it?'

'Nothing. Only what I've read in the papers.'

'I think you know more than that. Have you ever been to Guildford?'

Hill remembered that he had. He had been through the place on a train in October when the main line from Southampton was diverted. He told them. Underwood said he would see him later.

At about 8.30, Hill says, Jermey and Richardson came back and told him they had found explosives on his hands. He said it was lies. Going through his suitcase, they said, they had found letters about explosives. They told him his solicitor had been on the phone but they were not going to let him in. The sequence of events that night was confused by the fact that Hill, whose watch had been taken away, had no idea of time. The police denied that any interrogations had taken place after 5.15, but it was later established that inadequate records were kept at Guildford police station as to who had seen Hill when.

Hill remembers it as an eventful evening. 'Jermey, Underwood and a small, fat detective came to the cell. I was handcuffed and taken to a lift and taken to the first floor. I was taken to a room. On the walls were photographs of the bomb-damaged public house and plans showing the positions of the bodies. I was put in a chair facing these photographs about two feet away. I turned the chair sideways to the photographs. The fat one hit me a clout on the back of the head and knocked me off the chair... They began to shout at me, all at once, about the Guildford and Woolwich bombings. They took me to a window to look at police guards and people with cameras on the street. They told me this was all for me. Jermey took out my photograph and said it was worth thousands from newspapers... The questioning then went on, all of them firing questions at me and shouting names of people killed at Guildford. The name of Caroline Jane Slater was constantly mentioned. They said, "She was only 17 and you murdered her, you bastard"...

'I was put [back] in the cell and a blanket thrown in. I lay on the boards and tried to sleep but police kept coming to the door, kicking it and shouting things. A gun was shown at the flap several times. The cell light was kept on. After an hour, or maybe two hours, I was taken out again and taken upstairs to the same room and questioned constantly for about an hour by Jermey, Underwood and the fat one. They left after an hour or so and sent in another policeman in civilian dress carrying a black briefcase. I was sweating with the heat. He said "You have reason to sweat." He put the briefcase on the table and opened it and took out a number of large photographs of dead bodies of people on slabs, naked. Many were mutilated. He said, "We know you did it, and you and the girl are being charged. She's being brought in again." Jermey and Underwood came back and started the questioning again. They pointed to these photographs and mentioned the names of the people. I kept denying any involvement in the thing.'

He says he remembers two Metropolitan Police Bomb Squad officers coming to see him that evening to ask him about Woolwich and about the bomb at the Tower of London. At the Brian Shaw trial the following June, Detective Superintendent Peter Imbert of the Bomb Squad admitted that he had interviewed Hill in his cell on the night of November 28 between 10.15 and 10.25, and again, for three minutes, the following morning at 11.30. No record of these interviews had been logged by Guildford Police. Hill claims his clothes were removed for forensic tests and he was given a towel to wear. 'Another policeman came in, in civilian clothes. He said he did not think I would be charged but Belfast police would be over to see me. I got no sleep that night as they kept kicking the door all night and the light was left on... I was cold, with only a blanket and the towel, and no mattress, just bare boards.'

The next morning, Hill says that without breakfast or even a cup of tea, he was again questioned for some two hours by Jermey and a police officer he had not seen before. Jermey denies this. Hill says extracts of letters between himself and Gina were read out and sniggered over. After an early lunch of carrots, potato, meat and water he was interviewed by Underwood, who went through his Northern Ireland file.

Later that afternoon, Jermey brought Detective Chief Superintendent Wally Simmons to meet the prisoner for the first time; with them were Detective Chief Superintendent Albert James Cunningham and Detective Constable John McCaul of the Royal Ulster Constabulary. Cunningham was smoking a pipe and carried a briefcase. He told Hill they were inquiring into the murder of Brian Shaw at Arundel Street, Belfast. Hill denied all knowledge of it. Cunningham then gave him an account of what had happened. He was wrong about it, Hill later told his solicitor, but the points on which he was wrong were all too familiar: Cunningham's account was identical to the one he claimed to have given to Gerry Conlon and Paddy Armstrong in the Old Bell pub in Kilburn. Hill concluded that one of them must have grassed on him. He decided to make a statement. Records show that this part of the interview lasted no more than 10 minutes.

Hill was handcuffed and taken back to the room where he had been interviewed by Surrey Police the day before. He says he was taken up in the lift, past a reception area where he could see Gina; she had been rearrested and was sitting crying. Present in the interview room were Cunningham, McCaul and Jermey. Simmons came and went. Hill says there was talk of taking him back to Belfast that night on board an RAF plane. Cunningham took off his jacket and rolled up his sleeves. According to Hill, Cunningham put the questions and suggested the answers. Hill went along with them: his statement corresponded to the RUC's incorrect version of events.

In 1985 Hill claimed to the authors that both the interviews had been much longer than police records show: over an hour in the cells before he agreed to make a statement; four hours for the statement itself. He also said that Cunningham had done a deal with him: 'If I signed for Shaw they would let Gina go.' Whatever the truth behind this, events of the previous 24 hours had almost certainly taken their toll. Hill signed the statement without even reading it through.

'I signed it because I was exhausted, I was unable to think any more,' Hill told his solicitor. 'I just wanted to go and lie in my cell. I remembered the guns being produced... The Guildford thing was still to come and I had fears about why my girl was sitting downstairs and what would they do if I did not co-operate. I was relieved when there were no more questions.'

But if he thought that the relief would be permanent, he was mistaken. As Cunningham unhooked his jacket and rolled down his sleeves, his place at the interview table was taken by Wally Simmons. It was by now about 5.55 p.m. on Friday November 29. Jermey brought in an extra chair. A new police officer arrived — 'an Englishman in plain clothes' is how Hill described him — Christopher Rowe. 'Now he'll tell you about Guildford,' Cunningham said. Hill recounts how the two detectives from Belfast sat back and watched the first part of the interview, which was conducted mainly by Simmons.

Hill continued to deny knowledge of the pub bombs, but not for long. He told the authors in 1985, 'The threat was the same with Guildford as it had been with Shaw: Simmons said, "Confess, or we'll do Gina for it."' They both knew that she was still downstairs. 'They're right about the fact that after I finished making the Shaw statement there wasn't much of a delay before I started saying things about Guildford. I wasn't thinking logically at all. My mind was in complete confusion. I just kept telling myself it would never stand up when it came to it because I could prove I was elsewhere.'

The interview which, according to police, began at six, lasted until after 11 o'clock at night and at the end of it Hill was taken to London in order to point out locations. There is nothing in the bland phrases of the police record to suggest what the atmosphere must have been like inside Guildford police station that evening: the tension and the determination of the police officers to make something of this suspect from Belfast whom they now knew to have terrorist connections, and the incipient triumph as Hill started to confess.

'"I think you can help us on this matter,"' Simmons records in his report.

'He said, "I can't."'

'I said, "Two bombs were placed in two public houses in this town. I think you know something about the matter. That is why you are here."'

Hill has never alleged violence at this stage, and there is no record of how long the interview had been going on before Simmons reports him as saying,

'"All right. I'll tell you what I know."'

'I said, "Start from the beginning."'

'Hill said, "I came over with Gerry Conlon..."'

The statement describes how Hill came to England with Gina and his sister Elizabeth and stayed with his aunt Theresa. Later, he and Conlon stayed for a couple of days with Gerry's uncle,

Hugh Maguire. At a Camden Town pub, Hill met someone called 'Paul' (the name of a lad in the Quex Road hostel, he told his solicitor later) who instructed Hill and Conlon to report to the priest, Father Carolan, at the hostel in 'Quix Road'. Hill described how, in the company of one 'Dermot' (an invention, he says), he and Conlon were taken to Brixton to the flat of a girl called 'Marion' (chosen after his little sister's name) who showed them how to make bombs. 'There was a lot of explosives in there in plastic bags and it looked like brown sugar... It made my eyes water and caught my chest. It smelt like a bakery... She started fiddling with a square cardboard thing. There was a watch in the centre of the box like one you take out of your pocket. It had a white face and two hands, no glass and it wasn't ticking... I heard Marion talking to Gerry about wires... ' Photographs were supposedly shown of the Guildford pubs. The next day, 'Paul', 'Patrick Joseph Armstrong' and two girls came to call for Hill and Conlon and they drove to Guildford. The road ran past a racecourse. Armstrong knew you couldn't drive down the High Street on a Saturday, said Hill. At the station, Hill was told to get out and wait for someone who did not turn up. Armstrong collected him later and drove him back to 'Quix Road' before depositing him at Waterloo. As if this were not enough, Hill then volunteered that he had been asked to hide a container of 'yellow liquid' on the building-site where he worked, which was collected by Armstrong the day before the bombing of the King's Arms, Woolwich.

Hill explains this statement as an attempt to teach Conlon and Armstrong a lesson for telling the police about Shaw (as he saw it), while minimizing his own part in the affair. Apart from this, he claims, it was a mixture of fantasy and suggestions made to him by the police — some of them, such as the fact that Guildford High Street was closed to traffic on Saturdays, highly incriminating. He also tried to build in a fail-safe mechanism by naming people of proven antipathy to the IRA — Father Carolan; Hugh Maguire. But far from reinforcing the fact that his statement was nonsense, this was to have traumatic consequences for those he named.

For Hill's reasoning was tragically to underestimate the power unleashed by his confession. Within hours of his return to the Guildford cells after he had been driven around London in the early hours of November 30, police forces across London and the Home Counties launched a series of raids which led to one of the largest round-ups of suspects ever known in Britain. Among the first to be arrested were Hill's aunt and uncle, Anne and Frank Keenan.

'At approximately 5.30 in the morning on Saturday November 30,' Frank recalls, 'we were both awakened abruptly by the ringing of the bell and heavy knocking at the front door. I went and opened it and there were five or six armed plain-clothes officers and a dog outside. As soon as I opened the door one of the officers rushed in and pushed me against the wall and held me there whilst the rest of them rushed in to the remainder of the house. One of the officers... said to me, "When I get you to Guildford I'll teach you to tell lies, you Irish bastard." [This was a reference to the 'Patrick Benny Hill' confusion of the previous week.] I was then told to get dressed because I was still in my night-clothes. During the time I was getting dressed, officers and a dog had the run of the house... I left the house without having any conversation with my wife.'

Anne and her four-year-old son, Francis, were taken to Caledonian Road police station, where Detective Sergeant Day ordered them both to be searched. Anne remembers another, more sympathetic policeman saying to her, 'Just see what's in the lad's pockets.' She put her hand into the child's pocket and drew out a few sweets. Then, before she could be taken to Guildford, Anne flanked on either side by police officers, had to go and ask her sister Theresa to look after Francis. 'I was trying to persuade him that I was going to leave him with his aunt Theresa for a short time and that he shouldn't worry. Detective Sergeant Day then said to me within the hearing of the child, "You won't see him for a long time." I replied, "Will I not?" and then I turned my head towards my son and said, "I'll see you very soon, son... I have to go somewhere but then I'll come back, love."'

Another address to get a call in the early hours of November 30 was that of Hugh and Kathleen (Kitty) Maguire. Police arrived at their home in Westbourne Terrace Road, Paddington between 4.00 and 5.00 a.m. and hammered on the door. When Kitty opened it, they surged past her into the flat: Hugh counted 16 plain-clothes men, four uniformed officers, two WPCs, a dog-handler and a dog. He saw that the police were armed. After the police had searched them, Hugh, who suffered with an ulcerated leg, was allowed to put his clothes on and a dressing on his leg. 'When I went into the front room, Maureen [a 17-year-old girl who was staying with them] and my wife were crying. The place was torn to pieces. The drawers were out. There were policemen in the kitchen pulling all the tools and food out of the cupboards. There were policemen in the bathroom, police in the toilet... The dog-handler said he wanted to get the carpet up but there were too many police in the place for him to do it at the time.' His wife and Maureen were hustled out of the flat, but Hugh was kept behind for questioning before being taken to Harrow Road police station, then to Cannon Row. Like the Keenans, Hugh and Kitty Maguire were split up and driven to Surrey in separate cars. They were allowed to tell no one where they were going.

At about the same time as the raid on Hugh and Kitty, Sean Mullin and his girlfriend, Brigid Nicholas, drove home from a party and arrived at Sean's flat at 15 Rondu Road, Cricklewood, to find the police waiting. The flat was one where Hill knew Armstrong sometimes stayed and he had identified it to police as a bomb factory. Mullin's flat-mates, John McGuinness, Brian Anderson, Robert Carlisle and Alastair Cully, returned from the same party in Anderson's car at 7.30 a.m. to find the flat crawling with police officers. Of Sean and Brigid there was no sign, but they were all briefly reunited at West Hampstead police station before McGuinness, Anderson and Mullin were transported to Guildford. Cully and Carlisle were freed without much delay. Of the flat's five occupants, Cully and Carlisle were Protestants.

But the morning's most significant arrest was in Belfast: at 5.45, in Cyprus Street off the Falls Road, police came for Hill's old schoolfriend Gerry Conlon.

11
CONLON

'It would be like asking a wally to plant a bomb. No one in their right mind would want to have anybody involved who took LSD. It's nonsensical.'

Brian Rose-Smith, defence solicitor

In his mother's words, Gerry Conlon was 'no angel'; by all accounts he scarcely fitted the family mould. His father, Guiseppe (as he spelled it) — the name was bequeathed by an Italian godfather, Joe Raffe, who ran a chip shop in Divis Street — was regarded as a law-abiding man whose one rebellious act had been to jump ship on being conscripted into the Royal Marines during the war, an act for which he was never pursued. He had worked as a labourer until forced by TB to give up. He married Sarah Maguire and they settled in the Lower Falls of Belfast where their three children were born — Bridget, Ann and, on March 1 1954, Gerard.

Although they had been friends at St Peter's school — 'fairly close' friends, according to Gerry — Gerry Conlon and Paul Hill are very different as personalities. The IRA was all around them, but the cause did not intrigue Gerry as it did Paul. Conlon had thick, dark, unruly hair, large brown eyes and an expression much given to making people laugh, particularly at inappropriate moments. He was a talented schoolboy footballer and was watched by scouts for professional clubs, but he wasn't interested. He had dedicated his adolescence to having as good and as easy a time as West Belfast could offer and, as he grew up, his need for cash pushed him towards crime. In 1985, looking back on the beginning of the seventies, he wrote:

My life at this time was one of a petty criminal. I liked money, drink, gambling and girls and if I did not have money I couldn't enjoy myself, so I stole. I stole anything and everything I could: clothes, radios, records, watches, anything I could sell. I usually sold stolen goods in pubs in the city centre, pubs like the Bank Bar, the Tudor Bar, Kelly's Cellars and the Unicorn. I had the occasional jobs in '72, usually not through choice but because of my mother and father who worried about me and wanted me to start to settle down and keep out of trouble, or when the dole made me take a job or threatened to stop my dole money. I had a job, I remember, in Upper Queen Street as a store man in a linen warehouse... anyway, not long after I started working for this firm I started stealing from them. I stole sheets, pillow cases, hankies, tea towels, anything I could get hold of. I think I worked for about two months with them before I was sacked. But this was nothing new to me as every job I had I stole from the people I worked for.

So this was my lifestyle in '72 and of course I had the usual pull from the Provisional IRA about being a bit of a nuisance, and stealing. On one occasion I was told it wouldn't be a bad idea to join the Fianna as it might make me a better person. So for a few weeks, more like six weeks, I became involved with the Fianna. I used to have to go to the Divis Flats where in the links between the floors I would be drilled by the OC and his staff. All the orders for the drill were given in Irish and I didn't speak Irish, most of us couldn't understand it, so for days I would be told how to turn left, turn right, all things like this. We used to have to go to Fianna meetings three or four times a week and we would be either drilled or told the history of the Fianna and the IRA. You could not be sworn in without being able to parade and knowing about the IRA struggle. Sometimes you would be asked to count the foot patrols in the area and make sure they weren't up to anything. Also you would sometimes pick up the local hooligans and thieves and question them just like they questioned me.

Funny that. Well, I had been in the Fianna about four weeks
when I was sworn in by the OC. I was sworn in in a house in
Garnet Street. The following week the OC kicked me out for
stealing from a pub called Dan Lane's... Before I forget, in '72
before I joined the Fianna, while I was stealing and all that, I
used to go to a lot of clubs and discos and I started taking a
few pills, uppers and downers, mandrax and speed. Well, the
IRA don't like that sort of thing.

Anyway, E.B. and myself got found out by the Provisional
Fianna over Dan Lane's and were taken to see the OC who
gave E.B. a right bollocking but let him stay in the Fianna
(probably because he had older brothers in the Provisional
IRA). Me, I got suspended from the Fianna and was told if I
behaved myself for a few months I might be able to rejoin,
but in the meantime I was to keep away from members of
the Fianna and not get into trouble. Well, I was back to
square one. The only people who I knew who weren't IRA
were thieves, so I didn't have much choice about who I hung
around with, did I?... But to tell the truth I was glad to see
myself out of the Fianna because I would rather be gambling
than drilling; I'd rather be enjoying drinking and dancing than
standing on street corners worrying about the Brits.

With his friend Pat Kane, Conlon went to work in Manchester
between September and December 1972. He robbed a
leather-goods shop shortly before coming home for Christmas.
Of 1973, he writes that it was 'more or less the same as '72,
stealing, drinking, gambling and now and again the odd job. I
didn't get into any bother with the IRA, just my parents.' But
he did manage to get stabbed at Shelley's disco in a fight over
a girl from Derry and it was the £200 compensation money for
this injury that was to fund his trip to England in 1974.

The first half of that year was spent in Belfast with a gang of
shop-lifters, one of whom he says was Hill's friend Martin Skillen.
For this he was disciplined quite severely by the IRA and as a
result 'decided to stop stealing for the time being', while 'Martin

Skillen decided to join the IRA'. Gerry had begun going out with Eileen McCann and 'as things in Belfast looked bleak, no work, no stealing, I decided to go to London'.

He and Eileen set out on Friday August 3. Later that day Martin Skillen would die on the corner of Sevastopol Street.

Their original intention was to make for London, to which Gerry was no stranger, having visited with his grandmother as a child and spent holidays with his uncle and aunt, Hugh and Kitty Maguire. On the journey, however, their plans were changed by a chance meeting with a friend of Gerry's, Micky McQuade, who had a job as a chef on the ferry. Micky suggested that Gerry go to Southampton to see his brother Danny, who could fix him up with work and somewhere to live. Both these things Danny McQuade obligingly did; within a month of reaching England, Gerry found himself working for McAlpine's on the motorway near Romsey and living in a flat at Portswood. The chance meeting with Paul Hill in Southampton precipitated a split between Gerry and Eileen, whose relationship had been deteriorating in any case. Shortly, she returned to Northern Ireland, while Gerry threw up his job with McAlpine's and went with Paul to London.

At first they worked together 'on the lump' at Robert Hart's Arlington Road site, but the lures of London proved too much for Gerry and after October 11 he abandoned the job in favour of gambling, dope, drink — and, once again, crime, in order to finance these costly tastes. Hill did not go along with Conlon in his adventures, but he did accompany him to the Paddington Conservative Club — where Gerry's uncles Hugh and Patrick Maguire were members — and the two occasionally ate dinner with Hugh and Kitty at Westbourne Terrace Road.

Paul was also not averse to capitalizing on the proceeds of Gerry's crimes, the most unsavoury of which was a break-in at a prostitute's flat in Bayswater during the second week of October. The address was selected from among the sex ads in a newsagent's window next to Biddy Mulligan's pub in Kilburn High Road. Clad in a brown corduroy jacket of Hill's, Conlon broke into the empty flat and stole several hundred pounds which he found in a plastic bag in the wardrobe. He also strangled the woman's poodle before escaping through the window by which he had entered and taking a taxi back to Quex Road. He gave half the money to Hill.

One day merged very much with another. Hill's weekly departure for Southampton meant that Saturdays and Sundays were particularly hazy in Conlon's memory. He could remember little for certain about what he had done on October 5, the day of the Guildford bombings. Was it the day he had spent with Noel Marley after the dance at the Carousel Club in Camden Town, or had he met a room-mate, Patrick Carey, at Quex Road? The dance was ruled out, since it had happened the following week, while Carey remembered Hill's being present at the meeting at Quex Road, which also precluded October 5 as Hill had been in Southampton on that date. Besides, Carey's girlfriend maintained that she had been with Patrick on October 5 and that Conlon was nowhere to be seen. Gerry concluded he must have spent most of the early evening sleeping off drink in the hostel, to be woken around 6.15 by Carey who arrived with a stack of Country and Western records. The only verifiable events of the day were that he backed a horse called John Cherry which came in at 8–1 and that at around 9.00 p.m. he telephoned his parents in Belfast at a regular haunt, the Engineers' Club in Corporation Street.

But he never got through. It seems Guiseppe Conlon was buying a round of drinks at the time. Gerry, who had no more money, gave the hostel telephone number to the Engineers' doorman and spoke briefly to his aunt Bridget, who he thought sounded a little drunk. Guiseppe paid for his round and was called to the phone, but by the time he reached it Gerry's money had run out — and the doorman had lost the telephone number.

Hill and Conlon were waiting for their insurance cards to come through from the DHSS because they had heard about a good job at a building-site in Piccadilly. The cards would take some days to arrive, so the morning after the theft at the prostitute's flat they took the proceeds to Manchester and stayed for four days with one of Gerry's aunts. Gerry gave her some money to send to his mother and he and Paul blew the rest, returning to London on October 19 with about £60. Hill went straight down to Southampton, while Conlon returned to Quex Road, via the bookie's where he lost his remaining money. The follies of his recent lifestyle were catching up with him and Gerry felt miserable and homesick. The long-awaited cards from the DHSS had still not arrived, which made him feel worse. It was in this state of mind that he took some LSD and found himself pitched into a very bad trip. Trembling and terrified, he became obsessed with the need to go home to his parents. He went to see Father Ryan, the priest on duty at the hostel that evening, who did not tumble to the LSD but remembers the incident vividly:

'Gerard was a young, skinny, curly-haired youth and at this time he wore a sheepskin coat which came down to his knees. The edges were lined very conspicuously with white wool. His coat was totally unsuitable and made him look very conspicuous. He appeared very agitated, and under a great deal of stress. I formed the conclusion that he had a mental breakdown of some kind and was not in a fit state to travel. I tried to persuade him to remain at the hostel and I would arrange for him to see a doctor in the morning. I refused to give him any money. He went off and returned in about an hour. He had succeeded in getting almost all the money he needed to go home. He required another £5 to get him home. Seeing that he was going to go anyway, I thought I had no option but to give him the money... I was concerned for him as he left because the weather conditions in the North-West of England were very inclement. I had visions of him trying to hitch a lift over the M6 around the Shap and having problems of exposure. I was concerned for some time after he left and hoped he made it home all right.'

In fact, Gerry travelled via Holyhead and Dublin, having missed the connection for the Belfast ferry. At Holyhead he was stopped by a Special Branch officer who remarked that he had a Northern Irish accent and asked why he was returning to the Republic. Gerry explained that he had missed the boat-train and gave his correct name and home address. The officer searched his bag and, having found nothing of interest beyond a handful of letters from his mother and father, waved him on his way. He caught a train from Dublin and reached Cyprus Street on October 20.

Returning from Southampton to Quex Road that Sunday, Paul Hill found a note which said simply, 'Cracked up. Gone home.' He also discovered, to his annoyance, that his friend had taken with him Paul's brown shirt and a red and white jumper.

Back home, Gerry felt better. Over the next six weeks there were only two incidents to disturb the tenor of his usual happy-go-lucky existence. The first was a row that blew up between Conlon, his friend Pat Kane and a couple of IRA men outside a Falls Road chip shop. 'It was over something silly. We were probably drunk. A couple of nights later they came and picked us up. They took us to the Divis Flats and gave us a bit of a slap for our antisocial behaviour.' The second was nothing at all, really; just that Conlon had a visit from the IRA, after going out drinking with some mates on his return to Belfast. '... Paul Hill being in England would have been part of the conversation. That's why the IRA came to see me. They hinted that he had offended them in some way, but did not say how. I told them he was working in London and going down to Southampton to visit his girlfriend every weekend. They asked me who his girlfriend was. I told them.'

It is possible that Conlon's interview with the IRA might have found its way back to Army intelligence if the Provisionals were sufficiently displeased with Hill to frame him for the pub bombings. Hill says no one else knew him as 'Benny' or knew of his whereabouts in England. But Benny was a school nickname and could have come from a number of Belfast sources (it was used, for example, by Martin Monaghan, his co-accused in the Shaw murder case). It is also possible that military intelligence

on the look-out for Paul Hill had turned up details of his brother
Patrick. Patrick was undoubtedly recorded in police files since
he was wanted for a firearm offence, and this would explain
the confusion over police enquiries about Patrick 'Benny' Hill
at the Keenans' and the Smalleys'. The addresses in London
and Southampton could equally have come from IRA contacts
in Southampton, if the theory of the IRA's setting up Hill is to
be taken seriously: Ronnie McCartney had recognized Hill and
had communicated his whereabouts back to Belfast. Conlon has
also denied being the source of the incorrect account of the
Shaw killing picked up by Cunningham and McCaul. He and
Armstrong say that the meeting at the Old Bell pub in Kilburn
at which Hill claimed to have told them about Shaw never took
place. Conlon does mention Brian Shaw in his police interrogation notes, but there is no knowing whether he volunteered the
name or whether it was suggested to him. All in all, there is no
conclusive evidence that Conlon led the police to Hill.

On November 28, the Conlon family sat watching television.
The news came on. Someone had been arrested for the
Guildford bombing. Gerry later told the authors that although
the suspect was shown being hustled from a police car with a
blanket over his head, he thought he recognized Paul Hill by his
trousers and the two-tone shoes he was wearing; he knew they
were mauve and white and remembered Hill buying them with
some of the proceeds from the Bayswater burglary. He told his
family of his suspicion. The news elicited little sympathy from
his mother who had always regarded Hill as a troublemaker.
The following day, November 29, the news was confirmed when
Hill's mother, Lily, came up to Conlon outside Rosie's bakery
and told him of Paul's arrest.

They came for Conlon before six the next morning, a single
policeman and four or five soldiers. Guiseppe woke his son. But
Sarah Conlon describes his arrest as an almost casual affair,
unlike the raids that were simultaneously occurring in England.
The officers (she thought they were RUC, not Army) did not

even search the house, either then or later. 'He was left alone
to dress,' Ann remembers. 'His bedroom looked out over a flat
roof and at the back of it there were alleys. He could have been
out of the window and away in no time if he thought he had
anything to run away from. He could have escaped easily.'

But Conlon chose not to escape. He was taken to Springfield
Road police station and thence to Guildford. After three days he
started to confess.

Of the four who were to make confessions, Gerry Conlon is
the one who has given the most detailed explanation of how he
came to do so. His account is substantially different from the
police record. It contains allegations of violence by the police,
which were to form the basis of Conlon's defence at the trial.
The police denied them and the jury rejected them. From this
account, which was written for his solicitor in 1985, it is clear
that the claimed physical violence was only one of a combination
of factors that allegedly produced Conlon's first incriminating
statement. Its detail matches that of a previous account he gave
to his solicitor a decade earlier, despite his not having had access
to the material in the meantime. According to Conlon, the
officers interrogating him were Detective Inspector Timothy
Blake and Detective Chief Inspector Lionel Grundy. Blake was
to deny ever having interviewed him; it was a point that the
defence would contest.

> Grundy started questioning me again and when I answered
> as I had throughout [that he had had nothing to do with
> the bombing], Blake grabbed me by the balls and squeezed
> them really hard. I was screaming with pain and when he
> let go I fell to the floor — only to be lifted up again by the
> hair. I was again put against the wall. More questions from
> Grundy. Again, Blake grabbed me by the balls and squeezed.
> I was crying, in pain and confused. I started to lose all sense
> of time...
>
> I think I got a bit hysterical. I began screaming and crying
> and couldn't stop. Grundy told them to let go of me and sat

me down. He stopped yelling and started speaking to me normal. Grundy was saying things like, I was silly, they knew I did it, why don't you make a statement and get it over. I was going to prison anyway, but if I made a statement they would help me and I wouldn't get too long. All sorts of things like this, Grundy was saying. When I calmed down he... said he was going to see his boss and would be back shortly. Jermey put me back against the wall in the search position and began questioning me. When I didn't tell him the answers he wanted, Blake would hit me in the kidneys...

Suddenly the door flew open and in came two men, one very tall with a moustache (Rowe), the other small and dapper (Simmons). Simmons came and stood in front of me. He called me an Irish bastard, a fucking murdering bastard, and he hit me a terrible slap in the face, grabbed my hair and started screaming abuse at me. Rowe poked me in the chest with his finger and said I was guilty and he wanted a statement saying so. A few seconds later, he left... Simmons said he was going to get a statement out of me one way or the other. He slapped my face again. I started to cry and he laughed... Simmons then asked if my mother's name was Sarah... if I had a sister called Bridget. He was able to tell me that my sister worked on the Dublin Road and my mother at the Royal Victoria Hospital. He said something could happen to them, especially my mother as she worked in a dodgy place. He said he was going to make a phone call. He picked up the phone and asked them to get him Springfield Road station: Mr Cunningham... He asked Cunningham if an accident could happen... Simmons grabbed my hair and half pulled me over to the desk; he put the phone between our heads and I heard a Belfast voice say, 'I'm sure we can arrange something.' Simmons then pushed me away and said into the phone he would ring tomorrow and let them know if I was being more helpful. I was crying and frightened. Simmons said if I didn't make a statement he would ring Belfast first thing in the morning and I would never see my mother or sister again. The last of my resistance shattered when he said this. I was crying and shaking uncontrollably. I said my family hadn't done anything. I fell apart. Simmons said what happened to my family was up to me... I said I would make a statement like they wanted, but it wouldn't be true as I really didn't do it...

I started to write the statement but as I hadn't done the bombing I didn't know what to write. They knew this because when I finished the first page they read it and Simmons said I should make it more like Hill's. Jermey said it might be better for me if he went and got Hill's statement so I could read it and it would be easier for me to write mine. I said yes. Jermey left and came back with two of Hill's statements. I wrote a statement from what I had read on Hill's. I just wanted to get it over. I didn't care any more. I was tired, frightened, and to tell the truth I was beginning to believe that maybe I had done the fucking bombing. I just couldn't take any more. It seemed easier to do what they wanted. I don't know how long it took me to write the statement. I don't even remember writing it; everything seemed unreal. When the statement was done I was given a cup of tea and a fag while they read it and then I was taken back to the cells for the night.

Police say that Conlon started to confess much more quickly — on the afternoon of his arrival from Belfast. Detective Chief Inspector Grundy's notes run to only three pages before 'Conlon jumped to his feet and said, "All right. All right. I'll tell you the truth!"'

Simmons, who records seeing him for the first time the following day (December 3), after Conlon had made his first statement, describes their meeting as follows: 'Detective Chief Inspector Grundy introduced me, saying, "This is Detective Chief Superintendent Simmons. He is in charge of this investigation and he has seen the statement which you made yesterday concerning your part in this matter." Conlon said, "Yes, sir, but I've been telling these men more now, sure I have." I said, "I understand that, Mr Conlon, and I know you are now telling us some of what you say happened on the day of the bombings, but are you telling us the full truth yet?" He said, "Yes sir, I am. I wanted to get it off my chest. It's been worrying me for weeks now." I said, "Why didn't you tell us the whole story right away, then, if it was worrying you, instead of denying that you were involved?" He said, "I'm sorry about that, sir. It was because I was frightened of what might happen to me." I asked, "Do you mean you were frightened of the police?" He said, "No, no, I was frightened of what the Provies might do to me when I went home. I thought I'd get a head job for telling." I said, "But now you have changed your mind." Conlon said, "Yes. I want to get it off my conscience, honest I do.... "'

By this time, Paul Hill was on his fourth statement. He had made a confession involving Armstrong and himself at Woolwich which, though vague, was to form the basis of the Crown case for the King's Arms bombing. But the police were still not getting the hard information or the names they needed for Guildford. Conlon had said merely, 'There were eight or nine of us — Hill, Armstrong and some girls I didn't know,' while Hill said that Gerry and an 'old bird' had formed one bombing team, 'Paul' and 'Marion' the other.

Then, on December 3, there was a further breakthrough for the police, who were questioning both Hill and Conlon at Godalming police station. At 2.10 p.m. Hill is alleged to have told Detective Inspector Blake and Detective Constable Peter Lewis, 'Marion is Armstrong's girl, Carole.' Hill's own account of this is as follows: 'They would go out [of the room], come back and whisper. They said the "Anne" I refer to is Conlon's aunt. I said, no, I have no idea who she was. They also said "Marion" was Carole, Armstrong's girl.'

Ten minutes later, at 2.20, Conlon began an interview with Detective Chief Inspector Grundy and Detective Sergeant Jermey, during the course of which he is alleged to have said that one of the girls in the bombing party was 'Coral', Armstrong's girlfriend, and that another, who showed them how to make bombs, was 'my auntie Annie Maguire and she came with us to Guildford'. Of this, Conlon says, 'Grundy said Hill had told them my aunt Annie had showed us how to make bombs. I said no. Grundy said he wanted me to make another statement saying my aunt Annie had showed us how to make bombs. I said she hadn't and Hill was lying. Grundy said his boss [Simmons] believed Hill and wanted a statement from me saying she was involved and if I didn't he would have to tell his boss and I knew what his boss was like... I wrote what they wanted. I would have mentioned any name they wanted by now.' He says he copied from Hill's statement. For his part, Hill claims he was confronted with Gerry who, under police instructions, said, 'You know that's my aunt Annie.'

At 3.50, Hill began another statement in which he says that the 'old bird' is 'Annie who I met with Hugh Maguire in a Maida Vale club... She was in the bomb pair with Gerry.' Hill and Conlon independently claim that such collaboration continued all afternoon. 'Every so often another would enter, whisper something and that would be put to me to put down,' says Hill. 'This was normally shouted. "As it was," they would say, "it doesn't tally with what he [Conlon] said, and it had fucking better."'

By 5.30, the police could claim corroboration of three more crucial names. Back in North-West London, police moved in on Anne Maguire, Carole Richardson and her boyfriend, Patrick Armstrong.

12
ARMSTRONG

'I don't believe in what the IRA are doing because I am scared of getting shot. Everyone used to pick on me at school because I wouldn't fight back. I took hidings when I hadn't done it, and I was scared.'

Patrick Armstrong, in the course of examination under a
truth drug in prison, 1975

Patrick Armstrong was born in Belfast on September 24 1950, the second of four children. His father, a scaffolder who was never able to work satisfactorily after a serious fall almost cost him his leg, died when Paddy was 18. The family eked out a living on the wages earned by his mother, Eileen, as a cleaner at the university. For the first four years of Paddy's life they lived in the small Catholic enclave of the Short Strand before moving to the Lower Falls and thence into the Divis Flats. Eileen was a devout Catholic. Paddy was educated at St Comgall's Primary in Divis Street and at St Peter's Secondary Intermediate, Whiterock, where he was three years senior to Hill and Conlon.

But many of his friends were Protestants. His father's brother Billy had married a Protestant and Paddy's cousins were brought up Protestant. One of his early girlfriends was Protestant and lived off the Shankill Road. Paddy also worked with Protestants. He left school at 15, and between 1966 and 1970 worked for three months as a plumber's mate with John Dowling & Son, Upper Queen Street; for 20 months as a factory storeman with a clothing manufacturer off the Donegal Road; and for 18 months as a storeman at a cash and carry in the Falls Road. In the autumn of 1971 he worked briefly as a paint-sprayer with James Mackie & Son of Springfield Road. The jobs had low pay and low prospects and he quit each of his own accord in search of something better, paying the penalty of spending long months on the dole as a consequence.

As the sixties progressed, Paddy became aware that there was a particular reason for this; in fact his memories of the onset of 'The Troubles' are inseparable from those of the problems of finding work. 'It began to get much more difficult to get a job. They never openly asked you if you were a Catholic. They didn't have to. Catholics didn't go to Protestant schools so all they had to do was to ask you which school you went to and they knew whether you were a Catholic or a Protestant. If you were a Catholic, you tended to find that the job wasn't open to you.'

From his Grandma Mullin, his mother's mother, he heard stories of the IRA in the twenties. One that captured his imagination was the tale of Tom Williams, hanged for shooting a policeman. Six were involved in the shooting but only one could be hanged. Tom Williams, who was about 16 at the time, volunteered and was executed. 'Grandma Mullin liked telling stories like that, but to us they were only stories,' says Paddy dismissively.

'I suppose that the first time I knew that we were in danger from the Protestants was in 1969 when rumours began to circulate in the districts in which we were living that the Protestants were planning to attack us and to wipe out the Falls Road area. There had been civil-rights marches by Catholics and I remember one was ambushed... When "The Troubles" really broke out in 1969, about 10 Catholic streets were burned to the ground. The nearest one to us was Cashmere Street and four or five shops on the Falls Road were burned.

'I remember it very clearly on the 14th of August 1969. I was in my home in Milton Street and suddenly heard some chopping sounds, and I looked out of the window and saw some Catholics chopping down a telegraph pole as part of a barricade.' Paddy went round to his girlfriend's flat in the Divis and as he arrived the violence began in earnest. He spent the time looking after seven children in the flat — brothers and sisters of his girlfriend, and other local children — and his girlfriend's grandmother.

'That was the day that the Catholics in the Falls Road attacked the police barracks. The B men came out after the attack and about six or seven people were killed. It was the first time I had heard gunfire. One of the people killed was a nine-year-old boy who was shot dead by a bullet which went through the back window of the flat in which he lived, through two walls, and killed him. Somebody went round the Divis Flats shouting to get the women and children higher up. I grabbed a couple of children and went out of the door only to find that the B Specials who had an armoured car with a Bren-gun mounted on the top were firing indiscriminately in the Divis Flats area.' Bullets whistled close by and he dived back inside. Everyone threw themselves on the floor...

'The Army were cheered when they came in... The attitude to them only changed when curfew was imposed in 1970 or '71. I suppose we all knew the IRA would have to come back because we had to protect our areas against the Protestants. It was clear to everyone that the Catholics, being a minority, were not protected by the Protestant police force... I cannot really remember when I first knew the IRA were in our area. It was just something that happened.'

As the months passed, this atmosphere of violence became the norm. 'During the period 1971-72 I suppose I must have been stopped and questioned almost every day,' Armstrong remembers. 'Young men on the streets were automatically stopped by any Army patrol or police patrol and questioned. It became so commonplace that you never really gave it a thought.' But that didn't mean you were unaffected by it. Returning home to the Divis Flats at about 11.30 one night, he and a friend were shot at from the Army post in Albert Street. 'We saw two bullets hit the pavement in front of us... I suppose they could have hit us if they had wanted to. I think they were just shooting to scare us, but it really frightened me.' He describes a constant feeling of oppression, while his mother suffered a serious nervous breakdown and on two occasions had to be sent out of the city to recuperate. 'Living in a Catholic area surrounded by Protestants was not easy. Everyone's nerves were on edge; the slightest thing could trigger a shooting. There was often shooting — in fact you got used to it. Quite a number of people were killed who lived in the Divis Flats area; nobody I knew well, but people I knew none the less. I remember on one occasion we were not able to go out because they were firing the whole time. Eventually they called a truce on Sunday to allow people to go out and get food, but we were in our houses from 10 on Friday night until noon on Sunday.

'The Army raided our house on about four occasions that I know of; only once that I remember in Milton Street, but there were three searches of our house at Divis Flats. One of them, I remember, my mother was just going out to bingo and had gone next door to get the neighbour to go with her. I was sitting in the flat watching television and suddenly the Army broke the door in. They just simply broke the lock in. When they got in there they all had guns, and they said to me, "Where's your gun?" I said I hadn't got one. They said, "We saw you pointing it out of the window." At that point my mother came in and told them I had never had a gun and I had nothing to do with the IRA. The sergeant called my mother an Irish bitch. She invited them to search the flat, which they did, and they found no weapons. I wasn't taken to the barracks on that occasion.'

Like every young Catholic, Armstrong believed West Belfast should defend itself against Protestant raids. However, his own allegiance was to the non-violent Republican Clubs and to the Catholic Young Men's Association. In this capacity he helped organize events for charity and worked with elderly people. Not one of his brushes with the security forces resulted in a charge or even prolonged detention (another Patrick Armstrong resident in the Divis had affiliations with the Official IRA, and at least one of Paddy's arrests was a case of mistaken identity). Yet the possibility of detention filled him with dread.

In the event, his two dozen arrests took him no further than Springfield Road police barracks. His only visit to the Holyrood army barracks was for a football match. In the catalogue of events leading up to his decision to come to England, Armstrong makes no distinction between harassment by the security forces and by IRA gunmen. In one incident masked raiders broke into a bookie's in Divis Street where he was doing the marking up. One of them hit him on the elbow with a gun so that he dropped the bowl of water he was using to clean the blackboard. They took most of the money from the till. In another, men with guns burst into the Glen Chase pub on King Street and ransacked the tills. No one in the crowd of Friday-night drinkers tackled them.

'The main reason I left Ireland to come to this country,' he told his solicitor, 'was because I was fed up with "The Troubles".' His first trip to London was for six months in 1972. He worked as a hotel porter, but returned home because of his mother's ill-health, to more unemployment and the occasional casual labouring job. During a second spell at Mackie's machinery-part manufacturers, where he again worked as a paint-sprayer, he ran into an old acquaintance from school, Gerry Conlon. But beyond enjoying an afternoon at the bookie's together, the two were never especially close and they lost touch again when Conlon left the job.

In November 1973 Armstrong arrived in London a second time. The family were in arrears with the rent. Paddy was out of work again and when Father McKinley, their priest, came to talk to his mother about her financial problems he encouraged Paddy to return to England where he could get a better-paid job than in Ireland. Armstrong settled in the Kilburn area, renting a flat with a friend at 47 Chichele Road.

Although he managed to find casual work on building-sites, his good intentions of settling into a regular job were eclipsed by the excitement of London. To drink and betting-shops he now added drugs — which had been unknown to him in Belfast — pastimes incompatible with sticking to a routine. His employment prospects in any case suffered a set-back when on March 5 1974 he was arrested on a charge of burglary for stealing a television and placed on remand in Brixton Prison until May 8. When the case was heard at Middlesex Crown Court, Armstrong's landlord testified to having been with him at the time of the burglary. He was acquitted — remaining, ironically, the only one of the Guildford Four to have no conviction for petty crime, and yet becoming the only one to experience the inside of a British prison prior to being arrested for the bombing. Doubtless he also left behind him on police records his fingerprints and his photograph.

With the trial behind him and not a penny to his name, he left Chichele Road for a squat at 35 West End Lane, moving to Linstead Street — which was considered to be more salubrious — at the end of August. It was around this time that he first met John McGuinness and Sean Mullin, at a party in their flat at 15 Rondu Road, Cricklewood, to which he was taken by two mutual acquaintances, Patrick Docherty and Danny McKee.

Mullin, who got to know him well over the next couple of months, described Paddy as 'a quiet bloke' who 'didn't have much money and therefore didn't go out very often and was quite happy sitting in front of the television set. I never discussed politics with him and never heard him discuss politics with anyone else. He seemed to me a quiet, inoffensive bloke and totally not the sort of bloke who would get involved' with anything like a bombing.

Since his release from remand in prison, Armstrong had not worked with any regularity. For a few days at the beginning of October he took over a job at the Memphis Belle pub in Kilburn High Road from a fellow squatter, Jimmy Goodall, when Goodall left to go back to Ireland. The pub was a favourite haunt of the Linstead Street squatters, and Armstrong was swiftly and amicably sacked by the publican, Pat O'Rourke, under suspicion of drug-dealing (which Paddy denies) and when it was brought to O'Rourke's attention that several of the people who came to drink there with Paddy were under age. But for a few weeks as summer ended the Memphis was the focal point of Paddy's social life. It was there that Lisa asked him if she could hold her 16th birthday party at Linstead Street on September 6 — the party at which Paddy first met Carole. And it was there that Paddy ran into McGuinness again and asked him if he could hold his own birthday party, three weeks after Lisa's, at the flat in Rondu Road. It was to this party that Conlon and Hill were invited because they made an appearance — unusually for them — in the Memphis Belle on the day in question. Hill didn't go to the party but he registered the connection between Armstrong and the Rondu Road address.

Two days after Goodall's departure, on Sunday September 29, the police came to the house in Linstead Street looking for him in connection with a drugs offence. They searched the squat and took the names of everyone living there, including Armstrong's.

On October 20, Paddy and Carole left London in something of a hurry. Late on the Saturday night, October 19, two men had arrived at the house in Linstead Street. One of the squatters, Maggie Carrass, opened the door to them. When he heard their voices, Paddy dived out of the back of the house and disappeared. One of the men, whose name was Don Murphy, burst into the front room brandishing a hatchet. 'Tell Paddy that if he's not at the Memphis Belle tomorrow night we'll be back for him and we'll use this!' he yelled at Carole. After rampaging around the house for a while the two men went away. Half an hour later, Armstrong crept home. He refused to tell Carole what the row was about, but she was fully alive to its seriousness — money or drugs, she supposed. They spent that night at Rondu Road and set off north the following day.

As soon as they were out of London, their spirits rose. Carole was delighted to be on the road again; she had a dream of coaxing her lover away from the city and finding work with him in more congenial surroundings. Armstrong was equally enthusiastic. He had heard of good construction jobs — at a sensational £14 a day — on offer in North Wales. Hitch-hiking, they travelled north to Chester and Bangor and when the jobs, predictably, turned out to be a myth, headed south for Bristol via Caernarfon. They reached the south coast via Exeter and Poole and then travelled eastward — to Brighton, Newhaven,

Hastings and eventually Folkestone, where an incident occurred that was to have considerable importance for both of them.

Throughout the trip they had kept in touch with home; Paddy writing to McGuinness, to his two sisters living in England and to Jimmy Goodall who was now in prison. Carole wrote to Lisa and kept in touch with her mother by telephone. On this particular day, she had gone into a call-box in Folkestone and rung her mother, who had agreed to ring her back. A man was waiting outside the phone-box and after a while he grew impatient and hammered on the door. Carole opened the door and the man grabbed her by the hair and shouted at her that she was allowed only three minutes on a public telephone. Carole told him she would stay there as long as she liked, whereupon the man shouted, 'Get out the fuck!', grabbed her by the hair again and hit her head against the side of the box. Carole punched him in the face. Paddy came to her rescue, steered the man out of the box and shoved him towards the road. Carole, her conversation with her mother disrupted, ran into a shop two doors away and called the police. The man, meanwhile, had returned to the telephone-box and made his phone call, but on leaving found himself face to face with four workmen from a building-site across the road and two women, who had seen what happened. The workmen offered to 'fix' the man for Paddy, but Paddy replied that it was better to wait for the police. The police arrived and everyone went to the police station. Carole gave her home address and Paddy told the police he lived at 14 Linstead Street, NW6. Statements were taken and the man was made to apologize to Carole for assaulting her.

Their spontaneous appeal to the police over what was essentially a minor incident, and their giving their correct names and home addresses regardless of the fact that Armstrong's strong Belfast accent would have prompted the police to check their identities, were features that the Crown never sought to explain in its later portrayal of Armstrong and Richardson as two desperate terrorists, who in the latter part of October were on the run in the aftermath of a bombing.

Oblivious of any significance in their encounter with the law, the two travelled on to Dover, where they splurged some of the £30 remaining to them on a night in style — at Josef's Guest House in Folkestone Road. Mrs McMillan, who ran it, took a liking to Carole whom she described as 'a very nice homely girl'. The pair of them, she thought, were 'a very, very nice couple'. They told her they wanted to go to France.

But like so much in their lives, this too was wishful thinking. The next day they returned to London and travelled north to Hertfordshire where they visited each of Paddy's two sisters. Carole had the idea of going to Newcastle, but by the time they reached it their money had almost gone. Carole borrowed some from an aunt and they slept rough as usual, attempting unsuccessfully the next day to get some cash from Social Security. When this failed they realized the most sensible thing was to go back to London. The plan was to see Carole's mother and then travel to Belfast and get married; Paddy wrote to his mother from Newcastle with the momentous news.

But somehow this plan also evaporated. Approaching London, they split up in order to visit their respective families. On October 30, Paddy left his sister's and caught a bus into London, where his first act was to enter a betting-shop and lose all his money. He walked from Golders Green to Cricklewood and arrived, penniless, at 15 Rondu Road where John McGuinness told him he could stay on the sofa. This he did for the next 16 days.

Rondu Road was a rented flat and its inmates were somewhat different in outlook from the squatters, most of them holding down jobs that enabled them to run cars and enjoy a higher standard of living than their friends at Linstead Street. The flat was tiny: its five occupants — McGuinness, Mullin, Anderson, Carlisle and Cully — shared a single bedroom and a sofa-bed in the living-room. It was difficult enough for them to stay with their girlfriends there. The offer of accommodation to Paddy Armstrong was an act of true charity born, it appears, out of a vague sense of pity for him — though like many such acts it was accompanied by a hint of resentment. When records were stolen and gas meters broken into there was a feeling on the part of some of them that Paddy might have something to do with it. They were wrong: Armstrong's friend Gerry Conlon later admitted it was him.

Armstrong's own motivations at the time are unclear. Since returning to London he had not contacted Carole and in his second week at Rondu Road she turned up on the doorstep one night, furious at his neglect of her. Fortunately everyone was out and they were able to have the necessary argument in peace, before making up and settling down to watch television. At about midnight, the others all came home together with some friends. There was an instant decision to have a party and an expedition was launched to the Pakistani shop in Cricklewood Broadway for beer. They played records and sang and McGuinness, Anderson, Robbie Carlisle and Paddy smoked dope. The party broke up at about 3.00 a.m. Carole stayed the night with Paddy on the sofa. She left next morning after the others had gone to work, lending Paddy 50p. Peace had been restored, but there was no further mention of marriage.

It was shortly after this that Armstrong returned to Rondu Road one day — he habitually left the door open on going out because he didn't have a key — to find that the flat had been burgled and the meters broken into. Paddy caught the bus to Staples Corner, where McGuinness, Mullin and Anderson were working on a building-site, and told them what had happened; it was decided to call the police. The police arrived, took all the details and instructed them not to touch the mess since they would be back the next day to test for fingerprints. Paddy told them he would be in all day since he was not working. That night he won money off all the others at cards — but he lost it on the horses the next day. He borrowed £5 from Alastair Cully, lost that too, and decided that perhaps his credit had expired at Rondu Road. That night, November 15, he spent with Carole at her latest squat, 14 Algernon Road, before taking refuge in Hertfordshire with his sisters.

From that date until his arrest, Paddy based himself at Algernon Road, although Carole — with whom his former disappearance still rankled — left the squat herself, without telling him, in order to take a job in a hotel. Paddy was angry and relations between them grew frosty, though he did go out and find some work partly in consequence. At the end of November, Paul Colman, a fellow squatter at Algernon Road, asked him if he wanted to take part in a raid he and a couple of the others were planning on a local chemist's shop. Paddy declined, although he was happy enough to share in the proceeds.

'I went downstairs to see what they had: I saw masses of bottles of tablets and some syringes and almost immediately we started taking the drugs. That night [December 1] I had injections mainly, and took some 20 speed tablets. I was injecting Tuinal: I think I took about five tabs on the first injection and two tabs on the second one. I was up all night and got no sleep at all. On Monday December 2 we were on drugs the whole day... mostly speed and Tuinal. I had two injections that day, each of two tablets of Tuinal. I took an awful lot of speed; I can't remember how much. I didn't get any sleep that night, either, because the speed was keeping me awake.

'On Tuesday... we were really taking the drugs quite heavily. I must have had over 20 speed tablets and five or six Tuinal tablets... There were two different types of speed tablets, some were small and some big. I do not know the difference, although I assumed the bigger tablets were the more powerful ones.'

In the mid-afternoon, Carole and Lisa arrived at Algernon Road and they, too, joined in the feast. It was around six, when none of them was thinking at all clearly, that Carole suddenly remembered she had arranged to meet her mother at the bus stop on her way home from work. Too late: she had missed the appointment. This realization upset her. Emboldened by drugs and hating to let her mother down, Carole decided to brave the wrath of her stepfather, Docherty, and visit her mother at home instead. Loyal as ever, Lisa resolved to go too. It was a little after 6.30 when the two girls, stoned and nervous, approached the house in Iverson Road. Carole had not been there for weeks. They rang the doorbell and Docherty answered. Lisa remembers a sense of surprise. He was not unpleasant to Carole; he was positively friendly. What he actually said was, 'You'd better come in, Carole. There are some people here who want to talk to you.'

13
KILBURN
ROUND-UP

'I was with two girls. We roared with laughter. We thought
it was a huge joke.'

Brendan Dowd recalling in court the charging of the
Guildford Four

Lisa waited outside in the street for Carole and was startled
to see her reappear in the company of two policemen. Carole,
however, seemed unperturbed. She had told her mother as she
left the house that she would either call back later or meet her
for lunch the next day.

'I've got to go to the police station,' she shouted across at
Lisa, and asked the police if her friend could come too, since
they were going out for a drink afterwards.

'The police didn't ask me to go,' says Lisa. 'But I went anyway.
I realized Carole must be in some sort of trouble, though I had
no idea what. In the car they asked us if we'd heard of Judith
Ward. The name meant nothing to us. Neither of us thought any
of this was important.'

As soon as they entered Harlesden police station the two girls
were split up and led into adjoining interview rooms. Lisa asked
one of the policemen, 'What's it all about, anyway?'

'You're being arrested for murder,' he answered.

Lisa started laughing. 'I really thought they were joking. I'm
serious about this. It was such a stupid thing, I thought at that
time. I said to them, "You're joking!" and one of the police
officers kicked me up the backside. He did it hard. He told me
not to speak to his boss like that.'

It was now five days since the arrest of Paul Hill. Lisa says the police told her she had been to Guildford and asked if she knew Armstrong. 'They named lots of people and asked if I knew them... They said I had slept with Conlon and a few others had "fucked" me. They used those words. I was frightened. It was like a nightmare. I started screaming and shouting. Then one of the police officers, the same man who had kicked me on the backside, got hold of me by a big hippy crucifix which was hanging on a chain around my neck. He said, "God won't help you now," and ripped the crucifix from my neck... They told me they were going to arrest my mother.'

Meanwhile, Carole was being interrogated by Detective Sergeant John Donaldson of Surrey Police.

'"Bombings?"' he records her as saying, '"What the hell would I know about bombings?"' He asked her how old she was and she told him 17. He asked about her boyfriend, Paddy Armstrong, and she told him Paddy was squatting somewhere. Later she told him the address: 14 Algernon Road, Kilburn.

Carole says he showed her a photograph of Armstrong, which she identified, and then informed her they were both wanted for murder. 'I told him it was a load of bloody rubbish and he knew it.' Donaldson, however, records that at this point Carole burst into tears.

'When was the bombings at Guildford?' she asked.

'In October,' Donaldson told her. His statement continues: 'She said, "If I can see my diary it will prove I wasn't at Guildford." I said, "I think you were, but we'll talk about that later." The accused started to cry again and as I left the room she shouted, "Then you'll have to prove it!"'

Carole and Lisa were taken downstairs and put in cells next door to each other. 'I started hallucinating [from the drugs],' Lisa recalls. 'I kept hearing Paddy's voice. I was lying on the floor and screaming and shouting.' Carole heard her through the wall and tried to calm her down. The drugs, at this point, were having a relaxing effect upon her. 'I told her it was only the Tuinal. She told me, they've accused me of murder, and I said they've accused me of it as well, but they'll have to eat their words. Then a policeman came past and told us that if we didn't quieten down we would get 30 years apiece. We then both shouted abuse at the policeman and kicked and banged the door. About 10 minutes later Lisa was let out of her cell.'

At 9.25 the same evening, Donaldson, Detective Constable Vernon Attwell and officers from Surrey and the Metropolitan Police surrounded the squat at 14 Algernon Road. Its occupants had earlier dispersed for the evening: Robert Joyce and John 'Tonto' Boylen had gone to the cinema; Paul Colman to sell some of the drugs from his raid on the chemist's shop; Maggie Carrass was upstairs sleeping off the effects of their collective drug binge; while Pearce Bergin, Jean Caseley and Paddy Armstrong were, in Paddy's words, 'bombed' on speed and Tuinal, watching a television programme about Lady Randolph Churchill.

Pearce got up to leave and Paddy went with him out into the hall. Suddenly there came a shuddering thud at the front door. Bergin and Armstrong stared in astonishment as its panels splintered before their eyes and four policemen burst in. 'One of them had a crowbar in his hand,' Paddy told his solicitor. 'Two of them grabbed Pearce and two of them grabbed me.' Attwell, whom Armstrong later christened 'Dirty Harry', had a gun in his hand. 'Dirty Harry asked me my name and I told him "Patrick Armstrong". He said, "You're the one we're looking for." I was taken out by Dirty Harry and the other officer to a car which I think was a Ford. I was made to put my hands on top of the car and Dirty Harry pointed the gun at me throughout. He told me not to move. I was searched. The other officer with Dirty Harry who had seized me when they first came into the house put me in their car and told me to keep my hands on the top of the seat. Dirty Harry got in the front passenger-seat and another officer sat in the back of the car with me and another officer got into the driver's seat. Dirty Harry told me that if I moved he would empty the gun into me. I asked him what it was all about. He said, "You'll find out." I asked him again and Dirty Harry said, "Did you hear about the Guildford bombings?" I said yes. He said, "Well, you're nicked for them." I said, "I had nothing to do with them at all."' While Attwell took Armstrong to Harlesden police station, Donaldson stayed behind to supervise the arrest of the squat's other occupants.

At the police station, Paddy was ordered to take off his trousers, shirt, shoes and socks. He says he told the officers who searched him that he had never been in Guildford in his life; he didn't know where it was. The officers said nothing. Lisa, too, was stripped and searched and then allowed to sit on a bench opposite the room in which Paddy was now being interviewed. She could hear the sound of chairs screeching on the floor. 'I imagined that he was being hit,' she recalled later, 'though I don't know whether he was or not.' Into her confused brain came the voices of others — Maggie Carrass, from Algernon Road, and Carole, repeatedly asking for a solicitor. She remembers the police saying, 'No, you can't,' and Carole's voice again, insisting that it was her right, until she was told to shut up.

At about 11.00 p.m., Donaldson's vigil at Algernon Road was rewarded by the return of Paul Colman. He, it was hoped, was the 'Paul' mentioned by Hill in his statements. Donaldson accosted him on the basement steps and hustled him down into the house, informing him once they were inside that Colman was being arrested for the Guildford bombing. 'You're joking!' was the officially recorded answer.

The arrest of Colman completed the round-up of suspects at Harlesden. Lisa watched as the door of Armstrong's interview room opened and he was brought out into the corridor. Armstrong recognized one of the officers with Colman as a man called Pritchard who had been involved in his burglary case nine months previously. He had a gun in a canvas holster on his waist and was holding a crowbar.

'What's wrong?' he said when he saw Paddy. 'Lost your bottle?'

Armstrong was shaking with fear. He answered, 'You know I always shake like this because I did it the last time you questioned me. I always shake when I'm nervous.'

'Who got the TV?' Pritchard asked, alluding to the burglary.

'I don't know,' Paddy said.

Into the hall came Maggie Carrass. 'Look at all this trouble you've got us into!' she shouted when she saw Armstrong. She was crying.

'I haven't got anybody into trouble,' Paddy protested. The police told them both to be quiet. Armstrong was taken out to a car and driven away. Lisa saw Paul Colman put into a second car. Then Carole appeared. Through a confusion of faces, which included those of Maggie Carrass and Jean Caseley, Carole saw Lisa and shouted to her friend, 'Find my diary! See where I was!' The next moment she was gone.

In the early days of December over 40 people were arrested under the Prevention of Terrorism Act and held in police stations around London and the Home Counties. Twenty came from the Kilburn squats, 14 of whom were released fairly swiftly. Most of the rest were either relatives of the Guildford Four or people mentioned in their statements. But some had never heard of them, had nothing to do with them and appear to have been held for no other reason than that they were Irish and happened to be in the wrong place at the wrong time. Apart from those of Armstrong and Richardson, the arrests on the night of December 3 that were to have the most far-reaching consequences were not at the squats at all but at the home of Anne and Patrick Maguire.

At this point, however, the press were not discriminating. On December 5 the *Daily Mail*, for example, reported the raids on the Kilburn squats as a 'remarkable coup' in the hunt for the IRA safe houses, each raid producing clues to further addresses, as well as 'names, aliases, even some of the disguises favoured by the wanted men and women. Many of the suspects were caught in sleeping-bags — which terrorists carry around from one "safe house" to another to beat police raids... The problem facing Mr Rowe was that he had discovered IRA bombers in London were operating on the same pattern as they do in Ulster — all having several homes, so that if one home is visited and the wanted man is not there, then the alarm is given and all is lost.'

For Christopher Rowe, the round-up was a triumph. The *Mail* described him as 'confident it has shattered a tightly knit group of terrorists which began its bombing in London last August, 235 explosions ago'. However, the *Mail* added the caveat of a 'Bomb Squad member': 'There may still be some splinter fanatics.'

He spoke judiciously. The round-up in Kilburn was to have no effect at all on the wave of bombings that had terrorized London throughout November and was to continue unabated until the end of January 1975. The bomb at the Talbot Arms, Chelsea was thrown after Hill, Conlon and the tenants of the flat in Rondu Road had been taken into custody. At no time were those arrested at the beginning of December questioned about any of the November incidents — despite police insistence that they had arrested not only the bombers but the bomb-makers, 'Aunt Annie' Maguire and her household, at their 'bomb factory' at 43 Third Avenue, Harlesden, North-West London.

14
43 THIRD AVENUE

'I saw an officer who I now know as Simmons come past my cell. He... said, "You want to know about your son? Well, he's going to get 30 years." And then he said, "We'll see to it that you die in gaol."'

Guiseppe Conlon, deposition to the court at his trial

Since the arrest of Gerry Conlon, his parents back home in Cyprus Street had not been idle. Through the Association of Legal Justice they had engaged a Belfast solicitor, Ted Jones, and a firm of solicitors in London to act on Gerry's behalf. Jones made enquiries at Springfield Road police barracks on Sunday December 1, and was told Gerry would be leaving for Guildford that evening. The Conlons called several times at the police barracks, on one occasion delivering a set of clothes for Gerry at the RUC's request. They were told that if they returned by 8.00 p.m. they would be able to see their son; but when Ted Jones drove them back to the barracks, they learned that Gerry had already gone. In fact, according to the police record, he did not leave for Aldergrove Airport until 8.40 p.m.

Gerry says he actually caught sight of them. 'I was given a fresh set of clothes which I recognized as my own. I was told to use the bathroom and clean myself up. As I came out of the bathroom I saw my mum and dad at the end of the hall, talking to a cop. I tried to get to them but was dragged into the cell by McCaul and Jermey... ' In his deposition for the court, Guiseppe said, 'I can say for sure that if I had seen my son then I wouldn't have come over here on December 3.'

This, however, was what he now resolved to do. It was a momentous decision. Since his illness had forced him to stop work 11 years previously, his only exertions had been the occasional quiet drink or gamble, and the exercise of his skill at filling in his neighbours' tax forms and performing other kindly services which earned him local respect. Of necessity, his life had been uneventful. Later photographs show him as a sick man: bony-faced and stooping, with a tension about the shoulders. But Guiseppe's diffident, rather startled expression belied a determined spirit. He had a deep affection for Gerry and informed the RUC of his intention to follow his son to England. Sarah, his wife, begged him for the sake of his health to let her go instead. But Sarah was working and supporting the family, and Guiseppe was anxious lest she lose her job.

Ted Jones welcomed Guiseppe's suggestion that he accompany him and proposed travelling by air on December 2. Guiseppe agreed, but later decided to go by boat. He consulted his GP, Joe Hendron, before leaving.

Hendron was unhappy about the plan. Guiseppe's condition had been stabilized by a rigorous course of anti-TB drugs, but he had extensive fibrosis and calcification of both lungs and was in no state to travel. 'This man was too ill,' said Hendron. 'But he was terribly worried that his son had been arrested and he was determined to go.' The Conlons and Ted Jones had tried to telephone Sarah's brother, Hugh Maguire, but there was no answer. Hugh must be away for the weekend. Instead, Jones sent a telegram to the home of another brother, Patrick, at 43 Third Avenue, Harlesden, North-West London.

Ted Jones telephoned Guildford police and was told that it would be some days before Gerry Conlon would be allowed to see a solicitor. But before he could tell the Conlons this news, Guiseppe had borrowed a suitcase from his daughter Ann, packed a change of underclothes and some cigarettes for his arrested son and caught the overnight ferry for Heysham. Jones decided to postpone his trip. Guiseppe Conlon travelled to London alone.

The boat left at 9.45 p.m. Guiseppe sat in the lounge and dozed. About 10 feet away from him two men were chatting over a cup of coffee; their conversation was about what they were going to do in England. One of them said he was over on holiday, making for Manchester. The other was a lorry-driver; he was going to pick up a lorry on the coast somewhere.

The boat docked shortly before 6.00 a.m. on Tuesday December 3. The passengers shuffled down the single gangway and uniformed police organized them into a queue on the quay. It was grey and cold. The passengers were sent forward in small groups for immigration checks. Guiseppe saw the two men from the lounge just in front of him. There were half a dozen customs officers and Special Branch men doing the checking. Guiseppe's bag was searched thoroughly. He was asked for identity and showed his membership card for the Engineers', the mixed-religion club in Belfast at which the Conlons habitually met friends and family, and where Gerry had attempted to telephone his parents on October 5. Finally, Guiseppe was asked to empty his pockets. He took out his return ticket, his watch, a steel comb, pens, about £40 in cash and the piece of paper on which Ted Jones had written the name of the London solicitor — Simons, Muirhead & Allan of Bedford Street, Covent Garden. The official waved him through and turned to deal with the next passenger. Guiseppe found a seat on the train, which was rapidly filling up, and settled down to read his newspaper. The journey to London took just over five hours.

On reaching Euston station, he decided to go to Paddy's house in Harlesden rather than take a chance that Hugh had returned home; at Paddy's there was bound to be someone in. Sure enough, when he reached Third Avenue at about 1.10 p.m., Paddy Maguire opened the door. Guiseppe remembered Paddy as a schoolboy from the days when he was courting Sarah, but Paddy's absence from Belfast, first when he was in the Army and later after he married and went to live in England, had prevented them from knowing each other well. Sarah had not stayed in particularly close touch. Moreover, Gerry's more recent contact with the Paddy Maguires during his trips to England had not been a success. On the last occasion he had stayed with them he had been strongly suspected of stealing the children's pocket-money. Paddy made it plain to Guiseppe that Gerry's departure from Third Avenue was not exactly mourned; the boy had hit it off better with his uncle Hugh. However, this was a family crisis. Puzzled and concerned, Paddy asked Guiseppe to tell him what he knew. Since it was lunch-time, Guiseppe did not attempt to contact the solicitor, but leaving his suitcase in the living-room suggested to his brother-in-law that they go out for a drink.

They stayed in the pub until closing time. While they were out there was much speculation between Anne Maguire and her eldest son, Vincent, both of whom had meanwhile returned home, as to the identity of the unannounced and, in 16-year-old Vincent's opinion, rather smelly suitcase in the sitting-room. Paddy had not informed the family of the telegram from Ted Jones in Belfast.

When the two men returned, Anne was surprised to see Guiseppe, and on being told of Gerry's detention in Guildford she said she simply couldn't believe it. They discussed Hugh Maguire's continued absence and the fact that no one had been able to reach him or Kitty since Friday. Guiseppe suggested going round to see Hugh after supper. Anne telephoned a friend of Hugh's, Sean Tully, to find out whether he had heard anything. Tully promised to call at Hugh's flat. Paddy, however, who was rather drunk and getting increasingly anxious, slipped out of the house without telling anyone where he was going. He reappeared sometime before 7.00 p.m. and told his wife and brother-in-law that he had been to Harrow Road police station to enquire about Hugh, but the police had been unable to help.

After several attempts to call the solicitor, Guiseppe eventually got through at around 6.30 p.m., spoke to David Walsh and asked about arranging to visit Gerry. He made an appointment to see Walsh at 10 o'clock the following morning and called Sarah in Belfast to tell her the arrangements.

As evening fell there was much coming and going in the household. Supper was eaten in the kitchen. At 5.30 Vincent left for his evening class, and just after 6.00 Anne's youngest son,

Patrick, went out to the youth club. At about 6.30 Sean Smyth came in. He was Anne Maguire's brother, who lived with them; Guiseppe, who knew him merely as someone to say hello to, had not seen him for two years. They shook hands. Then Sean Tully walked, unannounced, into the house through the open front door; he had bad news. The woman who lived upstairs from Hugh Maguire had told him that Hugh and Kitty had been picked up by the police early on Saturday morning and had not been heard of since. Before the family could digest this shocking piece of information, there was another visitor: Pat O'Neill, a friend of Paddy and Anne's, arrived at the house with his three children, whom Anne had agreed to look after for a few days while their mother was in hospital.

Five minutes after O'Neill's arrival, at 7.05, Sean Tully drove away. His departure was noted by two people waiting outside; they were detective sergeants from Harrow Road police station. They watched Anne take her eight-year-old daughter, Anne Marie, and one of the O'Neill children down to Harrow Road to buy chips. They watched Paddy Maguire, Pat O'Neill, Sean Smyth and Guiseppe Conlon set out for the Royal Lancer for a drink sometime after 8.00 p.m. Anne said it was nearer 8.30.

Anne got the O'Neill children ready for bed and started to sort out the day's laundry. She was putting shirts into the washing-machine when the doorbell rang. Glancing through the window that looked from the kitchen out into the hall, she saw four men walk into the house and for a moment thought that the drinkers had returned early from the pub. But when the kitchen door opened, the man who stood there was a stranger.

'What is it?' Anne asked.

He didn't reply. But from behind him, a second man spoke. It was Detective Chief Inspector David Munday. He called her into the sitting-room. The hall was full of men and dogs. A dog was on its way upstairs.

'Do you know who we are?' asked Munday.

'You're the police.'

'We're the Bomb Squad.'

The children were hustled into a back room while police searched the house. The officers asked Anne if she knew why they had come.

'Is it because of Gerard Conlon?' she asked.

'What makes you think that?'

'Because his father arrived here today to get a solicitor for his son. He's been picked up for the Guildford bombings.'

'Yes, we know.'

At one point Munday asked her, 'What do you think about these bombings?'

'It's terrible killing innocent people,' said Anne.

Vincent, returning home from his evening class at about nine o'clock, saw two police vans and a car parked at the house. A man was standing outside. Vincent walked up to the front door and could see through it a group of men in the hallway. He also caught sight of a dog. The man outside told him to move on.

'What d'you mean?' said Vincent. 'I live here!'

The man called in to the others, 'Here's another of them.' He hauled Vincent into the house.

Vincent saw his mother in the front room, crying. 'What are they looking for?' he asked her.

'They think there's bombs here — that we're making bombs,' she told him.

'You've got to be fucking joking!' Vincent said, and realized it was the first time he had ever sworn in front of his mother. He was told to go upstairs and help the policemen search. Among other things in which police showed an interest was a kitchen drawer full of plastic household gloves which Anne said she wore because she suffered from dermatitis. The drawer was carried into the sitting-room.

Thirteen-year-old Patrick arrived home next. 'I knocked on the door. I didn't have my own key then; I was too young. I knocked, and a policeman opened the door (though I didn't know it was a policeman). There was people in the hallway... and I thought it was a party. This was the sort of thing that was going through my head. I didn't think the police would be in my house.

Then they told me who they were. I saw my mum in the front room. She was crying. They pushed me into the kitchen with my brother John, who was already there. They were searching the place, asking silly little questions like, "Where's the bombs? Where d'you hide them?"... Me and John thought it was funny, really funny. I remember John saying, "It's *Candid Camera!*"... But it wasn't.'

John, Anne's middle son, was dispatched to the pub to get his father. In the Royal Lancer the men had finished their first round and Guiseppe had bought a second. He had just paid for it when John pushed his way through the crowd and spoke to Paddy. It was a few moments before they all realized the boy was not alone. The four men trooped outside to find cars and dogs and crowds of police. They were asked their names and addresses and Guiseppe tried to explain that he had arrived that day from Belfast and had to see the solicitor the next morning. The officer he said it to wasn't listening.

They were put in separate cars and driven to Harrow Road police station, where their property was removed from them. Guiseppe's glasses were taken away and he could see very little. After two hours in a cell he was led to an interview room and questioned by Detective Sergeant Elbourne. Again he tried to explain about Gerry and the solicitor's appointment, but Elbourne took no notice. In answer to the question as to whether he had ever handled explosives, Guiseppe replied, 'I've never handled explosives in my life.'

He then had his hands swabbed by Detective Sergeant Laurence Vickery. Guiseppe did not know what this was for. He thought Vickery seemed nervous, dropping one swab on the floor and another on the desk before stuffing them into little plastic bags. Three kinds of swab were taken; the first with dry cotton wool, the second with what Vickery said was water and the third with something that 'smelt like ether', Guiseppe thought. Vickery then took scrapings from under Guiseppe's short, rather broken nails. He had his fingerprints and photographs taken and was put back in the cell. Guiseppe was very worried about letting the solicitor know that he wouldn't be able to keep his appointment and Vickery promised to make sure he was allowed a phone call in the morning. But he wasn't.

At about lunch-time the next day, December 4, Guiseppe was put in a van with Paddy Maguire and Sean Smyth — Pat O'Neill had been temporarily released — and taken to Guildford, where the three men were once again assigned to separate cells. Guiseppe saw a doctor who gave him some tablets and said he would get in touch with the GP, Joe Hendron, in Belfast. A few days later he returned and told Guiseppe there was little he could do for him. By this time Guiseppe was badly short of breath in his cell because he couldn't get enough air.

Anne remembers Detective Inspector Graham Powell saying to another detective at the outset of their first interview at Guildford police station, 'Meet Aunt Annie!' He told Anne, 'Gerard Conlon has made a statement saying you showed him how to make bombs.'

'Gerard Conlon is telling lies,' Anne retorted. 'I have not seen him for two years,' meaning he had not been to her house. She acknowledged she had seen him, possibly with Hill, at a dance in Camden Town.

On the night of Thursday December 5, Guiseppe Conlon was in his cell when he says he 'saw an officer who I now know as Simmons come past my cell. He shouted into Paddy's cell which was near mine. I heard him say, "You're a right bastard letting your sons get mixed up in this." I did not hear what Paddy said. Then he came to me and said, "You want to know about your son? Well, he's going to get 30 years." And then he said, "We'll see to it that you die in gaol." He also said to me, "I'll see you later."'

The first two of these taunts, if indeed Simmons made them, were to prove tragically close to the truth. But Simmons never did 'see' Guiseppe. Instead, he was interviewed the following morning by Detective Chief Inspector Lionel Grundy and Detective Sergeant Anthony Jermey.

'You've been arrested and are in custody for possessing explosives,' Grundy said. 'Have you any explanation to give?'

'There is no explanation,' Guiseppe said. 'I've never had anything to do with explosives.'

'We have certain evidence that you were in possession of explosives on or about the third of December.'

'That can't be right,' said Guiseppe. 'I only got here that day.' He told them of his journey from Belfast and the afternoon he had spent at 43 Third Avenue.

Jermey said, 'Do you remember having swabs rubbed over your hands?'

'Yes,' replied Guiseppe.

'That was a test to see if you had handled explosives recently. Do you know that that test has proved positive?'

'No, sir,' Guiseppe repeated. 'I haven't ever handled explosives... I've never handled explosives in my life... '

'Then how do you explain the explosives on your hands as a result of this test?'

'I can't,' said Guiseppe simply. 'I only came here to see my son.'

The questioning was the same, over and over. 'We know you have handled explosives recently. What we don't know is where. Why don't you tell us?'

'I don't hold with violence. I wouldn't have anything to do with it.'

'... If you don't hold with violence, tell us where the explosives are,' Jermey said.

'I haven't seen any explosives. I haven't touched any explosives. I don't even know what they look like.'

He was interviewed again in the afternoon, but gave exactly the same answers. Guiseppe later told the court that they called him names and that Jermey jabbed him in the forehead with a finger. 'They said they'd fix my son and that I'd never see him again.' He also said they repeated Simmons's threat that he would die in prison and that Jermey accused him of being 'over here getting a lorry full of stuff for the IRA'. They asked when he was going to pick up the lorry and Guiseppe told them he couldn't even drive.

'I said, "I've only got one story and that's the truth." I was seen three times altogether, twice on Friday and then on Saturday morning... On the third occasion... they wrote down what I said. I told them what I'd said before and that I'd come over to get a visit to see my son. It was not a long statement but when they wanted me to sign it I wouldn't until I got my glasses, and then I read it through myself and signed it.'

15
DECEMBER 4

'My conclusion after reading [Armstrong's statements] was that without corroboration in a case of this kind one is on very dangerous ground. Where there are additional problems about the way in which the interrogation was handled then one is on more difficult ground still. And the raising of those questions in the Armstrong case led me to spend the next 10 years being concerned about the management of interrogation and about confessions.'

Barrie Irving, Director, Police Foundation, 1986

By the morning of December 4, the Guildford Four were, for the first time, assembled together in the custody of Surrey Police. Hill had already been charged with murder at Guildford, but the new Prevention of Terrorism Act extended from two to seven days the period of time that the police could — with the sanction of the Home Secretary — hold suspects without charge. (Out of the first 594 applications for this extension, the Home Secretary refused only two.) In the event, none of the four was charged within the two-day period; all the charges could be said to be a product of the new powers. The Act provided no requirement for the police to allow suspects access to a solicitor during this protracted detention.

December 4 was to be a day of critical police interviews and confrontations, yielding a mass of information — much of it confused and conflicting — which was later to be picked over in the construction of the Crown case. The manifold nonsenses and contradictions, ignored for the most part by the prosecution, became central to the argument of the defence that the confessions were false and that the only verifiable detail relevant to the bombings was detail already known to police at the outset of the interrogations. The accounts that follow are taken primarily from police records. They differ from the defendants' own recollections which were to emerge at the trial.

The first event was a request by Paul Hill to speak to his girlfriend, Gina Clarke, about the alibi she had given him for the night of October 5. She was brought to his interview room at 11.35 a.m. In the short conversation that ensued, Hill apparently instructed her to 'tell the truth'. After a little prompting, Gina said, 'He didn't get down until about quarter past 10 that night,' adding to her lover, 'You told me that you had stolen something and that if I was asked, to say that you had been with me all evening.' Hill told the police he had not wanted to get Gina into trouble. When she left the room at the end of this short interview, his Guildford alibi had been severely damaged.

Hill then asked Detective Inspector Timothy Blake and Detective Constable Peter Lewis if he could make further amendments to his previous statements. 'The two girls, Annie and Carole, were in the cars when they picked me up in Quex Road.' 'Why didn't you tell us this before, Paul?' Lewis asked, to which Hill's answer was, 'I'm frightened to tell the full truth in case I get a head job. Armstrong would do it, you know. He'd kill me if he knew I was telling you this.'

He added that the bombs had been 'fixed' at about 4.00 p.m. in the countryside near Guildford; that he and Armstrong had stood on the corner opposite the Horse and Groom while the bombs were planted — Annie and Conlon carrying theirs into the Horse and Groom in a plaid bag, while 'Paul' and Carole entered the Seven Stars, Carole concealing their bomb in a white paper carrier; and that they had all left Guildford at about 8.10 p.m. and driven 'very fast' back to London. Hill said he had been dropped at Waterloo and had caught the train to Southampton.

While he was writing this statement, Donaldson and Detective Chief Superintendent Wally Simmons brought Armstrong into the room. It was a simple matter of identification. Hill confirmed that Armstrong was the man referred to in his statements, and Armstrong was given no opportunity to confront the acquaintance who had named him as an accomplice. The encounter appeared to have a decisive effect on Armstrong, however. Returning to his own interview room he began, weeping and shaking, to supply details of a past that claimed membership of first the Official and later the Provisional IRA. He now told his interrogators that his activities in Belfast had included the handling and firing of guns and taking part in raids on betting-shops. His 'lieutenant' had been someone called Connolly, and on being prompted Armstrong agreed this was the same person as Conlon. It was 'Connolly' who had contacted him in London, introduced him to Hill and shown him photographs of pubs they were to bomb.

On October 5, claimed Armstrong, the bombing party drove to Guildford in two Ford cars. One was possibly a Capri, the other a light-coloured Anglia; he had difficulty identifying them, he said, partly because he could not drive and partly because he was colour-blind. Paul Colman drove Carole, 'Connolly' and Armstrong in one; Hill took the other with 'Aunt Edith or Ethel' and 'two other Belfast boys'. They met together at a café in the centre of town, where they whiled away some two and a half hours, dispersing at about 7.00 p.m. to plant their respective bombs. Paul Colman parked by a pub with a 'horse on the sign', and 'Connolly' and Carole went in with the bomb in a brown paper parcel while Colman and Armstrong waited by the car outside. Carole carried a 'hippy shoulder-bag'. The two re-emerged after half an hour and they all drove at a 'normal speed' back to London. The bomb was 'all wrapped up' with Sellotape and string and he was not aware of its being primed.

After the bombing, Armstrong said, he and Carole started going out together and both were disturbed by what they had done at Guildford. Carole was 'on drugs'. At one point they had gone on a hitch-hiking tour together round Britain.

Two days earlier, Hill had implicated Armstrong in the Woolwich bombing, claiming that he had been driven to Woolwich in the back of a sports car, that Armstrong had been in the passenger-seat and that 'Paul' had driven. He claimed that Armstrong had thrown the bomb into the pub. Armstrong now told police he had been driven to Woolwich in a car that looked like an E-type Jaguar with Hill and 'Paul'. Hill had driven. He had waited in the car while 'Paul' got out and took photographs. This reconnaissance, he said, had been the extent of his involvement at Woolwich.

In between Armstrong's first admissions (which were made in the morning) and the production of his first statement in the afternoon, Detective Chief Inspector John Horton took Paul Colman to confront Hill. Hill said, 'No, he's not the Paul. I know him.' Armstrong's afternoon interview therefore began with his principal interrogator, Detective Chief Inspector Style, pressing him on the identity of 'Paul': 'My information is that [Paul Colman] is not admitting responsibility and says he can't drive.' Nevertheless, Armstrong insisted, 'That's him, so it is. I wouldn't put an innocent man in that position. He was there. I'll swear to it in court.' He offered as proof of Colman's ability to drive the fact that he was going to steal a car to 'do a chemist's shop' for drugs with 'Little Tonto and another bloke' (John Boylen and Robert Joyce, both of whom had been arrested following the raid on Algernon Road). Clearly, Armstrong was keen to impart as much information as possible — about anything. His afternoon statement proceeded with Paul Colman named as one of the drivers for the Guildford bombing.

At 1.15 p.m., a few minutes after Hill's confrontation with Colman, Detective Chief Inspector Alan Longhurst, Detective Constable Martin Wise and WPC Anita Mills began what was to be an interview of over five hours with Carole Richardson. Longhurst's note records no breaks, though breaks in interviews on subsequent days, written up in the same note, are recorded. It was just over three hours before she agreed to make a statement, which she wrote herself. In it, she said she had met and started going out with Paddy Armstrong on September 6; that on October 5 Armstrong had picked her up from 14 Algernon Road (not her address at that time) and taken her out in a

four-door saloon driven by a man with 'fuzzyish' hair, who had
a man with black hair sitting beside him. She was 'completely
smashed on downers' and could remember almost nothing
about the drive except for a series of fragmented images:
going to a public lavatory; passing a field with horses; stopping
somewhere for five minutes; stopping again for a can of Coke;
a brightly-lit shop; a flyover; and — lastly — she remembered
'possibly' entering a pub with 'red or orange lights, a timber
roof with wooden beams' and 'if I was in the pub the toilets
were downstairs'. This was Carole Richardson's first statement.
Although she finished it at 4.49, the interview continued for a
further one and a half hours during which she indicated on a
blank plan of the Horse and Groom the position of herself and
another person. The positions were not those of the bombers.
She signed the plan.

The police had been concerned about the need for the bomb
to have been primed. Armstrong said he had no recollection of
a priming, but the statements of Conlon and Hill allowed for the
possibility. Both, therefore, were driven round the countryside
— Conlon in the morning on December 4, Hill in the afternoon
— in an effort to find the place where this might have been done.
Each identified a different location.

Conlon's drive marked the end of his statements to the police.
At 4.47 p.m. he became the first of the Guildford Four to see
a solicitor. The meeting lasted a maximum of eight minutes.
Lionel Grundy reports that Conlon said: '"I want you to know
that this man here" (pointing to Detective Sergeant Jermey)
"has been very nice to me, and this man here" (pointing to me).
"They haven't punched or kicked me or anything and they've let
me have cigarettes. But that man there" (pointing to Detective
Chief Superintendent Simmons) "doesn't believe me and I've
told the truth."'

In fact, two solicitors recall meeting Conlon that day: Ted
Jones from Belfast, who had arrived in the wake of Guiseppe
Conlon, and David Walsh from Simons, Muirhead & Allan, the
London firm briefed by Jones. Conlon remembers only Walsh.

Both describe Conlon as being in a state of distress, though no more so than most young men about to be charged with murder. Walsh confirms Conlon's remarks about the police having treated him well, but records Conlon's adding that he had been 'tricked' by detectives at Springfield Road police barracks in Belfast and had told them things that were not true. Jones registered that Conlon was concerned about the treatment he had received at police hands. Both men record that there were no apparent bruises on their client, and that the meeting, which was very short, took place in the corner of a large room in the hearing of the police officers concerned. Conlon was asked later to explain to his solicitors the apparent contradiction between his remarks about the police having treated him well and his subsequent claim that he had been badly beaten. He told them that before that first meeting he had been warned not to complain about his treatment in police custody. He also alleged that he was subsequently beaten up for telling the solicitors that Simmons had not believed what he said. Again, the account he gave in 1975 of both incidents tallies with his description 10 years later.

Immediately after the meeting with the solicitors, Conlon was charged with the murder of Caroline Slater. He said: 'Not guilty.'

Hill and Conlon were then taken separately to confront Anne Maguire. Hill went first, at 5.13 p.m. Detective Inspector Powell, who was interviewing her at the time, records that Simmons asked Hill when had he last seen her. 'Hill replied, "The last time I saw her was in Guildford." Mrs Maguire said, "He did not see me!" Hill then said, "I am telling you the truth." Mr Simmons and Hill then left the room.'

Simmons returned a few minutes later with Conlon. Powell records: 'Upon entering the room Conlon looked at Mrs Maguire and said in a raised voice, "I wasn't the first to mention your name."'

'Gerry,' Anne cried to him, 'I've got four children!'

Conlon repeated, 'I wasn't the first to mention your name.'

Simmons said to Conlon, 'When did you last see her?'

Conlon's recorded reply is: 'I've already told you this in my statement.'

Conlon's own recollection is that 'Grundy said to me we are going to see someone who I knew and I was to say what I said in my statement. I was taken by Grundy and Jermey to another room and pushed inside. In the room was my aunt Annie. She looked at me and said, "Gerry, tell them I haven't done anything."

'"I know," I said.

'Grundy said to me, "Tell her she did it."

'I just said something like, "I'm sorry, Annie. I'm sorry."'

Anne Maguire's own memories roughly accord with Conlon's, except that she remembers no apology.

Anne also recalls that Armstrong was brought in to see her. 'He had both arms up his back and one of them had hold of his hair and he looked as though he just wasn't there.'

Up to this point in the day, the one of the four to have implicated herself least in the bombing was Carole Richardson. Now that was to change. As the evening wore on, Carole, still under the influence of the massive drug dose she had taken with Lisa and the Algernon Road squatters the previous day, became hysterical. A doctor was called to Addlestone police station, to which Carole had been returned after her interrogation at Guildford. His name was Kasimir Antoni Makos and he began his examination, in the presence of WPC Lesley Croxson, at 8.50.

Richardson told him she was addicted to LSD and took it by injection; her last injection had been two weeks previously. As a doctor, Makos ought to have queried this; LSD is not a physically addictive drug and is not taken intravenously. She also told him she was addicted to the barbiturate Tuinal, which she had most recently taken on December 2. According to Makos, she then said: 'The statement I made previously is all a pack of lies. I did lie to protect my boyfriend who was in possession of the bomb and *he did throw the bomb at the pub in Guildford*. I assisted *not knowingly* my boyfriend planting the bomb in the pub in Guildford where he took me in the car from my house and at the time of him collecting me from the house I had an attack of migraine.'[1]

The WPC also reported the gist of this conversation, though very briefly and with one important difference: she did not record Carole's suggestion that it had been a throw bomb, only her second assertion, '...He put the bomb in the pub.' Makos had no cause to report the throw-bomb remark unless Richardson had actually made it. As an outsider, he might not have realized the problem posed by such a comment: if after more than five hours of interview Carole Richardson had not appreciated that the bombing she was meant to have done had involved a time bomb and not a throw bomb, then either she was not taking in the basic facts of the crime or she was so confused that she was certainly not fit for further interview.

The second curious feature of the admission ascribed to Richardson by Makos is her alleged use of the expression 'not knowingly', which has a precise application in law to denote lack of guilty intent. Is it an expression that Richardson would have used? And if not, how did it come to be inside inverted commas? Croxson wrote, more idiomatically, '"... My boyfriend... put the bomb in the pub. I was with him, but I was on drugs that night. I didn't know what was going on."' The use of quotation marks in what became admissible statements meant that each purported to quote Carole Richardson's exact words. At the trial, the prosecution was to make much of her 'confession' to the doctor, yet the differences between the two statements meant that one, at least, must have been inaccurate, if only by omission.

The doctor's statement concludes with observations that other doctors reading them subsequently have sought to question. 'The clinical examination did not reveal that this girl was suffering from any injury nor any other diseased condition which would require treatment at the time of her arrest. She was considered by me to be fit for further detention. She was

[1] Authors' italics.

in a highly hysterical state, overventilating and trembling, but finally settled to bed very well, calmed down considerably and was in a state of complete mental control and in control of herself. She was given by me one capsule of Tuinal of 200 mgm (100 mgm of Butobarbitone and 100 mgm of Amylobarbitone Sodium). She made the above statements when she was in full control of herself and completely calmed down. I settled her on the couch and covered [her] with blankets. Before leaving the cell she asked for a cigarette which was given to her by the WPC. I left the cell when she was calmed and quite normal in her behaviour.'

With this endorsement of them, he passed her admissions about the Guildford bombing to the police.

16
CHARGED

'DCI: "Are you sure that what you told us up until now is everything you know?"

Accused: "Yes, sir, and I feel better for it. I am being fed and looked after here better than being in a squat."'

Detective Chief Inspector Thomas Style to Patrick
Armstrong, Guildford police station, December 6 1974
(police record)

The following morning, December 5, Style's opening gambit with Armstrong was to pursue the subject of bomb-making. 'When we spoke yesterday I asked you about the bombs — what they were made of and the like.' In fact, Armstrong had told him very little in their interview, beyond alluding to a 'magnesium timer'. He had disclaimed all knowledge of bomb composition and the police had not asked him to include the 'magnesium timer' in his statement. Instead, a new description appeared: '[Conlon] told me it consisted of gelignite or dynamite sticks with a detonator attached to it with a timer wired on to it' — a somewhat more detailed and more accurate observation, as far as it went.

Style now turned to the location of the bomb factory. Armstrong said he thought it was in Kilburn at one of the squats, 35 West End Lane, because 'from what I was told about explosives they had to be kept in a cool place and they used to keep them in these derelict houses'. This did not support the police contention that bombs were made in Anne Maguire's orderly and well-lived-in home off the Harrow Road, and Style did not pursue it. More helpful was Armstrong's supposition that the cars for bombing jobs were hired rather than stolen, but Style did not pursue that, either.

Armed with Carole Richardson's assertion to the doctor the previous night, the detectives returned instead to Armstrong's own part in the bombing. Attwell said, 'I feel that you went into the pub yourself and that's what's worrying you.'

'I took it in,' Armstrong blurted out. 'I put the bomb in.'

'What are you saying? That you placed the bomb in the pub and not Conlon?'

'He changed the plans when we got outside the pub and said I was to go in. I argued with him but he said, "You do it or you know what will happen." I knew he meant that he would shoot me.'

Armstrong described the place where he said he and Carole had sat. It was not the place where the bombers had sat. He then said they moved to make room for people as the pub filled up. This was the correct place. He marked them both on a plan. After an interview lasting two hours and 10 minutes, Armstrong began to make his second statement; it took 50 minutes to produce. This statement was to become the corner-stone of the case against him and the precise circumstances under which it was obtained were to be fiercely contested at the trial.

In it, he said: 'Me and Carole got out of the car with the bomb. I was carrying it under my arm. We went through the front door... As I had gone to get the drinks, Carole had gone over to an alcove by a fireplace. It had a juke-box and tables in it... The pub was quite crowded and the alcove as well... The bomb was on the seat between us. Conlon had told me to act normal in the pub. Both Carole and me were nervous. I sat nearest the outside wall and Carole was sitting on my right. After a few minutes some people came and sat by Carole and both Carole and me shifted round the seat so that both of us had backs to the outside wall and facing the bar. I decided to put the bomb under the seat where I was sitting. Because it was so crowded there Carole leant forward and bent down in front of me. I got hold of the bomb with my right hand and slipped it under my

seat. I pushed it as far as it would go. After that we sat there
having our drink. I saw Conlon come in and stand by the bar
opposite us by a pillar. He did not acknowledge or signal to us.
I saw him look at us, though. I saw him go to the bar and get
a drink. Carole and I then started necking. I put my arm round
her and she cuddled up. I started kissing her round her neck and
ear. We did this so we wouldn't get involved with other people
in that place and have to talk to them. After a few minutes I
noticed Conlon going towards the gents' toilet. I didn't see him
again in the pub. After about 20 minutes I decided we should go.
I said to Carole, "We'll go now." We got up and left... We left the
pub at quarter to eight.'

When he had finished this, his second and final statement
which, like its predecessor, he did not write himself, Style,
Attwell and Donaldson took Armstrong for a drive. Asked
to indicate the route they had followed out of Guildford,
Armstrong led the police around the block, past the pub a second
time, before leaving town.

Next came the vexed question of parking. On their respective
tours of the city centre, Conlon had identified a road off North
Street, near Maples — Leapale Road — while Hill had said they
parked actually in North Street, opposite the post office. But
Armstrong was obviously clutching at straws. In his previous
statement he had said they parked first of all outside the café
that had been their rendezvous, and secondly outside the Horse
and Groom itself. On being driven round town he now identified
the café as the Wimpy Bar in the High Street — a place they
could not have reached by car, let alone parked outside, since
the High Street was closed to traffic on Saturdays. It was
a contradiction of Hill's assertion in his first statement that
Armstrong (who Hill said was driving) 'knew' that he could not
get down the High Street on Saturdays.

'Where did you park the cars, then?' Style urged. The police
drove slowly down Quarry Street at the bottom of the High
Street and as they passed the end of Mill Lane snaking off to the
right, Armstrong said, 'This is where we parked, close up to the

wall. The other car was in front of us, just there.' The detectives' hearts must have sunk. Mill Lane is narrow and winding; there is barely room for two cars to pass. In 1974, parking was expressly forbidden between 8.30 and 6.00 p.m. and the restriction applied equally to Saturdays. No bomber in his right mind would have risked parking there.

At 2.20 in the afternoon, Carole Richardson was taken to Longhurst's office for another session with Longhurst, Wise and Mills. For all the spontaneity with which she had apparently confessed to the doctor the previous evening, it was now two hours before she agreed to make a further statement to the police. By this time Armstrong had implicated her in his first admissions, and in her second statement she implicated him. 'From time to time Paddy would say things about British soldiers, when he heard one had been shot, he would say that it was good, and it was a pity only one or so had been shot. He gave me the impression that he hated the soldiers in Ireland, and I had the feeling he belonged to a group over in Ireland.'

When it came, the second statement had far more flesh than the first. There is a description of the car — 'a creamy-coloured big car. I think it was a Ford car, a saloon sort of a car, and I think it had a radio in it.' (This was a familiar echo. Paddy had been pressed the previous day to supply further details of the car. Donaldson had asked him, 'Anything else about it at all? Did it have ashtrays or a radio, things like that?' 'Yes,' Paddy had said. 'The ashtray was in between the front seats on the floor, so it was. There was a radio. The seats were brand-new and I think they were light-coloured.')

Richardson also described the passengers in some detail; none of them bore any similarity to any of the other accused, although one — 'the passenger' — was to play a part in the operation similar to the one in which Armstrong had cast Conlon.

Apart from her account of the drive to Guildford, which took what some would say was not the most orthodox route — north via Hendon and thence on to the North Circular — Richardson's description of the day's events corresponded fairly closely to the one Armstrong had finished just 40 minutes before hers began: 'The passenger turned round and faced Paddy and said, "You're taking that into the pub," and looked at the parcel on the seat. He turned to me and said, "You had better listen because it concerns you, too." I said, "Why?" and he said, "Because you're going to blow up some British bastard soldiers." I said, "I am not." He said, "That's what you think!" I said, "I am not!" And he said, "If you don't you'll end up dead, like a few others in Ireland."'

She was now able to describe a meeting in the Wimpy Bar and a parking place similar to the one Armstrong had just identified in Mill Lane (although she was not taken for a drive to identify these locations for herself): '[The car] was parked in a side-street and we walked around a corner into the Wimpy. We had walked up a road and around a corner before we reached the café.' Then came another echo of information given by Armstrong earlier in the day. That morning, DCI Style had asked him if he knew John McGuinness, whom Hill had named as Armstrong's 'minder' and who had since been arrested at Rondu Road. Armstrong had been non-committal, saying only that there was mutual enmity between 'Connolly' and McGuinness. Now, however, McGuinness was suddenly introduced by Carole Richardson. 'When us four entered the café, I saw four other people... sitting together. Out of these I recognized a man with a beard, who I had previously met several times in Rondu Road, and he is Paddy's mate. I knew his name was John.'

She reported that they had discussed which group should bomb which pub, after which the parties had split up again and returned to their respective cars. 'We seemed to drive round and round. When the passenger asked for the parcel, Paddy handed it to him and he kept it for about five minutes. [This detail may have reflected the detectives' concern for the bomb to have been primed.] I don't know what he did with it. But when he handed it back to me he said, "We've got at least half an hour."' Thus equipped, she claimed, they entered the pub.

There was a further point on which Richardson's statement of December 5 mirrored Armstrong's: he had introduced a third member of the bombing team into the Horse and Groom, and now she did too. Armstrong had alluded to the presence of Conlon, surveying the 'courting couple' from a distance before dematerializing through the gentlemen's lavatory. But Richardson gave the third bomber a far more active role. She described how she, Armstrong and 'the passenger', after switching positions more than once in the crowd, sat together along the outside wall, she with the bomb at her feet. 'The passenger said, "Do your shoelace up." I said, "It's not undone." He then said, "Well, undo it and do it up again." So I remained sitting and just bent forward and Paddy pushed the parcel under his seat.'

In fact, the meticulous police work in the charting of customers in the Horse and Groom had ensured that there was no third man unaccounted for. The Crown were to solve this problem in the same way as they were to deal with most of the inconsistencies in the case — by ignoring it — but this example illustrates how information is almost inevitably passed from interrogator to suspect, and thus how one person's statement can influence another's.

Richardson's account concluded: 'The driver said, "Did it go all right?" The passenger said, "Yeah, but how much longer to go?" The driver said, "A few minutes." Paddy said, "What now?" Someone said, "Home."'... When we got back into London, they dropped Paddy and me behind the park on the corner of Hemstal Road and Linstead Street. Me and Paddy went home.' There was nothing here to lay the ground for the crucially timed alibi that was to form the core of her defence at the trial.

For this statement to be produced, Carole Richardson was interviewed for seven hours and 20 minutes, during which time she was given only two short breaks — one of 15, the other of 30 minutes. The session ended at 9.40 p.m. Considering that this followed the previous day's unbroken five-hour-five-minute interrogation, to say nothing of her youth, the influence of the drugs she had taken and her hysterical condition the evening before, there can be no question that she had lived through two extraordinarily stressful days.

Anne Maguire claims she was also under stress on December 5. 'They made me take my socks and shoes off when I was in the cell. Without socks and shoes and a very heavy period which I had at the time I was terribly uncomfortable. They made me stand against a wall with the tips of my fingers on the wall and my feet right back and apart. There was a hand-basin in the room and they turned it on and made it drip. The fat one did this. He made me stand there for half an hour or more and he kept saying, "Tell us, are you going to tell us?" And I said, "I don't know anything about anybody at all. I go to work and do my jobs and look after my kids and my home."

'I asked if I could go to the toilet and they said no. My two legs were weak and I kept falling down, and they kept telling me to get up. Then a policewoman came in who they called Babs or something. She was well-built. She kept saying, "Here's Auntie Annie who makes the bombs." And then one of them said, "We've been too lenient with you." After lunch the two women took me to the cell and said, "Walk down towards there," pointing. And as I walked, the woman lifted her foot and gave me a kick hard on the backside. I put my two hands out and hit the wall, which stopped me from falling. They brought me into another cell and the woman said, "Are you going to tell us? Because we are going to get it out of you." I said, "I'm an innocent person that you are picking on." The woman hit me a slap across the face. I was so shocked that I did not even cry. She said to the other one, "Look at the hard bitch; she doesn't even cry," and she dragged my two arms behind my back and threw me down on to the bed. I still did not cry. I was just too shaken. And she said, "Get out!" She picked me up and pushed me out and brought me to the other cell again. They kept on and on at me and I was completely confused and horrified by the end of it all.'

The following morning, December 6, Longhurst briefly switched his attentions from Richardson to Armstrong when

he, Donaldson and Attwell questioned Paddy in the cell passage
before the formal interview got under way. The encounter is
recorded by Attwell, but not by Longhurst in his own record of
subjects and timings of interviews over that period.

The detectives were capitalizing on Richardson's apparent
admission about McGuinness. Attwell said, 'Carole has been
talking and I believe you know one of the men involved in
the Guildford job quite well.' Armstrong did not answer. Then,
pressed further, he replied, 'All right. It was McGuinness. I tried
to tell you yesterday by saying one of the cars looked like his,
but he is a friend of mine and I wouldn't want to put him in it.'

'So now we have it right, do we?' said Attwell. 'There were
two teams of four involved in the Guildford bombing. Your team
consisted of Conlon, Carole, Paul Colman and yourself and you
did the Horse and Groom... The other team consisted of Hill,
McGuinness, Auntie Edith and the Belfast man. That team did
the other pub and used McGuinness's car. Is that correct?'

'Yes, that's it, so it is,' agreed Armstrong. 'That's the
complete truth.'

With this information Longhurst now returned to Godalming,
where Carole Richardson was being questioned. No time is
recorded for the start of Richardson's first session on December
6, but Longhurst notes that he interviewed her 'until 1.45 p.m.'
and again for three hours in the afternoon before she elected,
at 6.43 p.m., to make a third statement. This time she changed
her description of the driver of the car and named another of
the Rondu Road tenants — Brian Anderson ('Andy') — as having
been present in the café. She denied the involvement of Paul
Colman.

Immediately after the interview in the cell corridor,
Armstrong was taken to an interview room, where he
confirmed what he had said in the corridor to Detective Chief
Inspector Style. Further efforts to elicit information about the
'man from Belfast' failed, despite Style's prompting. Instead,
Armstrong volunteered further speculations on the seniority of
Paul Colman within the IRA — 'He must be something big.'

At 4.30 in the afternoon, Armstrong was taken into a room and made to sit down in front of Colman. Five detectives surrounded them.

Style said, 'Is this the man that drove the car when you were engaged on the Guildford bombing?'

'Yes,' replied Armstrong. 'There's no doubt about it.'

'Have you any doubt at all?'

'No. That's definitely him.' Armstrong looked straight at Colman and said, 'Why don't you admit it and tell the truth? You were there and you know you were.'

Colman said, 'Why are you doing this? You know it wasn't me. We didn't even know each other until three weeks ago.'

A short, bizarre argument ensued.

'Yes, you did,' Armstrong insisted. 'You came round to the house one night and spoke to me.'

'You answered the door,' Colman retorted. 'But I came round to see somebody else.'

'How did you know it was me if you hadn't seen me before?' asked Armstrong.

Colman shrugged.

Armstrong was returned to his interview room as adamant as ever that Colman had been involved. Colman, however, was released before the case came to court, with no evidence against him.

The detectives' other major preoccupation in the Armstrong and Richardson interviews of December 6 was bomb-making. Armstrong again suggested it had been done at 35 West End Lane by 'I would say, McGuinness, Hill, Connolly and Aunt Edith'.

'Were you there when the bombs were made up?' demanded Style.

'No. That's the truth.'

'How can you mention these names unless you have some idea that they could be involved in making the bombs?' There had still been no mention of bombs being made at 43 Third Avenue.

'Is there anything else you can tell us, however small, about the bombs?' he persisted.

Armstrong claimed he had seen 'a timer in West End Lane, something like a pocket-watch on a chain. It was in one of the drawers when I was looking for some clothing.'

Richardson's third statement contained a description of bomb-making at a new address, 50 Glengall Road, Kilburn (one of her former squats). Among those allegedly present was an unidentified woman with similar characteristics to Anne Maguire. Richardson described 'a creamy-yellow putty-like object' into which this woman pressed a piece of wood. One of the others 'passed the woman a clock which was tied face inward on to the wood and the putty with some shiny string'. Two lengths of silver wire were stuck into the putty: 'The end of the short bit was twisted round the second bit. The second bit was bent. I think the driver of our car picked up a piece of metal about twice as thick as the wire, which was attached to the longer piece of wire with a clip. The other end of the piece of metal was attached to the back of the clock. It was then passed to Andy and they started making another two the same except the clocks were different; one a small square travelling-clock, the other round and slightly smaller which could have been a pocket-watch.' While the bombs were being made, Andy and 'the driver' spoke in 'Irish'. 'This time,' she told her interrogators, 'I have not named anyone in connection with the bombings who were not involved.' It was a promise that would hold good for only two days.

With this third statement, Carole Richardson had gone almost as far with her confessions as she was going. But two days later, on December 9, she asked to see Longhurst again. Like its predecessors, the interview was witnessed by Wise and Mills. It began at 2.40 p.m. Three hours and 10 minutes later she began to make a fourth statement. In it, she retracted allegations against Andy, John McGuinness and the woman like Anne Maguire. Instead, Richardson introduced three new characters, two men and a woman, unknown and unidentified.

After depositing the bomb in the Horse and Groom, she claimed that she and Paddy had entered a second pub — the Seven Stars. Although she said she hadn't actually seen Armstrong plant the bomb, she now implicated herself fully in both bombings. It was an awkward admission for the Crown and they were later forced to dismiss it as untrue — a disavowal that was to have deep significance for the prosecution case. No serious attempt was ever made to explain why she should admit to something she patently had not done; or why, this admission being false, the others should necessarily be true.

On Saturday December 7, with Paddy Armstrong, Anne Maguire, Brian Anderson, Paul Colman and John McGuinness, Carole Richardson was charged with the murder of Caroline Jane Slater. She wrote to Paddy from Brixton Prison:

Dear Paddy, I really wish you would pull yourself together and name the people who were with you on the 5th. They wouldn't stop at putting you in it, in fact someone did. How did they have your full name and everything else if someone didn't talk?... It's only hitting me now just how bloody serious this is and you had better realize it pretty soon. Who are you afraid of, what can they do to you, whoever and whatever they are?... In Guildford they said I was probably at Woolwich as well. Jesus Paddy what have you got me involved in? I wouldn't believe them at first, until they said you said I was there — which I don't believe now, at least I hope you didn't say it. Tell Andy and John I'm sorry but the police said they said I was there, and there was nothing else I could do then.

All I do is hope and pray that you'll have the sense to tell the truth in court, and the same with Paul Hill and whoever else was there, that's if you and Paul were, and nothing either of you have said or done has made me think otherwise. I wouldn't mind, but as far as I can remember I have never seen Paul Hill before in my life. How many times have I seen Gerry, once maybe twice. How could you get involved in anything like this, you were always fairly quiet, oh Paddy it's cracking me up locked up nearly 20 hours a day. I'm used to being out all the time, never having to worry about a thing. I keep crying for no reason at all, I'll go mad if this doesn't end soon. I can't sleep at night and I have dreams, bad ones, most of the time. I feel like killing myself at times.

Well I'll close for now. Keep your chin up and please do all you can before I crack up. Write soon. All my love Carole xxxxxx

Bob Hope for President

17
FIGHTING BACK

'I know I wasn't in Guildford and you wouldn't believe me when I told you. I've got about 40 witnesses to prove it, but I don't know half of them.'

Carole Richardson to Detective Chief Inspector Longhurst,
Brixton Prison, December 31 1974

By December 9, 11 days after the arrest of Paul Hill, the admissions of the Guildford Four were substantially complete. Further interviews took place, and in the cases of Armstrong and Richardson, police record a reiteration by each of them that they had been involved in the Guildford bombing. Denying Woolwich, Armstrong told Donaldson and Attwell on December 11, 'I didn't do that one. The Guildford one, yes, I did that and I'll take what's coming.' Later that day he was permitted, for the first time, to see a solicitor. After that, there were no more admissions of guilt.

In Richardson's case, there is a record of her being interviewed by officers of the Metropolitan Police Bomb Squad — Detective Superintendent Peter Imbert and Detective Chief Inspector David Munday, the same team who had taken Hill's second statement on November 30. The record shows that they saw Richardson on December 12.

'I've said all I'm saying about the Guildford bombing,' she allegedly told them. 'My last statement is the truth... I was on the Guildford job. I'm not saying anything about anyone else.'

'You mean you were involved in the pub bombings in Guildford?'

'Yes... I've admitted to the Guildford bombing, which I did, but I haven't done any more.'

A mystery surrounds this interview. According to the date, it took place the day after Richardson, like Armstrong, had first been allowed access to a solicitor. 'I would certainly not have spoken to them after my solicitor had advised me not to answer any further questions,' Carole Richardson commented, when confronted with the notes of the interview later. 'The trouble is that some of the answers to questions they put could only have been made by me, and I have been trying very hard to remember who I gave those names to and when I did.' But more than that, she simply has no recollection of ever meeting Imbert and Munday. 'I was sick of the sight of Longhurst, Wise and Mills and someone different asking questions would be easy to recall. I believe I did tell the Guildford police the things that are contained in the statement of the Metropolitan Police, but I honestly cannot remember.'

Although they had left the field clear for Surrey Police as far as Guildford was concerned, officers of the Metropolitan Police Bomb Squad had been hanging around on the sidelines of the Guildford investigation ostensibly in pursuit of information about Woolwich and other London bombings. It was on this pretext that they interviewed Richardson, although their questions to her appear to convey little interest in Woolwich itself. Apart from Imbert and Munday, the Bomb Squad team comprised Detective Chief Superintendent Jim Nevill (who had seen Hill on December 1, the day after he had made his second statement) and Commander Bob Huntley, the team's head.

On December 10, Huntley, Nevill and Imbert interviewed Armstrong at Guildford police station from 11.33 to 12.25, in the course of which Armstrong gave them further details of his alleged photographic reconnaissance at Woolwich. Nevill and Imbert alone then went on to interview Paul Colman. Imbert and Munday completed their examination of the Guildford bombers by travelling, on December 17, to Winchester Prison, where Gerry Conlon had been remanded.

From the police record it appears Conlon was in fighting mood. Declining the offer to have his solicitor present, he said, 'I don't want anyone present. I can look after myself. I'm not going to answer any questions I don't want to, but I can tell you I'm not bothered about this charge. I've got a good defence. There are two people, a bloke and a girl, who will say I was with them when the bombs went off.'

'What bombs?' demanded Imbert.

'The Guildford bombs, of course. That's all I've been involved in.'

'Do I take that as an admission?' enquired Imbert.

'What do you mean?' Conlon asked.

'You say that is the only one you are involved in,' repeated Imbert.

'No. The only one the police have involved me in, I mean.'

Imbert was not going to leave it there. 'That was a slip of the tongue, then?'

'No,' said Conlon. 'I meant what I said. I have been involved in the Guildford bombs, but I have a good defence.'

'It sounds to me as if you slipped up then, when you said you were involved in the Guildford bombing.'

'What I meant was, I am not involved but the police have involved me in it by charging me. You're trying to trick me, aren't you?'

'No,' said Imbert. 'I want to ask you some questions, but not about the Guildford bombings. You've already been charged with those.'

'Yes, and I'll get out of it!' Conlon broke in. 'What others? I haven't been involved with any bombings at all, so there's no point in asking me any questions... But I'll tell you something. It is something when you bring my dad in here — he is a sick man — for possessing explosives. He's going to say you rubbed explosives on his hands.'

'When did he say that?' asked Munday.

'That's my business,' Conlon said. 'That's what he is going to say, so there's nothing you can do about it. I only admitted this because I had to.'

'What do you mean?' Munday pressed him.

'I'm not saying any more. You'll find out.'

'What about your father saying explosives were rubbed on his hands?' But Conlon refused to speak any further. Curiously, he denies this interview ever took place.

One of the other suspects to be interviewed by the Metropolitan Police Bomb Squad was Brian Anderson. On January 31 1975, three days before his release, he made a statement to his solicitor in which he said that on the day he was charged, December 7 1974, two Bomb Squad officers had come to see him. One took notes; the other did the talking.

'He told me I could do two years for nothing or 30 years for nothing. He wanted me to say I was spotting for others to plant a bomb at Euston. He knew I had been to Madame Tussauds because I had made a statement in September 1974 to the London Police and he wanted me to say I had been there to find a place to plant a bomb. He told me there were different scales in the ladder for involvement and it was up to me to take the bottom rung or the top rung. He said he would wash his hands of the Guildford thing if I would make a statement about the London jobs, and he would take me back to London that night...

'He then took me down to the cells and told me to think it over and he would come back again. He came later and took me upstairs again and I told him I did not want to make a statement about something I didn't do. I told him I was telling the truth and he said the truth was not helping me and why didn't I tell some lies? He said I would remember that day as the day I had the chance of my life. He told me not to think he would go away and forget all about it, but that he would be back every day to see me. I have never seen him since.'

Officially it looked like a triumph for the bomb squads of Surrey and the Metropolitan Police. Before Christmas, 13 people had been charged: Hill and Armstrong with murder at Woolwich; Hill, Armstrong, Conlon, Carole Richardson, Anne Maguire, John McGuinness, Brian Anderson and Paul Colman with the Guildford pub bombings; Patrick O'Neill, Guiseppe

Conlon, Sean Smyth and Patrick Maguire senior with possession of explosives. Sean Mullin of 15 Rondu Road had, with 'person or persons unknown', been charged with conspiracy to cause explosions. And Anne Maguire, on whose hands the test for nitroglycerine had originally shown a negative result, was now additionally charged for her alleged part in the manufacture of bombs, following the apparent discovery of traces of explosive on a pair of the plastic gloves she sometimes wore because of her dermatitis. Young Patrick and Vincent Maguire, arrested, released, rearrested and again released, were not to be charged with handling explosives for another two months — a full three months after the swabs had been taken of their hands.

The Crown contention was that, according to the statement of Gerry Conlon, the bombs had been made by Anne Maguire and members of the household at 43 Third Avenue. They were then transported to Guildford by a gang of eight people travelling in two cars.

But behind the impressive façade, all was confusion. The only solid evidence in police hands was the apparent forensic 'proof' that the alleged bomb-makers of 43 Third Avenue — Mr and Mrs Maguire and two of their children, O'Neill, Smyth and Guiseppe Conlon — had handled explosives. The house itself was clean. The search of the premises had yielded not a jot of evidence that there had ever been explosives there or, indeed, any of the paraphernalia of bomb-making familiar to the police from other 'bomb factories' — wire, detonators and the like. The picture was little better at the other alleged 'bomb factory' addresses — 15 Rondu Road, Cricklewood, identified by Hill, and 35 West End Lane, West Hampstead, guessed at by Armstrong — where the only discovery of note had been a Smith's pocket-watch at McGuinness's flat, similar to watches used as timing devices by the London Active Service Unit. Much was made of this find at the committal, although the discovery of one watch by itself was insignificant; by the time of the committal everyone connected with Rondu Road had in any case had the charges against them dropped owing to lack of evidence.

If the bomb factories were unproductive forensically, the 'bombers' themselves were even more so. Since no one else at Third Avenue matched descriptions given by the Guildford Four, the name of Anne Maguire was the only link between the two sets of arrests. Tests for nitroglycerine on the hands of all the other Guildford suspects proved negative. In short, what forensic evidence there was against the Maguire household was to prove highly controversial. But against the Guildford Four the forensic evidence was non-existent.

There was no identification evidence either. On December 13, Carole Richardson was put on an identity parade in the club room at Guildford police station. In the presence of John Avey, her solicitor's clerk, she was asked to stand in a line with eight other young women aged between 16 and 22. She chose a place between the fifth and the sixth in the line and stayed in the same position throughout, although she had been told she could move if she wanted to. Carole was wearing corduroy jeans, a brown patterned jumper and white plimsolls. Avey drew the police's attention to the plimsolls, which he felt might be revealing, and all the girls (including Carole) were instructed to remove their shoes.

The identity parade began at 11.50 a.m. One by one, eight witnesses from the Horse and Groom entered the room and walked down the line of young women. Each inspection took about two minutes. They were all customers who had noticed the 'courting couple' in an alcove and had given descriptions to the police. The first was Mr Burns. He was the man who, while too ill to speak, had nodded excitedly when the Roy Reynolds portrait of the courting couple had been shown to him in hospital. He walked slowly down the line and said, 'I'm sorry. I can't be sure.'

Mrs Burns came next. 'I can't recognize any of them,' she told the police.

'Are you sure?' she was asked.

'I'm sure.'

Her daughter, Carol, did no better.

Julie Spooner paused in front of Carole, but could identify no one.

Helen Jean Kettles peered very hard at the girl at one end of the line, and then retraced her steps to look again at the girl at the other end. She did not stop by Carole and made no identification.

Last came the paratroopers, Clerehugh, Cook and Lynskey. The last two had given police the fullest accounts of all about the courting couple. Cook took a long time. None of them made any identification. 'I can't see her there,' Lynskey said. Perhaps this was not surprising, since Cook and Lynskey had agreed that the girl was a 'natural blonde'. Carole Richardson has auburn hair.

Four witnesses from the Seven Stars were then brought in. None of them made any identification, either. In all, Carole Richardson faced 12 witnesses. The witnesses never saw Armstrong. Julie Spooner, who, it will be remembered, had given the fullest description of the man of the courting couple, described him as about 30, over six feet tall, thin, with dark, collar-length hair thinning on top, a sallow complexion, sunken cheeks, a long face, a prominent nose and dark eyes and eyebrows. Armstrong in those days was 24 and chubby-faced. He has lightish-brown hair and is five feet seven inches tall. The police decided — perhaps wisely from their point of view — not to repeat the exercise. It is worth noting that investigations in a case are made entirely on the initiative of the police; the suspect has no power to insist on an identity parade if he or she believes it will establish innocence. Having put Richardson on a line-up, the police might have felt that in fairness to Armstrong they should have allowed the same witnesses to identify — or fail to identify — him, but they chose not to do so. There were to be no identity parades with any of the other accused.

The only evidence left against the Guildford Four was their confessions to the police. McGuinness, Mullin, Anderson and Colman, who made no admissions, were shortly to be released.

Yet taken together, the 'confessions' present a curious picture. The detail on which they agree — descriptions of the pubs and the people in them, and the position of the bombers inside the pubs (or, in the case of Woolwich, outside the window) — is detail that was already known to the police at the start of the investigation. On all other material points the confessions differ radically from one another and offer endless contradictions, both internally and matched against the evidence of outside witnesses.

For Guildford, for example, Hill says that Armstrong drove a dark, four-door saloon and 'Paul' a lemon-coloured XL Granada. Armstrong says that Paul Colman drove a grey Ford, possibly a Capri, while the second car was a light-coloured Anglia. Later he says it was McGuinness's white Triumph Herald. Richardson says first, that 'Dodger' and, later, that a blond man with a Belfast accent drove a creamy-coloured Ford saloon.

Hill says the bombing party left London around midday and was back by 5.45 (later he says the bombs were planted at 7.45). Conlon says the team didn't leave London until 6.00. Armstrong and Richardson say they started out at 3.00. Hill says Armstrong drove Hill while 'Paul' drove Conlon and two women in a separate car. Conlon says he went with Hill and Armstrong, but that Richardson went in a separate car. Richardson and Armstrong say they went together. Hill locates the bomb-priming in a car-park at Wisley; Conlon places it almost a mile away at a junction on Ockham Lane. Richardson says it was primed while they drove around town. Armstrong says it wasn't primed.

On their arrival in Guildford, Armstrong and Richardson say, they all met in the Wimpy Bar. Hill has them going to the station. Conlon takes them straight to the pubs. Conlon says he went into the Horse and Groom with Carole while Armstrong waited outside. Carole says she went in with Conlon, but that Armstrong came too. Armstrong says he and Carole went into the pub and Conlon made a brief appearance once they were inside. Hill says Conlon went into the Horse and Groom with Anne Maguire, while Carole went into the Seven Stars with 'Paul'. Hill says the bomb was in a plaid bag. Armstrong describes it as a brown paper parcel which he tucked under his arm. Conlon says it was in a shopping-bag. Carole says it was 'like two shoe-boxes' and that she (not Armstrong) carried it in a 'hippy shoulder-bag'.

Even in their refined versions, the composition of the total bombing team is in all cases larger than would have been necessary to cover the two pubs. Hill says it comprised himself, Conlon, Armstrong, Richardson, Anne Maguire, 'Paul' and 'an old, balding man of 50'. Conlon names himself, Hill, Armstrong, Richardson and Anne Maguire and adds 'some girls I didn't know — eight or nine of us altogether'. Apart from himself, Armstrong lists Hill, Conlon, Richardson, Paul Colman, 'Aunt Edith', John McGuinness and another man from Belfast. Carole names neither Hill nor Conlon directly, but puts herself and Armstrong with five other people of shifting identities.

This was the raw material of the Crown's case against the Guildford Four. It was presumably in the hope of imbuing it with some sense that on the last day of December 1974, Longhurst, Wise and Mills visited Carole Richardson in D Wing of Brixton Prison, where she was being held on remand. The interview took place in the presence of Prison Officer Catherine Grew. Carole gave some information about a man she had known in Kilburn, Paul Guerin, but when they told her they were going to ask her some more questions about Guildford, she refused to answer them. Her record of the conversation is as follows:

'I said, "You know I was not in Guildford and I was forced to make those statements."

'Longhurst said, "Are you saying that I hit you?"

'And I said, "No. But you bloody well know who did," and I looked straight at Wise.

'He said, "Why didn't you tell us you were not in Guildford at the time?" and I said, "I know I wasn't in fucking Guildford and you wouldn't believe me when I told you. I've got about 40 witnesses to prove it, but I don't know half of them!"'

Carole Richardson had cause to feel more confident. Her pleas to friends and police officers alike to find her diary had drawn a blank; the diary in question was never found and was, in fact, burned by some of her fellow squatters after her arrest because they were afraid it might give evidence of burglaries and drug deals. (They also disposed of the Christmas presents she had wrapped early and labelled 'To Mum' and to her friends; they wanted no trace of her to be left in the squat.) But Carole's diary was not the only clue to her whereabouts on October 5. When Frank Johnson found out about her arrest during one of his regular trips to London, he returned to Newcastle pondering their movements in October. He worked back in his mind over the weekends and arrived at the night of the concert at the South Bank Polytechnic. 'I thought: "They were with me that night — Carole and Lisa... !"'

He rang up 'Mitch' Mitchell, a member of Jack the Lad, who confirmed the date of the concert. Then he made a careful written note of his recollection of the evening in question — where they had met and what had happened at the Elephant and Castle — with the purpose of conveying the information to Carole Richardson's solicitor. Having no idea how to reach him, Johnson walked into the office of a Newcastle solicitor he had heard of, Jeremy Beecham, taking with him the written note in the hope that it would cut out the necessity for expensive explanations. He did not find Beecham helpful. Without reading the account, Beecham referred him briskly to the clerk of the court in Guildford for the name of Carole Richardson's solicitor. Johnson telephoned Guildford, but the clerk informed him that there were instructions from some of the solicitors not to divulge their identities. Johnson rang the National Council for Civil Liberties, but the line was constantly engaged. He approached various friends, and even the local priest, and asked if they would go with him to the police station. It was just two years since he had been released from prison for possessing LSD and he knew enough about police stations not to want to walk in unaccompanied. Apart from what his own experience had taught him, he had learned a lot from the many Irish friends he had made at the de la Salle Catholic teacher-training college in Manchester where he had been a student: frequent trips to Derry and Donegal to visit them had familiarized him with the political situation in Ireland and with the experiences of young Catholics who came up against the law.

But Johnson could find no one to go with him to West End police station, Newcastle. He went alone. The desk sergeant told him to wait. He spoke to two local detectives, explained that he wanted to contact Carole Richardson's solicitor and gave an account of the concert on October 5. The second detective came and collected him a couple of hours later from his mother's and drove him back to the police station where, after a further wait of an hour or two, he was taken to meet Longhurst, Wise and a WPC who had arrived from Guildford to see him.

'They told me that I couldn't have been with Carole because she'd already made statements admitting that she was in Guildford,' says Johnson. 'The only way I could possibly have been with her was if I'd been in Guildford with her at the time. I wasn't worried about it because, well, it all seemed like a big mistake they were making. I knew where I'd been that night. I thought, it's just a matter of hours, or possibly, at the worst, days, and then they'll check up on what I'm telling them and realize it was a mistake, and that one of the people they'd arrested was the wrong person.' The interview lasted some hours and Johnson made a statement.

When he had finished it, he was arrested. His shoes and his belt were removed and he was put in a cell for the night. He could hear the sound of activity around him; drunks stumbling about. Johnson said that the light stayed on all night and that he was left without a blanket until the shift changed at 6.00 a.m. He remained there for most of the following day. Released in the evening, he went home to discover that his parents' home had been raided by a large number of police. His mother says they told her that traces of dynamite had been found in Carole Richardson's handbag. One of them added that Mrs Johnson would not see her son for a very long time unless he changed his story. They had taken away the notes he had made about October 5.

Prompted by Carole, Lisa Astin had been making her own enquiries. She rang both *Time Out*, which had advertised the concert, and the Students' Union at the Polytechnic to check the date. When she saw Longhurst and WPC Mills at Willesden Green police station, they pressed her to be specific about the time she and Carole had met Frank Johnson. Lisa was unable to be specific. 'I just said, well, I was with her the whole day... I felt really confident that everything would be OK and that she'd be released. In fact, from the time I discovered where we'd been that day I felt she'd be released within a few days.'

Carole clearly did, too. On January 7 she wrote to Paddy:

> Belfast Frank, Lisa and Geordie Frank were the only ones who believed I wasn't there even before it crossed their minds the concert was on the 5th. I didn't remember myself for about a week. I couldn't tell where I was without my diary and I couldn't have that. Anyway all's well that ends well I suppose.

In the new year, 1975, the 13 prisoners and their solicitors made weekly appearances at Guildford Magistrates' Court in Ward Street. Reporting restrictions on these hearings were not lifted and the press were permitted to give only the barest facts of who was charged with what. But the security of each hearing was so tight and the atmosphere in the town so antagonistic that the three local solicitors acting on behalf of Armstrong, Mullin and Anderson felt like traitors for daring to represent those charged.

Alastair Logan had been aware of this from the start. A one-man firm struggling to keep abreast of the divorces and property transactions of his clients, Logan had turned down the bombing case when, as Panel Legal Aid solicitor, he was first confronted with it; he knew the work-load would be enormous, too heavy for a man operating on his own. But at first no solicitor could be found in Guildford to risk his clients' goodwill by taking the case. Logan had no such sensitivities. A translation from Plato, framed on his office wall, has been the hallmark of a maverick career: 'Renouncing the glory at which the world aims, I desire only to know the truth.' When the buck returned to him, he reluctantly accepted it.

From his first visit to the police station to meet his client, Patrick Armstrong, he realized that something was wrong. 'As I was walking down the corridor Detective Sergeant Donaldson, escorting me, said: "I think that you will want to use the facilities." "What for?" I asked. "The man's got scabies and you've shaken hands with him twice." Then I noticed that he was wearing clear plastic gloves. If you want to prejudice somebody, that's a good way of doing it. First you say he's infected. He also happens to be Irish... and finally you add to that the offences, five counts of murder, two counts of conspiracy.' What struck Logan as distasteful was the policeman's assumption that his attitude would be shared. It wasn't just the police. The bombs had understandably struck deep at the heart of the community and the community had closed its ranks — and its mind. Logan admits that, being a local man, he probably felt more keenly than the other solicitors of the Guildford Four a sense of deviance.

The other feature of the case that gradually dawned on Logan and his colleagues was that all of them were being required to take part in a ritual that would transform their clients into guilty people; for it was a foregone conclusion, as far as everyone else was concerned, that the trial was merely a formality. Logan was the only qualified solicitor of the four; the other three were clerks. In the normal way this might not have mattered, but with the exception of the central London firm Simons, Muirhead & Allan, secured by Ted Jones for the Conlons, all came from local practices where matrimonial, conveyancing and petty-crime work filled the files. They and their senior partners had no idea of what lay ahead and no experience whatever of 'terrorist' trials. Since the language and the functions of the court were deceptively familiar to them, it was some time before the solicitors realized just how powerful were the forces now at work. Indeed, as Logan readily admits, they did not fully realize it until the case reached its conclusion at the Old Bailey. And by then, of course, it was too late.

18
ONGOING
BUSINESS

'He was Prime Minister when internment was introduced, so he was classed as fair game.'

Joseph O'Connell, on the bombing at Edward Heath's flat

December 11 — two days after the completion of the confessions of the Guildford Four — was the day of the promised debate on capital punishment in the House of Commons. In the wake of the horrific Birmingham bombings, both the motion and the main amendment came from local MPs.

Brian Walden (Labour, Birmingham Ladywood) introduced the motion: 'That this House, while recognizing that political terrorism requires a reappraisal of established attitudes, is of the opinion that a reintroduction of the death penalty would neither deter terrorists nor increase the safety of the public.' Jill Knight (Conservative, Edgbaston) moved an amendment calling for the reintroduction of capital punishment for acts of terrorism. Among her supporters were David Howell, the Conservative MP for Guildford, and Sir Michael Havers, the man who would shortly be chosen to lead the prosecution of the Guildford prisoners.

The Home Secretary, Roy Jenkins, was joined by a select band of Home Secretaries past and future, both Labour and Conservative — James Callaghan, William Whitelaw, Merlyn Rees and Douglas Hurd — in opposing the amendment, which was eventually defeated in a free vote by 369 to 217. Mr Jenkins said he believed 'that of all classes of killer, dedicated terrorists are the least likely to be deterred by the threat of execution'.

As if in endorsement of his point — and while the five-hour

debate was in progress — the Active Service Unit were back at work again, less than a mile from the House of Commons. At 6.30 p.m. Joseph O'Connell and Hugh Doherty threw a short-fuse bomb wrapped in nails through the courtyard window of the Long Bar of the Naval and Military Club in Piccadilly. The two men escaped down Curzon Street, firing twice from a .357 Astra Magnum into the cab of a pursuing taxi-driver. Harry Duggan, Dowd and Butler were waiting 200 yards away by Green Park. Thirty seconds after the explosion they raked the Cavalry Club with fire from an M1 carbine, a .45 Star automatic and a Sten-gun. The Sten-gun was Butler's: it jammed three times. Police cars gave chase but got stuck in central-London traffic. Remarkably, no one had been hurt.

On December 14 Dowd, in a Cortina, drove Butler and another member of the gang to the newly opened Churchill Hotel in Portman Square and led another brazen shoot-up. This time Butler's Sten was working. Bullets were also found from the Magnum and carbine used in Piccadilly three nights earlier. Three people were injured by flying glass. There were no subsequent charges.

On December 17 five-pound time bombs, activated by watches, exploded at three telephone exchanges between 9.00 p.m. and 10.00 p.m. Before one, at Draycott Avenue, Chelsea, a woman telephoned the *Daily Mirror* with a brief warning. Four policemen arrived in time to stop a post office engineer handling the bomb, which had been left on a scooter, but were injured themselves. There were no injuries at the second explosion at the exchange in New Compton Street, Soho, but the third, in Chenies Street, also in the West End, killed George Arthur, a telephonist, and injured five others. O'Connell and Butler later claimed responsibility on behalf of their Unit but were not charged.

Two days later, at the height of the Christmas-shopping season, O'Connell packed a stolen Cortina with 80 pounds of gelignite in 160 sticks and parked the car outside Selfridge's department store in Oxford Street. Three telephoned warnings enabled police to evacuate the area. When the time bomb, the biggest of the campaign, detonated the flash was seen two miles away and the damage to property was estimated at £1,500,000. There were no charges.

The following day, explosives experts defused a time bomb made by O'Connell and left in a brown holdall on a railway station platform at the military town of Aldershot. It was concealed under an issue of *Loving* magazine and a copy of the *Daily Telegraph*. This was the first unexploded time bomb to be found in the campaign. The independent Government forensic scientists at the RARDE scrutinized it minutely for similarities with the Guildford and other time bombs.

The device contained 14$\frac{1}{2}$ pounds of Irish Industrial Eversoft Frangex gelignite in 36 six-ounce sticks. The two detonators were wired in parallel and cut to lengths of nine and 12 inches. The timing-delay mechanism was a Smith's Combat pocket-watch. There was a four-and-a-half-volt Ever Ready type 126 bell battery with wire connections twisted around the terminal. The intercept position was set for between nine and 10 o'clock. The assembly material featured one-inch black matt PVC tape. The scientists were struck by two distinctive techniques, noting, 'These are very rare features and have not been observed in any other unexploded bombs': at the intercept pin the bared detonator wire was held under the watch lens by knotting and the watch's second-hand was bent back on itself. These features were to prove to be very telling indications.

Separately, the police lifted off a number of sets of fingerprints. In due course O'Connell, Butler and Duggan were convicted for the Aldershot time bomb. The Metropolitan Police were to claim years later that the fourth set belonged to the Irish-American William Quinn, although he has never been charged with the bombing. Hugh Doherty stood trial and was acquitted.

The next day, December 21, O'Connell and the ASU took as a public challenge a claim by Harrods that their department store was terrorist-proof. To evade security checks Butler wrapped 10 pounds of explosives around his waist and converted them into a bomb in a second-floor lavatory, placing the device in a holdall in the paint department in the hope of starting an extensive fire. The bomb was discovered before Butler telephoned a deliberately deceptive warning which referred to three bombs. The bomb was defused safely. There were no charges.

On the same day another unexploded time bomb was found and defused at the King's Arms in Warminster, Wiltshire. It had been left outside a pub disco frequented by soldiers from a nearby Army camp. Except for the fact that it contained 24 pounds of explosives it was identical to the Aldershot bomb. More fingerprints were found, but there were no charges.

The Christmas campaign culminated on December 22 with the fourth successive day of bombing and the most daring yet — the attempted assassination of Edward Heath, the former Prime Minister, on the night before he was scheduled to travel to Northern Ireland.

At 9.00 p.m. O'Connell drove Butler, Duggan and an unidentified man down Wilton Street, Belgravia, in a stolen Cortina and pulled up at number 17. The fuse of a throw bomb was lit and a bundle of explosives and nails was lobbed on to the first-floor balcony. It exploded two feet from Mr Heath's desk and caused extensive damage to his flat. Mr Heath was in his constituency conducting a Christmas carol concert.

Butler, as usual, carried a gun to cover the bomb-thrower. He recalled, 'We knew it was Heath's place but I wasn't sure if he was there at the time. I'm not sure where the information came from: it was given to the boss of our ASU.'

O'Connell later provided his rationale: 'He was Prime Minister when internment was introduced, so he was classed as fair game. It was just a frightener. We didn't know if he was in or not.'

Police briefly and unsuccessfully pursued the getaway Cortina which was found abandoned by Sloane Square underground station. Four sets of fingerprints were taken away. O'Connell, Butler and Duggan were subsequently found guilty of causing the explosion. Hugh Doherty was acquitted.

The brief Christmas and New Year lull ended on January 19 1975. Dowd stole two Cortinas to be used in the shootings at two more exclusive West End hotels — the Carlton Tower and the Portman. Butler and another man joined him. 'I did the Portman with the Sten,' Butler claimed. 'Must have fired 15 or 16 shots. Our intention was to shoot to kill.' The M1 carbine, now equally familiar to the police ballistics experts, was also used. Nobody was killed but 12 people were injured. There were no charges.

On January 23, Dowd and two others, using a stolen car, placed a 30-pound time bomb at the Woodford waterworks pumping station in North London. Three people were injured and three million gallons of water escaped. Damage was put at £160,000. Again there were no charges.

January 27 was the final frenetic night of what became known as the 'Phase One' campaign. O'Connell, Dowd, Duggan, Butler and Doherty together placed no less than seven time bombs, of approximately six pounds each, around London. The first, preceded by a warning, exploded at 6.30 p.m. in the doorway of Gieves, the military outfitters, in Old Bond Street. It had been placed by Butler and Duggan and caused £85,000 worth of damage. At 9.30 bombs placed by O'Connell, Dowd and Doherty exploded, causing minimal damage, at the Moreson chemical plant in Ponders End and the disused Enfield gas works. At 11.00 p.m., without warning, two more bombs — left by Butler and Duggan — detonated in front of Ratners jewellers in Kensington High Street and the City Girl boutique, Victoria Street. Two passers-by suffered injuries. Butler and Duggan gave a warning for the next time bomb, which they placed in the doorway of the Easyphit shoe shop in Putney High Street. Major Ronald Henderson of the Army bomb-disposal team defused it with two minutes to spare before its planned detonation at 12.30 a.m. Similarly, the warning given by O'Connell for his final bomb outside the Charco Grill hamburger restaurant in Hampstead, enabled it to be defused. As in this instance, the practical application of the ASU's policy of giving warnings designed to protect innocent bystanders appeared throughout the campaign to be quite arbitrary. The construction of the two unexploded devices matched tellingly with that of the earlier unexploded bombs collected by the police. The Charco Grill bomb additionally bore William Quinn's fingerprints.

This blitz ultimately attracted criminal charges — not for Dowd who made admissions on it, nor for Quinn, but for O'Connell, Butler, Duggan and Doherty in relation to the two unexploded bombs. All were duly found not guilty nearly two years later in what was to prove an intriguing jury decision.

This unprecedented campaign thus ended as suddenly as it had begun in October. The London ASU had effectively offloaded their barrage as a last fling before acceding to a cease-fire order from Dublin.

The war in Northern Ireland had been proceeding remorselessly in the meantime, with heavy casualties for both the Provisionals and the security forces. The IRA needed breathing-space to regroup and rearm and to take the strain off their volunteers in the North, so they jumped at the olive-branch offered by a delegation of Protestant churchmen to meet for a conference.

The venue was, by coincidence, in Harry Duggan's home village of Feakle in County Clare. On December 9 1974 the Provisionals sent to Smyth's Village Hotel a top-level team, including Ruairi O'Bradaigh, Daithi O'Conaill, Seamus Twomey, Kevin Mallon, Maire Drumm and Billy McKee. During the five-hour meeting the churchmen produced a hypothetical paper of British Government concessions in return for a cease-fire. Mallon, in particular, disapproved of such negotiations and before the IRA team could agree on a unanimous response, word arrived that the Garda Special Branch were also headed for Smyth's Village Hotel so the Provisionals left abruptly.

But the seed had been sown. On February 5 1975, Merlyn Rees, the Northern Ireland Secretary of State, announced to the House of Commons a series of measures aimed at reducing routine harassment at street level in the province and at effecting the gradual hand-over of policing from the Army to the RUC, conditional upon an end to IRA violence. Four days later the Provisionals' Army Council announced the suspension of 'hostilities against Crown forces'.

This allowed the London Active Service Unit a break before their luck ran out. They had left their fingerprints all over stolen cars and unexploded bombs; they had twice shaken off police chases and had even kidnapped a policeman, yet their identities and safe houses were still intact. They could congratulate themselves on having eluded intensive police efforts which had forced the Bomb Squad to utilize two-thirds of the manpower in New Scotland Yard's forensic and fingerprint departments and to increase its establishment, including the Special Branch, to more than 200 full-time officers.

Despite the numbers and expertise ranged against them, the ASU could still motor into the heart of the West End at 6.30 at night and blaze away like Chicago hoodlums with their Stens and carbines — and escape unscathed. They had generated fear and hatred among millions of ordinary Londoners and caused unimaginable grief to innocent victims and their families. But what of the old adage about a bomb in Britain being worth a hundred in Belfast? The IRA would have been entitled to ask themselves if they had not bombed the British Government into making concessions.

The cease-fire would end. The Active Service Unit would go back to work and redouble their carnage until inevitably their luck would run out and they would be caught. Once caught, they were headed for long life sentences, and by then their list of attacks would be so long and murderous as to make it pointless for the police to charge them with every stolen car, every shot fired, every bomb, even every killing. This is undoubtedly why, despite the overwhelming evidence against them, many of the incidents in the 'Phase One' attacks never reached the courts. Meanwhile, 29 of the 31 missions cited appear in the official police 'Incident Chart' of the ASU's activities. The ubiquitous involvement of Dowd and O'Connell's team is not in question.

What remains significant, however, in matching eventual trial and conviction to the outrages attributed to them is that none of them stood trial for any of the attacks that occurred before December 20 1974, despite fingerprint evidence dating back to early October. Indeed, Brendan Dowd, whose London record stretches from October 9 (when his fingerprints were found following the kidnapping of Basil Dalton) to the final seven-bomb blitz on January 19, has never been charged with any of the 'Phase One' offences.

It was during 'Phase One', of course, that the police were arresting, interrogating and preparing for trial the Guildford Four and the Maguire family — suspects who in turn had been so curiously exempt from questioning about the wave of terrorism breaking over the Home Counties.

19
NEAR MISSES

'I wasn't involved in the Tibble killing. It was an accident. It was our ASU though. We were lucky. There was a courier in the house that day.'

Eddie Butler

Brendan Dowd took immediate advantage of the cease-fire to go back to Dublin for a 'holiday' and for fresh orders from the Army Council. One result of the Unit's collective carelessness with fingerprints was that their continued freedom hung by a narrow thread at any port of departure from Britain to Ireland and back. Yet to forgo trips home meant consigning themselves to a permanent underground existence. Dowd had already passed both ways through Heathrow for his Christmas and New Year in the Irish Republic. Eddie Butler was another to cross the Irish Sea with forged papers for a 'holiday', during which he met two Provisionals wanted for terrorist offences, Eddie Gallagher and Marion Coyle.

But in London any sense of relaxation was fatally disturbed within three weeks of the cease-fire announcement — ironically as a result of London policing's returning to something like normality.

There had been a spate of burglaries in Hammersmith and West Kensington, and police street patrols in the district were accordingly stepped up. Around 1.00 p.m. on February 27 1975, three plain-clothes policemen, constables Blackledge, White and Wilson, became interested in the unusual behaviour of a man in Fairholme Road, Hammersmith. As the man crossed the road he repeatedly looked to his left and right; then he entered the basement flat of number 39. The policemen waited. After 40 minutes the man emerged and walked to a nearby bus stop.

Blackledge moved in, demanding to know where he had been. The man replied that he did not have to answer such questions but then gave his name as William Rogers, said he had been to a friend's house in Fairholme Road, and emptied his outer pockets showing a key-ring and some Irish money. Blackledge then threatened to call in more police if the man refused to submit to a further search. 'Why are you so nervous? What have you got to hide?' asked Blackledge. The constable insisted on searching the man's inside pockets at which he replied, 'All right, I'll take you to my friend's house if that will satisfy you,' and started to walk briskly away. Blackledge grabbed him but he wriggled free and broke into a run, pursued by the three constables.

By chance, another plain-clothes policeman — on a motor bike — joined in the chase. PC Stephen Tibble was off duty, having engineered a shift change the previous day. Tibble overtook the runaway man and headed him off at the corner of Charleville Road, where he dismounted and crouched down, ready to tackle him. The man then produced a Colt .38 from his coat and fired three times. One bullet embedded itself in a nearby front door but the other two hit Tibble in the chest. He died two hours later in Charing Cross Hospital with his wife at his bedside. He was 21 and had been in the Metropolitan Police for only three months.

A desperate search for the gunman ensued during which one police officer accidentally shot himself in the leg. A helicopter was sent up and the police ordered the power to be turned off on the Piccadilly Line around Barons Court as they scoured the tunnels. The gunman escaped, but the police were able to issue a prompt description of a 25- to 30-year-old man with an Irish accent, stockily built, clean-shaven with light-brown collar-length hair. A later description amended the gunman's age to 35. The police quickly broke into the front room of the basement flat of 39 Fairholme Road and found it stuffed with evidence of it's being a Provisional IRA safe house and bomb factory. Commander Robert Huntley of the Bomb Squad described it as 'the most important bomb factory we have ever found, and the first in London'. There were detonators, wires, batteries and watches which matched material gathered by the Bomb Squad from unexploded devices. There was a .45 Star automatic pistol, which ballistics experts soon matched with the weapon used in some of the West End shootings, and a Colt .38.

There was a host of familiar fingerprints which verified the links and some new ones as well. Cupboards and drawers yielded men's and women's clothing and wigs, English and Irish cash — and, under a carpet, an intriguing letter:

Dear Joe,

These are the address for collecting from McGill's man whatever weapons etc. that were not under Ben's control. 11, Leatherwood Rd, Hammersmith (either W12 or W6) Ask for Ernie Johnson and say 'Damage' sent you. Ask him to get the Army List from 'Spotter Murphy' & send it back to us through Liverpool.

Enclosed is also some information on possible targets. If you let us know when you need money too we'll send it via Liverpool. Everything at this end is now under Brendan's control so things should be O.K. When you write make it a proper letter — Dear Anne etc — just in case it gets opened in error.

Fowerboy House (By St. Paul's) all international calls, exchange for telex used by city dealers.

Cowboy Club — Picadilly (top serving officers) one girl with english accent dressed in tweeds to leave a suitcase for collection would do.

Fortnum and Mason, Cartiers of Bond St. Harley St.

Hotels — Savoy, Claridges, Grosvenor, Ritz & Berkely, all streets around Knightsbridge & Chelsea.

Bite lives in No. 2 the little Boltons.

Goodge Street Station on the platform if you look at the roof you see a large diam pipe with suppots around it. This carries a river which when shattered should flow on to the electric lines & fuck up at least that underground system.

Lewisham

There is a shop called ALPAT (it is a kind of pawn shop) on the pavement the same side as the shop about 20 yards further on you will see a large man hole (post office) inside 15 feet down (there are steps) is the main international London Link.

Walthamstow resovoir this has eight locks with tunnels connecting other which lead to hackney downs pumping station (there are two) a new one was built 2 years ago. Do intelligence on it with a view to poisoning lakes & blowing up pumping station. New Pumping Station is under large roundabout where North Circ Rd and A11 meet at woodford (I think).

London underground works on its own power station do some intelligence on it.

Frank, at 32 Grosvenor Crescent is still save should anything happen & you need it also Mick, 146 Sutton Court Rd, Hillingdon they are only for real emergencies.

In general keep clear absolutely of any arm or S.F. people in Brittian.

Get those two Belfast fellows home — clean them up, change them a bit & send them singley through Glasgow unless you can think of something better.

If you want any help let us know. There should be a drop Tuesday morning & Thurs. morning.

Mind yourselves.

Graine

PS. Some of the enclosed you probably have, I had difficulty decifering the writing so please excuse the spelling & any inaccuraces.

Among the easily solved inaccuracies of this handwritten and undated letter are that 'Fowerboy House' is Faraday House;

'Bite' is Sir Alfred Beit (whose art collection in Ireland had been raided by Duggan 18 months earlier); and the 'Cowboy Club' refers to the Cavalry Club which the gang shot up on December 11 1974. Other passages were to remain enigmatic.

Jawaid Ahmed, the bewildered landlord of 39 Fairholme Road, could now tell the police that the last remaining tenant was called Michael Wilson and that someone called O'Shea had left some time before. Furthermore, he had previously rented out flats to them and their friends in Hestercombe Avenue and Waldemar Avenue, two adjoining roads in Fulham. Wilson was Duggan and O'Shea was Dowd.

The police kept quiet about their discovery for 24 hours in the forlorn hope that Michael Wilson would walk into the stake-out they mounted at number 39, but he never did. Once more the trail turned cold as the Unit went to ground, abandoning West London in favour of North London.

The discovery of Fairholme Road was not the only near miss suffered by the British police in the hunt for the terrorists. Two months earlier, at 11.00 p.m. on December 23 1974, a landlord answered a neighbour's complaint about rowdy behaviour at 40 Westridge Road, Southampton, which he was renting out to a 'Mr and Mrs Phil Reynolds' — instead of whom he found two young men from Belfast, 'Walsh', 23, and Ronnie McCartney, 24. They were drunk. The police were called. Walsh first gave his name as McPharsand, proceeded to write it down as 'John McParland' and then panicked, producing a Colt .38. The two men shot their way out. As a second Panda car pulled up, PC Malcolm Craig was seriously wounded by shots to the stomach and pelvis. Another bullet struck the spectacles of PC Robert Harrigan but he was uninjured. The two young men escaped in a green Cortina and duly returned to Ireland, although not before the Colt .38 was handed to the London Active Service Unit.

They left behind a copy of Who's Who, a made-up 10-pound bomb and 11 sets of fingerprints, which included those of Dowd, O'Connell and Doherty. Another set matched prints found on the unexploded bombs at Aldershot and Warminster a few

days previously. The police appeared to have nipped a fledgling
Active Service Unit in the bud. It looked as if the London team
had been making the bombs and the Southampton team had —
unsuccessfully — been priming and planting them. McCartney
did not stay at large for long. In May he was picked up by the
RUC in County Tyrone in Northern Ireland and returned to
England and eventual life imprisonment for attempted murder
of the Southampton policemen.

But the Bomb Squad and Hampshire Police were increasingly
interested in 'Mr and Mrs Reynolds' and their fingerprints. On
March 13 1975, without any publicity, Hampshire Police issued
a warrant for the arrest of Patrick Joseph Gilhooley. The
document alleged that in December 1974 he attempted to cause
explosions at Aldershot and Warminster and that he caused
an explosion at the home of Edward Heath in Wilton Street,
Belgravia. He was also wanted for possession of explosives in
Southampton.

Hampshire Police knew exactly where Gilhooley was: a few
days earlier he had been arrested in Dublin for suspected
membership of the IRA when he had given a patrol-car driver
the false name of Conor McGrail. 'English Joe' Gilhooley had
been born in Lancashire but had become an Irish citizen after
settling in Dublin as a bus conductor in 1970. This enabled him
to thwart the Garda's initial attempt upon his arrest to send
him back to England on the mail-boat. Gilhooley was sentenced
to a year's imprisonment for IRA membership. He was released
after eight months in Portlaoise Prison, only to be rearrested at
the prison gates to face an extradition order served by Scotland
Yard. This was granted by an Irish District Court in December
1975 after sworn testimony from Mr Barrington Smith, a fingerprint expert from New Scotland Yard, that Gilhooley's prints
had been found on the Aldershot bomb. Gilhooley successfully
appealed to the High Court in Dublin; the outcome of the appeal
surprised no one, since the High Court had rejected 50 successive
extradition orders issued by the RUC and British police in cases
defined in Dublin as alleged 'political' offences.

The warrant for 'English' Joe Gilhooley is still outstanding. Despite the relaxation of Irish procedures over extradition in the wake of the 1985 Anglo-Irish agreement he has not been apprehended again.

The fuss over the failed extradition proceedings for Gilhooley was as nothing compared with the furore over the woman presumed to be 'Mrs Reynolds'. Hampshire Police took out two secret warrants on April 2 1975, alleging her involvement in the Aldershot bombing and her being in possession of explosives in Southampton. But then, in September, Scotland Yard went public in the most dramatic fashion, naming the woman and issuing photographs. The press instantly tagged her 'the blonde bomber' and 'Britain's most wanted woman': Ellen Mary Margaret McKearney, a 21-year-old ex-convent girl from Moy in County Tyrone, Northern Ireland.

Scotland Yard's accompanying statement was explicit: '... known to have been closely involved with terrorist incidents in this country since last autumn [1974]... probably the most dangerous and active terrorist operating over here... acts mainly in the role of terrorist courier, bringing supplies of explosives and money, and is known to travel extensively between here and Ireland. She also uses cars which she hires in assumed names producing false international driving licences. She has rented furnished rooms with or without male companions.'

Among the aliases said to be used by McKearney were Anne Kirby, Mary Davitt, Patricia Cooling and 'Mrs Reynolds'. She was wanted for questioning for a string of offences including the London bombings in the winter of 1974, the Southampton bomb factory and shootings and the murder of PC Stephen Tibble. It was not suggested that McKearney had shot him, but the police claimed that her fingerprints had been found both at 39 Fairholme Road, Hammersmith and at 40 Westridge Road, Southampton.

She was described as five feet three inches tall with blue eyes, 'a trim figure and well-shaped legs', brown hair dyed blonde and a collection of wigs and spectacles for disguise.

She was said to favour blue jeans and blue tights. Frank McManus, the former MP for her home constituency in Tyrone, who had once employed her at his advice centre, confirmed the glamorous impression: 'One thing I remember very clearly is that she was an attractive teenager. There were always groups of young fellows hanging about. They seemed to be infatuated by her.'

Nothing in her family background dispelled the suitability of her title as 'Britain's most wanted woman'. Her grandfather was a veteran of the IRA campaign in the 1920s. One brother, Sean, had been blown up by his own bomb in a bungled attack on a petrol station; another brother, Patrick, was serving five years for planting a bomb in an Irish meat factory. Yet another brother, Thomas, had just completed a year's imprisonment in the Irish Republic for illegally possessing a firearm. In due course, Thomas would be sentenced to life imprisonment in Northern Ireland for killing a soldier and would join the first — aborted — hunger strike at Long Kesh. For good measure, Margaret McKearney herself was already wanted by the RUC in connection with the killing of a member of the Ulster Defence Regiment.

Within 24 hours, Michael Nicholson of Independent Television News had found her and filmed her arriving by car at the home of Daithi O'Conaill, the Provisional IRA Chief of Staff, in Ennaforth Park in Dublin. O'Conaill himself was two months into a 12-month prison sentence for membership of the IRA. His wife, Deirdre, was driving the Volkswagen, which abruptly sped off as McKearney hid her face. Nicholson reported seeing two pairs of the now infamous blue tights hanging up in the front room.

All this fuelled near apoplexy in the popular press and on Conservative back benches, although it was repeatedly pointed out by the Irish Government and police that Scotland Yard had neither forewarned them of their publicity launch nor, more pertinently, issued an extradition order. The release of one of the photographs of McKearney — described by Commander

Roy Habershon of the Bomb Squad as 'a bloody good one'
— generated more diplomatic unease. The Press Association
quoted Scotland Yard as saying that the photograph had been
'taken in Southern Ireland by an information source who seized
a unique opportunity to snap a quick picture'. This suggested to
some Irish politicians that the Metropolitan Police were illegally
operating a spy in the Republic. Within the next 24 hours
Scotland Yard denounced the account of the taking of the
photograph as 'a complete fabrication'. This, in turn, prompted
the editor-in-chief of the Press Association, David Chipp, to
issue a statement maintaining that the account had been given
verbatim by a Scotland Yard senior press officer to one of his
reporters who 'has a note of the quotation and we stand by his
account of what he was told'. Scotland Yard finally announced
that the photograph had been found in a house in Manchester
and, with regard to the Press Association, said, 'There may have
been a misunderstanding over the scope of our conversation.'

The extradition row continued when a senior Garda official
in Dublin announced, 'All Scotland Yard has to do is pick
up a telephone and ask. Under the terms of extradition
arrangements between the two countries, we can hold someone
for 72 hours while details of a warrant for arrest are sent to
us. Then it is up to the courts to order a further remand or
not.' For their part, Scotland Yard could reasonably conclude
that, given the Irish Constitution and the recent rulings of the
Irish High Court, there was no point in bothering. Nevertheless,
they were roundly criticized for their handling of the affair
in editorials at both ends of the political spectrum of the
British press.

The *Daily Mirror* asked: 'Did Scotland Yard bungle the
timing of its dramatic appeal about Margaret McKearney? It
now looks as if the alarm was raised after the quarry had already
bolted. Police seemed so confident that she was still in England.
Why else the public appeal? But did they check closely enough?
Newspapers and TV got a lead on her movements without much
difficulty. And Irish Special Branch men appear to have had a

good idea where to find her. Didn't Scotland Yard ask them before showing its hand?'

The *Daily Telegraph* concluded: 'To all this must now be added the rumour (can it possibly be true?) that Scotland Yard's sole interest in the supposedly dangerous terrorist Margaret McKearney, is to keep her out of the country in order to avoid the embarrassment of arresting her.' The *Telegraph* did not enlarge on the intriguing speculation that the prospect of McKearney under arrest could actually prove embarrassing. Scotland Yard insisted that they were not simply trying to scare her off: 'We know absolutely that is the girl we are after.' Whatever lay behind it all, no one expected to see Margaret McKearney paying an early visit to England.

Her parents seemed relatively unperturbed by the furore and gave a photograph of their daughter to the *Daily Mail*. They said she had never been to England and that they were treating it all as a joke. Although they later announced that they would be suing all the newspapers who had printed what was unquestionably a grave *prima facie* defamation, the writs never arrived — except at *The Sun*, who had printed a photograph of a completely unconnected girl in a Dublin street and claimed that they had found Margaret McKearney. The press finally caught up with McKearney again in a Dublin pub and were rewarded with the quote: 'I hate blue tights anyway.'

One tragic outcome of the McKearney fiasco was the death of a Catholic couple in their sixties, after the illegal Protestant paramilitary Ulster Volunteer Force had announced in Belfast that Margaret McKearney was on their intelligence files and on a death list. On October 23 Peter and Jean McKearney were shot dead at their farmhouse in Moy, County Tyrone. They were not related to Margaret McKearney.

Next the Garda detained McKearney and a friend, Mrs Grainne Cooling — the sister-in-law of Daithi O'Conaill — in December 1975 at the wedding reception of a man who had recently served a prison sentence for IRA membership. The women were released without charge after 48 hours. A week later they signed a statement that read, in part: 'We, the friends and relatives of political prisoners in Portlaoise Jail endorse the prisoners' demand for a public sworn inquiry into the brutal behaviour of the Portlaoise governor and his minions.'

In September 1977 McKearney married James O'Neill of Belfast in St McArtan's Cathedral in Monaghan in the Irish Republic. Among the guests were Ruairi O'Bradaigh, the then president of Provisional Sinn Fein, and Daithi O'Conaill. Mrs Deirdre O'Conaill was matron of honour. Margaret McKearney was last reported to have a daughter and to be living in rural Ireland.

There was, however, one successful, if highly contentious, extradition relating to the mainland IRA campaign of 1974-75. As the London ASU scattered in the wake of the Tibble killing and the discovery of the Fairholme Road safe house, the Irish-American member of the team, William Joseph Quinn, went to Dublin. There, he was arrested by the Irish police in April 1975 and charged with assaulting a policeman and with membership of the IRA.

On May 14 Quinn appeared briefly at the Special Criminal Court in Green Street, a few hours before his case opened. He was unaware as he was hustled into the dock between two policemen that he was on a clandestine identity parade. PC Adrian Blackledge, who had attempted to arrest the killer of Stephen Tibble earlier in the year, was in court with the Irish police. He had been flown to Dublin and told that he would have the chance to identify a suspect for the Tibble killing. Before him were three groups of three men; in each group was a man in plain clothes flanked by two uniformed men. Blackledge identified Quinn from one of these groups as the man he had confronted in Fairholme Road. Blackledge was unable to recognize Quinn's voice, since in court the latter spoke with an unmistakable American accent, while Blackledge had earlier described Tibble's killer as having an Irish accent. Nevertheless,

Blackledge was certain he had made a positive identification of Tibble's killer.

Quinn was duly acquitted on the assault charge and sentenced to a year in Portlaoise Prison for membership of the IRA. The British authorities made no attempt to extradite him upon his release nine months later, and a British warrant issued in June 1976 lay dormant. Quinn, still unaware of his covert court-room identification, stayed on in the Irish Republic. During the next two years he was regularly picked up for questioning by the Irish police, but was released without charge on each occasion. The British police were informed of these moves but took no action, explaining later that they regarded extradition proceedings as unreliable and that they had hoped Quinn might return to England and lead them to his accomplices.

Instead, Quinn returned to the United States in February 1979, moved in with his aunt in San Francisco and took a sales job at Serramonte's, his uncle's stationery store in Daly City. He began saving money for an eventual return to Ireland. He told friends he wanted to buy a farm in the countryside. On September 29 1981 three FBI agents walked into the shop and bought notebooks and paper handled by Quinn. They then arrested him outside the store on a Californian warrant issued on behalf of the United Kingdom.

Within a month, the United Kingdom formally requested Quinn's extradition on a series of charges: the killing of Stephen Tibble; conspiracy to cause explosions dating back to January 1 1974; and bombing incidents, including three letter bombs in 1974 — to Judge John Hazzard, Sir Max Aitken and Bishop Gerard Tickle.

The British affidavit, filed by Detective Inspector Alan Lewis of the Metropolitan Police Anti-Terrorist Squad, further cited the unexploded time bombs left at Aldershot British Rail station on December 20 1974 and at the Charco Grill, Hampstead on January 27 1975. The basis for the bombing charges was the claimed presence of Quinn's fingerprints on the devices and at Fairholme Road and other London safe houses.

Quinn made no attempt to deny the charges in the Californian courts. Instead, his lawyers mounted a protracted struggle to prove that the offences were 'political' and therefore not subject to the prevailing extradition treaty between the United States and the United Kingdom. His family, previously apolitical, now moved behind him. 'I wish he'd never gone over there,' declared his father, 'but if he did those things, it's like any soldier would do in a war. It's not right the way they talk of him being a terrorist. I would say that he's a freedom fighter and I don't think they should be holding him at all.' His younger brother Jim, a Vietnam veteran, said, 'My brother did what was right for him and right for the Irish. He had his war; I had mine. But I'd say his was a hell of a lot more just.'

Quinn spent five years in a small cell in the San Francisco County Jail as the proceedings dragged on. At one stage he was within 24 hours of being released on a magistrate's order, but it was swiftly overruled. Thereafter, Quinn's optimism failed: 'I'm almost resigned now to going back,' he said in a prison interview. 'It seems to me that Uncle Sam is out to suppress Irish support in this country and I'm going to be a sacrificial lamb for that policy... I'm locked up in my cell here for 23 hours a day and yet, just about every night, I dream I'm out walking on the streets of San Francisco.' His one outing was in chains to his father's funeral. The charges were reduced to conspiracy and the Tibble shooting and, finally, after five years of wrangling, Quinn's extradition was ordered by a judge in the US Ninth Circuit Court, who observed, 'Clearly the evidence... linking Quinn with the Tibble murder is not overwhelming. If that were all the evidence introduced at a murder trial, Quinn could not be convicted.' The evidence of the secret identification parade had not been laid before the American courts.

Quinn was flown into England by the RAF in October 1986. He was now past 40, his dark hair greying. It may have crossed his mind that he was the first subject of successful extradition proceedings relating to the mainland bombing campaign: Peter McMullen, in New England, and Margaret McKearney and

'English' Joe Gilhooley, in the Irish Republic, had all seen British warrants and extradition attempts founder and continued to enjoy their freedom.

Quinn's eventual trial, in early 1988, centred on the admissibility of the identification by Blackledge at the Dublin Special Criminal Court nearly 13 years before. After lengthy legal submissions away from the jury and the press, the judge allowed the evidence. Quinn pleaded not guilty to the murder of PC Stephen Tibble, but was convicted and sentenced to life imprisonment. Beyond smiling to his distraught aunt and mother in the public gallery, he remained outwardly impassive. His London solicitor, Gareth Peirce, said, 'It must have been the worst ever identification anywhere in the whole world... The whole arrangements were so suggestive as effectively to point Quinn out to him [Blackledge].' Peirce further noted that Blackledge had been brought into the Dublin court down a corridor that afforded a first sighting of the man in the dock; that none of the normal English safeguards of a properly constituted identity parade had been applied; that the Irish chief superintendent in charge of Quinn's Dublin case had kept no records of the physical appearance of the other two men making up the parade, one of whom had allegedly had a moustache while Quinn was clean-shaven; and that none of the eyewitnesses to the Tibble shooting had been asked to identify Quinn.

Whatever the confusion surrounding the process leading to the all-important identification of Quinn, or, indeed, caused by the conflicting police accounts of the age and accent of the gunman, there was no argument over the presence of Quinn's fingerprints in Fairholme Road and other safe houses; no argument that he was a fully fledged and unrepentant member of the London Active Service Unit. His American lawyer, Colleen Rohan, told the *Los Angeles Times* at the outset, 'Our position is that he was obviously a member of the IRA and that his motivations in all this would have been clearly political.'

William Joseph Quinn was even more explicit: 'I wanted to help out if I could. I'd do it all over again. I'm afraid I would. I guess that nice American boy wasn't happy with the television culture and that Disneyland world. I guess he was looking for a new identity and better sense of values and just happened to find a worthy cause to be devoted to.'

20
A CRITICAL
WITNESS

'I was willing to sign anything. They said, we'd like you
to make a statement and I said, just rewrite whatever
you want. I'll admit to doing the whole thing on my
own if you want... Because I thought... I'm going to
be safer in prison than I am in this place with these
fellers.'

Frank Johnson, 1985

The resumption of hostilities by the London Active Service
Unit in the second half of January 1975 brought a new *frisson*
of fear to Guildford. It was generally felt that for as long as the
city was obliged to host the regular court appearances of its
own bomb suspects, Guildford was a prime target for the IRA.
Siege measures included regular inspections of the Ward Street
public lavatories close to the Magistrates' Court; the frisking of
customers at the North Street Berni Inn; searches of everyone
entering the Civic Hall and the sports centre; spot checks on
people and cars in the vicinity of North Street; and tighter
security than ever around the tiny court itself. For the people of
Guildford, one consuming question was the venue of the eventual trial. Three days before the committal, police announced
that security considerations ruled out the holding of a full
trial at Guildford. Eyes turned towards Winchester, where the
Price sisters had been convicted, but Winchester shopkeepers
were less than enthusiastic. Douglas Bylett, President of the
Chamber of Commerce, told the *Surrey Daily Advertiser*,
'The Guildford bombings didn't happen on our cabbage patch,
so we will protest most strongly if the trial is held here. The last

one totally disrupted our lives and we don't want that to happen again.'

It was to Guildford in this atmosphere that Frank Johnson was brought, by air from Newcastle, on January 22. Johnson took his status as an alibi witness seriously and in anticipation of his court appearance had shaved off his beard and found himself a new job, cleaning out pigs' guts in an abattoir. Leaving work one evening, he encountered — with little surprise, he says — one of the Newcastle detectives who had questioned him previously, a man called Ryans, leaning against a smart, red, unmarked police car. They drove to West End police station, Johnson acutely conscious of the pigs' guts underneath his fingernails. He was not to wash his hands for two days.

Ryans's demeanour was less congenial than at their previous meeting. The police were interpreting the discovery of the notes he had left in his room at home about his activities on the night of October 5 as proof of his attempt to cook up an alibi for Carole Richardson. Johnson says he was put in a cell without blankets or supper, although this did not worry him unduly since he was used to sleeping rough. When the shift changed half-way through the night, the new officer gave him a blanket. The next morning, Longhurst and Wise came to see him. They told him that unless he changed his story he would have to go with them to Guildford. They drove to the airport and boarded a plane. Johnson ate two breakfasts because the turbulence put the detectives off their food. On arrival, he was installed in a police car next to Wise and handcuffed to a hook on the floor. At Guildford police station he was informed they were holding him under the Prevention of Terrorism Act on suspicion of having been involved in the Guildford bombing.

In his first statement — the one he had made to Longhurst and Wise in Newcastle before Christmas — Johnson had said that he had arrived at the Charlie Chaplin pub in Elephant and Castle at about 6.00 or 6.10 p.m. and that the two girls had joined him about 15 minutes later. They had stayed at the pub for a further 10 minutes or so and then sauntered off to the Poly, which would have meant arriving there at about 6.40.

'I've seen lots of people and you've got your times wrong,' Longhurst said to him now.

Johnson agreed that he was unsure of the time and that it could have been 7.00 p.m.

'We have checked thoroughly. We've checked all the times. It wasn't 7.00 p.m. that night,' Longhurst insisted. 'It was about 8.00 p.m. when you arrived at the college... You've tried to alter the times back at least an hour.'

The police record of the interview shows a constant return to the question of the time and a steady berating of Johnson for 'IRA sympathies' and for fixing the alibi. Johnson says that this record, extracts of which follow, is a paraphrase of events, since the interview lasted all day and was resumed the next day. According to police, the morning session took two hours five minutes and the interview continued for one hour 47 minutes in the afternoon.

'You're in a horrible predicament,' said Longhurst. 'From what you said before and what I have found out. If it was true you would not be here now, but you have told deliberate lies to get Carole out of trouble. You did not think this up on the bus. You told someone before that, that she could not have done it as she was with you.'

'How was that? I couldn't have told anybody that.'

'Do you know Ray Laidlaw?' asked Longhurst.

'Yes,' said Johnson. Laidlaw was the drummer with the band.

'Has he got anything against you?'

'No, I don't think so.'

'Do you remember what you said to him when you met?'

'No.'

'You said, "Sorry we're late; we have just walked from an underground station." That was at 8.00 p.m.' This was untrue. Laidlaw's statement says clearly that he saw Frank Johnson arrive with Carole and Lisa at 7.45.

'That wasn't me. I don't remember that,' said Johnson. But he added, 'I did come and see him, though.'

'Lisa said to you Carole had been arrested for the bombing and she had admitted it. Did she say that?'

'Yes.'

'It seems coincidental that you afterwards remembered she was with you.'

'Yes.'

'You said when you were in the pub you played on a tennis machine, didn't you?'

'Yes.'

'But Lisa says it was a football machine.'

'That's what I call a tennis machine,' said Johnson, stubbornly.

'Has Lisa seen you?' Longhurst asked.

'No, but she phoned me a couple of times.'

'Have you been in touch with Carole?'

'I don't know how to get in touch with her.'

'You thought when you made that statement, Carole would walk out with Lisa backing you up... Do you know where Lisa met you that night?'

'Yes,' repeated Johnson miserably. 'In the Charlie Chaplin.'

'No it wasn't,' said Longhurst. 'What do you know about bombs?'

'Only that they kill people.'

'You did know something about bombs before the fifth of October.'

'No, I didn't!'

'You checked all this out beforehand, didn't you?'

'I didn't check anything out,' said Johnson. 'It was straight-forward. If I'd thought it was more complicated, I would have checked more thoroughly.'

'This was well thought out, Frank,' Longhurst assured him. 'It was not a complicated one, but very simple and good. But now we know what the real truth is. You have underestimated what people like us would do about it. The only thing unanswered is whether you were here [in Guildford] or not.'

'You can check that, like you have checked everything else,' Johnson told him bitterly. 'I can't say anything.'

'Because of putting this alibi up you have really involved yourself. It may be that you, Lisa, Carole and others were all here in Guildford.'

'I know I wasn't there,' Johnson insisted.

'You can't prove you were not there.'

'I can't think about it!'

'Nobody in the Charlie Chaplin remembers you,' said Longhurst. 'The only thing right is that you were at the South Bank Poly by 8.00 p.m. Time enough to plant bombs in Guildford and get there at that time.'

Johnson said nothing.

'You know that what I've been saying is true, Frank.'

'You appear to have done your homework,' Johnson conceded. 'It may be that I got the times wrong, but I don't think so.'

'You knew there was going to be bombings, didn't you?' Longhurst said.

At this point the police notes record Johnson's reply as, 'I had a good idea.' Johnson is adamant that he never said this, and that he never said other things that are ascribed to him in the next part of the interview:

'... When I'm in Ireland people ask me if I can get anything of use to them.'

'Like what?'

'Guns, ammunition, two-way radios and things.'

'You have said "I" and not "we" went to the Poly. I told you to be careful of your choice of words. You are getting confused, Frank, about lying and telling the truth... '

And later, in the afternoon:

'Carole was in Guildford during that time, wasn't she?'

'I suppose she was... '

And later still:

'Frank, tell me the truth.'

'I made it up. I didn't think Carole was there.'

'What time was it you got to the Charlie Chaplin?'

'I don't know.'

'You knew it was a lie about the time?'

'Yes.'

'It was later than 6.30 p.m., wasn't it?'

'Yes, it was much later.'

'How does Lisa know about it?'

'I don't know. I didn't discuss it with anybody. I made it up on my own.'

At 5.10 p.m. Johnson made a statement. He was held overnight and questioned for a further two hours 25 minutes the following day before being released at around tea-time, but there were no further changes or admissions. In his January 22 statement he opened by saying that some of the things in his previous statement were untrue. He admitted discussing Carole's arrest with Lisa at a squat in Kenilworth Road. On the subject of timings, he said, 'When I arrived at the Charlie Chaplin public house it was dark and the street lights were on. I don't remember how long I waited in the pub for Lisa and Carole to arrive, but it could have been as long as 40 minutes. When the girls arrived at the pub we had one quick drink and a game on the tennis machine. We stayed there no longer than 10 minutes and then walked quickly to the Poly... I had fixed the times earlier because I didn't believe that Carole could have done such a thing and I wanted to help her. I am sorry for all the inconvenience I have caused to all the people concerned.'

Johnson's two days in custody had elicited three important changes in his story. First, he admitted a degree of collusion with Lisa over the alibi. Secondly, he now claimed that everything had happened substantially later than he had said in his first statement. Thirdly, he was now admitting to playing a direct role in IRA activities.

Lighting-up time on October 5 was 7.01 p.m., so for it to have been 'getting dark' (as he had said) when he left Brixton and 'dark' on his arrival at the Elephant, Johnson would have to have reached the pub at 7.15 at the earliest. The addition of a possible 40 minutes' wait before the girls joined him brings the time to 7.55. With '10 minutes' for the drink and the game on the machine and a further five minutes for the 'quick' walk to the Poly, the time would by then have been 8.10 p.m. — at least 10 minutes after the latest estimate of his arrival by witnesses for the prosecution. So Johnson's timing now erred on the side of being implausibly late. On the matter of his IRA activities, these are recorded in his interview notes but, significantly, not in his statement. If the admissions were in fact made, it is curious that they do not appear in his statement, and even more curious that after making them Johnson should have been released from custody and told to make his way home. He says one of the police officers gave him cash for the journey.

If, on the other hand, no such admissions were made (or made voluntarily) in the course of the interview, then what else is unreliably recorded in the notes? At the end of the second statement appears a postscript which reads: 'I would like to add that I have no complaints about treatment in Guildford police station on Wednesday 22nd January 1975.' Johnson had, of course, signed the postscript. But once out of Guildford police station he was to give a very different account of what had happened there.

21
COMMITTAL

'It's Guildford CID that haven't got their heads screwed the right way round. Not BRITISH JUSTICE, that doesn't come into it until the trial... '

Letter from Carole Richardson to Paddy Armstrong,
Brixton Prison, February 28 1975

In early 1975, as the committal hearing approached and the Crown honed its case, clues emerged as to the course it would be steering through the evidence. Sean Mullin, arrested at Rondu Road the previous November and released on bail on January 27, was acquitted on February 3 of the single charge of conspiracy to cause explosions. The murder charge against Brian Anderson was dropped on the same day and he was released. McGuinness and Colman also had their charges dropped and were set free. Lord Hamilton of Dalzell, the Chair of Guildford Magistrates, acknowledged that he had given bail to Colman, McGuinness and Mullin with the approval of the counsel for the Director of Public Prosecutions (DPP), but these were not developments to which the police submitted calmly. Rumblings of anger at Guildford police station over the prizes lost spilled out in angry questions in the House of Commons from David Howell, Guildford's Conservative MP, and David Lane, the Conservative Home Affairs spokesman. 'I shall be taking steps to find out why this decision was taken,' said Howell. Lane added that he hoped there would be an explanation soon: 'People are very upset.' The reason for the releases was patent lack of evidence, but although the police were to stifle their dissatisfaction, it was to burst out in an intriguing political row at the end of the trial.

On February 24, the murder charge against Anne Maguire was dismissed. A spokesman for the DPP told Guildford magistrates,

'In the light of all the available evidence, counsel has advised that evidence against her is insufficient to justify the prosecution asking for her committal for trial.' Anne collapsed, sobbing with relief. 'I thought I was going home,' she remembers. 'I came out of court and we were in the hall and they told me that because of the nitroglycerine on my gloves I had to stay in prison.' Worse, it was on this same day that her two young sons, Patrick and Vincent, were charged with possession of explosives.

The release of Anderson, McGuinness, Colman and Mullin put heart into Paul Hill. On February 3 he wrote to his mother:

> Well Mum, as you will know by now four of the other people charged with me have been cleared and I am now a bit happier as at least something is happening in the case and it will make people think... Don't worry Mum, as you know some people don't want to believe that we did not do it. All I can say is thank God they ain't judges... Gerry Conlon cracked up in court today and started shouting that he never did it and he was crying like hell. I can't blame him but I cheered him up a bit as he will only make himself worse 'cos I know what it's like...

Conlon, for his part, was maintaining a cheerful front to his family. On February 15 he wrote:

> Our committals are coming up in about three weeks time, and Dad and I must stand a very good chance of getting bail or even a very slight chance of getting completely off, but it is very hard to say what will happen, but with a bit of luck and God's help it will work out all right in the end.

The defendants' only chance to see one another was at the weekly court appearances. In fact, these appearances were the only occasions on which it can be said with complete certainty they ever met together at all — before or after their arrest. Paddy Armstrong was no letter-writer. It was therefore not until now

— and through the arbitration of Lisa Astin — that Carole was finally assured of his innocence. Her relief was boundless. On February 1 she wrote:

> Dearest Paddy, I have just seen Lisa and she told me what happened, of course I believe you weren't there. The way the police put it, it made me think I was there. But when it's all over we'll show them. Lisa will be up again next Wednesday and I told her not to worry about me but to get to see you whenever she could. She won't take my advice I know but I wish you all the luck in the world, because I didn't think you would have done such a thing and I'm really glad now I know for sure...
>
> Paddy just answer me one question, why did you make a statement against me? I don't think you did now and the way everything is going we'll be making statements to the press fairly soon. It'll be good to walk down the road with you again though. Maybe we can go hitch-hiking again. I still want to see the palm trees in Wales...

No record exists of Armstrong's ever answering her question; perhaps he did not even remember how he first came to implicate her. But under the influence of a truth drug later that year he was to recall that he had denied her presence at Guildford until Detective Chief Inspector Longhurst came into the room and told him she had admitted to being there herself, at which point he agreed that she was.

Whether or not he ever explained this to her, she was clearly prepared to forgive him. On February 15 she wrote:

> I really miss you. At least they let me see you for a few minutes in court. It's so hard to put my feelings down on paper but I'm sure you understand what I mean. At least I know a bit more about Guildford now and what happened in the police station. I didn't know what or who to believe at first but now I know. I don't blame you if you went through

the same ordeal as Paul and Gerry. God I hope you didn't though, it didn't sound very nice at all... All I hope is the truth is believed in court. Because I'm sure Anne and Paddy are, and I know you and me are, so we have nothing to worry about really. It's surprising how you get to know someone in a few weeks, Anne's a really nice person. I wonder if I'll ever see her when I get out, or should I say when we get out.

Towards Hill she was a little less charitable. February 20:

How could Paul Hill make statements against me? I don't even know the guy, I think I saw him once with Gerry walking down the road. Oh well liars can never remember all their lies so the truth will come out in the end and I just hope it's bloody soon.

What are you going to do when it's all over, stay here or go back to Belfast?

They ought to bring back hanging then it might all quieten down and save taxpayers a lot of money, what do you think, because in over about 50 years only about 3 people have been wrongly hanged but it makes judges and juries think and listen a lot more.

But the strain was telling on her nerves and her next few letters are full of wild swings of mood. February 25:

I'm really starting to miss you bad, when we get committed God only knows when I'll see you again. It's not fair why didn't they pick on Gerry or Paul's girlfriends, why the heck me. It's not fair but this bloody world isn't fair to anyone that does any good in it, is it? Anyway why worry, we know the truth and that's all that matters. I know where I was and you know where you were I think, so the truth's got to come out that we weren't there.

February 26:

Beware I'm in a bad mood so if you don't want to be driven mad don't read any further. Why the hells name did you pick on me to put in your blasted statement? I'm really in a bad mood with you at the moment, well not just you but mainly you. Why did you hold a party for Lisa's birthday and why did I meet Frank Egan. If I hadn't met him I wouldn't have been at Lisa's party and I wouldn't have met you and then I wouldn't be here it's all his fault...

[The IRA] are bloody fools the lot of them. I wish they'd all blow themselves up so there'd be no more trouble because it's only innocent people who get hurt or blamed for it and them Bastards don't give a damn. Oh god why did they have to pick on me, I can't stand it any longer it's driving me mad, people don't seem to understand. They can make mistakes but God forgive them for what they've put me through. I'm just not strong enough to stand it any more.

February 28:

I'm really fed up, this is starting to get me down. I'm cracking up. What you said about British Justice. It's Guildford CID that haven't got their heads screwed the right way round. Not BRITISH JUSTICE, that doesn't come into it until the trial, sorry about the writing but my hand's shaking like a leaf and I can't concentrate properly.

March 3:

I just feel like finishing it all, and I hope to god that Longhurst and Wise can carry it on their conscience. All they are is animals, they don't care about humans. I know I'm innocent but them bastards just keep pushing, bloody CID all they are are animals the bloody lot of them. How are you anyway, you didn't look too good. It's hit you harder than what you let on hasn't it. I know you're innocent but them animals don't know the truth. When I was making them statements every time I lied they said it was the truth and when I told the truth they walloped me, bloody animals that's all they are.

Sorry about that outburst Pad, but I keep getting the feeling no one gives a damn whether I get out or not. I know it's not true but I can't help it. I'm so fed up it's just unbelievable. I must have read every book in the library twice and all my letters about 50 times at least. Oh blast I've just dropped a bottle of orange on the floor, it's all blooming sticky, that's not concentrating but so what.

My blooming memory's terrible. I can't remember who I've written to and who I haven't, everyone probably reads the same thing two or three times. I went to the dentist today and had another 5 fillings and one's fallen out...

March 14:

Dearest Paddy, I really miss you. It's not fair, why can't they have double cells, and your not being allowed an engagement ring is ridiculous just because you're not married. It's so silly — what's the use of an engagement ring after you're married? Anyway we would be by now if everything went according to plan and you had kept your job and we hadn't been arrested... How's the 'lieutenant' going? [By now she had read Armstrong's statements and knew how he had described Gerry Conlon.] Your statements are unbelievable in some places, the names you called Gerry I wouldn't be surprised if he didn't attack you when he gets his papers and I wouldn't blame him. Mind if he did I'd have a go at him the next time I saw him myself...

They're playing 'Jack of Hearts', Bob Dylan, off his new album 'Blood on the Tracks'. It's brilliant. There are so many good albums coming out around now and I'm missing them all, but I'll hear them when I get out I hope. But that's one album I'm gonna get as a reminder of Brixton Prison, Guildford CID and the bloody IRA.

Oh I feel like screaming, in fact I think I will, it'll clear my mind a bit. I'll ask Anne to join me though because I'll feel a fool screaming on my own. When do you think this will all be over? I ask myself but can't find a suitable answer so you tell me. I'll close now because I've got a visit, so see you soon. Love to all, especially you. Chin up. Look after yourself. All my love

Carole

PS. I wish you were dog-sitting then I'd know I was back home.

PPS. Jack of Hearts reminds me of you Piggy.

March 15:

When will I be able to walk down the street again and go into a shop and buy a packet of fags? I think I'll go over to Shishkidan when this is all over. It's in Holland about 9 miles down the canal from Amsterdam, it's a really far out place. John and Leslie Anne went there when they went hitch-hiking round Europe and they said you can't beat it, it's even better than Amsterdam they said, tariff boards with dope prices all over the pubs. Sounds too good to be true but at least I'll or we'll be doing nothing illegal over there because you can't be had for dope, and I doubt if anyone will start planting bloody bombs over there.

How are you anyway? Gerry said in his letter you wouldn't have a haircut, mind if you saw his first I don't blame you, what a state, the barber of Seville getting to work again. Oh well at least he didn't cut his throat, and sell him to be made into meat pies, what a thought. I shouldn't have thought of that it's made me feel sick...

I keep wondering who's gonna crack first. Paul I doubt, maybe Gerry — his letter's a lot different from his last one — maybe you, maybe me, but I reckon it'll be Gerry.

March 12:

Dearest Paddy, You looked well today, you weren't shaking quite so much. Next week at least I'll know what the police think they have on me other than everyone's statement. Gerry is really mad and his hair, what a state. But it will have grown out by the time this is all over, worse luck...

[The] thought of what this is all about is really bad but when it ends I'm going to get a job in some stable in the country and you are not going back to Belfast, that's the worst place to go. You'll be found innocent of this but if there's any trouble round the Divis flats you'll be one of the first to be picked up, because we'll all be watched for a good few years when this is all over and no matter where you go there will be someone behind you. Anyway what's wrong with this country?

I've just written to Gerry. I can't concentrate on anything. Next week will be a good week... there should be quite a commotion on Monday, Tuesday, Wednesday if they last that long. Because no court is gonna believe what those lying sons of bitches have said. But who cares. Let them say what they like, I know we all know the truth, well I do anyway...

After various prognostications and postponements, the committal proceedings opened on March 17 — St Patrick's Day. A police cordon was thrown around the High Street for the hearing in Guildford's ancient Guildhall. This was to be the first public airing of the case and police were expecting crowds of spectators; 24 seats had been allocated in the public gallery for the first in the queue. However, excluding the young woman with a push-chair who was denied access because no children were allowed, only two people turned up.

Outside, the High Street was quiet. Two police officers with dogs patrolled discreetly. As the defendants were led into the court through the back entrance in North Street, two women shoppers stopped to watch and shout angrily at them. It was a minimalist demonstration. Clearly, Guildford had had enough.

Inside the court, the three magistrates listened while the junior prosecuting counsel for the Crown, Mr Michael (now Sir Michael) Hill, read out a long opening statement of the Crown's case against the Guildford Four:

'It is the prosecution's case here that as part of the extension of their bombing campaign from Northern Ireland to Great Britain, the Provisional IRA decided that one of their targets in Great Britain would be a number of servicemen's public houses, and that those would be bombed by active service units without warning,' he began. It was an interesting opening in view of the fact that never at any stage did the police seriously investigate the possibility that the Guildford Four could have been connected with other IRA bombings, or that any other IRA bomber could have been connected with the Guildford or Woolwich bombs.

'On the afternoon of 5 October last year,' Michael Hill continued, 'a terrorist gang of some eight persons in two cars travelled down from London to Guildford arriving some time before 5.30 in the afternoon... These four defendants were members of that eight-strong gang [and] have been involved in the planning of and the preparation for this attack for some time...

'There is a certain amount of evidence in the papers as to the background of these crimes. Part of it comes from what each of the defendants told the police, and part of it comes from direct evidence.' (It is unclear what he meant by 'direct' since there was no evidence apart from the confessions.) 'As the interviews with these defendants are read and the statements that they made considered, it rapidly becomes apparent that at no one stage was any one of them telling the whole of the truth. What also becomes apparent is that there were two reasons in the minds of each one of them for not telling the whole truth. Of course, the obvious reason — a desire to minimize his or her culpability which I would trust is different from involvement. Secondly, what becomes clear is that there was a deliberate attempt to impede and confuse investigations by the police made by each one of these defendants in the interviews and the statements where they were admitting taking part in the bombings.' The Crown inferred, he added, that there had been advance planning of this counter-information technique.

He proceeded to give examples of it. Hill, he said, 'deliberately lied' about the vehicle used for Woolwich (the silver sports car), 'knowing that the bombers had been seen, as had their vehicle' — a 'red or maroon Mk II Ford Cortina'. While as for Carole Richardson, in claiming to have placed the bomb in the Seven Stars as well as the one in the Horse and Groom, 'it may well be that [she] has admitted doing something which she simply did not do.' In other words, the Crown had decided to deal with the inconsistencies in the statements by selecting some parts of them as true, in order for its case to stand, and some parts as 'deliberately false', in order for it not to conflict with the known facts. Michael Hill declined to speculate as to what could have prompted this extra admission, or to elaborate on why the Crown had misgivings about it.

After rehearsing the details at some length, he concluded, 'The prosecution say that the evidence in this case shows quite clearly that at the very least they were members of the team that deliberately planted a bomb in the Horse and Groom with intent to kill; that it matters not in those circumstances what specific part in that bombing raid they played; if they were members of that team they are guilty of murder.'

Although the four counsel for the defence declined to make submissions on behalf of the accused, two witnesses, Frank Johnson and Lisa Astin, were called to give evidence of Carole Richardson's alibi. Johnson, for whom a trip to Guildford had uncomfortable associations still fresh in his mind, none the less returned to his former position: that he had met Carole

Richardson and Lisa Astin at the Charlie Chaplin pub at such
a time as would have precluded Carole's driving back from
Guildford to reach the South Bank Poly by 7.45 p.m. He faced
the three magistrates, gave his evidence fully and clearly and
refused to allow the prosecution to rush him. Lisa maintained
simply that she and Carole had been in London together
all day.

Lunch-breaks during the committal were unsophisticated
affairs in which counsel disappeared together, leaving the solicitors to their own devices. Alastair Logan remembers that on one
of the two days of the hearing they were hunched around a table
in the dreary Market Street Wimpy Bar (not the one enshrined
in Paddy Armstrong's police statements), that conversation ran
on the morning's proceedings and that at last they began to
divulge to one another their feelings about the case.

'I don't know who started it. It may have been me, I can't
remember,' says Logan. 'But someone ventured — it came out
almost apologetically, as I recall — that they believed their client
to be "not guilty". And suddenly everyone sat up. And everyone
looked at each other for the first time. And everybody spoke
at once and said that, yes, they too believed it; each of us had
independently reached the conclusion that we suspected our
clients had told the police a lot of rubbish, and that all four
had absolutely nothing to do with the Guildford and Woolwich
bombings. There we were in the middle of Guildford and we
believed our clients to be innocent. It was like admitting to
heresy!'

The four legal advisers were alone in this conviction. The
hearing concluded with the referral of the case for trial. The
defendants were dispatched to prison. Guildford, glad to see the
back of them, relaxed its security precautions.

On April 16, Anne Maguire was at last given bail and allowed
to return home to her children to await trial in January 1976.
One day earlier, on April 15, Paul Hill was charged at Crumlin
Road gaol in Belfast with the murder of ex-soldier Brian Shaw.
The *Surrey Daily Advertiser* (April 21/22 1975) published

a short report linking Hill with both cases, which would have been seriously prejudicial had any juror at the Guildford trial read it.

The trial opened on June 17 and ran for seven days at the Belfast City Commission before Mr Justice Kelly. There was no jury. Hill pleaded not guilty. The sole evidence against him was the statement he had made to the two RUC officers, Cunningham and McCaul. The judge found him guilty, although his two co-accused got off more lightly. Hector Young, who had been with Shaw when they entered the bar in the Divis Flats complex from which Shaw was later abducted, found himself acquitted on all three counts of murder, conspiracy to murder and intimidation. Martin Monaghan was sentenced to three years' imprisonment on charges of intimidation and membership of the IRA. Sentencing Hill to life, the judge said that he was satisfied beyond reasonable doubt that Hill had aided and abetted the murder. He had not pulled the trigger on Shaw, but 'It was clear Hill was a member of the Provisional IRA and a willing party to an execution squad sent out to kill Shaw.' As Hill was led from the dock, he shouted to the judge, 'Good-night... you bastard.'

At the end of the committal, Carole Richardson wrote:

Dearest Paddy, Not long to go till freedom now I hope. It'll be great to get out again, straight to the pub for a drink, a luvverly scotch and lemonade, I haven't had one for ages, or a Guinness and black... There's a rumour going round about June 2nd for the trial, maybe I'll be out for my birthday...

But her optimism was short-lived. June 2 was nothing but a rumour. At the beginning of May she was moved to Risley Remand Centre, in Cheshire, where she was to stay until the trial. It was there, on June 19, that she celebrated her 18th birthday. The move to Risley seems to have triggered a change in Carole. As the trial approached she no longer spoke of the case; her raw anger and bewilderment — the natural perceptions of someone on the 'outside' — had been stifled. Her letters are brittle, flippant, full of fantasies and the latest music. It was becoming dangerous to feel too deeply. One of her last letters before the onset of this new mood was written to Paddy on May 8, immediately after her arrival:

Dearest Paddy, I really feel sick. For a while I thought everything would be alright even if I did only see you once a week, but now I won't see you for months, until we go to court. Why did they have to move me? It's worse here than Brixton. From what I've heard I'll be locked in all day except exercise. I'm about 200 miles from London so I very much doubt if I'll get many visits and the rules are so different. It was bad enough when you were in Winchester. It's even worse now, I don't know what I'm going to do. Why the hell did they move me, it was enough even to be in prison in London but now I'll go completely mad. I'll get none of the privileges I had in Brixton or anything.

How are you anyway? Keeping well I hope and not getting too depressed. I don't know if I'll get my Vallium or night medicine. It'll drive me up the wall worse, even the stuff at Brixton wasn't that good.

I really cried coming up here. We came the same way near enough as when we were hitch-hiking around past Birmingham. St John's Wood, even within half a mile of the old squat, past the Red House, the Swiss and everywhere, it was awful. I haven't even a photo of Little Sister [her name for Lisa] or any of my papers. My solicitor is going to go mad because he wants me to read them until I know them off by heart. I don't think he will like having to come all the way up here twice a week either, he hasn't even got a car. Now I'm starting to wish Anne didn't get bail, at least I'd still be in Brixton. They don't seem to take into account the cost of going backwards and forwards for everyone concerned. I'm down to my last packet of fags. I can't do any knitting so bang goes your jumper and the baby clothes for Patsy. I think I'm going mad already, I'm sure I heard a cow just now.

I really miss you. I don't know, you seem so far away again. At least in Brixton you were only over the road. It's so stupid, an 8 hour journey for 15 minutes, so that means my mum won't be able to get up, Nan and Grandad won't, Lisa won't, it's really sickening. But Guildford CID will pay for it in the end, they know now it wasn't me but they are too pig-headed to admit it, but the truth always comes out in the end so they'll pay and pay damn well.

Look after yourself,
Love and peace always,
Love Carole xxx

God Bless the Innocent
And May the Guilty
Be Brought to Justice.

22
DOWD'S ARREST

'My luck just ran out.'

Brendan Dowd, July 10 1975

In the spring of 1975, in the wake of the Tibble shooting and the loss of the Fairholme Road safe house, Brendan Dowd returned to Dublin for a spell, during which he dyed his hair blond. His next instructions were to go to Manchester and establish a new active service unit in the North-West, adopting a new identity as a postgraduate student courtesy of an international driving licence in the name of Dennis Power. He rented a flat at 7 Mitford Road and kept in touch with Dublin by telephone.

To assist him, he was sent a mixed bag of volunteers, which threw into perspective the professionalism of the London ASU. Either the Army Council of the Provisional IRA was running out of high-calibre men or it had failed to absorb the lessons of the highly successful London team. The new Unit was a risky cocktail of North and South; of experience and hot-headed youth; and in its most notorious member contained a man whose name, appearance and fingerprints were already well known to police on both sides of the Irish Sea: Sean Kinsella.

Kinsella, 28, a former barber notable for his black Castro-style beard, came from Legnakelly, County Fermanagh in the North. A year earlier he had been gaoled for life in Dublin for the murder of Senator Billy Fox, a senior Protestant member of the Irish Government. Within two months Kinsella, his brother Michael, the notorious Eddie Gallagher and 16 other convicted Provisionals used explosives and helicopters to break their way out of Portlaoise Prison. After a number of lucky escapes on the run, Kinsella successfully found his way to Manchester.

Paul Norney was also on the run, having escaped from custody while awaiting trial for the alleged murder of two soldiers in his native city of Belfast. He was 17. Even allowing for the speed with which young Provisionals move into key Brigade and Battalion positions, especially in Belfast, the decision to send a 17-year-old — however precocious — to an undercover unit in England was extraordinary.

Stephen Nordone was another teenager, aged 19. He was born of Irish parents in Erith in Kent and brought up in Dundalk, County Louth, just south of the Northern Irish border and the 'bandit' country of Newry and Crossmaglen. Nordone claimed to have joined the Provisionals there at the age of 14. He was reported to be virtually illiterate but a skilled bomb-maker.

The fifth member was Noel Gibson, 22, a Gaelic football enthusiast from County Offaly in the Irish Republic. The five men set up initially in separate flats in Manchester and began assembling a formidable cache of arms, ammunition and explosives: 1,600 rounds of ammunition, 168 detonators, 17 clocks, a Swiss light machine-gun, a Swiss automatic 7.5-mm rifle, an Armalite, a Sten-gun, revolvers and automatic pistols. The 458 pounds of gelignite they accumulated indicated that the North-West was also serving as a major distribution point. They compiled a fresh list of targets. Their orders were to sit tight and await the inevitable end of the cease-fire.

Before then, and before they could put their armoury to use, there was an unnecessary and disastrous lapse of discipline. On the evening of June 30 the three youngest members of the team — Norney, Gibson and Nordone — got drunk in the Rusholme district of Manchester and went for a meal at the Indiana restaurant in Wilmslow Road. The manager, Shatiqur Choudhury, refused to sell them a bottle of wine to take away. The infuriated trio later returned to the restaurant and Norney, the 17-year-old, opened fire through the window, narrowly missing a table of late-night diners. Within minutes a patrol car pulled up alongside Norney and Gibson as they headed back to Gibson's bed-sitter in Brighton Grove. The two Provisionals drew their pistols and shot and seriously injured the driver, Inspector Emlyn Watkins. They were captured shortly after by a back-up team of police, but Nordone managed to escape.

The Brighton Grove flat yielded target lists and a number of addresses. Dowd hastily evacuated the remaining arsenals, and with Kinsella and Nordone ferried the guns and explosives in a hired car to a first-floor flat in Oxford Road, Liverpool beneath Miss Ada Cunningham, a 70-year-old retired schoolteacher. For the moment they seemed to have escaped. Then, a week later, Dowd made a reckless mistake of his own: in the early morning on July 9, with Kinsella and Nordone in the car, he drove through a red traffic-light directly opposite the headquarters of Merseyside Police. A patrol car went after the three men in the hired Marina and flagged it down. Dowd calmly apologized and correctly recited the date of birth on his illegal driving licence, but when it came to Kinsella's turn he had not done his homework. After he had stumbled through three attempts to get the date of birth on his licence correct, the police informed the three men that they would have to go to the station. Kinsella opened fire, injuring one of the officers. Dowd sped off and they abandoned the car as soon as they were out of sight.

Dowd knocked on the door of a ground-floor flat in Canning Street. 'Police. Open up!' he shouted. As the door opened, the three gunmen burst in. They found themselves in the home of Michael Townsend, a 36-year-old fitter, and his 11-year-old son, James, who was awakened by their unceremonious entry. Dowd turned on the radio for the news bulletins, which indicated that the gunmen had got clean away. Townsend was then dispatched to buy food, cigarettes and a full set of newspapers, leaving behind his son as security.

According to Townsend, Dowd said, 'Look, we're not going to hurt you. Behave yourself and you'll be OK. We're in trouble and we need your place so just behave yourself. We just want to stay in your house until things quieten down and then we're going to leave.'

Townsend was reassured: 'I made them all a cup of tea. We all sat talking and I said I sympathized with their cause but not their methods. Kinsella said that to them it was a war and in any war innocent people get hurt.'

The three spent the whole day at the flat in Canning Street. At 6.30 p.m. Dowd ordered Townsend to telephone for a taxi. Townsend was remarkably unperturbed: 'Towards the end we were getting on great. Just before the taxi came Dowd gave me £5 and my kid some pocket-money. Actually, it was quite emotional, you must understand. They all shook hands with me and said, "Thanks very much."'

Possibly overcome by this budding relationship, the North-West ASU had made their final blunder. The taxi-driver who took them back to Oxford Road in the Waterloo district was traced, and in the early hours of the following morning the red-brick house was surrounded by 25 officers from Special Branch and the Serious Crimes Squad.

As the first wave of police dashed up the stairs, the Provisionals fired through the door, injuring Detective Sergeant Tommy Davies in the stomach. The detectives fired back through the door and regrouped. A second burst of police fire hastened the end of the battle. Dowd, outnumbered, outgunned, with no plausible escape route and without the leverage of hostages, gave the order to surrender. 'My luck just ran out,' he told his captors.

Media interest fastened on the prodigious arms find and on Sean Kinsella, author of the spectacular mass break-out from Portlaoise Prison, but it was Brendan Dowd who captured the attention of the police. He was wearing a watch that belonged to PC Lloyd, the young constable kidnapped in Semley Place, near Buckingham Palace, the previous October. In one of his safe houses was a photograph of Margaret McKearney. His fingerprints matched a set found in the Fairholme Road safe house and on a number of items connected with the unsolved wave of London bombings. Within 48 hours, Detective Chief Superintendent Jim Nevill of the Metropolitan Police Bomb Squad had travelled up to Liverpool from London to interrogate him at St Anne's Street police station.

Throughout three lengthy interviews in Liverpool and at HM Prison Strangeways in Manchester, Dowd was alternately open and guarded about his time in London. Later, in court, he was to dispute the accuracy of his signed statements. (In particular he took exception to a statement attributed to him in which he claimed that his hands were too big to make time bombs, offering to the judge to demonstrate his ability there and then in open court — an offer declined.) He disclaimed most but not all of the first wave of the London bombings. In particular, he denied responsibility for any bombings that had resulted in death or injury.

The list of incidents about which he was questioned included the fatal throw bomb at the King's Arms, Woolwich, an offence for which Paul Hill and Patrick Armstrong were soon to stand trial. Detective Chief Superintendent Nevill had personally heard their confessions to the bombing.

Dowd admitted to having lived in Fairholme Road with 'Michael Wilson' and in earlier, abandoned safe houses. He admitted to making what he called 'nail bombs' which had bolts attached, notably the two that had been thrown at the Talbot Arms public house (only one of which had exploded). He admitted to having been involved in the night of the seven time bombs, as maker and planter. He admitted to ownership of guns he knew were now in police hands, including a snub-nose undercover Colt .38 special. He gave a full account of the kidnapping of PC Lloyd, whose watch he had kept.

One way in which Detective Chief Superintendent Nevill checked the truth of what he was being told was by asking about the cars stolen and used on various missions: their make and the places they had been stolen from and dumped. Dowd several times stated that he could not place the thefts or the dumpings: 'We stole so many... They're easy to nick, those old Fords.' Repeatedly, on being asked the model, he replied, 'Corsair or Cortina.'

23
PHASE TWO

'GHQ decided the truce was off for us... We had our orders.'

Eddie Butler

The fragile cease-fire of 1975 was never expected to last. The Provisionals had always viewed it, partly out of cold expediency, as a chance to regroup and restock. Anti-Catholic atrocities such as the Miami Showband massacre in Northern Ireland strengthened the case of the militarists in the inner circles of the IRA leadership. The political development towards power-sharing did not appeal to the Provisionals and the calls for renewed action became irresistible. The reverses in Birmingham and the North-West made the London Active Service Unit the natural choice to carry out a resumption of the mainland bombing campaign.

O'Connell, Duggan, Butler and Doherty were holed up in safe houses in Crouch Hill and Stoke Newington, well away from the hastily abandoned bomb factory in Fairholme Road. They, too, had re-equipped during the cease-fire and had stockpiled 250 pounds of explosives.

On three successive summer nights the centre of London was rocked by explosions. On August 28 a booby-trapped time bomb detonated harmlessly outside Peter Brown's in Oxford Street. O'Connell later admitted that he had positioned it in the hope of its being noticed and drawing in an explosives expert. The following night the tactic worked: this time a telephoned warning brought an Army explosives team to a time bomb left in a plastic bag outside the K Shoe Shop in Kensington Church Street. It contained an 'anti-handler micro-switch'. O'Connell, the bomb-maker, later described the technique: 'The bomb was boobied with a flick-switch at the bottom. The circuits are false and are concealed in the bomb itself, in the hollowed explosives. We set it in the car and parked about 100 yards away. It was boobied to catch anyone trying to defuse it.'

Captain Roger Goad was working on the bomb when O'Connell's flick-switch tripped. Goad was blasted into the air and killed outright. Butler, who had been standing guard as the bomb was placed, boasted, 'Our intention was obvious — to get an expert, an explosives expert. We succeeded, didn't we? He didn't take his precautions.' In fact, according to police, Captain Goad was working as fast as possible on the primed bomb because of the danger to a gathering crowd of onlookers. He was awarded posthumously the George Cross.

The next bomb in the sequence exploded at night in the doorway of the National Westminster Bank in High Holborn on August 30. There was some damage to the bank but no injuries. According to O'Connell, 'We did it just to keep the Met. on the run three nights running.'

O'Connell next made and placed the 10-pound time bomb that killed two people and caused £175,000 worth of damage in the foyer of the Hilton Hotel on Park Lane on September 5 — the worst explosion since the one at the Horse and Groom in Guildford 11 months earlier. O'Connell was to claim that the bomb was not intended to kill anyone and that a properly coded warning had been telephoned in time to clear the lobby. Cross-examination at O'Connell's subsequent trial revealed that a 20-minute warning had been given but that the Metropolitan Police had neither telephoned their own warning to the hotel nor insisted upon its evacuation. Accordingly, the jury acquitted O'Connell and his Unit of the murders while finding them guilty of manslaughter instead. The Hilton Hotel bombing was the last incident in the Phase Two campaign to be preceded by a warning.

But it was a bomb outside London, with which the Unit announced its return, that held the greatest resonance. The

1st Battalion, Welsh Guards had just returned to barracks at Caterham in Surrey after a four-month tour of duty in Northern Ireland. Butler had established that the Caterham Arms public house, a quarter of a mile away, was popular with the troops. It was marked down as a 'military target'. O'Connell made a 10-pound time bomb, with his distinctive Smith's Combat pocket-watch timing mechanism. On August 27 Duggan and Doherty drove to Caterham and placed the bomb, concealed in a bag, beneath a bench seat in the bar. Eyewitnesses subsequently recalled 'two shifty-looking Irishmen' in the pub, but the Unit had calculated correctly that the slackening-off of terrorist activity during the cease-fire would enable them once again to infiltrate a soldiers' pub without being challenged.

There was no warning. About 120 customers were packed into the discothèque when the bomb exploded at 9.20 p.m., ripping through the roof, showering victims with splinters of mirror and glass, flinging people into the air and tearing off limbs. Guardsman Stephen Ollerhead recalled: 'I was thrown across the floor into the middle of the dance-floor and when I came to a few seconds later it was all smoke and bits of dust settling and bricks all over the place. I thought I was all right at the time so I started to clear the rubble off and get out but I saw my leg was blown off below the knee and there was just a shin-bone remaining.'

Somehow, no one was killed, but the blast injured 23 civilians and 10 soldiers. Eight victims, including five women, were left critically ill. The 'shifty-looking Irishmen' were widely reported to be the principal suspects, although police were also speculating that the bomb could have been the work of the still uncaptured Kieran McMorrow and Marlene Coyle.

With the prompt departure of two senior Surrey detectives for Belfast the following day, Detective Chief Superintendent Wally Simmons held a press conference at which he announced that the Surrey Bomb Squad had been reformed. 'It's too early to say yet who is responsible,' he told reporters. 'But the bombing is consistent in size, type and method with the blasts at two Guildford pubs last October.'

It was an inescapable fact that Phase Two had opened in exactly the same way as Phase One — with a characteristic time bomb placed surreptitiously under a bench seat in a Surrey public house frequented by soldiers. Equally inescapable was the fact that the four people held responsible for the Guildford bombings were securely locked up, within three weeks of the opening of their Old Bailey trial. Simmons's first impressions of the nature of the bomb itself were soon borne out by the forensic scientists at the RARDE — the Caterham Arms device was, indeed, a carbon copy of the two at Guildford.

24
THE CASE FOR THE CROWN

'The whole truth will probably never be known.'

Sir Michael Havers QC

Shortly after dawn on Tuesday September 16 1975, sniffer dogs toured the Central Criminal Court looking for explosives. Police marksmen took up positions on adjoining roofs. Electronic detectors scanned every vehicle for explosives as it entered the court car-park. A squad of City of London policemen, ranged in a semicircle in the hall of the Old Bailey, allowed no one up the marble staircase to Number Two court without an identity pass, body frisk and baggage search, a routine maintained throughout the five and a half weeks of the case.

The IRA had bombed the court precincts in 1973, so the precautions were by no means idle. No one attending was left in the slightest doubt that a high-profile terrorist trial was opening as the defendants were swept through the gates in an impressive motorcade of two prison transporters sandwiched between Rover police cars with blue lights flashing — or, perhaps, that these were highly dangerous defendants. Even by the standards of the nation's most famous criminal court it was a dramatic show. The defence team recall the atmosphere as never less than daunting. Several defence witnesses found it terrifying.

Mr Justice Donaldson presided. Sir John Francis Donaldson — now Lord Donaldson, Master of the Rolls, arguably the most influential post in the judiciary — was a highly controversial judge in the mid-1970s. His spell as President of the ill-starred National Industrial Relations Court so enraged trade-unionists and the Labour Party that 188 MPs launched an attempt, unprecedented in the twentieth century, to have him impeached for alleged political bias. Michael Foot accused him of having a 'trigger-happy judicial finger'. Less eloquent Labour MPs called the former Conservative councillor a 'Tory stooge'. Variations of the charge have followed him throughout his career.

What was not in question was his ability. A product of Charterhouse, Cambridge and the Guards, he was only 46 when he was appointed a High Court judge (with the traditional accompanying knighthood) — the youngest in the country. His judicial reputation was clever; fast but occasionally impatient; original and fair. In September 1975 his career was at a crossroads. The Labour Government had abolished his National Industrial Relations Court on reaching office the previous year, and his expected promotion to the Law Lords had not materialized. He had suffered the minor indignity of a recent profile in *The Times* entitled 'Where Are They Now?', in which he was described as being found in 'obscurity' as an ordinary judge in the Commercial Court of the Queen's Bench Division. This was very much his speciality even if *The Times* referred to the posting as 'judicial Siberia'. If he was in any need of rehabilitation, a high-publicity trial would afford it. In fact, this was the first time Mr Justice Donaldson had ever sat at the Old Bailey.

The four defendants were produced from the cells and seated in the dock. The clerk of the court read out the three-page arraignment: 'You are charged in an indictment containing 11 counts. In the first count, you are all four charged that on days between the 1st November, 1973, and the 4th December, 1974, whilst within Her Majesty's dominions, you unlawfully and maliciously conspired together and with other persons whose identities are unknown to cause by explosive substances explosions in the United Kingdom of a nature likely to endanger life or to cause serious injury to property.'

The 11 counts, stripped to their essentials, amounted to the following: all four were charged with murder at Guildford; Hill and Armstrong were charged with murder at Woolwich; and Armstrong alone was charged with an unlawful reconnaissance of the King's Arms, Woolwich. Interestingly, while the conspiracy charge and the Woolwich murder charges mentioned 'persons unknown' as having been involved, the Guildford charges did not.

Armstrong, Richardson and Conlon successively pleaded not guilty to each charge. Hill, however, immediately made a bad impression. 'I refuse to take part in this,' he replied to the first charge. 'I refuse to defend myself. Your justice stinks.' He repeated this to his second charge and stayed silent as the remaining charges were read to him. Sir Michael Havers QC, leading for the Crown, was straight on to his feet with a technical legal point as to whether a jury should be impanelled forthwith to determine whether Hill was 'mute of malice'. Mr Justice Donaldson turned to Hill's counsel, Mr Arthur Mildon QC, for clarification on Hill's plea and was not, at first, rewarded: 'My Lord, I have had instructions as recently as last night,' Mr Mildon replied. 'I am seeking confirmation of those instructions. When I have that information, I shall be able to assist your Lordship.' The court paused as Mr Mildon confirmed his instructions. 'My Lord, the instructions to which I refer were that there would be a plea of not guilty to all counts concerning my client, and those instructions have just been confirmed.'

While a lay observer of the English court system may think it surprising to find a defence barrister being instructed in a mass-murder case the very night before a trial (itself commencing 11 months after the prosecution began preparing its case) and then arriving in court still unsure as to how his client was pleading, this is not thought to be remarkable by the Bar or its rule-making bodies.

Sir Michael Havers, Conservative MP for Merton, former Solicitor General — and now, in 1975, shadow Attorney General — Master of the Inner Temple Bench and a QC of 10 years' standing, led for the Crown. He was, at 51, at the height of his adversarial powers and destined to become Lord Chancellor, and was himself to become the target of an IRA bomb.

After the all-male jury had been sworn in and told of the charges and uniform pleas of not guilty, Sir Michael took two days to outline the prosecution case.

'This is an IRA case,' Sir Michael began. 'The prosecution evidence will satisfy you that Armstrong, Conlon and Hill are all members of the IRA. The girl, Richardson, is English and joined the enterprises about September of last year... These were carefully planned crimes with photographic reconnaissance done in advance and photographs of the targets prepared.' Hill and Conlon, he claimed, had come to Britain specifically for the bombings. Richardson and Armstrong, he added, were the 'courting couple' who had planted the Horse and Groom time bomb. It was a crime of 'military precision'.

There were 59 prosecution witnesses waiting to support these claims, so it was a powerful opening, but it is in the nature of opening addresses that the quality of evidence to support the claim is not immediately made clear. The evidence of IRA membership came only from the confessions. There was no exhibit produced of photographs or cameras from the alleged reconnaissances; again the claim stemmed from the confessions alone. There was no corroborative evidence of pre-planning. Perhaps the boldest claim was that Armstrong and Richardson were the 'courting couple'. Sir Michael Havers told the jury that they would be identified from the descriptions given by soldiers in the Horse and Groom. He did not tell the jury that the eight witnesses who had given the fullest descriptions of the 'courting couple' had already failed to pick out Carole Richardson on identity parades and that Patrick Armstrong had never been put on parade at all. Nevertheless, Sir Michael said of Private Jonathan Cook that his descriptions were those of Richardson and probably of Armstrong. 'It was a very observant description by Cook. He had seen them leave the pub at about 6.55 p.m.'

Private Cook had attended the identity parade. In his two statements to the police — in the second of which, certain details of timing had changed — he had been insistent that the girl had 'natural blonde' hair. Carole Richardson is a natural brunette, as evidenced by the photograph of her taken backstage at the South Bank Polytechnic concert on the night of the bombing. Unless she was wearing a 'natural blonde' wig for the bombing, the 'very observant description' by Private Cook served to clear her rather than incriminate her. The Crown never sought to suggest that Richardson might have used a wig. As for the male member of the 'courting couple', Private Cook twice described him as having 'wavy', dark hair. Armstrong had completely straight, long, fair hair. Yet, Sir Michael Havers's announcement was dramatic enough for the ITN news report of the opening of the trial to lead with the claim that Richardson and Armstrong would be identified as the bombers. They never were.

In fact, the prosecution produced no evidence beyond the admissions to tie any of the four defendants to the bombings — with two exceptions. As Sir Michael Havers described the make-up of the Guildford bombs he referred to 'significant fragments' of a Smith's pocket-watch found in the debris, and immediately proceeded to reveal that police had taken away a Smith's pocket-watch from the Rondu Road flat where Armstrong had once stayed for a fortnight. This appeared superficially damning, but it transpired that there were more than a million of this type of Smith's pocket-watch in circulation; that there was no evidence to connect it with Armstrong rather than with any other member of the household; and that no other items potentially linked with bomb-making were found there or elsewhere. Mr Justice Donaldson presumably found this evidence so circumstantial that he made no reference to it in his lengthy summing-up.

The second, and more direct, piece of evidence against Armstrong came from his fellow squatter, 17-year-old Brian McLoughlin. McLoughlin was produced from Borstal to testify that Armstrong had invited him to blow up a pub and that on another occasion he had opened a parcel of Armstrong's, which he had presumed to contain drugs, to discover two guns instead. Mr Justice Donaldson in his summing-up made it clear how discredited a witness McLoughlin was: 'The Crown invite you to think that is very powerful supporting evidence of their case. And so, members of the jury, it is, if — and this is a very important "if" — it comes from a reliable source. I would be the last person in the world to try and hold against him his previous convictions, but he has rather a large number for somebody of his age and they are offences which in one way or another can be regarded as offences of dishonesty. So he does not start, really, in the best of lights as a reliable witness.

'Then you get the extraordinary point that on 8th October he was apparently living at Linstead Street [the squat] and yet he says that he never heard about these bombings until January of 1975. Members of the jury, is that really on?... If there is any doubt about it then surely, members of the jury, it is at least as likely that McLoughlin is a young man who, having got himself into trouble with the police on several occasions, is now trying to earn his passage back to righteousness in a most unrighteous way, by making up some evidence about Armstrong and telling the police about it, and saying, "Look what a reformed citizen I am,"... you would think that the fairest thing to do would be to put McLoughlin's evidence on one side and say that it does not really help you at all.'

In the light of this judicial demolition of McLoughlin's credibility — his being effectively denounced as a prison grass — it does not reflect well on first the police and then Sir Michael Havers to have relied upon the Borstal boy's claims as 'very powerful supporting evidence', but that area was not explored.

Thus, the Crown case came to rely exclusively upon the confession statements. There was no identification evidence, no forensic evidence and no fingerprint evidence. McLoughlin apart, there was no third party to incriminate any of the defendants. The long list of witnesses turned out to be police officers involved in the arrests and the taking of the statements; customers from the bombed pubs and scientists with their calculations about the nature of the bombs. All this was important in establishing exactly what had happened at the bombings so that it could be set against the versions given by the defendants.

Victims from the Horse and Groom supplied graphically distressing accounts of the explosion and its aftermath, which in turn provided highly emotive copy for the court reporters and underlined to the jury what a gruesome offence it was. It threw up nothing new against the accused: no one was disputing that the bombs had detonated to terrible effect.

Exactly which of the defendants did what on the alleged bombing trip to Guildford was, claimed Sir Michael, immaterial. Once the defendants became members of the team, knowing what was intended, it did not matter what part each played. This interpretation saved the prosecution the difficulty of saying which of the confession statements actually presented the true picture of who had bombed which pub, since none of them was wholly consistent with any other, not least in the references to the four people who had originally been charged with murder as a result of the statements and had subsequently been freed without charge.

The confessions, according to Sir Michael, veered from 'startling accuracy' to the 'deliberately misleading'. He described how Carole Richardson, when supplied with a blank diagram of the Horse and Groom interior, had marked the position of the time bomb with 'startling accuracy' (although she had twice marked the police diagram incorrectly in previous attempts). On the other hand, when the police had driven Paul Hill around London and he had identified an innocuous house in Brixton as a bomb factory, this was an example of being 'deliberately misleading'.

As the confession statements were recited, such discrepancies became the central problem for prosecution, defence and jury. As often as ostensibly accurate detail emerged, so too did palpable nonsense. Everyone agreed that the statements were not wholly accurate and consistent, but did the accurate detail outweigh the inaccurate or vice versa? Whatever the inaccuracies, what could explain away the correct detail if the four had not been involved? If, as Sir Michael Havers insisted, the inaccuracies were part of a concerted IRA counter-interrogation technique to deceive the court, why should the defendants have made any accurate admissions at all? After all, the police insisted throughout that there had been no duress involved in the taking of the statements. The freedom with which the defendants had admitted involvement had not surprised Detective Chief Superintendent Walter Simmons, head of Surrey CID. He told the court that this was not unusual in his 26 years' experience. In four murder inquiries he had conducted in the last three years, most of the defendants had readily admitted their guilt.

Detective Sergeant Anthony Jermey of Surrey Police allowed that most of the confessions amounted to 'fairy-tales'. He now realized that most of what the defendants had told the police was 'a mixture of fact and fiction'. He concurred with the hypothesis that the defendants had inserted false detail into their statements to confuse the police.

This was a dilemma that could be resolved only by the jury. The defence could not deny that the statements contained detail about the interior of the public houses that was accurate. The prosecution called forensic scientists from the RARDE, who confirmed that the defendants' descriptions of the bombs were accurate. In short, they had admitted the bombings in the detail that surely only people closely acquainted with the explosions could have provided. The prosecution case rested on the quality and quantity of that detail.

On the fourth day, proceedings were delayed for 45 minutes when Paul Hill failed to appear. He eventually arrived in the dock sporting a bruised, swollen and grazed eye. No reference was made to this in court. The police announced outside court that a full-scale inquiry had begun to establish how this had happened, but nothing came of it.

The prosecution case ended with the acquittal of Patrick Armstrong on the charge of unlawfully and maliciously assisting in a reconnaissance of the King's Arms, Woolwich with intent to cause an explosion. This followed a legal submission from Mr John Leonard QC, Armstrong's barrister. The Woolwich murder and conspiracy charges against Armstrong remained.

The fifth and eighth days of the trial were each marked by explosions by the seemingly unstoppable London ASU. On September 22 they returned to the Portman, which they had shot up the previous winter. Now they placed a time bomb on the outside window-ledge of the hotel coffee shop, which caused a number of minor injuries. Three days later they struck at another soldiers' pub, the Hare and Hounds, near an Army barracks in Maidstone. A trooper's stag-night party was in full flow when they arrived and the building was so crowded that they aborted their plan to leave the bomb inside. As they left, Sapper David Campbell thought that the two men (O'Connell and Butler) were behaving suspiciously and followed them outside, where he noticed a holdall left alongside what proved to be the landlord's car. The pub and nearby houses were hastily evacuated, preventing injury when the device exploded shortly after 10.00 p.m.

But at the Old Bailey, all such extraneous matters were peripheral to what was developing into the sole issue: the confessions. If they had been properly obtained they were, despite the inconsistencies, utterly damning. By the end of the second week it looked like an open-and-shut case. Gerard Conlon, who had been told by his QC to expect 30 years, was already resigned to conviction. Carole Richardson, in contrast, still assumed blithely that everything would be all right. Beneath the ledge of the dock they passed the unfolding days and hours playing 'hangman'.

25
IN DEFENCE

'I never done no bombs at all.'

Patrick Armstrong

The defence argued on two main fronts — alibi and duress; that the accused had provably been elsewhere at the relevant times and that the confession statements to the police had been extracted under varying degrees of duress and, accordingly, could not be relied upon; that the defendants had had nothing whatsoever to do with the terrible bombings.

On six successive days of the trial, officers of Surrey Police stood under oath in the witness-box and unanimously testified that all the interrogations had taken place without the slightest impropriety. There had been not a single threat or instance of violence throughout. The defence had no objective evidence to offer against this insistence. Since all the interrogations had taken place without a solicitor present, there was no uncommitted witness to the allegations. Just as the defence could not prove that duress had occurred, nor could the police prove that it had not. Somebody was lying.

As the intensive cross-examination of the police and their equally consistent denials of violence proceeded, Mr Justice Donaldson suggested that it would be helpful to know how many police officers had been engaged in the investigation, as this would indicate the degree of collaboration needed for a conspiracy. Mr Christopher Rowe, Assistant Chief Constable of Surrey, gave the figure as more than 100.

This point was later picked up by Sir Michael Havers, who claimed that if the accusations 'of the most appalling kind' were true, then there must have been 'a really gigantic conspiracy'

between two police forces — Surrey Police and the Bomb Squad
— involving officers of all ranks, including Commander Huntley
of the Bomb Squad, Detective Chief Superintendent Walter
Simmons — the head of Surrey CID — and Surrey Assistant
Chief Constable, Christopher Rowe, and culminating in 'a most
appalling perversion of justice'.

The hypothesis posed by the judge, the senior police officer
and the prosecuting counsel does not, in fact, strictly require
more than 100 co-conspirators. According to police records, the
number of police officers present during those interrogations
resulting in confessions at which duress was alleged totalled 17.
It was the defence case that confessions made without accompanying claims of duress (as, for example, to officers of the Bomb
Squad) were all made after confessions where duress was alleged
and that the defendants were still too frightened to retract
their false confessions. The hypothesis remains appalling but the
required scale of perversion was not so great as purported by Mr
Rowe or Sir Michael Havers.

The four defendants, notwithstanding the absence of corroborating evidence, each made sustained claims of police impropriety.

Detective Sergeant John Donaldson was cross-examined for
90 minutes. He denied that Patrick Armstrong had been
'softened up' as a prelude to making his first confession
statement. He denied that Assistant Chief Constable Rowe and
Detective Chief Superintendent Simmons had each assaulted
Armstrong, or had even been in the interrogation room during
questioning. He denied that Armstrong had been told about the
dismembered bodies of the victims of the Horse and Groom
with the threat that he would face the same fate if he did
not confess. He denied that Armstrong had been told that
it would be all right to confess because Conlon would take
the repercussions in Belfast for 'squealing'. He denied that
Armstrong's confession consisted merely of material supplied by
the police. Everything, Detective Sergeant Donaldson insisted,
was volunteered freely.

The detective was reminded that upon Carole Richardson's arrest she had insisted that she could prove where she had been on the night of the Guildford bombing if her diary was fetched. Why had this not been followed up? Donaldson replied that his one objective at the time had been to find Armstrong and that he had not thought of pursuing the matter of the diary.

Detective Sergeant Anthony Jermey faced two hours of questioning by Lord Wigoder QC, counsel for Gerard Conlon. He consistently denied a series of allegations: that while in custody Surrey Police had stripped Conlon, hit him in the kidneys, squeezed his testicles, stood him against a wall and ridiculed him, while not injuring him sufficiently badly for him to require medical attention. Lord Wigoder accused Jermey of using a trick learned 20 years earlier in the RAF of pressing his thumbs behind Conlon's ears to cause extreme pain. Jermey denied all knowledge of such a technique. Jermey further denied that Conlon had made a first statement disclaiming all knowledge of the bombings which had been torn up by the police and thrown into a rubbish bin. Lord Wigoder suggested that as Conlon had continued to deny the bombings Jermey had threatened to bring an officer called Tim into the interrogation room to make him see things 'a little clearer'. Jermey replied that there was an officer on the force called Tim Blake who was a large man but that he had not entered the room while he was with Conlon.

Jermey further denied that the RUC officers who had arrested Conlon in West Belfast had variously hit him, spat in his face, called him a 'murdering bastard' and threatened to abandon him in the Protestant Shankill Road. Lord Wigoder claimed that Conlon had been threatened that the Army in Belfast would be instructed to put the word out in the Lower Falls that Conlon was a 'tout' so that the IRA would take reprisals against the Conlon family. Again, Jermey denied it. In fact, Jermey claimed, when the Conlon's family solicitor, Ted Jones, eventually visited Conlon in custody, Conlon had praised Surrey Police, volunteering that he had not been punched or ill-treated and singling out Jermey as having been 'very nice' to him. Lord

Wigoder suggested that Conlon had been afraid of reprisals if he complained about the police and that, if anything, this had been a hint that he was being abused. 'I took what he said at face value,' replied Jermey.

Lord Wigoder alleged that Conlon's statement had been dictated to him by police officers and written only because he had become terrified. To say that there had been no pressure or persuasion was 'rubbish'. Jermey replied that he was speaking 'the absolute truth'; Conlon had 'not [been] touched in any way'.

Detective Sergeant Jermey did make one admission to Lord Wigoder. He acknowledged that notes of a conversation he and another officer [Detective Chief Inspector Lionel Grundy] had with Conlon were not written out until seven hours after the conversation had started. There had not been time to write it down as they went along as this would have disturbed the flow of questioning.

There was further cross-examination of Jermey about the treatment of Paul Hill. He strongly denied that his colleague Detective Chief Inspector Brian Richardson had brought a gun into Hill's police cell. He repeatedly denied that police had threatened to charge Hill's pregnant girlfriend Eugenia Clarke, then in custody, with the bombings. He also denied putting suggestions to Hill who had then assented to what he was told. Jermey insisted that everything in the statement was what Hill himself had said. Hill had protested his innocence for 24 hours after his arrest and had then suddenly changed his mind and decided to tell the police everything. Jermey did, however, admit that notes he made of his conversation with Hill before he agreed to make a statement were actually written down *after* the statement had been made. It had, said Jermey, taken Hill three hours to make the statement.

When Detective Inspector Timothy Blake was called, his evidence threw up two disparities for the jury to resolve. Conlon had known that Blake was a Roman Catholic and that he had a tattoo of a dagger on his arm, yet Blake told the jury that he had not interviewed Conlon: 'I have not seen him.' He did not know how Conlon knew that he was a Roman Catholic and denied saying to Conlon, 'I am a Catholic and you make me sick.' (In a later cross-examination Blake recalled having a conversation with one of the accused's visitors outside Winchester Prison in which he had revealed that he was a Catholic.) Lord Wigoder asked Blake to remove his jacket and show his tattoo to the jury. Had he not similarly taken off his jacket to set about Conlon, stripping him, punching him and squeezing his testicles? Blake replied that apart from passing a remark to Conlon at a court appearance he had never spoken to him. He added that Godalming police station, where Conlon had then been held, was centrally heated and that sometimes when he was working in his own office he did take his coat off and roll up his sleeves to be comfortable. Blake further denied that he had slapped Conlon and poked him in the ribs on a later occasion and that a threat had been made in his presence to take Conlon to an Army camp where he would be left for the Army to 'get him'.

Blake faced further allegations of brutality against Paul Hill from Mr Arthur Mildon QC.

'Did you haul him down on the floor?'

'No.'

'He got up from the floor and you knocked him down again.'

'No.'

Blake strongly denied Mr Mildon's suggestion that he had sat astride Hill while he was on the floor with a knee on each shoulder and shaken his head by the hair. At this denial came an outburst from Hill in the dock. Blake insisted, 'I never used violence towards him at all.' He further denied seeing guns present during Hill's interrogations and testified to having been unsurprised at the willingness with which Hill had made statements to him and Detective Constable Peter Lewis on three successive days. 'He seemed to take a liking to Detective Constable Lewis and me,' said Blake, adding that on several occasions Hill had said he could trust the two officers. Lewis confirmed Blake's evidence. There had been no violence.

The statements had been made freely and without pressure.

Detective Chief Inspector Lionel Grundy was accused of knowing that Conlon had been assaulted by Blake and threatened by Detective Chief Superintendent Simmons. He denied both this and the further allegation that he and Jermey had made up facts about an interview with Conlon after he had made a statement.

Detective Chief Inspector Brian Richardson, who had been present at Hill's arrest, denied that he had ever shown a gun or pointed it at Hill. He agreed that he had been armed at the arrest but testified that his gun had remained in its shoulder holster, covered by his jacket, throughout the time he was with Hill — at the arrest, in Southampton police station and on the journey to Guildford.

A further series of accusations — all denied — was made against Wally Simmons, the head of Surrey CID. Lord Wigoder claimed Simmons had made two undisclosed visits to Conlon in Godalming police station, at which he had repeatedly threatened Conlon and had suggested that the Army would spread a rumour in Belfast that Conlon had been 'touting'. 'No, my Lord,' Simmons replied.

'And you banged on the desk and put on an act of being a wild man saying you would kill him if you came around the desk.'

'Certainly not, my Lord.'

Simmons further denied allegations of brutality laid against his immediate superior, Christopher Rowe. Lord Wigoder asked him about a visit made with Rowe to Conlon in Winchester Prison. Why had no record been kept at the interview? 'Mr Rowe hoped we could prevent further bombings by finding a cache of explosives we had reason to believe was still in this country,' Simmons replied.

Yet more allegations were made against the Surrey Police officers who had interrogated Carole Richardson. Detective Chief Inspector Alan Longhurst revealed to the court that the 17-year-old girl had not been told during her first five days of custody that she had not actually been arrested and was free to walk out if she wished to; nor had she been allowed to speak to her mother on the telephone when, according to Richardson's QC, Eric Myers, her mother had been telephoning the police station constantly and being fobbed off; nor had the girl been informed that she could have the advice of a solicitor. Longhurst next agreed that on December 4 Richardson had been interviewed for just over five hours, but denied that she had been in an unfit condition for interview.

Mr Myers claimed: 'In the course of this interrogation she was reduced by your repeated accusations and refusal to believe her until she became completely brainwashed and would agree to anything if only your officers would leave her alone.'

'No, sir.'

'You were putting to her things you thought and believed were true over and over again to indoctrinate her and they came back to you as if she were telling you.'

'No, sir.'

Mr Myers suggested that after five hours and five minutes Richardson had needed a doctor in a hurry. Longhurst replied that she had not needed one in his presence. He had not sent for one but he knew that a doctor had come later. He agreed that Richardson had sobbed, put her head on the desk and talked during the interview of taking Tuinal. He said he understood that the doctor had been called in to consider the question of drugs, but reaffirmed that he would not have questioned her unless he had been sure that she was fit for interview. Asked if he had discovered he had a drug addict on his hands, he replied, 'Not to the best of my recollection.'

Longhurst further denied that his colleague Detective Constable Martin Wise had punched Richardson and that WPC Anita Mills had shouted 'murdering bitch' at her, hitting her with the back of her hand. Mr Myers claimed, 'It was in the shadow of this attack, condoned by you, that all the following interviews took place.'

'It didn't happen,' Longhurst replied.

WPC Mills refuted any suggestion of assault on Richardson. Mills, however, agreed under cross-examination that during a subsequent interview in Brixton Prison Richardson had complained of being assaulted. Why, asked Mr Myers, had Mills not referred to the complaint in her notes of the interview? Mills replied that she did not know but had thought that the interview was over when the matter came up.

Cross-examination of Detective Constable Wise established that the unrecorded prison interview was as follows:

'Why did you admit it?'

'Because you hit me and called me a liar and a murderer.'

'No one hit you.'

Wise testified that this conversation took place after the interview had finished. He reiterated the denials of his colleagues that Richardson had been indoctrinated, brainwashed or assaulted: 'Nobody laid a finger on her.'

As Christopher Rowe was Assistant Chief Constable of Surrey and in charge of the case, the allegations of brutality against him were, perhaps, the most serious. They were uniformly denied. It was suggested that on one occasion when he had visited Paul Hill in Woking police station, he had instructed Hill to spread his arms and legs against a cell wall and then kicked his legs even further apart. Rowe denied visiting Hill on the date cited. He had been present during part of Hill's other interrogations but had asked only one question, namely whether Hill was all right, to which Hill had replied, 'Yes, sir.'

John Leonard QC accused Rowe of hitting Patrick Armstrong and calling him a bastard: 'Did you not say "You were not there at the finish when people were lying there with no arms and no legs."?'

'No, sir.'

'Did you not go in while the statement was being made that day [December 4] and tell him that he had until 7.30 p.m.? And you said "I suppose you were proud of yourself you Irish bastard," and kicked him on the right thigh and then said, "You had better tell the truth or we will kill you."?'

'No,' replied Rowe. 'I never saw the man until he was charged.'

John Leonard QC then submitted Simmons to sustained cross-examination. He suggested that Rowe had hit Armstrong with his left fist under the prisoner's right eye. Simmons denied it. Leonard claimed that Simmons had intervened when Rowe again moved in on Armstrong. Simmons denied it. Leonard asked Simmons if it was true that Simmons had said, 'We will try the other side now,' and had then hit Armstrong with the back of his hand on the left of his face — not hard, but just touching the eye. Simmons again denied it. Simmons finally denied that five policemen had crowded round Armstrong, repeatedly firing questions at him until he was reduced to tears.

Lord Wigoder asked Rowe why Conlon had not been charged until 24 hours after his first statement when the Judges' Rules stipulated that police should prefer charges as soon as they had enough evidence to do so. Rowe replied, 'We had a number of prisoners in custody and a number of enquiries and checks had to be made. I do not think the delay made any difference.' The Assistant Chief Constable concluded his stay in the witness-box with an unequivocal statement of confidence in the integrity of his force: 'The officers under me were specially chosen and I knew I could trust them. I am quite certain there was no impropriety.'

The four defendants now gave their versions of the effect of the alleged duress. Armstrong said, 'I was compelled by force and fear to make the statements and the statements were taken by question and answer. The questions were put in such a form as to suggest an answer, to which I assented.' He claimed in evidence to have been high on drugs when arrested: 'I had taken barbiturates, Tuinal and speed... The first I knew was a crowbar coming through a window... Two of the officers carried guns. One was Detective Constable Attwell. He put it to my head and said, "Don't move or I will empty the chamber into you." The other had a gun at the other side of my head.'

Armstrong claimed that in Guildford police station Rowe and Simmons had repeatedly called him a 'fucking lying bastard' and punched and kicked him; that Attwell had come in and warned that other officers 'will come in here and throw you out of the window and put it down as suicide'. 'I was crying and shaking,' Armstrong said. 'I started to make the statement. Being hit and thrown against the wall had affected my mind.' He told the jury that his confession statements were almost 'entirely untrue', the exceptions being his immediate personal particulars and the details of his hitch-hiking holiday with Carole Richardson.

As for his claimed IRA background and exploits, Armstrong now said it consisted of information he had picked up from living in the Divis Flats in Belfast; he had got the idea of the armed raids on bookmakers' shops from an occasion when he had been working in a bookmaker's shop when it was held up. He wanted the police to believe his statements so that they would not carry out their threats. Armstrong claimed that the apparent accuracy of his geographical knowledge of Guildford derived from the police question-and-answer technique on his hand-cuffed drive around the town. The overall motivation for what he claimed were false confessions came from a combination of a drug overdose, violence and the threat of greater violence, and from a fear of authority instilled by his Belfast experience of being picked up for questioning and being roughed up by the Army.

Sir Michael Havers QC cross-examined Armstrong for a morning session. Armstrong began answering questions calmly and quickly but by the end he was close to tears. 'I never done no bombs at all,' he protested. Why had he confessed? Because he had been afraid of what the police might do. Why had he said he was in the IRA? Because he had known it was an IRA job. Why had he implicated Carole Richardson? Because he had heard that she had admitted it. Why had he involved Paul Colman if he knew he was innocent? For something to say. Why had he said there were two cars involved if he was inventing details? Because he had seen it in Hill's statement. Why had he lied in his statements? Because the police had kept ignoring him when he pointed out mistakes. Why had he been able to mark a sketch plan of the Horse and Groom with the places where the bombers had sat? Because he had seen plans of the pub interior on the police-station wall.

Sir Michael Havers said to Armstrong, 'You have committed murder — multiple murder — because you were frightened into it. You say you were frightened of the Surrey Police. So why did you not tell the Metropolitan Police when they interviewed you about this?'

'I was scared they would go and tell the Surrey Police.'

'Would you also have lied to Sir Robert Mark, the Police Commissioner?' enquired Sir Michael Havers.

'Yes,' replied Patrick Armstrong.

Paul Hill, like Armstrong, made numerous allegations of violence and impropriety against Surrey Police, but he argued that it was not the violence that had prompted his confessions, insisting that his six statements sprang from fear that the police would charge his pregnant girlfriend, Gina — who had also been held by Surrey Police — with the bombings: 'I made this [first] statement because my chick was being screwed up. This was my sole reason.' He explained the subsequent alterations and additions to the first statement as attempts to convince his interrogators that he really had taken part in the bombings. The information in the confessions, Hill claimed, was a mixture of lies, guesswork, detail he had picked up from the statements of his co-accused and facts fed directly to him by the police. He denied having anything to do with the Guildford or Woolwich blasts.

'You made six statements, the total effect of which is that you were involved with both,' said Arthur Mildon, his QC. 'Tell the jury what the reason is for your having made these statements.'

'Because they told me they would screw my chick up for them,' Hill repeated.

Under cross-examination by Sir Michael Havers, Hill proved a belligerent, even impudent, witness. 'Do you read James Bond detective stories?' asked Sir Michael.

'No, I only read the *Mirror*,' said Hill.

He was questioned about his description in one confession of the alleged route taken by the bombers from London to Guildford. How did he know they would pass a racecourse, some road-works and dense woods on the journey? Most of it was guesswork, said Hill, but he had seen a racecourse from the train. Sandown Park racecourse is skirted on either side by the British Rail Waterloo to Southampton line, which Hill used regularly on his visits to Gina Clarke, and the A3, the alleged route taken by the bombers.

Sir Michael wanted to know why Hill had not informed the Metropolitan Police of the way in which Gina had allegedly been threatened. 'Because they were policemen,' said Hill. Sir Michael was most persistent on the question of why Hill had concluded his statement with the phrase that he had made it of his 'own free will' when he must have known that he would one day be confronted with the statement in court. Five times Hill replied that it had made no difference what he put down.

'And is that the attitude I can expect throughout?'

'Yes.'

The importance Sir Michael attached to the inclusion of the phrase 'own free will' seems misplaced. If any confession is false and improperly obtained it is hardly to be expected that a dishonest police officer would allow a prisoner to state that it was not made freely. Besides, Hill had already made the point that he was attempting to persuade the police that he really had been involved and, on the basis of that criterion, it was just the sort of phrase he could be expected to have inserted or assented to. By the end of the cross-examination Hill had maintained his innocence as unswervingly as Armstrong. He had been consistent throughout.

Gerard Conlon's account was one of considerable brutality in both Belfast and Surrey. He accused two RUC officers,

Cunningham and McCaul, of punching him on the jaw, kicking him, swearing at him and dragging him by the hair. Both officers had earlier testified that there had been no ill-treatment of Conlon. He accused the two Surrey policemen who had come to Belfast — Jermey and Grundy — of spitting in his face and producing a statement by Hill that named Conlon. Conlon described being pressurized into giving a statement and being sick over Jermey's trousers on the trip to England, where he spent his first night, he said, naked in a freezing cell in Addlestone police station in Surrey.

All this and the alleged ensuing assaults by Blake were not what induced his first confession, Conlon insisted. He attributed it instead to two interventions by Detective Chief Superintendent Simmons in the cells at Godalming police station. Conlon claimed that Simmons had first threatened to have him shot by the SAS if he did not make a statement and had then said he would arrange to have Conlon's mother shot on her way to work; that it would be put down as an accident and that all Simmons had to do was to telephone Cunningham and McCaul and they would arrange it. 'I have seen the SAS operate,' said Conlon. 'They would have done it.'

Whatever the plausibility of this alleged threat, 1974 was a year of numerous sectarian killings in the Lower Falls where the Conlon family lived. Conlon claimed that the threat bore enhanced menace owing to Simmons's revealing the knowledge that Mrs Sarah Conlon walked daily to work at the Royal Victoria Hospital, a quarter of a mile from the family home in Cyprus Street. Conlon further knew that the shift patterns were such that his mother regularly had to make the journey alone, late at night or early in the morning, when the streets were dark and deserted.

Conlon said he had written out a truthful statement which was thrown into the rubbish bin by the police with the words, 'If that's the truth, you had better start telling lies.' When Simmons had allegedly threatened again to telephone Belfast, Conlon now agreed to confess: 'There was nothing I could do then but make a statement because they would have shot my ma... Someone stood behind me reading out on a piece of paper what I had to put down.'

Under cross-examination Conlon told Sir Michael Havers, 'The first time I was ever in Guildford was when the police first brought me there.' Why had he implicated others beyond his allegedly threatened family? 'If they told me to put your name down at the time, I would have done it to save my people. It's as simple as that.'

Sir Michael, who had been propounding the theory that a sophisticated counter-interrogation technique was the explanation for the nonsenses in the confessions, now offered a new theory. He suggested that it was only when Conlon had woken up to the realization that he had confessed to a terrible crime that he decided to pull the wool over the jury's eyes by filling his account with inconsistencies.

'I have no need to pull the wool over the jury's eyes,' replied Conlon. 'I am telling the truth.'

'Did you enjoy leading the gang which blew up those people in Guildford?' Sir Michael asked as his final question.

Conlon reiterated that he had never been to Guildford before being taken there by the police, adding, 'If they told me to put down the Pope's name, I would have done it. I would have put down anybody's to save my ma.'

The protracted cross-examinations of the three men had failed to elicit any damning admissions. Sir Michael Havers's acknowledged skills could not break down the persistent claims of innocence. Yet Surrey Police had encountered no such difficulty. Had they not all confessed freely, pleased to rid their consciences of the crimes? Sir Michael attributed this unanimous turnabout to the defendants' joint realization that it was the only way to give themselves the remotest chance of being found not guilty and that they called up 'the most magnificent imaginations'.

Carole Richardson did not go into the witness-box. She has always claimed that she was willing to submit to cross-examination under oath. The team of defence solicitors was also prepared for her to testify but her QC, Eric Myers, opposed the move. She was only 18 and her demeanour in the dock had fluctuated wildly from apparent deep depression to juvenile frivolity. Against a barrister of the skill and intensity of Sir Michael Havers it was an unpredictable risk.

Her statement was read out instead. Shortly before her arrest she had taken nine Tuinal tablets. She had begun by insistently denying any involvement in the Guildford bombings and asking for a lawyer and for her diary to be fetched. 'At one point Longhurst made a reference to "mad Irishmen". I began to smile at the words "mad Irishmen" and Mrs Steer [formerly WPC Mills] hit me on the jaw with the back of her hand and hurt me. I was again accused of being at Guildford and denied the accusation. Wise then hit me on my left jaw. I lifted my arm to my face to protect myself and then he punched me in the ribs. Mrs Steer shouted at me that I was a murdering bitch and how did it feel to murder people.'

'Longhurst simply sat there saying and doing nothing. Wise then looked at me and said, "If Alan left the room I would splatter you all around it." Longhurst simply said nothing and simply kept silent. It was Longhurst's attitude in saying nothing that was the worst part of it. Later on Wise hit me in the face. Mrs Steer then said, "You think you are a hard little bitch, don't you?" I did not answer her... I was shaking and very scared. My jaw was hurting and the Tuinal was beginning to wear off... and I was afraid of what they would do and whether they would hit me again. Longhurst then said, "Were you there?" I said, "Yes, I was. I was smashed out of my head on barbs and I don't know what happened. I was out of my head." When I said this I was shaking like a leaf and I said it partly out of panic and also out of a feeling that to agree with what they wanted would stop them getting at me. I said this but it was not true...

'They were so positive that I was at Guildford I knew that they would not believe my denials. The answers and statements which the police have given in evidence against me are not true.

The statements which I wrote were virtually dictated to me and I wrote down what they said and suggested to me. When I wrote out my statement I did not know what to write. Longhurst asked me questions and made suggestions and would indicate that I should write down what he said. I was forced to go along with what was happening because I was terrified of them and of what further treatment I would get if I continued to deny my involvement. I was kept at the police station without a solicitor and without being allowed to see my mother and I had no alternative but to go along with them... I was not in Guildford on 5th October and I have had no part in any agreement or conspiracy to cause any explosion whatsoever.'

26
ALIBI

'It is not for the accused to prove that they were elsewhere, it is for the prosecution to satisfy you that they were at Guildford or wherever it may be... '

Mr Justice Donaldson

All four accused presented defences of alibi for Saturday October 5, the night of the Guildford bombings, and Paul Hill, who alone was charged with being at Woolwich on Thursday November 7, claimed a defence of alibi for that night as well.

As the arrests had taken place seven weeks after the Guildford bombings, the defendants (and other potential witnesses) had had a long interval to bridge to be confident of what they had been doing and where on October 5 — a difficulty doubtless increased by the unregulated nature of their lifestyles. Alternatively, if, as Sir Michael Havers claimed, 'military precision' had been the hallmark of the operation, then there had been ample opportunity to organize coherent fabricated accounts of their movements.

What emerged was neither a collective collapse of memory nor a watertight set of alibis — pre-arranged or otherwise — but a mess. As Mr Justice Donaldson was to point out, a defendant can hardly be blamed for producing a less than perfect alibi. It is a normal state of affairs for any citizen to have difficulty in proving absolutely what his or her movements at a given time might have been after a lapse of seven weeks.

This was Gerard Conlon's problem. He claimed to have spent all day in London but could call nobody independent to substantiate his account at the crucial times. The judge summarized Conlon's evidence as follows: '"On 5th October I woke up at about 10.30 a.m. I left the hostel about 12 o'clock after I had done some washing and had something to eat. I went to the shops. After shopping I went to the Memphis Belle. Paul [Hill] and I went to the pub. Patrick Kerry [Patrick Carey] came past with his brother. I left the pub at one o'clock and went to another pub. I left with Hill. I did not stay with him all day. We separated about 3.00 or 3.15 p.m. He was going to get the train to Southampton. I went to the bookie's and then to bed. I was drunk. I had been drinking pints and shorts. No one was there when I got there. Paul Kelly [Patrick Carey] came in after 6.00 p.m. and woke me up. He told me the time. He stayed until 7.45 and then went. I went downstairs to watch television. I stayed in for the rest of the evening. During 5th October I went nowhere near Guildford."'

Conlon's evidence was wholly consistent with his known lifestyle but for a court it was hopelessly flimsy. Patrick Carey, if he had testified to this effect and satisfied the jury as to his honesty, would have given Conlon an absolute alibi. But Patrick Carey was not in court. He had gone home to Northern Ireland and had told Conlon's solicitors that he had not the slightest intention of giving evidence in a terrorist trial, adding that he simply could not remember the night in question anyway; two quite understandable reactions which gave no help either way as to whether Conlon was telling the truth or lying. For good measure, Carey's girlfriend told both the police and Conlon's solicitors that Carey had not gone back to Quex Road hostel that evening. With the hindsight of knowing that not one of the 11 alibi witnesses called by the defence was ultimately believed, one might speculate that the absence of a young man from Northern Ireland was immaterial. Patrick Carey would not be the only alibi witness who was not produced in court.

The reluctance to be seen testifying on behalf of accused terrorists was underlined by two of Patrick Armstrong's supporting witnesses, Tom and Jacqueline Walker, who had lived with Armstrong and Carole Richardson in the Linstead Street squat. They asked for their address to be withheld in open court and thereby to be kept out of the press. The request was refused, although other witnesses concerned with the alibi evidence — both prosecution and defence — were granted this privilege by the judge.

Armstrong claimed to have spent October 5 in a similarly dissolute fashion to Conlon: rising at midday, drinking at the Old Bell pub in Kilburn High Road, borrowing some money, going to a betting-shop and to the Kilburn Snack Bar and arriving home at the Linstead Street squat between 5.00 and 5.15 p.m. 'Carole Richardson and the others were there. Lisa [Astin] and Carole did not stay. They left just after 6.00 p.m. I was asked to dog-sit by Carole. The dog was Carole's. The others joked about it. I did not go out. I sat and smoked joints, cannabis in cigarette form. Others were with me — John Brown, Tom Walker, Jacqueline, two friends and two girls. They were visitors. We played records... Later on I got a bit high and I decided to go to bed. I went back to my own room. There was no one there and I got into the sleeping-bag. We only had a mattress. I went to sleep. I got into the sleeping-bag after 10.00 p.m.'

Thomas Walker was the first to confirm Armstrong's account. After an afternoon on which he and his pregnant wife begged for money for drugs in Kilburn High Road, he had returned to the squat: 'I got back at 5.30 or 6.00 p.m. I went to the room which I and Jacqueline had and Paddy was there. I was jealous. There was an argument and Paddy left.' If Thomas Walker's recollection was true, there was insufficient time for Patrick Armstrong to have gone directly to Guildford and spent 30 minutes in the Horse and Groom before leaving at 6.55 p.m. (quite apart from the time that the prosecution alleged the bombing team had spent in a Wimpy Bar prior to entering the pub).

Jacqueline Walker corroborated Armstrong's presence in the squat at the relevant time: 'He was in most of the evening. He came up and lent me his radio at 6.00 or 7.00 p.m. I am not too sure how long he stayed there.' But there was a conflict between husband and wife. While Tom remembered having the row with Armstrong, Jacqueline did not. She said she had not seen

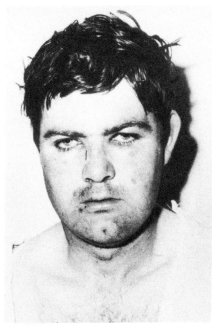

Members of the London Active Service Unit: Harry Duggan (above left), Brendan Down (above right), Joseph O'Connell (below left) and Edward Butler (below right).

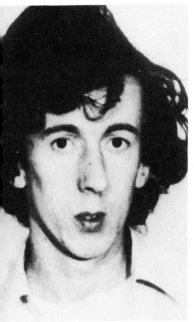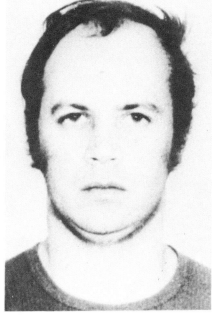

Contents of a suitcase found at a London Active Service Unit safe house, Stoke Newington, London

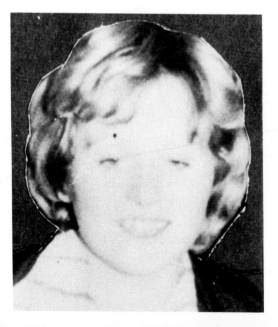

Margaret McKearney, still wanted by Scotland Yard for bombings and shootings in autumn 1974

Unexploded bomb, Aldershot railway station, December 1974: the work of the London Active Service Unit

Unexploded bomb, Lockets Restaurant, October 1975: the work of the London Active Service Unit

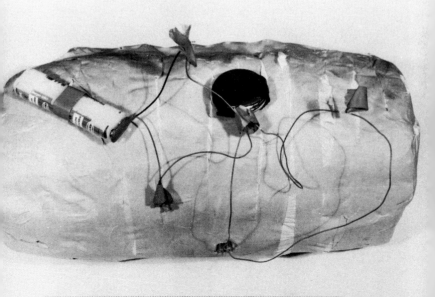

The Horse and Groom pub, Guildford, after the bombing,
October 5 1974

A victim of the Seven Stars bomb, October 5 1974

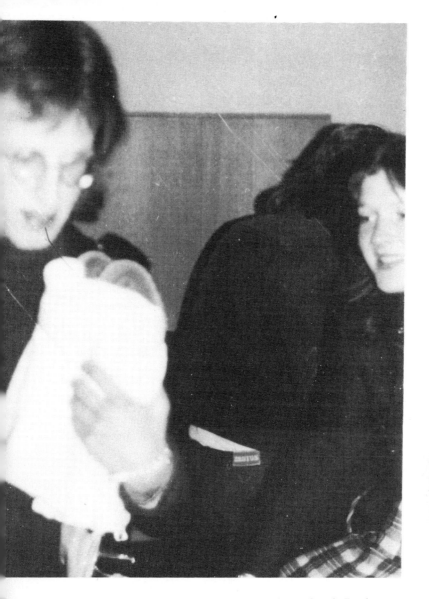

Ray Laidlaw of Jack the Lad and Carole Richardson, South Bank
Polytechnic, October 5 1974

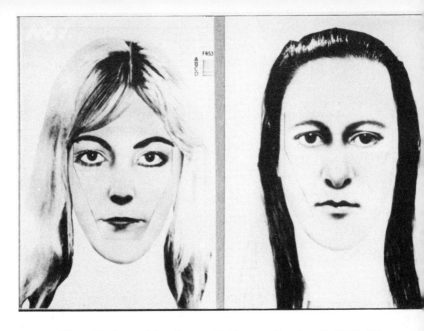

Photofits issued by Surrey Police on October 7 1974. They were withdrawn after being identified as those of bomb victims. The blonde one was said to have been taken to be Paul Hill (below right) but it bears a striking similarity to a photofit of Marlene Coyle (below left), wanted since 1973 for conspiracy to cause explosions

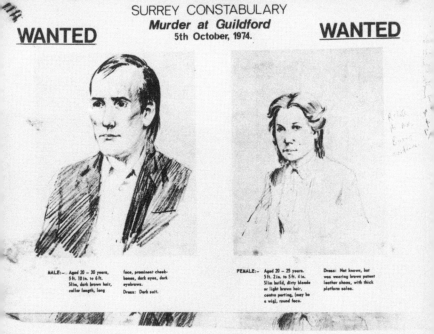

Roy Reynolds's 'extraordinary likeness' of the 'courting couple' in the Horse and Groom, said to resemble Armstrong and Richardson, below

Gina Clarke with Paul Hill's baby, born 1975

Paul Hill, HM Prison Gartree, 1985

Carole Richardson (right) and Lisa Astin, summer 1974

Anne and Paddy Maguire at their wedding, Belfast 1957. They left Northern Ireland immediately afterwards and have lived in England ever since

Sarah and Guiseppe Conlon with Ann as a child

Gerard Conlon

Detective Chief Superintendent Walter Simmons of the Surrey Bomb Squad (left) and Peter Imbert, member of the Bomb Squad investigating the London Active Service Unit and pub bombings in 1974 and Metropolitan Police Commissioner since 1987 (right).

Below left: Sir John Donaldson (right) at his introduction into the House of Lords as Baron Sir John Donaldson of Lymington, 1988, together with one of his sponsors, Lord Eustace Roskill. These two judges presided over the trials and appeals of the Guildford Four and the Maguire household. *Below right:* Sir Michael (now Lord) Havers, prosecuting counsel in the Guildford and Maguire trials, Lord Chancellor in 1987

her husband until 9.00 p.m. Individually, they had both given evidence that could clear Armstrong but their accounts were not wholly reconcilable. The Crown argued that neither could be relied upon.

Brian McLoughlin, who occasionally shared the downstairs room with Armstrong, Richardson and Lisa Astin, confirmed the dog-sitting story: 'I remember the golden Labrador belonging to Carole and Lisa. They were out and Armstrong was baby-sitting for the dog. We were talking, listening to records and smoking pot. Armstrong was high. He went to his room. I thought he went to bed.' McLoughlin, however, had already been demolished as a credible prosecution witness, so the defence could hardly now rely upon his evidence of alibi.

Yet another member of the Kilburn crowd placed Armstrong in the Kilburn squat at the time the Horse and Groom bomb was planted. Thomas Leniston testified: 'I think this was a weekend, Saturday or Sunday night. I don't remember the date. That day I went to see some friends at about 3.00 p.m. at South Penge. I got back to Linstead Street between 6.00 and 6.30 p.m. There were quite a few people there, including Paddy.'

The glaring deficiency in Leniston's evidence was, of course, the all-important matter of the date. How could it be tied to October 5? Leniston recalled a late-night fracas in the street outside the squat which involved the police and dog-handlers arriving at the scene. This recollection also featured in the evidence of Tom and Jacqueline Walker, Brian McLoughlin and Armstrong himself. They were, it now appeared, all talking about the same night. But on the last day of the trial Sir Michael Havers sprang a dramatic surprise. He called rebuttal evidence that the police had no record of any such incident in Linstead Street that night. Much was made of this eleventh-hour intervention. It made them all look like liars.

The jury had a choice of three ways of interpreting Armstrong's witnesses. Were they all honest but mistaken? There were surely too many similarities for that, notably the time they all agreed that Armstrong had been in the squat and the common recall of the street fracas. Were they all, then, covering up for their friend? If this was the case they had completely failed to adopt an agreed story. There had been ample time for Tom and Jacqueline Walker to co-ordinate their accounts of their movements; for Thomas Leniston to be certain about the date; and for Lisa Astin, who frankly admitted that she could not remember whether she had or had not seen Armstrong that evening, to have joined in the collusion. Further, by fraudulently attempting to establish a false alibi they would have been taking a grave risk of implicating themselves in a conspiracy to pervert the course of justice in a terrorist murder trial, a strange course of action if they knew or suspected that Armstrong was guilty.

The third alternative was that the inconsistencies in their accounts could, in the context of the time lapse, the drugs and the unregulated lifestyles, be seen as imperfectly remembered truth — and the more plausible for not being rigidly identical — and that the police record of arrival at the street fracas had never been entered in the incident book or had simply gone missing. Under cross-examination the police had allowed that the log was not always kept as exhaustively as it might be.

To a conventionally-minded juror, the squatters may not have appeared an attractive selection of witnesses. At any rate, Mr Justice Donaldson simultaneously raised and disposed of the point: 'It is certainly right that you should not hold it against any of the accused if they have been obliged to call some people in support of their alibi who, you may think, lead lives of which you would not wholly approve.' The judge further scotched the suppressed mirth in court at the notion of dog-sitting at the heart of Armstrong's alibi: 'Although there have been smiles at the idea of dog-sitting, those of you who have friends with dogs will know that it does happen. People have to look after dogs and there is nothing very improbable about that.'

The jury was to reject Patrick Armstrong's alibi. It was not until after the trial that Armstrong's solicitor, Alastair Logan, found a police officer who had taken part in a late Saturday-night fracas in Linstead Street — it had not been the collective invention of the squatters. The police had been quick to deny that any such incident had taken place, but this policeman was now able to find records of the event. However, what he also claimed was that the incident had occurred on a subsequent Saturday. Armstrong still insists today that the disturbance in Linstead Street was on Saturday October 5, but as things stood in court he joined Gerard Conlon as a man without an alibi.

Paul Hill, alone, had to account for himself on the nights of both the Guildford and the Woolwich bombings. His version of Thursday November 7, when the prosecution claimed he had been present in Woolwich at the throwing of the bomb into the King's Arms at 10.17 p.m., was relatively straightforward. He claimed to have been at the home of his aunt and uncle, Anne and Frank Keenan, 12 miles from Woolwich, at 91C Brecknock Road, Kentish Town.

Hill remembered the television programmes they had watched that evening: *Top of the Pops* and *Six Million Dollar Man*. 'I watched *Six Million Dollar Man* up to the time when I went out to telephone my girlfriend. It was nine-ish. I went to Kentish Town tube station to do so. I walked. It is about nine minutes' walk from Brecknock Road. I talked to Gina for 20 minutes to half an hour and then I walked back to the flat. I got back between 9.30 and 10.00 p.m. I didn't go out that night again. I lay on the bed watching television. The first time I am positive I heard of the bombing was the next morning, but I could have heard it at the end of *News At Ten*.'

Frank Keenan's evidence matched Hill's exactly, apart from the detail of the telephone call. He thought Paul had left at about 9.30 p.m. and was back 20 minutes later. Anne Keenan testified that Hill left sometime after 9.00 p.m. and was back 15 minutes later. She also remembered watching *Monty Python's Flying Circus* and seeing a newsflash about the Woolwich bombing before going to bed. She could not recall the time of *Monty Python* or when she went to bed.

The television programmes and the newsflash established that they were talking about the correct night. The first ITN reference to the bomb was at 10.26 p.m., nine minutes after the explosion. Frank and Anne Keenan were each certain that Hill was back in the house for good by 10.00 p.m. at the latest, so the minor discrepancies between Hill's own evidence and the Keenans' as to the length of the telephone call were immaterial. None of the accounts enabled Hill to be in Woolwich at 10.17 p.m. — a good half-hour's drive away. He could not have been in two places at once.

Mr Justice Donaldson's conclusion on the Keenans' alibi was not helpful to Paul Hill: 'Members of the jury, you will have to consider in view of that slightly muddled situation, whether it would have been possible for Hill to have gone out and gone to Woolwich, whether Mrs Keenan would have remembered, whether Mr Keenan would have remembered and, of course, whether Mr and Mrs Keenan are telling the truth anyway. Those are matters which you will have to take into consideration. So much for the alibi.'

In fact, the 'slightly muddled situation' bore no relation to whether Hill could have gone to Woolwich. There was no muddle in the Keenans' evidence as to where Hill had been from, at the latest, 10.00 p.m. onwards. As to whether they 'would have remembered', it was their clear evidence on oath that they did, and the supporting detail of the television programmes confirmed their statements. The only real question for the jury was whether they were telling the truth. If they were, Hill was innocent of the Woolwich bombing. If they were not, Frank and Anne Keenan had colluded in presenting a false alibi.

Hill's alibi for the Guildford bombings was altogether more complex and unsatisfactory: 'During the morning I was at Quex Road [the Roman Catholic hostel in Kilburn] in bed. I got up and put two coats into the dry-cleaners. Lunch-time I spent drinking with Gerry Conlon in the Memphis Belle and the Old Bell. I finished when the pub closed at 3.00 p.m. I then went back to the dry-cleaners and collected the clothes. I took them back to

Quex Road and then went to Waterloo. It was before 4.00 p.m.
I went to Southampton. I got there at half past five-ish. I went
to Stainer Close on a bus. I met Gina and in the evening we went
out for a drink. I arrived at the Target public house at about 8.00
p.m. and left at closing time, 10.30 or 11.00 p.m. We then went
back to Stainer Close. I think both Crosbies were still up. Mrs
Crosbie was there when we arrived. Gina and I went to bed at
about 12.00 midnight, maybe after.'

Gina Clarke had made a statement to the police on November
28, the day of Paul's arrest, which corroborated this: 'I had seen
Paul on 5th October. I saw him at about 6.15 that evening and
he stayed until 12.00 [midday] on the Sunday. He rang me on
the Friday evening. The arrangement was the same as usual.
I saw him at the bus stop near Stainer Close. I had gone out
because I thought he was a bit late. It was the 6.20 bus. We
went back to Stainer Close. My sister and her husband were
there. Mr Crosbie was in the bedroom. He was in bed. He spoke
to Paul from the bedroom. We had tea and then left about 8.00
p.m. We went to the Target public house. We had meant to go
and see my brother but it was a bad night, it was raining. We
stayed there until closing time, 11.00 p.m., and then returned
to Stainer Close. We watched the end of the film, had tea and
went to bed.'

Kathleen Crosbie appeared in court to substantiate further
that Hill had been in Southampton and not in Guildford. She
said Hill had arrived at Stainer Close between 7.00 and 7.10
p.m. (later than in Gina Clarke's account), stating that Gina had
expected him at 5.00 or 5.30 p.m. She acknowledged that she
had first been unable to distinguish the weekend of October 5
for the police, but had subsequently placed it because of a row
she had had with her husband the following day, an incident
confirmed by Gina Clarke's evidence.

Thus far, Hill's alibi appeared consistent with his witnesses'
accounts, but the prosecution purported to be able to blow two
substantial holes in it. The first was the alleged conversation
involving Hill and Gina Clarke — in police custody — and

Detective Inspector Tim Blake on December 4. According to Blake, Hill said, 'Look, I want to see Gina. She has nothing to do with the bombings and I told her to give me an alibi. If I don't tell her to tell the truth she may be in trouble and I don't want that.' Gina was produced and the following conversation allegedly ensued:

Hill: 'Gina, tell them the truth.'

Clarke: 'I have told them the truth. You were with me since seven o'clock that night.'

Hill: 'You know that is not true. I have told them the truth about everything. You tell them what time I really came down that night.'

Clarke: 'Are you sure, love?'

Hill: 'Yes, I want you to tell them. I am not putting words in your mouth.'

Clarke: 'He didn't get down until about quarter past ten that night. He may have come before. I met him off the bus.'

Hill: 'What did I tell you?'

Clarke: 'You told me that you had stolen something and that, if I was asked, to say that you were with me all evening.'

If this conversation took place without duress on either party, then Hill's alibi for Guildford was worse than worthless. Gina Clarke's account is critically different: 'The police said that Paul had already told them what had happened at Guildford and told me to tell them. Paul said to me, "Tell the truth about what happened." Simmons showed me a paragraph of Paul's statement. Some time later I agreed that it was true. I agreed because every time I said what happened, they didn't want to know.'

Mr Justice Donaldson decisively interpreted the evidence: 'So what Gina is saying is that Detective Inspector Blake has got it right as to what happened. She is saying, of course, that her original statement [October 28] was untrue and that the statement she was making at the time of this meeting [December 4] between the two of them was untrue. But she does not support Hill's statement that he had put the words into her mouth in any way. She supports the police recollection of what occurred.'

This damning analysis is seriously flawed. First, Gina Clarke's evidence does not support the police version. She twice alluded to the police's having shown her part of Hill's contested confession, something that does not exist in the police account. Further, Gina Clarke's explanation of her statement of December 4 was that she agreed to make it only after the police had repeatedly refused to accept what she had insisted all along was true — that it was, in effect, the result of pressure. This, again, was significantly different from the police version.

Secondly, Gina Clarke was not telling the court that her original statement of October 28 was untrue. On the contrary, her evidence in the witness-box was that the original statement *was* true; that she had retracted it on December 4; and finally that it was her retraction — under the double duress of Hill's insistence and police pressure — that was untrue. There was no quarrel about whether the substance of what had been said at the confrontation of December 4 was accurately recorded but, rather, over the circumstances that had prompted it. Hill bluntly insisted that he put the words into her mouth at the insistence of Blake. So the real question for the jury was again whether they believed the police claim that no improper duress had taken place. Paul Hill and Gina Clarke were consistent if the jury accepted their joint allegations of pressure together with Hill's insistence that he had felt he had to convince the police he was really guilty to save Gina from being charged.

The greatest damage to Hill's alibi for Guildford came from an unlikely source: British Rail. According to Gina Clarke, Paul Hill had explained his late arrival on the bus to the stop near Stainer Close as the result of British Rail maintenance work on the Waterloo to Southampton line. This had meant the train had had to terminate at Eastleigh, on the outskirts of Southampton, from where passengers travelled the last stretch into Southampton by bus. However, Sir Michael Havers produced evidence from British Rail showing that the first train to be affected by this work on the line had been the 8.42 p.m. departure from

Waterloo. Still, Gina Clarke insisted from the witness-box that
Paul Hill was with her before 7.00 p.m. Hill's own statement
made no reference to the train's having terminated at Eastleigh.
He said that he had arrived at Southampton in the usual way.
Unless the British Rail records were wrong, it is impossible to
reconcile Gina Clarke's knowledge of the bus from Eastleigh
station with Hill's arrival on an earlier train than the 8.42 p.m.
The implication must be that Hill had, in fact, been on the 8.42
p.m. train and that Hill, Clarke and Mrs Crosbie were at best
mistaken and at worst lying. Hill's defence team could produce
nothing to contradict Sir Michael Havers's discovery. In the
years following the case, Gina Clarke has continued to insist that
she was not confused by the fact that the Eastleigh diversion was
still operational on the Sunday at lunch-time when Hill returned
to London; and that Hill arrived early on the Saturday evening
having been affected by the maintenance work at a time earlier
than British Rail records show that he could have been.

However, the point was made that everyone involved in the
alibi had agreed that Paul and Gina had gone for a drink at the
Target public house, and Mr Justice Donaldson observed, 'If it is
right that Hill went for a drink and he is very insistent about that
on a number of occasions, then he could not have caught the 8.42
train, unless the pubs in Southampton are open surprisingly late.
It really would have been difficult, if not impossible, for him to
have got into a pub at that time of night.'

In 1974, the Southampton pubs closed at 11.00 p.m. on
Saturdays. The 8.42 p.m. train reached Eastleigh at 10.15 p.m.,
still 15 minutes away from its scheduled arrival at Southampton
station at 10.30 p.m. Assuming — to Hill's disadvantage — that
the train was on time and that the connecting bus was ready
and kept pace with the original train schedule — all of which
must be unlikely — Hill could not have been ready to catch
a second bus to a stop near Stainer Close, more than four
miles away across the River Itchen in Sholing, before 10.30
p.m. After he had caught the second bus — again assuming
there was a bus ready and waiting — it would, as the

judge noted, have been 'difficult, if not impossible' for Hill and Gina to have reached the Target in time for last orders.

Nevertheless, if Paul Hill, Gina Clarke and Mrs Crosbie could not be relied upon for accuracy in the matter of Hill's arrival time in Southampton, then the jury had no need to accept their insistence that they had gone to the pub, either. Hill's alibi for Guildford was in tatters.

27
ELEPHANT AND CASTLE

'You can work out the times for yourselves.'

Mr Justice Donaldson to the jury

Carole Richardson had what appeared to be the strongest alibi evidence of all, not least because two critical timings were established by prosecution witnesses. The Crown had relied upon Privates Jonathan Cook and Paul Lynskey as the most reliable eyewitnesses from the Horse and Groom. They had been waiting for the so-called 'courting couple' to vacate their seats in the alcove and were watching closely. Cook testified that they had arrived at 6.45 p.m. and that the 'courting couple', whom the Crown alleged were Carole Richardson and Patrick Armstrong, had left 'seven or eight minutes later' — at 6.52 or 6.53 p.m. Sir Michael Havers put the time at 6.55 p.m., which would be more convenient to Carole Richardson's case than 6.52 p.m., but the earlier time makes more sense on the evidence.

The second important time was given by Simon Moodie, an accommodation officer at the South Bank Polytechnic, who had been checking free-pass arrivals at the Polytechnic for the Jack the Lad concert on October 5. He recognized Carole Richardson and testified that she had arrived at '7.30 p.m.... No, between 7.45 and 8.00 p.m.'. Two members of Jack the Lad, who had seen Carole Richardson shortly after her arrival, inside the building, put the time of their meeting at, respectively: between 7.40 and 8.00 p.m.; and about 7.45 p.m. within 15 minutes either way. Richardson's QC, Eric Myers, concluded that she had reached the building as early as 7.30 p.m. and 'beyond peradventure no later than 7.45 p.m.'. Taking 7.45 p.m. as — being in the middle of the range — the fairest estimate of Carole's arrival time at the South Bank Polytechnic, the jury had to be persuaded that she could have travelled from the Horse and Groom in Guildford to the South Bank Polytechnic, near the Elephant and Castle in South London, in 52 or 53 minutes.

The obvious way was on the A3, a very different road in 1974 from the present route, which comprises unbroken dual and triple carriageway from the outskirts of Guildford to Putney. There were stretches of dual carriageway in 1974, but the bulk of the trip would have been made on two-lane roads: through Ripley village, where the old A3 has now been downgraded to the B2215; through a succession of traffic-lights in Esher; past the then notorious bottleneck of dual roundabouts known as the 'Scilly Isles'; and then via a choice of routes to cut across South London to the Elephant and Castle, at a time on Saturday evening when there could reasonably be expected to be a steady flow of traffic heading towards the West End. More than half of the 32-mile journey was subject to speed limits of 30 or 40 miles per hour.

The defence commissioned Mr Martin Cornberg, an articled clerk, to see how long the trip took in 1975 when the speed limits were slightly lower. Mr Cornberg drove the route in a hired car at the equivalent time on a Saturday, observing the speed limits throughout. His journey took 64 minutes. On that basis, Carole Richardson could not have been the girl in the 'courting couple'.

PC Heritage, a traffic-control driver, also covered the route, in what he agreed was a 'very nippy' car, a six-cylinder Triumph 2.5. Ignoring the speed limits, he claimed a time of 45 minutes, fast enough for Carole Richardson to have been the Horse and Groom bomber. But would a getaway car have risked speeding when the bomb was not primed to detonate until 8.50 p.m., an hour after the supposed journey? Mr Justice Donaldson considered, '... anybody who has just planted a bomb would be extraordinarily stupid to drive back to London with no limits. It would be inviting detection by the police and some awkward questions.' But the nippy police car also drove the route observing the 1974 limits, and registered a time of exactly 52 minutes. Regrettably, the court did not establish whether this journey was made on a Saturday evening at the correct time, but 52 minutes was within 60 seconds of the time needed to beat the 7.45 p.m. deadline and allow Carole Richardson to be the bomber.

There were also what became known as the 'end times'. The 'courting couple' had been seen leaving the Horse and Groom at 6.52 or 6.53 p.m. Carole Richardson had been seen at the entrance of the Polytechnic at 7.45 p.m. But the timed runs had been measured from Guildford to the Elephant and Castle. To put the matter to Carole Richardson's advantage there was at least a five-minute walk from the Horse and Groom to any of the various locations where the getaway car was supposed to have been parked, and a further five-minute walk from the nearest edge of the Elephant and Castle to the front door of the Polytechnic — an extra 10 minutes of journey time which put it beyond the capability even of a nippy car breaking the speed limits. Even assuming that Carole Richardson was driven from doorstep to doorstep, by a car that had been waiting illegally on North Street outside the Horse and Groom — and there was no evidence given of her getting in or out of a car at either end — then the journey time must have been increased by at least two minutes for the drive on from the Elephant and Castle by narrow backstreets or one-way main-road dog-leg to Borough Road and the Polytechnic. 'You can work out the times for yourselves,' the judge told the jury. 'They are fairly fine. You will have to consider whether it is possible at all.' What is certain is that if the jury accepted the time driven by the solicitor's clerk, it was quite impossible.

All the calculations about the journey times, however, would become redundant if Frank Johnson was correct in his assertion that he had met Carole Richardson for a drink at the Charlie Chaplin public house on the far side of the Elephant and Castle complex from the Polytechnic. Because he claimed that this meeting and drink had occurred directly before the walk to the concert and the 7.45 p.m. sighting by the doorman and prosecution witness, Simon Moodie, Carole Richardson was unquestionably innocent — if Frank Johnson was telling the truth. It did not matter what time the meeting in the Charlie Chaplin had taken place. If it had taken place before Moodie's sighting, then there was insufficient time for Carole Richardson to have made the journey from Guildford on any estimate. Frank Johnson's credibility became crucial.

This was immediately understood by Sir Michael Havers. His first three questions elicited honest but damaging information: that Johnson had two convictions for possession of LSD; that he supported the aims but not the methods of the IRA, an organization in which Johnson allowed that he may have had friends — 'I don't know'; and that he was a member of the Newcastle branch of the Anti-Internment League because he opposed the principle of imprisonment without trial (a laudable enough principle, perhaps, when applied to most jurisdictions, but more sensitive in the context of Northern Ireland). At this point Mr Justice Donaldson's note-taking let him down, for when he came to summarize Johnson's evidence to the jury he stated incorrectly that Johnson had been 'subject' to imprisonment without trial, which he never has been. Even without the judge's mistaken innuendo that Johnson was a former internee, the agreed facts made the headlines: 'Alibi Witness Was Pro-Republican'. Frank Johnson, now established as pro-Republican and a criminal, had next to explain why he had changed his story not once but twice — which on the surface made him look, at best, hopelessly confused and unreliable; at worst, a perjuring liar.

His first statement cast him in the role of either honest alibi witness or cunning plotter: Frank Johnson walking into Newcastle police station out of the blue and declaring that Carole Richardson had been with him at the Charlie Chaplin at such a time as to demolish utterly the Surrey Police case against her. His second statement, signed after two and a half days in Guildford police station, declared — among other things —

that he had lied to protect Carole; that he had met her in the
pub 40 minutes later than first claimed; and that the time spent
drinking together had been significantly shorter — a quick drink
rather than a 20-minute one. His third account, now given to
the court under oath and sustained under cross-examination,
essentially reverted to the first — that he could not be precise
about times because he did not have a watch, but that between
6.30 and 7.30 p.m. he had met Carole Richardson in the pub,
had a 20-minute drink with her and Lisa Astin and taken 10
minutes walking to the Polytechnic. Johnson reconciled the
three versions by saying that the middle account was untrue,
the product of sustained psychological and physical pressure by
the police.

Johnson told the court how Detective Chief Inspector Alan
Longhurst had threatened to throw him off the roof of Guildford
police station unless he changed his story; how Longhurst had
asked him, 'How would you like to see your mother go up in
flames in her wheelchair?'; how Detective Constable Martin
Wise had hit him below the ear. Under cross-examination
Longhurst agreed that he knew that Johnson's mother was
disabled and confined to a wheelchair, but both officers wholly
denied any impropriety and insisted that the statement had
been voluntary as signed. Neither prosecution nor defence
seemed interested in pressing Johnson for further details of
his two-and-a-half-day detention at Guildford police station. Sir
Michael Havers, however, was intrigued to know why, if these
terrible claims were true, Johnson had not made a formal complaint to the police, to his MP or to the National Council For Civil
Liberties. 'I was too frightened,' Johnson replied. 'I just wanted
to forget about the whole thing.' Frank Johnson has never been
able to forget about his time in Guildford police station. He was
to give a much fuller account later.

In the confusion of the various timings — Johnson never
claimed to be precise about any of them — and the ensuing
attempts to prove his overall unreliability as a witness, prosecution, defence and judge failed to fasten on to one undisputed

fact common to all his statements: the fact that he had met Carole Richardson, at whatever time, for a drink in the Charlie Chaplin prior to presenting himself with the two girls to Simon Moodie, the Polytechnic doorman, at around 7.45 p.m. So even if the defence had been forced to rely on the contested statement given to Longhurst and Wise at Guildford, the question as to whether Carole Richardson had had enough time to travel from Guildford was still alive — but no one fully pursued it.

No one was disputing the time taken to walk from the Charlie Chaplin to the Polytechnic: 10 minutes. This placed Carole Richardson in the pub at 7.35 p.m. In his first account and under oath, Johnson said they had passed 20 minutes drinking together, but even according to his second, retracted statement in which he reduced the drinking time in the pub to 'no longer than 10 minutes', the alibi still held good. Had they spent no longer than five minutes in the pub, Carole Richardson would still have had to arrive there at 7.30 p.m. Not even the fastest recorded time trial between Guildford and Elephant and Castle — the 45 minutes claimed by the police driver ignoring speed limits — could have delivered Richardson from the Horse and Groom at 6.52 p.m. to the Charlie Chaplin at 7.30 p.m. The journey was shown to be impossible on the basis of the central timing given by the prosecution witness Simon Moodie and the one account by Frank Johnson that the police relied upon as true.

The statement given by Frank Johnson at the end of his stay with Surrey Police further invites the question as to why he has never been charged with being an accomplice to the Guildford bombings, or with perjury. DCI Longhurst told the court that he had brought Johnson to Guildford under arrest for involvement with the bombings. By the end of his interrogation Longhurst had a statement, produced as voluntary and true, that Johnson had, in effect, conspired to concoct an alibi — a cold-blooded attempt to pervert the course of justice in a major terrorist case. Yet no sooner had Johnson made this self-incriminating statement than he had been released without charge. Longhurst informed the court that this had been because of 'insufficient evidence'. The idea of charging Frank Johnson with perjury or with conspiracy to pervert the course of justice is not a fanciful one; this has happened to witnesses offering false alibi evidence in numerous major criminal cases in London. Another anomaly was that during interrogation, according to sworn police records, Johnson had volunteered that he was involved with the IRA in the matter of guns, ammunitions and two-way radios. This remarkable admission had stimulated no further questioning at the time, failed to appear in the eventual statement and was of no interest to Sir Michael Havers when it came to cross-examination.

An unusual feature of Carole Richardson's alibi was that the police and not the defence were the first to hear of it. She had maintained all along upon her arrest that she could not remember what she had been doing on Saturday October 5 but that if someone could find her diary her movements would be established. The police conceded in court that they had taken no action on what might have appeared to be a simple and straightforward course. Perhaps, if the diary had been located and had shown an entry for the concert on October 5 the jury would have been entitled to surmise that it had been doctored to provide a false alibi. At any rate, the brown diary was never produced.

Accordingly, the first indication that Carole Richardson had a plausible alibi came from Frank Johnson's intervention at Newcastle police station. In such circumstances there is a duty upon the police promptly to inform the defence of the existence of a potential witness. They did not. Cross-examination revealed what Richardson's counsel bluntly denounced as 'dirty tricks' by Surrey Police. After Johnson's sudden revelation, the police interviewed the members of Jack the Lad. Their recollections of seeing Carole, and the times at which they had seen her, meant that the survival of the Crown's case against her depended on Johnson's claim to have met the girls beforehand in the Charlie Chaplin pub. It had been the middle of February before the defence team found out that Jack the Lad had been interviewed by the police. Frank Johnson, after his failed attempts to interest a solicitor or the clerk of Guildford Magistrates Court, had walked into Newcastle police station on December 20 1974.

Eric Myers QC asked DCI Longhurst if he recalled telling the group of musicians that it was unnecessary to communicate with the defence solicitors because the police would see they got copies of the statements.

'No, sir,' replied Longhurst.

'It's a fact that no one on the prosecution side breathed a word to Miss Richardson's solicitors that the group had been interviewed.'

Longhurst replied that he did not know.

'This was straight out of the dirty-tricks book because of the nature of the case,' Myers continued.

'No, sir,' replied Longhurst. He agreed that the police had been aware that photographs had been taken backstage by the brother-in-law of one of the musicians, and when Myers produced a colour photograph agreed that it showed Carole Richardson at the concert on October 5.

'The police knew all about Carole Richardson's alibi long before she or her solicitors knew,' Myers insisted.

'I can't tell you,' replied Longhurst. The point was taken no further.

Whatever the jury made of this and whatever their overall impression of Frank Johnson's conflicting statements, they still had before them the unequivocal assertion of Lisa Astin that from the moment she had woken up in an adjoining sleeping-bag to Carole Richardson at 11.30 a.m. on October 5, to the time the two girls had climbed back into those sleeping-bags around midnight, they had been together all day and had gone no nearer to Guildford than the Charlie Chaplin pub.

Lisa Astin was now 17. She scarcely looked it. In the witness-box she gave the impression to at least one court reporter of a young, immature schoolgirl — small and barely audible. Nobody in court could have been impressed when

Gerard Conlon pulled a face at her from the dock and Lisa Astin could not suppress a nervous giggle. The basic facts of her evidence, however, stayed wholly faithful to the account that she had first given to Carole's solicitors after she had telephoned *Time Out* magazine to ascertain the date of the concert. They matched Richardson's own testimony to the court. The two girls had gone to the launderette together; they had returned to Linstead Street together; they had travelled to the ABC bakery together; they had caught a bus to the Swiss Cottage swimming-baths together; they had returned to Linstead Street together to change for the concert; they had taken the tube to Elephant and Castle together, met Frank Johnson at the Charlie Chaplin, gone to the concert and gone home together; in short, a complete alibi for the whole day.

There were discrepancies along the way. Lisa Astin, in court, was no longer sure whether it was that Saturday that she and Carole had bought or stolen the doll that was given to Maura Kelly at the bakery. The fact that one of the band remembered Carole with the blue bean-bag doll that Maura had given to Carole in return suggests that Lisa's first recollection was, in fact, correct. She had never remembered Carole asking Paddy to dog-sit for Leb. Now, under cross-examination by Sir Michael Havers, she was no longer as sure as she had been that Armstrong was in the squat when the girls returned from Swiss Cottage.

Sir Michael made a particular point of pressing her about the electronic machine that Frank Johnson and Carole Richardson claimed to have played at the Charlie Chaplin. Frank Johnson had persistently described it as either a tennis or a football machine — 'I'm not sure which'. Quite apart from the time lapse, his uncertainty was understandable in that the principle and layout of the two games, both popular in pubs in 1974, were almost identical: each player controlled an electronic blocker to intercept and propel an electronic ball across the screen with the purpose of eluding the opponent's identical electronic blocker. Bypassing the defensive block resulted in a point in tennis or a goal in football. According to the sole newspaper court report of her evidence in the *Surrey Daily Advertiser*, Lisa Astin agreed that she had told Surrey Police that Frank and Carole were playing electronic football. The judge's notes of proceedings record that she denied having told anyone that it was a football machine. One of the defence solicitors had a secretary in court taking notes of the proceedings. These record Lisa as stating, 'I am not sure whether it was tennis or football.' Sir Michael Havers triumphantly produced a representative of the machine's distributing company to testify that on October 30 1974 the Charlie Chaplin publican had exchanged a tennis game for a football machine. Sir Michael put it to Lisa Astin that she had not been to the Charlie Chaplin until November and then, for the purpose of concocting a false alibi for her friend Carole Richardson, she had inserted the detail of the football machine. Astin denied it. Sir Michael at different times during the trial suggested that the alibi had been concocted prior to the night of the Guildford bombings and, here, that it had been put together after the switch of the electronic machines. He did not suggest to the jury how Carole Richardson could have been party to this alleged concoction.

Nor did he dwell on the fact that Simon Moodie, the doorman, and the members of Jack the Lad remembered Lisa Astin as clearly as they remembered Carole Richardson. Their evidence confirmed the truth of what Lisa Astin had been claiming throughout about the two girls' movements from 7.45 p.m. onwards. To dismiss her evidence the jury had to accept that she was being truthful about the latter part of the evening and untruthful about the afternoon and early evening, despite the ample detail that corroborated Carole Richardson's account. Sir Michael Havers concluded by establishing that Lisa habitually took LSD, barbiturates and amphetamines, and that she was high on the night of the concert — facts that were irrelevant to whether the two girls had spent the day together.

As the most definitive alibi witness for Carole Richardson, Lisa was to get surprisingly short shrift from Mr Justice Donaldson, who dealt with her in just over a page of his summing-up. He introduced her as 'a young lady who I am sure you will all remember', and peremptorily paraphrased her evidence, concluding without further comment, 'That is Lisa Astin.'

As the jury were to reject the alibi evidence of Lisa Astin and Frank Johnson it is reasonable to assume they must have agreed with Sir Michael Havers that it was concocted. It is worth contemplating what that would have entailed. Carole Richardson was the last to claim that she had an effective alibi, having failed to recall either to police or to her own solicitors what she had been doing on October 5. Were the jury to believe that she had first concocted it and then forgotten it? Or even, to take the concoction at its most devious, that somehow the plot had been formed after the event and that all the detail had been imparted to or from Carole Richardson while she was held on remand in Brixton Prison? This would have required Lisa Astin and Frank Johnson to risk severe personal consequences if Carole were found guilty, from the danger of rehearsing in court their illicit drug habits to that of being joined as parties to the principal offence. It would have required Carole to be prepared coolly to risk the freedom of her friends and the worsening of her own position if the plot were exposed at a time when the only evidence against her was her own confession. Above all, it would have required co-ordinating a convoluted plan in ignorance of the central character, the prosecution witness Simon Moodie. They had no idea who he was; whether the police had found him; or whether he remembered seeing them and at the right time.

Above all, the putative deception, with all the nerve, foresight and elaboration it demanded, had inexplicably accounted for only one of the four. Why had the IRA gone to such trouble to concoct alibis for her alone? Why, in what Sir Michael had claimed was a meticulously planned operation, was there no comparable alibi constructed for the others? There are no rational answers other than that Frank Johnson and Lisa Astin told the truth at the Old Bailey in October 1975. Thirteen years on they tell the same story — as do the Keenans and Gina Clarke for Paul Hill. They have not resiled on any detail of their testimony. It is a remarkable concoction that is tumbled by a jury but persists for 13 years. Indeed, other witnesses not produced or not willing to testify at the trial have now come forward to support the alibis. Their accounts will be examined later.

Finally, and perhaps irrationally, there is the photograph of Carole Richardson (reproduced in the picture section), indisputably taken at the South Bank Polytechnic on the night of the Guildford bombings. It was taken at a time that does not exclude her from being the bomber, so the fact of its existence is wholly circumstantial beyond proving where she was after the bomb exploded. She is wearing the clothes that Lisa Astin claimed she was wearing. In its original colour it shows the red and white strap of a shoulder-bag that does not belong to the 'Scorpio' bag she was alleged to have taken into the Horse and Groom. She has brown hair, not blonde or dirty blonde hair. 'She was very happy and carefree that day,' Lisa recalled. But, according to Surrey Police, Sir Michael Havers and the jury, this is the 17-year-old girl, too young to buy alcohol in a pub, who earlier that night had sat for up to an hour on top of a steadily ticking, highly volatile gelignite time bomb and would shortly discover that it had killed five young people who were not much older than her.

The hearing of the various alibi witnesses was punctuated by two more time bombs in central London. The first, on October 8, went horribly wrong. Joseph O'Connell had assembled a gelignite device, wrapped in coach bolts, intended for the Ritz Hotel in Piccadilly. Eddie Butler was to place it but found the hotel too busy. He carried the bomb into a cubicle in the toilets of Green Park underground station nearby, defused it, waited and then set about priming it again. 'Then some guy in the next toilet looked over the toilet to see what I was doing. He was a total stranger. I thought he'd seen me so I ran out, threw it down at the bus stop, and ran off.'

The virtually instantaneous explosion killed Graham Tuck and injured 20 other bystanders. The three members of the bombing team scattered, and although one was blown off his feet by the blast, they escaped successfully yet again. 'The detonator was pulled out,' O'Connell later claimed. 'It shouldn't have gone off.'

Four days later, the Unit placed a 26-pound coach-bolt time bomb at Lockets Restaurant in Marsham Street, Westminster. As usual, Lockets was full of Conservative MPs and senior civil servants. Two elderly women spotted a suspicious-looking holdall wedged between railings and a restaurant window, and the manager was able to evacuate the building. The bomb was defused with three minutes to spare to reveal, on subsequent inspection, the ubiquitous fingerprints of Joseph O'Connell.

28
'ENTIRELY A
MATTER FOR YOU'

'I would not have made a false confession but Armstrong
may be different from me.'

Mr Justice Donaldson

By definition, a judge's summing-up cannot be exhaustive. When
Mr Justice Donaldson began his on Monday morning it was the
beginning of the sixth week in court and there were 22 days of
evidence, argument and speeches to summarize before the jury
could consider their verdict; it was by no means the longest
trial ever heard at the Old Bailey, but it was still of exceptional
length. It was Tuesday lunch-time before Mr Justice Donaldson
finished and his speech had run to 126 A4 foolscap pages of
transcript.

As it is a common complaint of any losing side in a court case
to claim that its best points have been improperly put or not put
at all (to which the only complete answer is for the whole case
to be repeated at full length to nobody's clarification), it should
be stated immediately that Mr Justice Donaldson's summing-up
was, in many ways, a model of its kind and faultless in its expo-
sition of the law. But it cannot pass without critical scrutiny. As
the last words the jury were to hear and, by the nature of the
adversarial system, the first piece of perceived neutrality, it is
obviously of crucial importance.

Mr Justice Donaldson promptly acknowledged the elusiveness
of perfect objectivity: 'The purpose of the summing-up is to tell
you what the law is which you have to apply and to try to give
you some assistance as to the facts. But when I say "give you
assistance as to the facts" do not misunderstand me. I know

there is a popular view that juries get some assistance from the judge as to what the proper verdict is, but that is quite wrong... It would be contrary to human nature if I had not my private view on the matter, but you are not concerned with that at all. If you think you can detect what my view is, ignore it.'

There is indeed, as the judge surmised, a popular view that judges, unwittingly or otherwise, do steer juries towards verdicts — popular enough for the view to be embraced by many regular observers of our courts in action — and it is a rare jury that does not, unwittingly or otherwise, absorb the judicial message, however properly forewarned. The message may be passed through a facial expression, an emphasis or an intonation — none of which enters the official record — or even in a sentence couched with impeccable caution.

When Mr Justice Donaldson says, 'That, you may think — it is entirely a matter for you — has all the hallmarks of being a voluntary statement and not a suggested statement — you have to weigh it up,' he has reminded the jury three times in a single sentence that they are the sole arbiters of fact but has simultaneously imparted a powerful value judgement. The technique can work for either side — and in this case did. What is futile is to pretend that the technique is not at play and that there is not to some extent a highly influential 'thirteenth member of the jury'. The mantric use by Mr Justice Donaldson of the phrase 'it is entirely a matter for you' merely legalizes the innuendo.

Nobody could dispute that the bombings had taken place, that they amounted to murder or that a participant in the bombings was guilty of conspiracy. This left one simple point at issue. Were the defendants involved? But before this point could be explored there was a difficult intellectual notion for the jury to grasp. Mr Justice Donaldson explained it with admirable lucidity: 'None of the accused has gone into the witness-box and said that any of the others are involved, so there is no evidence from any one of the accused which is any evidence against the other accused.' This meant that the jury had to put out of their minds the knowledge that each of the defendants' confessions was damning of his or her co-accused. The difficulty of maintaining this fiction was exacerbated by the reading of lengthy extracts from the confessions with the theoretically non-existent references intact. Mr Justice Donaldson was scrupulous in reminding the jury of this awkward point at each juncture.

He also alluded to the notorious Maxwell Confait murder case which had just concluded: 'It is a case in which the Court of Appeal — and I speak purely from what I read in the newspapers — has set aside convictions for murder based on statements made to the police by accused people, which in the light of subsequent investigation the Court is satisfied were false confessions. This, of course, is a very disturbing matter in the general interest and no doubt it will be very thoroughly investigated... What you may really think it amounts to is this: that that was an example, that case, which proves what has never been disputed so far as I know — that you can, in exceptional circumstances, get people agreeing that they committed crimes which they did not, in fact, commit... It will give you, no doubt, long and anxious consideration. You will have to consider how it is this sort of thing can happen... It appears that two of the three people concerned in that case were young men who were congenitally retarded, and that may have had some bearing on the matter, I do not know.'

The defence might have preferred the judge to have focused on the behaviour of the police rather than on the mental state of the convicted which, doubtless inadvertently, differentiated it from the matter in hand, but otherwise the point was fully made. It was not reiterated, however, when the detailed analysis of the Guildford confessions began.

Mr Justice Donaldson took each defendant in turn, beginning with Patrick Armstrong: 'What the Crown say about Patrick Armstrong is this: they say that he was an active member of the IRA. They say that he came to England knowing that three attacks, of one sort or another, were planned and that he came over to take part, wholly or in part, in those attacks... The

Crown does not suggest that Patrick Armstrong threw the [Woolwich] bomb. They do not suggest he was at Woolwich at all on 7th November when the bomb was thrown. What they say is that... he assisted in its commission by joining and helping the party who did the photographic reconnaissance... But, of course, the photographic reconnaissance really begins and ends with his statement in which he says that he went on the reconnaissance. He now denies it and the only evidence you have got is from his statement... Patrick Armstrong's case, of course, his defence, his answer to these charges, is relatively simple. He says that he had no part whatsoever in either the Guildford or the Woolwich bombings.'

The confessions, of course, were the crux of the case: 'It is the same problem that you find running through the whole of this case in relation to all of the accused: are these original statements made to the police in substance true?... He [Armstrong] says that they are almost entirely untrue and that the only true parts are his personal particulars and the account which you will find of his hitch-hiking activities. He says that the reason why he signed those false statements was he was high on drugs when he was arrested and when the effect of them wore off thereafter, he said, he was induced to sign them because he was very frightened of the Surrey Police officers... I would not have made a false confession, but Armstrong may be different from me.'

Armstrong's counsel had suggested that a Belfast upbringing might have conditioned him to be afraid of authority to which the judge now added another of his hypotheses: 'I suppose an alternative view would be that the background of somebody from Belfast might cause him to fear authority, but equally, to be more prepared to stand up to it, I do not know. That would be entirely a matter for you... '

It would probably have been irrelevant, but the judge's musings about Belfast might also have mentioned the numerous independent reports that were currently uncovering a systematic practice by the security forces of subjecting suspects to prolonged sleep deprivation, restricted diet, hooding and prolonged noise and enforced standing positions. (Such practices during Armstrong's late teenage years in Belfast were definitively confirmed at the European Court of Human Rights in 1978. They can have been no secret to anyone on either side of authority in Belfast at the time.)

Armstrong's confession statements were repeated to the jury almost in full. For some reason Mr Justice Donaldson supposed: 'Perhaps you will not feel that much importance should be attached to the first two lines... in fairness to him.' Nevertheless, he quoted them. According to the police, Armstrong's first recorded words were: 'I am pleased to have been caught. It's nice to tell someone all about it. I'm going to tell you everything I've done right from the beginning.'

Alternatively, it is arguable that these words could be subjected to the three differing interpretations that could be placed upon the entire body of confessions: that Armstrong was genuinely pleased to have been caught for a crime that had got wholly out of control — in which case a true account might be expected to follow; that Armstrong, as the hard-boiled IRA terrorist the prosecution had sought to portray, was setting out from the start to make a statement full of red herrings; or that he was simply giving the police what he assumed they wanted to hear. For whatever grade of terrorist Armstrong was supposed to be, the words have a corny ring — not quite what one would expect of a Provo mass murderer.

Mr Justice Donaldson interrupted the recital of the confession by reminding the jury that the Crown's forensic expert, Mr Donald Lidstone, had said of Armstrong's description of the Guildford bomb that it was 'a fairly accurate description of what a bomb would look like'. Armstrong's description was: '... it consisted of gelignite or dynamite sticks with a detonator attached to it with a timer wired on to it.'

In respect of Armstrong's claim under oath that the statements had been, in effect, extracted under terror by Surrey Police, the judge seemed intrigued as to why Armstrong had not complained to the Metropolitan Police when they came to interrogate him. He allowed that being in the continuing custody of Surrey Police might have provided the explanation, but did not suggest that Armstrong might have thought that a complaint to any police force was pointless. However misguided it may be, there is a long-standing and popularly held view that complaining to the police about alleged police violence is a waste of time.

Mr Justice Donaldson summarized succinctly the internal contradictions in Armstrong's statements: 'The Crown does not maintain and, indeed, they obviously could not maintain, that everything in those statements is accurate. Some of it clearly is not.' The judge had nothing more to say on this: no speculation as to why someone so 'pleased' to confess had proceeded to include a pack of lies and impossibilities; no indication of the magnitude of the inaccuracies which ran so deep as to implicate innocent people and contradict the Crown's considered version of who had driven to Guildford, in what sort of car and in what numbers, of where the car had been parked, of who had gone into which pub and so on. The judge made no comment on Sir Michael Havers's theory that the inconsistencies represented a new and sophisticated IRA counter-interrogation technique (which, in itself, begs the question as to why a suspect should confess at all if the meat of the subsequent confession serves only to undermine, deliberately and elaborately, the original, overall admission) — a technique, incidentally, that has never been attributed to the IRA before or since.

There was no speculation as to why certain changes in succeeding statements had so curiously coincided with changes in the statements made by the co-accused. Even Sir Michael Havers had been struck by this and had said, 'It's almost as if they were allowed by the police to sit together for a couple of hours to plot out the next instalment of this exciting story,' hastily adding that this was not, in fact, what had happened.

After considering Armstrong's alibi evidence, which with the benefit of hindsight one may dismiss as worthless, the judge turned to two contentious matters — the alleged violence of

Surrey Police and the alleged quality of detail in Armstrong's confession statements: 'You have seen these officers in the witness-box and you may like to ask yourselves whether this evidence [of brutality] could be true. If it could be true, then you might like to go on to ask yourselves whether — if you can visualize these officers offering him violence — it would be sufficient violence to make him confess to murder... The second question you might like to ask yourselves is where you have two confessions which are as detailed as these, could the detail be wholly explained by the form in which the police asked the questions or the suggestions that they made?... But, members of the jury, could that really explain — and this is what you have to ask yourselves — the wealth of detail that is contained in these statements? If you do not think that is a useful question, do not ask it of yourselves, but if you do, you may want to consider the answer.'

There were further useful questions that might have been put to the jury at this point. Why had all four defendants, once in court, retracted apparently voluntary confessions? Was there anything in the 'wealth of detail' that was outside the knowledge of the interrogating officers? If not, could it not all have been suggested to the prisoners, even unintentionally? What were the general dangers of relying on uncorroborated confessions, let alone ones obtained before the defendants could see solicitors? Equally, the prosecution were entitled to ask why, if the confessions were false, were glaring inconsistencies allowed to remain in the final statements? Or, to put it at its bluntest, if there had been a fit-up why was it such a shoddy one? As will be seen, the confessions of Patrick Armstrong were to play a seminal part in a future Royal Commission on Criminal Procedure which brought about changes in the law on interrogation, but the issues raised and the reforms instituted can not be made retroactive to the events of 1974.

The judge concluded by raising three further points about Armstrong's confessions. Why, when the drugs that had allegedly played a part in his first confession had worn off, did he still admit involvement? Why, when interviewed by the Metropolitan Police away from the claimed duress applied by Surrey Police, did he apparently again admit freely to the bombings? Why, if the duress was so intense, did he admit to Guildford and insist on his innocence for Woolwich? In his final remarks on Armstrong, Mr Justice Donaldson attached considerable significance to these questions while taking his customary care to include Armstrong's explanations, which were, in effect, that he had become so terrified and had dug himself into such a hole that, irrespective of drugs or police pressure, he feared even more trouble if he began retracting while still in police custody without access to a solicitor. As for the final point about Woolwich: 'It is fair to remember that Armstrong by and large denies that... You may not like the man, you may not like his way of life, but that is nothing to do with it. He is entitled to be acquitted if you have real doubts. But if, of course, you have no real doubts, then it is your duty to convict. So much for Patrick Armstrong.'

Mr Justice Donaldson followed a similar line with Carole Richardson, reciting lengthy extracts both from her confession statements and from her statement read from the dock which was not subject to cross-examination: 'Carole Richardson is not to be criticized, any more than any other accused is to be criticized, for not giving evidence on oath, or, for that matter, for not remaining silent. She had a free choice, she has made it and that choice points to neither guilt nor innocence. You may take her statement that she made from the dock as part of the matter which you have to weigh when you are considering a verdict. Whether you think it carries the same weight as it might have done if it had been tested by cross-examination is a matter entirely for you.'

Similarly, the judge gave an account of Richardson's alibi witnesses, with a reminder to the jury to search for the truth and to set aside the notion that 'you may not find them very attractive'. As no one apart from the judge had raised the question of how attractive they were, it appears to have been an unnecessary aside. 'You have heard Lisa Astin's evidence which, on the face of it, confirms Carole Richardson's present statement. You have heard Frank Johnson and you have to decide whether he confirms Lisa or whether he does not. You have to decide whether, really, when you take account of his previous statements and the way he gave evidence in the witness-box, he amounts to anything at all. We are not concerned with Frank Johnson's character. You are not concerned with it.' Mr Justice Donaldson had returned to the topic once again, solely to remind the jury that it did not matter.

Once more the jury was left with the dilemma of whether the apparent quality of detail in Richardson's confession was the best proof of her guilt or whether to believe her account that the statements had been dictated under duress. The judge all but brushed aside what was, perhaps, the most incongruous claim in any of the confessions: that she had been part of the team that bombed the second Guildford pub, the Seven Stars. The judge was content to accept the Crown's generous view of this confession: 'As far as the Seven Stars is concerned, the Crown do not suggest that she was, in fact, anything to do with planting the bomb there. They do not suggest that she went into the Seven Stars, although her fourth statement suggests that perhaps she did.'

The fourth statement went rather further than the possibility of a suggestion. It made the unequivocal claim that after leaving the bomb in the Horse and Groom she got in the car and drove for a while: 'I would say about five minutes. The road in which we stopped was badly lit and I didn't see any cars pass us or going in the opposite direction. The road was about 12 to 14 feet wide... We entered the pub which was, or looked like, old brick with, I think, a flat front... Inside the pub it wasn't so bright and the people seemed younger and I could hear music. The bar was curved round into a corner. The inside wasn't as nice as the Horse and Groom. I think there was a cigarette machine on one wall. There was a man standing at the bar, he was plump and he stood on my toes... We finished our drinks, left the pub and went back to the car.'

Sir Michael Havers had already told the jury that it did not matter who went into which pub, so why should the Crown want the jury to disregard such a statement? It contained a wealth of accurate detail about the width of Swan Lane and about the architecture, mood and layout of the pub — surely the sort of detail that only someone who had been inside could provide; the sort of detail that a false confession could not deliver. It was totally incriminating and it came from Carole Richardson's final statement which, otherwise, the Crown most relied upon. Yet at both the committal proceedings and the trial the Crown had been careful to stress that they did not wish to accept Carole Richardson's claim to have entered the Seven Stars. Why should she admit to more than even the Crown wanted to pin on her? Why was the Crown so reluctant to accept that this detailed confession, claimed as wholly voluntary by the police, was true?

The obvious answer is that if the Crown had accepted this part of the confession it would have so radically reduced the time available for the dash back to the South London Polytechnic as to make an implausible journey downright impossible. A five-minute drive, four minutes at the bar and time for a drink would have cut between 10 and 15 minutes at least off a journey time that the judge had already described as 'fairly fine'. When Carole Richardson made the statement about entering the Seven Stars, the police and Crown knew nothing of the prosecution witness Simon Moodie, whose evidence would make the getaway time from Guildford so crucial.

Richardson's claim to have bombed both pubs had to be discounted for the case against her to survive. As the prosecution denied the truth of her statement about entering the Seven Stars, they were bound to acknowledge that it could have come only from invention or suggestion. The Seven Stars statement, like the others, contains a mixture of accurate geographical detail and personal recollection such as that of the plump man treading on Richardson's toes. Invention? Suggestion? Truth? A real experience from another time and place transposed to the Seven Stars?

Discussing an earlier statement, Mr Justice Donaldson had examined the phrase 'I came out from the loo, where I bumped my head'. He told the jury that it had 'all the hallmarks of a voluntary statement and not a suggested statement'. The jury could have been excused a sense of confusion in trying to reconcile why a defendant's head bumped in the loo of one pub should sound authentic while a plump man treading on her toes at the bar of another should not, but the judge did not invite them to make the comparison. No attempt was made to explore the difficulties the Crown case would have been left in had they accepted Carole's presence in the second pub.

But more pertinent still were the correct architectural and geographical details about the Seven Stars itself. How could an invented statement guess accurately the width of Swan Lane or the internal layout of a pub, now that the defendant was no longer supposed to have entered it? Richardson's explanation was that all such detail had come via police dictation. The police denied it. Any suggestion of dictation would, of course, have demolished the case against Richardson and the rest.

Much had been made of the fact that Carole Richardson had been the only one of the defendants (or witnesses) to lodge a complaint about alleged police brutality in custody. But now Mr Justice Donaldson was to turn the point on its head: 'If, in fact, Carole Richardson were right in her allegations, you may wonder whether the police officers would ever have admitted that she had made a complaint. But, you know, she did make a complaint at Brixton Prison and those officers readily admitted that she had made a complaint. You may think that gives some pointer to the reliability of the police officers' evidence in this matter, although it is entirely a matter for you... Is it not significant that there is no challenge that the matter was reported? Members of the jury, would the complaint have been reported if Detective Constable Wise was the sort of man that Carole

Richardson says that he was?' Mr Justice Donaldson's triumphant crescendo was, at this point, impeded by a rare interjection from the defence team. Eric Myers QC gently pointed out that prison officers had been present at the interview in question so 'it really goes to whether the police really had any choice, if that is the right way of putting it'.

The judge generously conceded that this was the right way of putting it, that the police had had no choice but to report the complaint as the prison officers might have testified to it independently. Nevertheless, the judge's interesting idea that '... you may wonder whether the police officers would ever have admitted [a defendant's complaint of brutality]' was not advanced on behalf of any of the other defendants.

As with the others, the case against Carole Richardson ultimately stood or fell on the confessions — on the quality of detail they contained and on the disputed method of their taking: 'The only people who can substantiate those allegations are the police officers and Carole Richardson... All those officers deny on oath that there is any truth in those allegations of brutality whatsoever. Carole Richardson has alleged it but, of course, the allegation is made in a statement from the dock and is not on oath. You will have to weigh the matter.'

For Hill and Conlon, Mr Justice Donaldson followed the same pattern of reading their confession statements at some length; recalling their explanations from the witness-box; and reviewing their alibi evidence. The arguments and counter-arguments were by now familiar but in the case of Hill, as the one to have confessed first and thereby set off the chain reaction of arrests and confessions, it was especially important to understand why he should have made false confessions in the first place. 'What he says is "I did not do it [confess] because I was battered into a pulp by the police or anything of that sort." He says, "I could have stood all that, but they made it perfectly clear that they were going to charge Gina and I made these confessions to stop them charging Gina."'

Was this plausible? 'Certainly they were in love,' the judge allowed, 'no doubt about it, no dispute about it, but would he have been prepared to confess to murder to get her off the hook and what sort of hook was she on anyway? She may, perhaps, have been under suspicion by the police, but why should Hill have thought she was in any real danger of being convicted? You have to weigh the possibilities in this. You may like to go on to consider too, even assuming that he thought that she was going to be convicted of murder if he did not do something, and even if he thought that in these circumstances it was right for him to confess to murder, why would that get her off the hook?'

These were hard questions to answer. Hill's QC had put forward the additional suggestion that Hill was a compulsive and imaginative talker, by implication a fantasist who proved to be his own worst enemy. There were numerous theories about why Hill may have wanted to avoid returning to Belfast but these could not be introduced without prejudicing the present case (besides, Hill had always denied fearing reprisals from the IRA in Belfast). For his part, he has maintained to this day his claim that everything sprang from the fear that his pregnant girlfriend would be falsely implicated. By the judge's reasoning it was a less than compelling argument, although if Hill was innocent and found himself in the dreadful position of being wrongfully charged with mass murder then anything must have seemed possible. It would have been much easier for Hill, then or now, to have blamed his confessions on the brutality he claimed to have suffered, but he has always insisted that this was incidental.

The judge drew particular attention to the end of Hill's second statement: 'Something which you may think is important, but it is a matter for you, is that at the end of this statement Hill wrote in his own handwriting: "I knew what was going on and pubs would be blown up and people would be killed. I am sorry now as I had no option, as I knew what would happen to me. I have made this true statement under no pressure or threat and what I have done I will now pay for in a court of law."' Under cross-examination Hill agreed that there had been no pressure, just suggestion, repeating his cynical view that 'It made no difference what I said.'

Quite apart from the subjective question of whether the postscript rang with the authentic tones of a newly repentant IRA terrorist, its significance is surely no more nor less than that of the content of the rest of the confessions. If, as Hill claimed throughout, he was trying to tell the police what he thought they wanted, indeed to convince them of his involvement, it is just the sort of addition he would have complied with or even volunteered.

Mr Justice Donaldson's final words cannot have given Paul Hill much optimism: 'Finally, as with all these confessions, you may wonder how it is possible to produce quite so detailed a confession if it is not true. You will wonder whether there is any other reason, because certainly none has been suggested, for making such a suggestion, other than it was true. There it is.'

The summary of the case for and against Gerard Conlon was the shortest. There were only two confessions to recite and there was no third party to corroborate his alibi. Although Carole Richardson's case was possibly distinct in that she appeared to have the strongest alibi, it was clear that the cases against the three young men from Belfast would stand or fall together. 'You will take account of the fact that he could have disappeared to Eire or somewhere else after the bombings but did not do so, that he was at home, his own home, when he was arrested. You will take full account of the fact that he left England under his own name. How much weight you think proper to give to those matters is, of course, entirely a matter for you, but it is right that I should remind you that those points were made. It is also right that I should remind you... that in these statements, Conlon's statements, there is no sentence in his own handwriting saying that the statements were made of his own free will. It is entirely a matter for you whether you think that is significant. The officer who took the statements said it was not his practice to invite the person making the statement to so include such a sentence. Perhaps it occurred to you that if you have a situation in which, as Conlon says, he was so scared that he was prepared to confess to murder, whether the same amount of scaring might not easily cause him to add a sentence that the statement was made of his own free will. But at any rate, if that point has any validity, no doubt you will take the fullest account of it. I will say no more about Conlon's case.' The judge here seemed unaware of any double standard set alongside the significance he had attached to the fact that other defendants had added just such handwritten testimonies of fair treatment.

It was approaching 11.20 a.m. on the second day of the summing-up. Mr Justice Donaldson was now on his 126th and final page: 'These crimes which were undoubtedly committed at Guildford and Woolwich are abominable crimes and there is no doubt about that, but the issue is not whether they were abominable crimes, it is not whether they were committed. The issue is whether any of these four accused were guilty of committing them. You have to look at these statements and you have to make up your minds how they came to be made. You may think the statements, on their face at least, disclose an extraordinary knowledge of the detail of the way in which these offences were committed. You may well wonder whether these particular people, three of whom you have seen in the witness-box, are the sort of people who would confess to murder when they had nothing whatever to do with it... But if, of course, in the end you have real doubts about the guilt of any of them, then naturally you will find them not guilty because the Crown would have failed to prove the case. But if, on the other hand, you are sure at the end of your discussions, then it is plainly your duty to bring in verdicts of guilty.'

The four defendants were returned to their cells in the bowels of the Old Bailey and the jury retired to consider their verdicts.

29
VERDICTS

'The English language is rich in words but no single one can adequately describe your crime.'

Mr Justice Donaldson, October 22 1975

The all-male jury was out for 27 hours. At Sir Michael Havers's prompting, the Old Bailey jury bailiff was posted outside their retiring-room — an unsettling final reminder of the high-security overtones of the case. They were taken to their London hotel under armed escort, and there was further armed protection at the hotel overnight. They had been told by the judge that it was of the greatest importance to the Crown, to the defendants and to the public that unanimous verdicts be reached.

At 2.07 p.m. on Wednesday October 22 they returned with unanimous verdicts on every charge. As each of the 33 outstanding charges was recited, the foreman said, 'Guilty.' The clerk of the court turned to address the four defendants: 'You severally stand convicted of murder. Have you or any of you anything to say why the court should not give you judgment of imprisonment of life according to the law?' There was no reply. Carole Richardson buried her head in her arms and began to cry. She was comforted by a wardress.

Christopher Rowe, the Assistant Chief Constable of Surrey, now returned briefly to centre stage to inform the court of Paul Hill's murder conviction from Belfast. The four defence barristers offered what mitigation they could muster — not an easy task when the defence had maintained throughout that their clients were totally innocent.

Eric Myers QC reminded the judge that Carole Richardson

had been only 17 at the time of the offence which meant that there was no flexibility in setting her murder sentence. It had to be detention during Her Majesty's pleasure. Arthur Mildon, QC for Paul Hill, said that if — as the jury must believe — the statements were essentially true, then his client, only 20 at the time, must have been operating under orders. John Leonard, QC for Armstrong, had a new document to place before the court, a report prepared by, according to the judge's description, 'a distinguished consultant psychiatrist of a London hospital'. It revealed that his client 'was always timid and has often been ragged... To sum up, Armstrong is a timid man who avoids trouble, in particular physical violence. He appears to be frightened of authoritarian figures, perhaps particularly those in uniform. It is unlikely that the drugs Armstrong has taken seriously impaired his judgement at the time he was making his statements, but fear of violence by the police and the fact that he had been deprived of sleep may have greater relevance.' Lord Wigoder, QC for Conlon, said, 'I do not think it would be appropriate or helpful to address the court on behalf of Conlon.' Mr Justice Donaldson then retired for 20 minutes to consider his sentences and closing remarks.

Carole Richardson was sentenced to life imprisonment on the charges of causing explosions and on five counts of murder. There was no sentence for the conspiracy charge. 'It will be for Her Majesty's Secretary of State to decide how the order in respect of the murder convictions is implemented... You may go.' According to one report, Carole Richardson blurted out, 'You bastard,' before disappearing from sight.

Mr Justice Donaldson turned to the three young men from Belfast: 'Your crime was not directed at those you killed, it was directed at the community as a whole, every man, woman and child living in this country. You obviously expected to strike terror into their hearts and thereby to achieve your objectives. If you had known our countrymen better, you would have realized it was a vain expectation... The English language is rich in words but no single one can adequately describe your crime... It was a callous crime, it was a cowardly crime and, in particular, it was a completely pointless crime and one which will be remembered only for its infamy.

'Having been sentenced to life imprisonment, you may think that you can expect to be released in 12 to 15 years. That is a widely held view, but it is also a very dangerous view... The idea that life means 12 to 15 years dates from the days when the sentence for murder was death. Only when there were extenuating circumstances were murderers reprieved and sentenced to life imprisonment, and it was the reprieved murderers who were released after such a period. None of you three men would have been in this category. You would have been executed. The sentence of life imprisonment in your cases must be altogether different... it must be doubtful whether any question of release will arise during the lifetime of the trial judge.' Mr Justice Donaldson had celebrated his 55th birthday during the trial.

For Gerard Conlon this meant life with a formal recommendation of not less than 30 years. 'But I must stress the words "not less than",' said the judge. 'I do not mean by my recommendation to give you any reason for hoping that after 35 years you will necessarily be released.'

Patrick Armstrong's life sentence was longer — not less than 35 years, with a similar warning: 'I do not mean by this recommendation to give you, either, any reason for hoping that after 35 years you will necessarily be released.' In this instant Armstrong became the recipient of the longest minimum recommended sentence under the Murder (Abolition of Death Penalty) Act 1965. The dubious honour of holding this record was not to remain his for long.

'Paul Hill,' Mr Justice Donaldson declared, 'your case is by far the worst... The wording of the 1965 Act is such that I cannot formally recommend that you never be released... In my view your crime is such that life must mean life. If as an act of mercy you are ever to be released it could only be on account of great age or infirmity. Very well.' The trial was over.

Hill, Armstrong and Conlon were taken below without reaction. Mrs Lily Hill, who had attended most of the trial, shouted out from the public gallery, 'Don't worry, son. You won't have to do it.' Outside, Mrs Hill tried to reassure Hill's girlfriend, Gina Clarke, who was nursing Paul's seven-week-old baby girl, Kara, born a week before the trial opened. Gina Clarke eventually left with a reporter from *The Sun* who had been observed helping with the baby in the Old Bailey corridors as the trial was in progress.

The following morning's press was wholly unquestioning about the verdicts and the police investigation that had secured them. As discussed in Chapter 10, there was widespread confusion as to how the first arrest had been made — unsurprising since even now the authorities seem unable to agree.

Interviewed by Barry Penrose for BBC Television's *Nine O'Clock News*, Detective Chief Superintendent Wally Simmons provided a less colourful story than that printed by Fleet Street the following morning. 'Very early in the inquiry,' Simmons said, 'we received some information from an intelligence officer in Belfast naming a suspect [Hill] and from there... we sent officers across to Belfast to follow up this information. We started getting addresses in this country at which he could be found. We followed a lot of them up — they were false leads — until eventually we got the information that he was in Southampton and they brought him back.'

Simmons was not claiming that the entire team had been caught. 'I believe there were others,' he told Penrose. 'We are still making enquiries along those lines... I have grave suspicions as to the identity of the other people.'

'Do you think also that you know the identity perhaps of the second girl, the missing girl, in the other bomb party?' Penrose asked.

'Yes, I do,' said Simmons. 'I believe we know the identity of her. There's a great difference, of course, as you well know, between knowing and being in a position to prove a fact.'

This was, perhaps, a little defeatist on Simmons's part. Under a legal system that allowed extended detention under the Prevention of Terrorism Act and conviction on the basis of uncorroborated confessions alone, the public might have expected a criminal of this order to be detained for questioning — provided she was in the country. The fact that she was appeared to be established the following morning in the *Guardian*: 'The Surrey Police believe they know the names of the other people involved and that two of them are now in Southern Ireland while another girl is in England.' These tantalizing details seem to have stimulated very little action by Surrey Police in the following years, for there have been no further charges despite the continuing freedom of three suspects whose identities are supposedly known to the original investigating force. Technically, the case is still open, but no officer is assigned to it.

Anne McHardy, the *Guardian* reporter who was for many years the newspaper's Northern Ireland correspondent and who covered a series of major terrorist trials in Belfast and London, now recalls two other impressions of the case, which she sat through from the beginning: 'I have always felt a sense of unease about it. There was something not quite right about the defendants. They didn't seem to have the right calibre, the right stuff for these sort of offences. They didn't have the self-contained air of tough Provos. But there was never any doubt throughout the case that they were going to be convicted... '

Amid much speculative and colourful reporting, nobody had found any fresh information to tie the defendants to the IRA. Frontline Provisionals are consistently picked, for security reasons, from families with long-established histories of active Republicanism. Neither the press nor the police attempted to link the Guildford defendants with any of the other unsolved terrorist offences of the previous autumn. The Metropolitan Police Bomb Squad had nothing to say to the media. Surrey Police took the glory.

'Surrey Police were publicly delighted with themselves,' the *Guardian* reported. 'Even subsequent events, including the dropping of the murder charges against four people, have not dimmed their certainty that they had penetrated the heart of the terrorists' organisation.'

The *Daily Mail* and the *Daily Telegraph* both led on Carole Richardson. The *Mail* featured an interview with her mother, Mrs Anne Richardson, who said her daughter had talked of studying in prison to be a veterinary surgeon but had jokingly ruled it out because the course of study supposedly involved chemistry and 'she wouldn't be able to study that at the moment'. This anecdote of Carole's joke prompted the banner headline 'Terror Girl With No Pity'. The *Daily Telegraph* topped their background piece with 'Girl Who Planted Explosives In Army Pub Had Tried To Join WRAC'. The implication was, as it had been in court, that Carole Richardson had used the job application as reconnaissance for IRA purposes. The problem with this notion was that it had been her friend Patsy Melody's idea in the first place and the interview had taken place four months before Carole Richardson met any of her co-defendants and before their arrival in England. Further, the prosecution had never sought to establish that Richardson was a long-time accomplice of any group or had been involved in anything prior to the day of the Guildford bombings.

The Sun boasted its exclusive pictures of Paul Hill's baby and a letter from Carole Richardson to Lisa Astin, written in the Old Bailey cells. Her understanding of the dynamics of the case was naïvely different from that of the court reporters and defence solicitors, who had all been certain that the verdicts would be guilty:

It's dinner time, thank God. My backside is killing me. Six weeks on these chairs will seem like a lifetime. At least it will be over soon. Book a barrel of Newcastle Brown Ale and a pint mug somewhere... God Bless the Innocent and May the Guilty be Brought to Justice.

Lisa Astin gave Barry Penrose a sharply edited interview for
BBC Television news, although she remembers it was not
before she had had rather too much to drink. Penrose wanted
to know whether she might have been involved in the Guildford
bombings herself, under the influence of drugs.

'No, I don't think it is possible. Only it could have happened,
but I think I would have remembered by now.'

'But,' Penrose persisted, 'do you think, looking back to a year
ago, that you were being used by IRA men in London?'

'Well, if we were,' she replied, 'I certainly wasn't conscious
of it.'

The *Surrey Daily Advertiser*, meanwhile, was on the
streets of Guildford on the afternoon directly following the trial
sentences. A front-page editorial gave voice to the prevailing
local attitude towards the bombers and the police:

> The quality of mercy is strained to the limit in attempting
> to feel anything but loathing and revulsion for those who
> have been convicted of the mindless carnage at the Horse
> and Groom in Guildford last year. One must regard these
> people as the most warped among the dregs of humanity,
> yet they are aged between 18 and 24 and could pass in a
> bar as ordinary, normal human beings. Our society will be
> rid of them for a very long time and we hope that the cry
> for political amnesty will not, one day, be used as an excuse
> to free them. This was the crime of planned, callous murder.
> In Surrey, aside from the numbing horror of the facts them-
> selves, most concern will be felt over the many calculated
> attacks on the police which were made at the Old Bailey. This
> is the classic defence of prisoners who have nothing else to
> rely on. In pursuit of justice, defending counsel have a duty to
> make these allegations and the press to report them. Today,
> when the trial is over, we hasten, on behalf of the people of
> Surrey, to assure the police of our boundless admiration and
> gratitude for the vigorous and determined way they handled

the case. Our confidence in them is increased, not diminished. We dismiss the contemptible accusations of brutality and intimidation and congratulate the police witnesses on the fortitude and patience with which they bore them. Surrey is proud of its police and the way they rose to this ghastly challenge. It is the one cause for satisfaction in this nightmare crime.

The Editor

Christopher Rowe, who had just been awarded the Queen's Police Medal in the most recent honours list, phlegmatically told the paper that the outcome was satisfactory: 'We don't get worked up about verdicts but they justified 12 months of hard work by police officers and civilian staff... I am quite sure we have not got the lot. It was planned from Northern Ireland and we have not got the men above. There must be others involved.' Rowe did not divulge the grounds for his knowledge or for the theory that the offence had been planned from Northern Ireland. He confirmed his belief that Paul Hill's first statement 'was basically true', except in its saying the bomb factory was in Brixton — and that this was to divert attention away from North London. He admitted that without the Prevention of Terrorism Act, which enabled police to detain suspects for up to seven days, their task would have been 'very difficult'. With regard to the accusations of brutality against him and his force, Rowe was remarkably sanguine: 'This is the classic IRA defence; in fact, it is their only defence, which means we must have done our job well. Anyone who contemplates losing his temper when interrogating may as well give up the police force.'

Rowe had two final thoughts: 'The situation in Northern Ireland will probably change in a couple of years and they'll all be released as political prisoners! All we want to do now is solve the Caterham bombings.'

In contrast to the diplomatic public pronouncements of Rowe and Simmons, the private anger of Surrey Police at what they saw as the enforced release of McGuinness, Anderson, Colman and Mullin — the four men originally charged with the Guildford bombings but freed owing to a lack of any evidence against them — now spilled over into a remarkable unattributable briefing to Colin Pratt of the *Daily Express*. On October 23, the *Express* splashed the startling headline 'Bomb Police Muzzled: How Government Veto Let Suspects Go Free'. The story claimed: 'Surrey Police were given written instructions from the office of the Director of Public Prosecutions. These indicated that the Government believed that charges of conspiracy left open too many avenues of doubt.

'The police were anxious to file charges of conspiracy to murder against a number of people,' the *Express* continued, but '... after weeks of grinding detective work the police had to drop a line of inquiry which could have resulted in a number of conspiracy charges. In the words of one senior detective, "We were forced by the very people supposed to be responsible for law and order to let some right villains get away with it." The reasons were never meant to be made public. But such was the outrage of the detectives who worked round the clock to bring the bombers to justice that the word was leaked out.'

The allegations produced an angry reaction in the House of Commons. The Home Secretary denounced the story as 'false, irresponsible and malevolent', but the *Express* refused to retract. The row bubbled on for a week. The Solicitor General, Peter Archer, made a statement reiterating that all the charges against McGuinness and the others had been dropped because of insufficient evidence; this statement was supported in Parliament by Sir Michael Havers. But the *Express*, largely unrepentant, concluded its editorial reply, 'Lord Hailsham believes... it is the Government's intention to retain the charge of conspiracy in dealing with terrorism. We hope that's true. It goes against what we have been told by men who are in the front line in the fight against terrorism. They, too, are honourable men.'

Most of the remaining morning press coverage concentrated on the severity of the sentences and on the police route to Paul

Hill. One fresh point emerged from the Press Association, the country's most trusted news agency. Bernard Scarlett, the chief crime reporter, noted that Paul Hill would serve his sentence in England and not in Northern Ireland, where he had been sentenced to life imprisonment for his part in the Brian Shaw killing: 'He was safer, police felt, in an English prison, because the IRA had sentenced him to death for "squealing".'

On their first morning as convicted terrorists, the Guildford Four did not have the front pages to themselves. The end of the trial coincided with the beginning of the Monasterevin siege in the Irish Republic. Nobody suspected that the two events might have been connected, however remotely. The siege showed the IRA at its worst. Eddie Gallagher and Marion Coyle (first cousin of Marlene Coyle) had kidnapped Dr Tiede Herrema, a Dutch industrialist working in Ireland, and were holding him captive in appalling conditions in a council house in Monasterevin, County Laoise. His ordeal was to last 36 days. For much of the time he was kept bound and blindfolded, with his ears plugged. Gallagher knocked out one of his teeth with the butt of his gun.

Gallagher and Marion Coyle represented a breakaway faction of a brand that intermittently afflicts the IRA during internal debates about the level of violence to be maintained. They had lost the argument over the ill-fated cease-fires at the beginning of 1975 and were now operating independently. They saw themselves as heroic, unswerving Republicans, but in the eyes of everyone else — including the Army Council of the Provisional IRA — they were fanatic gangsters. Senior Provisionals were particularly anxious to get their hands on the proceeds of an Irish bank robbery staged by Gallagher and Coyle in June 1975 at Navan in County Meath. A sum of £97,000 was missing from IRA funds. Gallagher, former deputy director of operations and a key figure in setting up the 1974 active service units, was *persona non grata*.

The split dated from the Feakle talks between the Provisionals and Protestant clergymen in County Clare in December 1974. Daithi O'Conaill, then Chief of Staff, had sought a Christmas cease-fire to allow a twin-track of political initiatives and military regrouping. His main opponent was Kevin Mallon, who had wanted outright war and refused to speak to the clergymen in Feakle. Mallon was Marion Coyle's lover. When Kevin Mallon was arrested for IRA activities, one of which was a prison break-out staged by Gallagher, and sentenced again by the Irish courts in the summer of 1975, Marion Coyle openly denounced O'Conaill as a tout. Now, from the besieged house in Monasterevin, the price for Dr Herrema's life was the release of Mallon and Dr Bridget Rose Dugdale, the former English heiress who had staged the Beit art robbery with, among others, Harry Duggan. Eddie Gallagher was the father of Dugdale's baby and they were later to marry in prison. As the siege dragged on, Scotland Yard announced that they wanted Gallagher in connection with recent unspecified bombings in England — but not the latest wave that had begun with the Caterham Arms explosion. Gallagher and Marion Coyle were duly captured and sentenced in Dublin to 20 and 15 years respectively.

As Marion Coyle was led away to begin her sentence after three years on the run, her mother shouted 'Nazis' at the court officials. Mrs Susan Coyle declared, 'As far as I am concerned Marion is the greatest girl in the world.' The Coyles were a remarkable Republican clan from Bogside in Londonderry. Marion's brother Philip was then serving five years in Northern Ireland for a firearms offence; her late Uncle Joe had been a staff captain in the IRA with a *cumann* (branch) named after him in the city. His daughter Marlene, whose photofit had been prematurely released by Surrey Police in the immediate aftermath of the Guildford bombings, and who was wanted in conjunction with Kieran McMorrow, has never been arrested.

McMorrow was eventually arrested by Irish police in a St Patrick's Day gun battle in a quarry in County Cavan near the Northern Ireland border. He was gaoled in Dublin for 10 years on firearms and explosives charges, after refusing to plead, dismissing his lawyers and conducting his own defence in Irish. When he was released in 1987, Scotland Yard took no extradition action against him on the 59 terrorist offences — including the M62 coach bombing — with which they had publicly associated him in the 1970s.

The concluding irony of the newspaper reports on the end of the Guildford trial in 1975 was that the publication time of the *Surrey Daily Advertiser* enabled it to carry one other story on its front page which had broken too late for the national morning press. The bombers of the Caterham Arms — and, by their own account, of the Guildford and Woolwich pubs — had struck again. It was, perhaps, their most wretched killing. The previous day, one of the London Active Service Unit had telephoned the home of Conservative MP Hugh Fraser, enquiring what time he left his London home in the morning. The Frasers' cook unsuspectingly told the caller that it was usually at 9.00 a.m. Joseph O'Connell had devised a new sort of bomb with a device known as a micro-switch — 'a button that was safe when it was pressed down. When it was released it went up.' In the face of ever-increasing public alertness to IRA bombings, the device avoided the difficulty of placing time bombs in public places and the hazards of fast getaways from short-fuse throw bombs.

During the night after the Guildford convictions, Eddie Butler went to Campden Hill Square in North Kensington with an unidentified member of the Unit and placed a micro-switch bomb under the front wheel of Hugh Fraser's Jaguar, which was parked outside his house: 'I covered the man who was setting that one down. It was in a very small carrier-bag, or shoulder-bag or something. We picked that particular car and that particular area because it belonged to Fraser. He was a target. He'd been put on our list by the Active Service Unit. We'd been told to get certain politicians but we weren't told names. We just picked Fraser on our own. The bomb would have exploded when he revved his car. It was about 14 pounds of explosives.'

Hugh Fraser never reached his car. Shortly before 9.00 p.m. the package was spotted by a man walking his dog — Professor

Gordon Hamilton-Fairley, an eminent cancer specialist at St Bartholomew's Hospital. Bending over to investigate, he activated the micro-switch and was killed outright by the explosion. Joseph O'Connell, Eddie Butler, Harry Duggan and Hugh Doherty were subsequently convicted of the killing. O'Connell told the police, 'We turned to killer bombs for effect. Our targets were establishment targets and we wanted to cut down on hurting innocent people, and just get the targets. We didn't mean to get the professor. He must have pulled it out or something. The target was Fraser.'

But for the moment the Metropolitan Police had no idea who had planted the Campden Hill Square bomb, and Surrey Police had no idea who had placed the Caterham Arms bomb. Whatever satisfaction the public might have derived from the record sentences meted out to the Guildford defendants, it was swiftly overtaken by this gruesome reminder of the continuing potency of the London Active Service Unit.

30
MAGUIRES ON TRIAL

'I am innocent, you bastards. No — no — no!'

Anne Maguire, on hearing the verdict at her trial, March 4 1976

The trial of the Maguire household for unlawful possession of nitroglycerine opened on January 27 1976 and lasted for over a month. There was, said the judge, no connection between their case and that of the Guildford bombers, beyond the fact that some of the accused were related to Gerry Conlon and that one of them claimed to have come to England on hearing of Conlon's arrest. He quite properly did not remind the jury that Anne Maguire had originally been held for murder at Guildford; or that, thanks to remarks attributed by police to her nephew and reported at the trial by the media, headlines had splashed across numerous newspapers in Britain about 'Aunt Annie's Bomb Kitchen'. Nor did he mention the further connection, namely that at the Guildford trial, as now, the prosecution had been led by Sir Michael Havers and he himself, Sir John Donaldson, had presided.

In the absence of other firm evidence, the prosecution case rested on the reliability of the tests for nitroglycerine that had been carried out on the defendants' hands. Apart from Pat O'Neill's children, 10 people had been at the house in Third Avenue on the afternoon and evening of December 3 1974. Six of them had apparently been found with traces of nitroglycerine. The exceptions were Anne Maguire herself, her second son, John, her eight-year-old daughter, Anne-Marie, and Hugh Maguire's friend Sean Tully. But Anne had been charged on the grounds that nitroglycerine had been found on at least one household glove belonging to her.

'Unless you are satisfied by the scientific evidence that nitroglycerine was present on those people's hands or, as the case may be, on the gloves, it would be quite unsafe to convict any of them,' Mr Justice Donaldson told the jury at the start of his summing-up. 'In other words, if you are in real doubt as to whether the material which was analysed was nitroglycerine or [another substance], that must be the end of the case because you must be in doubt about whether any of them had anything to do with nitroglycerine at all.'

From the outset, therefore, the judge impressed upon the jurors' minds the importance of the principle at stake. The prosecution was claiming that in the test for explosives that had been performed on the hands of the accused, the behaviour of nitroglycerine was unique and could not be confused with that of any other substance.

The judge told the jury that they must be 'sure' the prosecution had proved its case, and he went on to explain this: 'What is meant by "sure" is that [the prosecution] must make you sure that the offence has been committed. If you are not sure; if you have a reasonable doubt, not a fanciful doubt but a real doubt about the matter... you must bring in a verdict of not guilty.'

It was not enough, of course, for the members of the jury simply to accept that the test indicated traces of nitroglycerine; they also had to satisfy themselves that these traces were part of a larger body of explosive that had been handled knowingly by the accused. The judge had been careful to make this point early in his summing-up; the prosecution had to convince the jury to the extent that they were 'sure' that this larger 'bulk' of explosive existed. The fact was that no such bulk had ever been discovered, either in the house or in the neighbourhood.

One curious feature was that the search of the house in Third Avenue had been incomplete. The attic had been left untouched. The boarded-up fireplaces had not been ripped out. Even Guiseppe Conlon's suitcase was found by his wife, Sarah, when she arrived a week later, unopened, undisturbed. Did the police seriously believe this was a bomb factory, given that their search was so perfunctory? It was a point to which the judge alluded only when pressed by counsel for the defence.

But, in the end, underlying the prosecution case was the contention that IRA bombs were being made or stored at 43 Third Avenue. The arrest of Gerry Conlon and the disappearance of Hugh Maguire had 'produced a state of crisis or panic' in the household and, in Sir Michael Havers's phrase, it had been 'all hands to the pump' within the 'closely-knit group' to move the nitroglycerine in expectation of a raid. The explosive, which has a consistency similar to that of marzipan, had been 'kneaded' and packed into small bags in such a way that it was said to have become impacted under the fingernails of all the defendants except Anne. (Vincent, young Patrick and Pat O'Neill were allegedly found to have traces under their nails but not on their hands.) So there really was no possibility, the Crown argued, of an innocent contamination — such as through chance contact with a doorknob or a towel.

Where, then, was the nitroglycerine and when had it been spirited away? Having raised this vital question at the start of his judgment, Mr Justice Donaldson failed to return to it directly, except in dealing with the misgivings of the principal witness for the defence, John Yallop. Yallop had identified several disturbing features about the case which, in conjunction with his misgivings about the test itself, had brought him to a conclusion that it would not be safe to convict. The first of these was the anomaly of six people with nitroglycerine on their hands moving around in a house in which no trace of explosive had been found; it was 'decidedly queer', he considered, that they had not extended their professional expertise in cleaning the house to cleaning their own hands. He was further puzzled by the fact that nothing else was ever found — no explosives, detonators, timing devices, batteries or wire. Then there was the inexplicable matter of how the police sniffer device — and dogs — had entirely failed to detect traces of explosive vapour in the drawer where Anne's contaminated gloves had been stored. Yallop said he would have regarded the sniffer as a confirmatory test for explosive — and it had registered negative. Finally, he found it hard to believe that knowing the dangers of handling nitroglycerine, Anne Maguire should apparently have been alone in protecting herself with gloves. Nitroglycerine is rapidly absorbed through the skin into the bloodstream and gives the handler a blinding headache, known to scientists as an 'NG headache'. Would Anne Maguire have worn gloves while allowing her children to use their bare hands? The judge interrupted Yallop in this catalogue in order to comment that this was hardly 'expert' evidence.

In his judgment, Mr Justice Donaldson commented, 'One possible thought that may occur to you is that the material was not in the house but somewhere else, we just don't know where.' He then discussed Yallop's point about the missing detonators: 'If somebody was concealing explosives... it would be a bit silly to leave the detonators behind, so was not Mr Yallop perhaps searching around rather desperately if that really was a point which bothered him?... So you may think that these last points don't amount to very much.' In dismissing the detonators he omitted to mention the far more crucial question of the 'bulk' of explosive. Thereby was one of the major flaws in the prosecution obscured for good.

The comings and goings in the house had been so many that it was not possible, on agreed timings, for everyone to have been working on the explosive simultaneously; but there was one period, said the judge, when Paddy Maguire, Guiseppe Conlon, Pat O'Neill and Sean Smyth had admitted spending time together: '"We went down to the pub; we had a very short time there; we got through one quick round; we were about to start the second round when we were interrupted by the police."' From before 7.00 p.m. the house had been under surveillance by the police. The defendants insisted they had left home some time after 8.00 p.m., fastening the time on to Mrs O'Neill's telephone call from the hospital to her husband, which had been prearranged for eight o'clock. But the police evidence was different. According to the judge, the men 'were seen going to the pub at 7.45 and the arrest in the pub must have taken place after 8.45, between 8.45 and 9.00'.

The fact that the men agreed they had only just begun their second round when the police arrived was viewed by the judge as significant. 'Contrasting time for a fairly quick pint and moving on to the next pint within an hour, and in the light of the drinking habits of which you have heard from Mr Maguire at any rate, can those two timings stand together? There is something wrong there somewhere, is there not? It is a matter for you. And if in fact the four accused are not telling the truth about the time they were in the public house, why aren't they telling the truth?... At any rate, that is a period of time to which quite obviously you will want to give rather special attention.'

The suggestion inherent in this was that the men had used about half an hour of their time in the pub not for drinking but for disposing of the 'bulk' of nitroglycerine in a hiding-place so secure that it was never to be found; and, furthermore, that this had been achieved under the noses of the two police officers who had been sent to keep 43 Third Avenue under surveillance. The disputed period became known as the 'missing half-hour'. The judge had instructed the jury that they must decide the case exclusively on the evidence they had heard, yet he had used the confusion about the amount of time spent in the pub to open the jury's minds to new and unsubstantiated possibilities as to how the 'bulk' could have been shifted — despite the fact that the Crown had produced no evidence that the men had ever left the pub prior to being arrested there. And since he did this in the closing pages of his judgment it was, in effect, his final comment on the missing 'bulk'.

But on another matter the judge was far more explicit, returning to it several times. This was the statement by Vincent Maguire that he had found a long, thick stick of chalk under the bed on the day in question when looking for scattered playing-cards. Vincent knew perfectly well it was chalk, but on being told that traces of nitroglycerine had been found on his hands,

casting about for a possible explanation and hearing his young
brother, Patrick, crying in the next-door cell, he had said to DC
Bray, who was questioning him, 'The only thing I can remember
is a candle thing I found under Sean's bed... about eight inches
long and smooth like a sort of wax. I could get my fingers right
round it. I don't know what it was, it had bits broken off one end.
It was like a big candle really.'

When this description was read out to him in court, Douglas
Higgs, the principal scientific officer for the Crown, commented,
'Well, it doesn't suggest a candle... In my experience, having seen
things which perhaps fit more aptly the description you have giv-
en, there are sticks of gelignite with white wrappers about eight
inches long, one inch in diameter... These are sticks of explosive
which are wrapped in wax paper and therefore they would have
that waxy appearance which would seem to fit in... '

In his summing-up, the judge reported Vincent's account of
the context of his admission about the chalk: '"Harvey ran at
me with his forearm against my throat up against the wall. He
twisted my head. He hit me in the stomach. It hurt and I cried.
There was no other violence. I decided to tell the story about the
candle when I heard Patrick scream... " Do you think the police
officers really have got it wrong? Do you think they are lying? If,
of course, you think that Vincent really did talk about a candle
and wax, do you think that he was beaten up, and do you think
he said it because he was beaten up?... You no doubt will consider
whether, if he was really beaten up like that, he would not have
complained to somebody at the time... But really, in the end, of
course, what you will want to make up your minds about is this:
was it true that Vincent handled something which Mr Higgs says
is a good description of gelignite? It was young Patrick who was
asked about the stick of white material and he said, "It is chalk.
I got it from school. The gym master gave it to me." And young
Patrick, you know, he also alleged that he was beaten up... If it
is untrue, why is he lying? Why is Vincent lying? Is young Patrick
simply supporting Vincent in a lie? And what about Vincent? Is
he lying because he regrets now having told the truth about this

stick of gelignite? Well, it is a matter for you... ' Vincent himself had never suggested that the stick might be gelignite. But with this extrapolation the judge deftly planted in the jury's minds the impression that the stick of chalk was a stick of gelignite. In his apparent obsession with this spurious piece of evidence, he did not see fit to repeat the fact, acknowledged by Higgs in cross-examination, that the chalk could not possibly have been gelignite or the sniffer would have detected it.

The 'candle' affair was an illustration of how sinister inferences were drawn from incidental details in the case. There were other examples. Some emphasis was laid on the claim that in an inflamed and drunken argument with a housing officer, Paddy Maguire, whose relations with Anne had at times been tempestuous, had once demanded that his name be removed from the tenancy of the house in Third Avenue because it might be 'blown up'. The judge returned to this incident twice in his judgment without referring to Maguire's explanation that the house had a dangerous, faulty gas meter.

The immigration officer at Heysham alleged that Guiseppe Conlon had told him he was going to Surrey to pick up a vehicle. Conlon contended that the officer had confused him with the passenger he had overheard talking on the ferry, who had been just ahead of him in the queue. The fact that before his departure Conlon had informed the RUC at Springfield Road police barracks of the real reason for his journey failed to dispel the impression endorsed by the judge that Conlon had lied to immigration control. It was not until 1981 that a letter was obtained from the RUC confirming that Guiseppe had indeed told the RUC exactly where he was going and why.

When the telegram announcing Conlon's arrival reached Third Avenue, Paddy Maguire had neither informed his wife nor telephoned the solicitor in Belfast, which struck the judge as suspicious — though to a lay observer it demonstrated nothing more odd than the lack of close ties between the Conlons and the Paddy Maguires, which Gerry Conlon's antisocial behaviour in their house had served only to accentuate.

The discrepancy between the timings in the accounts of different members of the household was a further matter that the judge chose to make much of. Conversely, the behaviour of Pat O'Neill, John Maguire and Sean Tully was never cited by the judge in favour of the defence. These three had all been in the thick of activities either at the house in Third Avenue during the period when the explosives were supposed to have been packed up or during the contentious 'missing half-hour' at the pub. All three had been allowed to continue going about their business and had done so in a manner that indicated nothing but their total innocence. (O'Neill was released and later rearrested when the scrapings from under his fingernails were found to be positive.) Tully and John Maguire were never charged. Tully's car, which had left Third Avenue at a time considered by the prosecution to have been crucial to the disposal of the nitroglycerine, was found to be clean.

The behaviour of Pat O'Neill is worth particular comment in this respect. Released from police custody, he returned home to Brixton and reported to work, where he explained what had happened. He arranged to have time off work in order to look after his children, and visited his wife in hospital. In the words of his solicitor, Harry Disley, 'He had some three days in which he could quite easily have left the country. It never occurred to him to do so. If [he had] been handling explosives and been subject to forensic tests, he must have known the game was up and presumably he would have got the hell out of it as quickly as he could. But he made no move to do so and was arrested in his own flat in the early hours of the following Saturday morning.'

But in the end, all these matters, together with the disquieting absence of the 'bulk' of explosive, became secondary. As the trial progressed, the belief in the guilt or innocence of the seven had, in effect, been reduced to the belief — or lack of it — in the TLC test. This consideration obscured the different and more important question, quite properly identified by the judge at the outset, of whether the prosecution had proved that the defendants had committed the offence. If there was any 'real doubt', they would have to be acquitted. But it was much easier to demolish 'real doubt' about the TLC test than about the wider issue of the Maguires' guilt.

To begin with, however, the jurors had to get to grips with this test — thin layer chromatography (TLC). In 1974 samples swabbed from the hands and from under the fingernails were immersed in a strong solvent — in this case, ether — and a small drop of the solution applied to a specially prepared chromatographic plate. Alongside the spot to be tested a second spot was applied, this time of nitroglycerine. This 'standard spot' was for the purpose of comparison. The end of the plate with the two samples on it was then immersed in a tank containing an 'eluent', which in the Maguires' case was toluene, a liquid considered by scientists performing the test to produce the most accurate readings for nitroglycerine. The eluent was drawn up the plate for 10 or 15 minutes as if it were blotting paper, carrying with it the two spots. Sprayed with a developer known as Griess's reagent, the two spots materialized once more on the plate; the position at which they did so and the degree of pink they now adopted was measured on a scale and compared. The result would indicate whether the unknown substance swabbed from the suspect's hands was the same as the 'standard spot' of nitroglycerine.

Scientists for the Crown and those for the defence disagreed on the all-important question of the test's infallibility. How 'sure' could one be that because a sample reacted in the same way as nitroglycerine it necessarily *was* nitroglycerine and not some other substance? In a case where there had been endless discussion of the burden of scientific proof, the judge took pains further to define this concept of sureness: 'You would be making a great error... if you simply said, "Well, we have great experts here; they disagree. Who are we, as mere jurymen and jurywomen, to decide between them? Where two experts disagree there must be a doubt." Now that would be an entirely wrong approach to your function. It is your duty to assess the evidence... [and] consider the way in which the expert witnesses gave their evidence... For example, the word "sure" is a common enough word; you know what it means in your everyday life. One of the things that you have to consider here is whether a scientist means exactly the same thing and perhaps in particular whether [one of the scientists who gave evidence for the defence] meant exactly the same thing when he was talking about possibilities and sureness. Was he talking about sureness in the way in which you and I regard it, or was he talking about scientific certainty, which is a quite different concept... You have to take that evidence as a whole and form your view upon that evidence as a whole. Perhaps most important of all in relation to all the witnesses, particularly the experts, you want to have a look at their line of reasoning. Does their line of reasoning make sense to you, or doesn't it?'

At some points the jury could have been forgiven for thinking that defence and prosecution were not so very far apart. Mr Justice Donaldson summarized the argument of Elliott, one of the scientists at the Government's RARDE at Woolwich who had performed some of the tests, as follows: '"On the information which I had and the work which I had done, I said on the balance of probabilities the result was nitroglycerine, but one cannot be sure because there is a possibility that there was no nitroglycerine. The only way to be sure that the substance is nitroglycerine is to run more than one test. When I did these tests I did not think that any further tests were necessary."'

Douglas Higgs, a principal scientific officer at the RARDE and Elliott's boss, was prepared to go further. 'I seek to establish that the TLC test is infallible and I believe it to be,' he said. 'I think we have now reached the point at which we have tested enough by TLC to exclude other substances. In a purely scientific sense the chances of a rogue elephant turning up are one in 10,000. In the real world they are millions to one.'

He had brought with him to the witness-box evidence to support his claim, which Mr Justice Donaldson was to make much of in his summing-up for the jury. Under RARDE supervision, said Higgs, TLC tests had been carried out by police all over the South-East of England on more than 900 volunteers from all walks of life. Every one of the tests had been negative. 'I came to the opinion from this survey that there was no substance from a very wide range of personal occupations, habits, hobbies and all sorts of circumstances that could arise, including smoking habits; they did not give rise to a substance which on the TLC procedure appeared to stimulate the nitroglycerine reaction.'

In addition to these tests, 110 swabs had been taken from employees at the Woolwich RARDE itself — a place where explosives were known to be stored. None of those tested had actually been working with explosives, so the point of the sampling had been to establish whether people working in the vicinity of explosives could become innocently contaminated. Again, all the results had been negative.

Further experiments at another government research station, at Waltham Abbey, had established that only those coming directly into contact with explosives showed positive results in the TLC test. Finally, tests had been carried out on some 175 substances (out of 200) in the nitro group of chemicals and none, allegedly, had been found to demonstrate any confusion with nitroglycerine. The evidence appeared persuasive.

For the defence, John Yallop had performed tests of his own. As Higgs's predecessor, a former principal scientific officer at Woolwich with 34 years' experience of working with explosives, he ought to have been a formidable witness. An examination of the Maguire case had raised serious doubts in his mind about the TLC test — and the significance of this was all the greater because he was the man who had actually developed the test in the first place. In an explanatory paper for the defence, he had written: 'No competent scientist could do other than conclude that the hypothesis is incorrect; namely, that the pink spot is not due to nitroglycerine. To do otherwise would be unscientific, illogical and pig-headed.' He repeated his opinion in court.

One major feature that had caused him to reassess the reliability of his own test was the result of the swabs taken from Paddy Maguire. Before their hands had been swabbed

with ether, all suspects, it will be recalled from Guiseppe
Conlon's account, had had their hands swabbed with dry cotton
wool. Yallop explained that within 20 minutes of handling
nitroglycerine it will become absorbed through the skin into
the bloodstream — hence the need in performing the test to
penetrate the skin with ether. The dry swab, therefore, was no
more than a preliminary test; if nitroglycerine were present in
the dry swab it would be highly irregular for it to be absent in
the ether-soaked subcutaneous swab. Maguire's ether swab had
been negative. 'At the end of three to four hours,' Yallop told
the court, 'he apparently had sufficient still on the surface to
come off on a dry swab but none at all came off on an ether
swab and this is just not how nitroglycerine behaves.' He
explained that since the dry swab had been positive the process
of absorption would still have been continuing. It was, he said,
'an extraordinary anomaly'.

To bear witness against his own test — and against eminent
colleagues — in a high-profile terrorist trial was a courageous
stand to take. It amounted to risking the reputation of a lifetime
for a deeply-held belief. This was scarcely the concern of Sir
Michael Havers, however, who in cross-examination attempted
to ridicule Yallop's sudden conversion. 'It is on one result of the
seven accused, or six accused whose hands were positive, that
you turned round and started running back down the road you
have been travelling for years.'

'That is not the only one, if you remember,' Yallop said.

'This must be the one that struck you first.'

'Yes, that was the one that struck me first.'

'This is the one that not only stopped you but turned you in
your tracks.'

'No, I don't think that is quite the right way to express it. It
gave me to pause and therefore caused me to carry out a critical
look at the whole thing.'

At the outset of his testimony, Yallop had set his work in context, explaining that the TLC test had originally been designed
as a means of identifying traces of explosive where an explosion

had already occurred, but that he had never contemplated its use as the sole evidence in a case. 'It was always drummed into me by my explosives police liaison officer that our scientific work was only part of the story,' he said. The testing of all chemicals under a single system using toluene was, in Yallop's view, of limited use: 'You can only draw the conclusion... that the questioned substance *may* be chemically the same as the control; what you cannot do is to say that it *is* the same.'

For the purposes of this case he had therefore set about investigating the house itself and the possibility that some common substance in it could produce results in the TLC test similar to those produced by nitroglycerine. He had tested every household chemical found at 43 Third Avenue, from air-fresheners and Dab-it-off to tinned ham and tobacco. In tests with toluene none had yielded pink spots in a similar position to those yielded by nitroglycerine, but in tests with methynol and alcohol the nitroglycerine spots were identical in colour and position on the scale to those produced by Players No.6 and Benson & Hedges cigarettes.

The judge waved these last results away. 'It means nothing to me and it may mean nothing to you. They are not toluene and they produce this confusion... If tobacco is the nigger in the woodpile, let us not get too theoretical with this one, but remember... John is the heaviest smoker and John swabbed clean; and what about the 900? Were there no smokers in the 900?' He was referring to the RARDE tests.

In his summing-up, the judge compared Yallop's efforts to isolate an innocent 'substance X' unfavourably with Higgs's survey of the 900 volunteers. 'So what is this substance X and where is it, and how does it come to affect these accused but not the 900? If you could point... to some grouping which affected the six accused... what is the other factor which affects these six and did not affect any of the 900? Well that is a possibility which you will have to think of. The Crown say, of course, the answer is simple: there is no substance X and the 900 did not handle nitroglycerine and these six did. But there it is.'

In a trial fraught with abstract scientific concepts, the idea that exclusively negative results had been produced in a survey of 900 ordinary citizens must have had a powerful effect upon the jury. It certainly appeared to have convinced the judge. 'You have to decide on the scientific evidence whether there is a non-explosive substance which could have affected the hands of the six,' he told them. '... If there was such a substance... you may think that they were singularly unfortunate; it appears never to have happened to anybody else as far as the evidence shows. So let me go on now to assume that you are satisfied that it was nitroglycerine... ' Although he attempted to set it in context, the implication of this assumption on the judge's part must have appeared to the jury to be a signal of his own belief.

Throughout the judgment, Mr Justice Donaldson had displayed a clear preference for the reasoning of the Crown scientists over that of the scientists for the defence. But in his personal conviction that no other substance produced a result in toluene comparable to that produced by nitroglycerine, the judge was ignoring a crucial argument in the defence's favour. It had come to light only at the last minute and became known in the trial as 'exhibit 60'. On the very day Mr Justice Donaldson was to begin his summing-up, John Yallop had managed to find a paper whose existence he had half remembered: a report by Elliott at RARDE, dated June 1974, which demonstrated that the performance of nitroglycerine in the TLC test was not, after all, unique. Another explosive, Pentaerythritol Tetranitrate (PETN), produced identical results in toluene: a pink spot of the same intensity at the same point on the scale at the same rate of climb. Elliott certainly knew about 'exhibit 60' when he gave his evidence. Higgs, as Elliott's boss, should have known about it when he spoke of the odds being 'one in 10,000' against.

The fact that no one had suggested that any of the accused had PETN on their hands caused the judge to dismiss the finding as irrelevant. 'It now being the case that there is no suggestion by either the prosecution or the defence that PETN was in fact the substance which was found on the swabs or gloves, you can ignore that part. Substance X, if it exists at all, is not PETN.' But although it may appear a nicety, the underlying principle of this finding was important for the defence. Even when, in the absence of the jury, the collected defence counsel spelled out as clearly as etiquette permitted that the judge had entirely missed the point, he apparently failed to grasp its significance — that the existence of any substance that performed in the same way as nitroglycerine demolished the very 'uniqueness' on which the Crown case depended.

There were other disturbing aspects about the conduct of the tests. In 1983 an independent forensic scientist, Dr Brian Caddy of Strathclyde University, reran the tests in toluene demonstrating the identical performance of nitroglycerine and PETN. Interviewed by Yorkshire Television, Caddy expressed his further concern over several technical omissions, among them the fact that only one 'standard spot' of nitroglycerine had been applied to each plate, whereas, owing to the variable rate at which the spots were liable to climb up the plate, two or even three 'standard spots' ought to have been present for there to be any certainty. Most notably, however, he was concerned at the absence of any confirmatory tests on the hand swabs. He told Yorkshire Television unequivocally, 'It is at the source of forensic science that you should confirm your results by an additional test. If one had made the statement that this was based on the evidence of one test then that is fair enough, but to say categorically that this was a positive result is not acceptable... I would not be prepared to go to court without a confirmatory test.' In the Maguire case, the only confirmatory test to have been carried out was on Anne's gloves, which had originally been tested by an 18-year-old apprentice. The swabs and tests on the hands and gloves of all the accused were subsequently destroyed, so they could be neither confirmed nor rerun.

Throughout the discussion of the forensic aspects of the case, there was one possible explanation as to how the Maguires' tests could have registered positive that the defence, doubtless for tactical reasons, never suggested. It was an idea advanced by several people who have examined the case, and summarized here by Christopher Price MP (*New Statesman*, March 9 1984): '... [the possibility] that there really was nitroglycerine on the swabs and scraping — and that some persons unknown, between the time the swabs were taken by the police and the time they were finally processed at Woolwich, doctored them. This is a possibility not hitherto publicly advanced, because it cannot be substantiated by any available evidence, and it would seem to involve wicked interference with the processes of justice.' In other words, a fit-up.

In fact, the judge himself had touched on the issue in relation to Anne's gloves, which were not taken direct to Woolwich but passed through Scotland Yard. 'All right, suppose somebody was authorized [to have access to them],' Mr Justice Donaldson speculated. 'Where would they have got nitroglycerine on their hands and so contaminated them? It is a matter for you, members of the jury, but you may think it is somewhat unlikely, to say the least of it, that those gloves became contaminated in police custody... '

No possible explanation was suggested to the jury at the trial, of course, but Dr Caddy and others have proposed one since. Nitroglycerine is commonly used in a range of medical preparations for heart conditions; it would, in Caddy's view, have been a simple matter to distil enough nitroglycerine from such pills to contaminate the swabs.

In 1984, Chris Price drew the Home Office Minister's attention to the possibility of contamination, but David Mellor's response was understandably dismissive. 'I do not think you will be surprised when I say that we could not agree to take action in a case on the basis of purely hypothetical propositions of this sort. I remain, in this as in other cases, always ready to look carefully at any new evidence. But the criteria for a free pardon cannot be met, and no useful purpose would be served in referring a case to the Court of Appeal unless there is new evidence or a new argument with real substance behind it.' The likelihood of such evidence arising so many years after the event is remote when the sole evidence in the case was destroyed for ever by the very people who analysed it.

But this is to jump ahead. The jury, unfortunately, did not have the deliberations of Dr Caddy at their disposal. They left the court with Mr Justice Donaldson's final words ringing in their ears: 'But if, members of the jury, having considered all these matters, you are sure, then it is your duty, your duty in accordance with the oath that you have taken, to bring in a verdict of guilty.'

The jury took almost two days to reach a decision. On March 4 they gave a verdict of guilty against all the defendants, unanimous except against young Patrick. They found him guilty by a majority of 11 to one. In contrast to his conduct at the Guildford trial, when he had passed no comment on the verdicts, Donaldson told the Maguires that in his opinion they had been 'rightly convicted'. Anne and Paddy Maguire, supposedly master bomb-makers who gave lessons in the kitchen of their council house, were sentenced to 14 years' imprisonment — the maximum possible sentence for possessing explosives. Guiseppe Conlon, father of convicted bomber Gerard Conlon, who had set the 'alarm bells ringing' at 43 Third Avenue with the news of his son's arrest, Sean Smyth, the lodger and willing collaborator, and Pat O'Neill, who had used his children as a cover for his activities, received 12 years each. Vincent Maguire, by then 16, was given five years, and 14-year-old Patrick four years' youth custody.

Mr Justice Donaldson concluded, 'It is not only the man or woman who pulls the trigger or plants the bomb who is the terrorist. Anyone concerned at any stage shares the guilt of using violence for political ends. There can be no greater offence than this, for it strikes at the very root of the way of life for which generations have fought and, indeed, died to preserve.'

Anne's son Vincent told the authors, 'My mother couldn't even put a plug together. She was nearly blind. She had to wear real strong glasses to see what she was doing. I don't even think she could put a screw in a plug, let alone make bombs.'

Once again, the newspapers went to town on 'Evil Aunt Annie' Maguire. *The Times* reported, 'To the Provisional IRA she was a senior armourer who taught their half-trained recruits the art of making bombs when they were posted to London on active service.' Peter Matthews, Chief Constable of Surrey, expressed his satisfaction with the verdicts. 'We have cut off a major pipeline to the terrorists,' he said. 'We are only sorry we did not find the bombs.'

31
THE BALCOMBE STREET SIEGE

'We've been pretty close to each other for a long time. We're going to have to meet pretty soon now.'

Detective Chief Superintendent Peter Imbert on the telephone to Joseph O'Connell

On December 6 1975 Eddie Butler took the afternoon off and went to a football match. He stood in total anonymity amid the crowd of 36,000 at Highbury Stadium to see Arsenal lose 2–1 to Leeds United — despite a goal from Arsenal's new Irish international star, Liam Brady. It was a short walk back from the ground down Blackstock Road and up Crouch Hill to the top-storey two-bedroom flat at number 61 he was now sharing with Hugh Doherty.

They had been in the flat since August 22, having found it through the accommodation columns of the *Hornsey Journal*. They gave the landlord, Mr Benjamin, no trouble and paid the £12 weekly rent on time, via his estate agents — who knew Doherty as John Anderson and Butler simply as Farley. There were 15 people in the late-Victorian house, including five other Irishmen, whom they studiously avoided. It was just the right mix of normality and anonymity.

Comfort and decoration were sparse. Butler and Doherty slept in sleeping-bags on top of bare mattresses. The stuffing spilled out of the one comfortable armchair. The television didn't work. A poster of an Irish showband singer adorned one wall, crudely cut-out colour photographs of the footballers Peter Bonetti and Stan Bowles another. They had just painted one of the walls orange.

When Butler reached home he found the kitchen was bare except for a packet of sausages, bread, milk and butter. The flat was strewn with stub-filled ashtrays and empty cigarette packets of the Irish brand Carroll's No.1. Butler was an incessant smoker. Doherty had left earlier, his pockets weighed down with 40 Ford car keys, to steal a car for tonight's operation.

It was too early for the late edition of the *Evening News* with the classified football results to be on the streets, so Butler passed the time fastidiously working on his guns. He remained the cover man, under standing instructions to open fire rather than be arrested. The M2 Sten-gun was his principal covering fire and he prepared two 24-round magazines for it, taking out each bullet in turn and polishing it with his handkerchief. Butler was worried about the Sten. It was liable to jam. After half an hour he went out to the newsagent's, following the routine he maintained for even the most banal shopping expedition by tucking a loaded Colt .38 into his waistband.

Doherty returned with the car — a four-door Cortina, the Active Service Unit's preferred model. This one was dark blue and he had taken it from a quiet side-street in Hammersmith, a favoured location for stealing cars. They drove two miles to 99 Milton Grove in Stoke Newington, where Joseph O'Connell and Harry Duggan were waiting in their safe house.

O'Connell's M1 carbine joined the Sten in a black holdall on the back seat. He also brought a .357 Astra Magnum pistol. Duggan carried another Astra Magnum and a 9-mm Browning automatic. Both Butler and Doherty took their Colt .38s. With Duggan driving, they set off down the Essex Road at about 8.00 p.m., looking like any carload of young men headed for a Saturday night out in the West End.

Had they read a copy of the previous Wednesday's *Evening News* they would have known that they were pushing their luck to its limits for, to the horror of New Scotland Yard, someone had leaked to the paper what was essentially the blueprint of the biggest dragnet yet mounted to catch them — Operation Combo.

Operation Combo was the brainchild of Wilfred Gibson, Deputy Assistant Commissioner (Operations) of the Metropolitan Police, and Ernie Bond, the first head of the Bomb Squad and now leading the CID hunt for the bombers. The police plan sprang from the first discernible pattern of behaviour the Unit had fallen into. For in the last six weeks they had launched five attacks at night in the heart of the West End, and on three successive occasions had thrown bombs at what O'Connell was later to call 'ruling-class' restaurants.

On November 12 they had thrown a shrapnel-packed bomb through the window of Scott's Oyster Bar in Mount Street in Mayfair, killing John Francis Batey. Six days later an identical attack had killed Audrey Edgson and Theodore Williams at Waltons Restaurant in Walton Street in Knightsbridge. The police plan was costly, but simple enough: to flood the West End with police and wait for the bombers to enter the web.

Gibson and Bond commandeered 800 men from every level of the Yard's resources, including officers who were normally desk-bound and the more cerebral members of the Fraud Squad. In the centre of the West End they placed 246 pairs of plain-clothes CID men for street surveillance, unarmed because of the risk of opening fire on an unrecognized colleague. These men were backed up by an outer ring of uniformed and armed police in cars and vans and on motor bikes, waiting at the main roads out of the West End north of the river. A detachment of the Special Patrol Group guarded each of the bridges south across the Thames.

Operation Combo ran for the first time on November 27. Everyone waited from 6.00 p.m. until midnight, when the exercise was called off. Nothing had happened in the West End but, well outside the carefully positioned police ring, Duggan and Doherty were hiding in the bushes outside the home of Ross McWhirter, in Village Road, Enfield. McWhirter, one of the twins who had founded *The Guinness Book of Records*, had launched a £50,000 reward for the capture of IRA terrorists, as part of a 'Beat the Bombers' campaign. Butler later told the police, 'That man thought he lived in Texas. He put a bounty on our head. He asked for it.' Duggan shot McWhirter twice with his Astra Magnum, killing him, while Mrs Rosemary McWhirter, who had been forced at gunpoint to let the men in, cowered in the kitchen.

Undeterred by this and by the leaked report in the following Wednesday's *Evening News*, Gibson and Bond sent their 800 officers back for what proved to be another fruitless vigil, on Thursday December 4. When they decided to run Operation Combo again two days later, on December 6, one newly promoted Superintendent in the Bomb Squad, Peter Imbert, trusting that the IRA would not be stupid enough to hit the West End on a Saturday night, set off for a weekend in the country.

O'Connell had not bothered to make a bomb for this sortie, although there was plenty of material left in Crouch Hill. Given the team's appalling record it was just going to be a minor Saturday-night shoot-out. It would achieve little beyond adding another notch to their catalogue of attacks — with none of the sensation of the assassination attempts on Edward Heath, the former Prime Minister, nor the bravado of some of their bombings — but it would stoke up the siege mentality in the capital fostered by outrages that had been running, on average, at one a week throughout the winter of 1975. It would reinforce the apparent invulnerability of the Active Service Unit. After 18 months and nearly 50 missions, still no one knew who they were or where they were based.

Perhaps they had grown complacent. Perhaps they were simply running out of ideas. Perhaps the strain of living under cover, heroes of their cause but anonymous and unacclaimed, had given rise to a subconscious wish to get caught. But, whatever the reason, their target tonight, December 6, was so reckless as to be suicidal. Not only were they retracing their steps to the West End for another 'establishment' attack, but O'Connell, the leader since Dowd's departure, had sanctioned a return to the scene of a former crime. It had happened before, for they had twice shot up the Portman Hotel, but those two attacks had been 10 months apart. Now they were heading back to Scott's Oyster Bar, Mount Street, still partly boarded up from the time they had hit it less than a month ago, but newly reopened for the holiday season and defiantly decorated with Christmas baubles.

Two plain-clothes policemen were posted in Mount Street. Just after 9.00 p.m. they watched the blue Cortina drive along the street in the direction of Park Lane and slow down opposite Scott's. PC John Cook spotted what looked like a rifle butt in the hands of one of the passengers in the back seat and, just as he radioed through this information, O'Connell leaned out of the front passenger-door window and fired two rounds from the carbine — harmlessly — through the plate-glass frontage of the restaurant. Butler's Sten-gun jammed again before he could get a burst off. The car accelerated away. The Sten and the carbine were stowed into the holdall. What the four did not realize was that the police had seen them and that Operation Combo was instantly activated.

Further down Mount Street, Detective Inspector John Purnell and Sergeant Philip McVeigh, both on foot, unarmed and in plain clothes, picked up the radio message and passed on a description of the car and its registration number. Then, as the Cortina turned north towards Marble Arch, the two policemen were lucky enough to hail a taxi. Jumping in, they ordered the driver, 'Follow that car!'

Butler was the first to sense that the black cab was tailing them. O'Connell dismissed the notion. What could be more natural than being followed by a taxi in the West End?

Duggan stopped at a set of traffic-lights and the taxi pulled up behind. When he set off again it was still following. They turned left into Alpha Close. It was a cul-de-sac. Pulling up, they watched the taxi carry on for 30 yards along Park Road and pull up too. The gunmen got out and started walking. Duggan, as the driver, had the responsibility of clearing the car of incriminating material, but the situation was now desperate and he left the holdall behind. They no longer had any doubts as to what was happening.

Purnell and McVeigh walked calmly after them. The four men reached the junction of Rossmore Road and broke into a run. As the two unarmed officers gave chase they were joined by a Flying Squad car and a transit van, both full of armed police. Operation Combo was now tightening around Marylebone. The four started shooting, Duggan trying to provide covering fire from one side of the road as the other three sprinted on. Detective Inspector Henry Dowswell realized he was five yards from Duggan's Magnum and threw himself to the ground.

Running down a flight of steps the men found themselves in Balcombe Street. Duggan caught up with the others. The gunmen fired off more than 20 rounds, but they were trapped: there were police at either end of the street. The men dashed into the joint entrance of numbers 22–24, a set of council flats. Butler and Doherty frantically tried to find a way out at the back. There was none. The only alternative was the stairs. They charged up one flight and pressed a front doorbell at random: Flat 22B. John Matthews, a 54-year-old post-office worker, had been watching *Kojak* on television when he was interrupted by an extraordinary burst of police sirens and flashing lights in the street below. Stepping from the lounge on to the narrow balcony to see what was happening, he was yelled at to go inside. His 53-year-old wife, Sheila, was laying out some clean laundry; she wanted to do some ironing before having a bath and going to bed. When the bell rang, John Matthews, expecting it to be the police, promptly went to open the door.

The four men, with guns drawn, burst into the flat and propelled John Matthews back through the hall into the lounge.

The Matthews had the impression that the men knew what they were doing as if they had rehearsed for such a moment. With scarcely a word they moved swiftly and ruthlessly. The Matthews were shoved on to their settee, where John

Matthews's hands and feet were tied with his wife's tights; the front door was blocked with furniture; the gas fire, the television (still broadcasting *Kojak*) and the lights were all switched off. When the doorbell rang once more and a policeman's voice called for the Irishmen to come out, Duggan promptly dragged Mrs Matthews into the hall with his gun pressed to her neck. 'Fuck off, you bastards,' he shouted through the door. Mrs Matthews screamed at the police to go away: 'He's got a gun at my head.' The police withdrew.

The gang now moved to barricade themselves completely into the small lounge of the Matthews' flat, deliberately cutting themselves off from the kitchen, bathroom and lavatory. This had the effect, intentional or otherwise, of preventing individual members of the Unit from being picked off in adjoining rooms by police marksmen and of deterring any attempt to storm the room without serious risk of wounding or killing the Matthews in a shoot-out. Butler later claimed, 'If the police came in shooting to get the hostages out, we weren't going to give them the satisfaction of taking them out alive.'

The cold-bloodedness was tempered by occasional consider-ateness. When, for instance, the team built a small bonfire of their forged driving-licences and identity papers, they respected Mrs Matthews's request to burn them in a metal waste-paper bin rather than on her best carpet.

After 30 minutes O'Connell telephoned 999 and asked for Sir Robert Mark, the Commissioner of the Metropolitan Police. He was put on to Jim Nevill, head of the Bomb Squad. 'We're the IRA. We've got hostages. We want a minibus and a plane to take us from Heathrow to Ireland.' A deadline was set for midday the following day.

Duggan taunted Mrs Matthews: 'Ever been to Ireland?'

'No, but I've always wanted to go,' she replied.

'Well, you're fucking well going tomorrow,' said Duggan.

Although the Matthews had recognized the accents as Irish, only now did they fully comprehend that they were being held captive by the IRA. 'Nothing registered. We were just too horrified. We were too scared to ask questions. They were so disciplined. They seemed to know instinctively what to do.'

But the gunmen were nervous, too. John Matthews noted how Duggan's hands were shaking as he tied up his hostage. The four men must have realized instantly from the rapidly gathering police strength outside that their options were stark: surrender meant the certainty of a lifetime in prison; a shoot-out the equal certainty of vainglorious death. The notion of safe escort to a waiting aeroplane and a welcoming airport in Ireland or anywhere else must have seemed fantastical.

Butler, at least, realized this much: 'We had an idea from the start we wouldn't get a safe passage, so we decided to play for time to see if someone would clear out our flats and get the gear.'

By midnight a small army of policemen had moved into position in and around Balcombe Street. Floodlights were brought in to illuminate the flat and its balcony, and 25 families in adjoining residences or in the line of potential fire were evacuated to a local hotel. The startled customers of Balcombe Street's pub, The Portman Arms, found themselves bundled without warning into the cellars for two hours, before being sent scurrying to safety past the cordons that now sealed off the street and Dorset Square. Marksmen positioned themselves on roof-tops and in rooms with a vantage point towards the Matthews' windows. Number 22B was destined for a while to become the most famous address in England, as the national and international media rushed as fast and as close as they could to the centre of the drama.

Having turned off the television as soon as they had moved into the flat, O'Connell's men were unaware of how quickly the first newsflashes of the siege had been broadcast and how rapidly the press had responded to the story. At 10.30 p.m. the Matthews' telephone rang, and an enterprising reporter from the *Sunday Mirror* at the other end of the line offered optimistically to act as a mediator. His exclusive interview was brief. 'Can you help... hell!' O'Connell shouted, slamming the receiver down. Butler was so exasperated by this incident, coupled with a succession of calls from anxious friends and relatives of the Matthews, to whom O'Connell gave equally short shrift, that the receiver was soon taken off the hook.

The Matthews were, however, astonished on that first night at the nonchalance with which O'Connell and Butler curled up on the floor and went to sleep. Duggan sat guard at Mr Matthews's feet, opposite Mrs Matthews to whom he had given the remaining armchair not used in the barricade. The two embarked on a series of staring contests which Duggan always won. Doherty set himself on the floor beneath the window-sill. The Matthews spent a sleepless night. The guns were to hand and loaded throughout.

Police set up their operational headquarters in Marylebone railway station nearby. They also took over the flat next door to 22B and nicknamed it 'Fort Belfast'. Gibson, whose plan had cornered the gang, was in overall charge and he appointed two men for the key roles of negotiators. Jim Nevill, already familiar to the British public from his television appearances as operational head of the hard-pressed Bomb Squad, was on call that night and had been involved from the first radio messages. He was assigned the night-shifts. Detective Chief Superintendent Peter Imbert, Nevill's deputy, who had confidently predicted that the terrorists would not be so stupid as to attack central London again on a Saturday night, hurried from his weekend retreat in the middle of the night to prepare for the day-shift.

Although these two men had worked closely together for the last 18 months hunting the nameless men now cornered in Balcombe Street, Imbert, more stolid than his urbane colleague, had not been in the public eye. When he was a young man his ambition had been fired by his reading Walter Thompson's book *I was Churchill's Shadow*, and he now had considerable Special Branch experience — work he unashamedly relished. By 1975 he had embarked on a steadily accelerating rise through the Met, but it was his role at Balcombe Street — within a month of his promotion to Superintendent — that was to project him into the line of succession for the post of Britain's most senior policeman, Commissioner of the Metropolitan Police.

It was the present incumbent of that title, Sir Robert Mark, who had established the ground-rules for police conduct in such a siege. The paramount rule was 'no deals' — an imperative shared by politicians and police. The strategy required the police to play a patient waiting game with the intention of freeing the hostages unharmed and capturing the gunmen alive or, if necessary, dead. However, if the gunmen tried to break out, the police were prepared to risk killing the hostages to prevent the gang from escaping. Similarly, if the gunmen started to kill the hostages, then the police would go in with no holds barred. Whatever happened, there was no scenario in which the gang might break out, get rescued or board a plane bound for the airport of their choice. For as long as possible the police were prepared to stand back and exert tightening physical and psychological pressure through negotiation, deprivation and fatigue. These had been the tactics employed at the Spaghetti House siege in London two months earlier. Gibson, who had been in charge on that occasion, had brought about a successful outcome after five days in which the police had learned a good deal about surveillance and siege psychology.

In the early morning Nevill dialled the Matthews' flat to find the receiver back in place, and spoke successively to O'Connell, Doherty and Duggan. Neither side mentioned the threatened noon deadline for a getaway aeroplane and it was never referred to again. As Butler had recognized, 'The odds against were too high.' The men agreed to accept a field telephone to establish uninterrupted communication, and the Post Office line was cut off.

An effective channel of contact was a satisfactory first step for the police, although they were no wiser as to the identities of the men inside 22B, or even how many there were. Four had got out of the car, but several witnesses were certain that only three of them had disappeared into the flats — and the gunmen weren't saying. Indeed, one unfortunate eyewitness caught running away from the gunfire in Balcombe Street had had an uncomfortable overnight grilling before satisfying the police that he was not a terrorist.

Fast work elsewhere confirmed to Nevill and Imbert that holed up in Balcombe Street were at least some of the men they had been so fruitlessly hunting. The stolen Cortina and, left inside it, the *Evening News* with the football results and the Sten-gun in the bag dropped by Duggan variously yielded fingerprints and forensic clues that linked the men with the McWhirter killing and the shots fired at three West End hotels a year before. Furthermore, the fingerprints matched some of those taken from the Active Service Unit's safe house at Fairholme Road so hurriedly vacated at the start of the year after the shooting of PC Tibble. These were unquestionably the men they were hunting, and they included 'Michael Wilson', whoever he was, who had been publicly called 'the most wanted man in Britain'.

The midday deadline passed innocuously. At 2.00 p.m. on Sunday the field telephone was lowered down from the window of the flat above. O'Connell, calling on his experience with Marconi in the Irish Republic, promptly dismantled it to check for a bug and, satisfied there was none, reassembled it with equal expertise.

Something of a technological battle of wits ensued. Press speculation attributed to the police a whole range of fanciful devices: parabolic and laser-beam microphones, a button-sized fish-eye camera lens and robotics. Certainly, the police took aerial photographs, lowered a remote microphone from the flat above and attempted to insert bugs through wall drillings from their sandbagged post in the adjoining flat. This had been anticipated by the gunmen when they sealed themselves off in the lounge and removed the ceiling-light attachment to prevent bugging from the flat above. They were perhaps mindful of the recent Monasterevin siege in the Irish Republic, where Eddie Gallagher and Marion Coyle had been captured after holding hostage the Dutch industrialist Dr Tiede Herrema. Gallagher and Coyle had used the whole building and had been successfully spied upon by the Garda.

For the first time in public the police deployed the D11 unit, the 'Blue Berets', instructors and volunteers from the firearms unit of the Metropolitan Police, each granted the privilege of choosing his own weapon. An armoured Saracen personnel-carrier, more familiar to the streets of Belfast than to London, lumbered into an adjacent mews. Two SAS men arrived on the scene to offer their services, which were politely but firmly declined. The Met were quite clear that it was they who were running the show.

Imbert made the next psychological breakthrough. 'Tom', as the police called O'Connell, used the field telephone to ask for water. 'Get it yourselves,' retorted Imbert. O'Connell replied, 'Your fellows are all over the place aren't they?' This revealed to Imbert that the gunmen were all confined to one room. He was shrewd enough and quick enough not to lie outright and thereby risk the trust and rapport he was trying to establish.

'We've been pretty close to each other for a long time. This is the closest we've ever been. We're going to have to meet pretty soon now. Why don't you let Mrs Matthews out to get some water? Perhaps we can make a deal that we'll let her return.'

This enabled O'Connell to believe that the police had already penetrated the surrounding rooms. The press jumped to the same conclusion upon the police announcement that the terrorists were confined to a single room. The trapped men were following television and BBC radio news bulletins on the unfolding siege, so any lingering thoughts of relaxing their self-imposed denial of the food, water and toilet facilities elsewhere in the flat were effectively ended.

Inevitably, sanitary conditions in the lounge deteriorated rapidly. The gunmen emptied the drinks cabinet of glasses and jugs for urination. Mrs Matthews was left to relieve herself where she sat. The bottles of gin, whisky and sherry were ignored, in disciplined observance of the Unit's anti-alcohol strictures, although they used the whisky to clean their teeth. The discipline was selective: with no sense of rationing, the men consumed all the bottles of tonic water and dry ginger mixers by Sunday evening. Mrs Matthews was allowed to drink some whisky and succeeded only in giving herself a nasty headache.

Initially, no one in the room was concerned about food. The Matthews were too tense to feel hungry. When Doherty gave Mrs Matthews a chocolate from a box that her husband had won in a Christmas raffle, she promptly choked. Doherty consumed the rest of the box himself. He was the only non-smoker in the room. At the start of the siege Mrs Matthews had five packets of Embassy and Mr Matthews a pouch of roll-up tobacco. Butler, a virtual chain-smoker, was principally responsible for finishing the supply, and when it ran out was prepared to untie Mr Matthews's hands so he could roll up the dog-ends into more cigarettes.

Cigarettes soon became part of the besieged men's demands over the field telephone, and Imbert and Nevill exploited their craving. They adopted a policy of refusing food and cigarettes until there was an agreement to free Mrs Matthews, both because she was in poor health and because she had become the focus of public concern. Furthermore, all international siege strategy insisted that the first hostage release represented a vital breakthrough. O'Connell allowed Mrs Matthews briefly to tell Imbert, 'I'm all right,' before grabbing back the telephone. But this encouraging moment was never repeated.

At 10.00 p.m. on Sunday the police lowered a sanitary bucket and water-container to be pulled in through the window. To the gunmen's irritation there was no food or cigarettes. Before drinking, they made the Matthews sample the water for potential poison or soporific additives. Then they all watched Sir Robert Mark's televised press conference, at which he announced, 'The decision not to send in food will not be reversed until the police receive advice that it should be.' The police had nutritionists as well as psychologists to advise them. Sir Robert added that the terrorists weren't 'going anywhere except a cell in Brixton prison'. Mrs Matthews considered this a dangerously provocative remark. Gradually, she became obsessed with the certainty that she would die. She received no reassurance from 'Tom', 'Mick' or 'Paddy' on the point.

Doherty, despite his greed with the chocolates, seemed to Sheila Matthews the most compassionate of her captors. That night he gave her a sheet from her bundle of ironing for warmth. 'Don't overdo it,' warned Duggan, whom Mrs Matthews recalled as 'the good-looking one... there was something sadistic about him'.

After the first 24 hours the siege turned into what was to be a long stalemate. The permanently drawn curtains had the unsettling effect of making day and night almost indistinguishable, as daylight and floodlight penetrated the oppressive room with similar intensity. Everyone took fright when the floodlights suddenly failed, fearing the flat was about to be stormed. Jim Nevill quickly got on the telephone to reassure the occupants that it was simply that the generator had broken down.

Duggan and Doherty rarely moved from their positions and rarely spoke. Duggan, in particular, seemed to the Matthews not to need sleep. Butler was conspicuously the most restless; he counted his money, repeatedly cleaned his Colt .38 and made neat arrangements of his ammunition. O'Connell, for all that he appeared to the Matthews the weakest and palest, had shown himself from the start to be in charge. He took command of the field telephone, on which his end of the conversation was invariably curt and abusive. Imbert and Nevill were not budging from their basic offer — the exchange of hot food and cigarettes for Mrs Matthews. When the whole room heard a radio appeal by Sheila Matthews's sister Joan to keep calm, O'Connell took the transistor radio and listened to the news bulletins close to his ear. They relieved the tedium by playing selections from the Matthews' record collection — Engelbert Humperdinck and Gilbert O'Sullivan — and watching the occasional football match or film on television. The hapless John and Sheila Matthews had to endure *Ned Kelly*, the portrait of the murderous Australian outlaw.

Although the whisky and gin remained untouched to the end, the gunmen relaxed sufficiently to drink the sherry. One night O'Connell drew up a spoof will and showed it to his compatriots, and they all had a laugh before he burned it. But the good humour was quick to snap. During his time with Special Branch, Peter Imbert had mugged up on Irish Republican history, and on the Tuesday he tried to deploy his expertise to forge a more sympathetic relationship with 'Tom' and tighten the psychological screws. But when he suggested that the men were betraying the Republican heroes of the past, O'Connell lost his temper and threw the field telephone out of the window. Anxious to make amends for this blunder, police lowered sandwiches and cigarettes to the flat almost immediately, but O'Connell was not to be placated and he ignored the offering. The police had to resort to negotiating by loudhailer.

The next day O'Connell optimistically demanded a five-course hot meal, cigarettes and tablets for Mrs Matthews, who was suffering increasingly from headaches and sleeplessness. The police responded with sandwiches, hot coffee, 40 cigarettes and the tablets. O'Connell kept the cigarettes and tablets and contemptuously flung the coffee and sandwiches into the street. The police retaliated by cutting the power supply — with the principal effect of denying television, since the lights were in any case permanently off. That night they erected scaffolding and a large blue nylon screen across the street. Ostensibly its purpose was to catch any ricocheting bullets, but there was speculation that its construction was intended to implant fresh fears in the gunmen that the police would end the siege by storm.

Imbert and Nevill turned the loudhailer to their own advantage. They encouraged the Matthews and taunted the terrorists: 'Your so-called friends in Ireland don't want anything to do with you... Any coward with a gun can stay in a flat with a middle-aged working-class couple. It takes courage to make the decision to come out.'

The two negotiators studiously avoided the use of the word 'surrender' with its overtone of humiliation. The BBC radio broadcasters, now the team's sole source of information, also agreed to the police request to refrain from using the word.

On Thursday the men betrayed the first crack in their united front. O'Connell had for two days held to the demand for a hot meal and repeatedly refused the proferred sandwiches. Now the police tempted them with hot soup, provoking a disagreement among them, which was picked up in a blurred form by the listening devices. Imbert immediately exploited the moment over his loudhailer: 'This is a public announcement. Food is being lowered but you are refusing it. The press will know. Push the window open now. I have imagined you have closed it because you and your comrades can't make up your minds.'

After 15 minutes — and after five days without food — the men relented. The sandwiches and soup were pulled in, but O'Connell defiantly rejected the cigarettes as 'too small'. The Matthews were again used as guinea-pigs, but apart from the samples they were made to test they got nothing; the Provisionals ate the rest themselves. That night, for the first time, the police passed down a replacement sanitary bucket.

The following morning O'Connell suddenly resuscitated the Heathrow plan. He got John Matthews to hand over the keys to his car — ironically, a Cortina — which was parked below, and ascertained whether it had two or four doors and how much petrol was in the tank. Mr Matthews's legs were untied for the first time since Saturday night, and he and his wife were walked around the room to restore their circulation. 'You're going out,' said O'Connell. But the plan to frog-march the Matthews out to their car with pistols in their mouths never materialized. The gunmen realized it was hopeless. What they did not know was that the police had, in any case, taken the simple precaution of deflating the tyres of the Matthews' Cortina.

The Heathrow plan was the Unit's last hope. Some credence was given to the notion of their resistance having been broken by an erroneous radio report that the SAS had moved into Balcombe Street, but their options were the same as when the siege had begun: surrender to a lifetime in prison or shoot their way to suicide. While they had shown scant regard for the Matthews, there was nothing to be gained by harming them. The six days had given their cause unprecedented international publicity, but none of them was ready to die. The patient police strategy finally paid off. O'Connell called out for the field telephone to be reinstalled.

The Metropolitan Police had decided early on to film the key moments of the siege. Now one of their cameras fixed on Superintendent Peter Imbert for the critical conversations that were to follow. Imbert was ready. In jacket and tie and with a clean white handkerchief peeping out of his breast pocket, he proceeded to give an assured performance in the art of negotiation. Over the next two hours he talked out the gunmen and the Matthews without loss of blood or a shot being fired. It was one of the Met's great moments — no less for the television pictures that beamed the denouement of the Balcombe Street siege around the world. Either triumph or catastrophe was poised to unfold for all to see. Imbert admitted later to feeling an electric tension. His steady voice betrayed none of it.

He began by reverting to the tactic that had resulted in O'Connell's throwing the last field telephone out of the window: dipping into his knowledge of Irish Republicanism.

'What's the idea of sticking it out now? Can't you make up your mind? What would Daithi O'Conaill think of you holding a couple of people like that? He'd say it was kid's stuff, wouldn't he?' David O'Connell — Imbert used the Irish version of his name — was the Provisional IRA Chief of Staff and no relation to Joe.

'OK.' replied O'Connell. It was 2.15 p.m. Imbert came straight back.

'Let's get it straight then, so there's no mistake. You'll let Mrs Matthews go. I don't want her to make any moves yet. Now, I've got to tell everyone what's happening. OK?'

'Her feet are stiff.'

'Her feet are stiff? Well, there's not much of a walk. There's about 15 feet. She knows the way. If she turns left and walks along the balcony there'll be somebody there to meet her.'

'Somebody'll have to go with her.'

'You can send Mr Matthews.' It was worth a try.

'If one of our men walks by the window and comes back again can you give him safe passage?' O'Connell had a particular reason for asking.

'Yes,' Imbert replied instantly, without consulting his superiors. It was a cool decision. While he was apparently deferring to a terrorist request, his agreement preserved the tentative rapport that was being re-established on the field telephone. It gave the gunmen the security of retaining Mr Matthews as an insurance against a shoot-out. It gave Imbert Mrs Matthews. Roy Habershon, former Commander of the Anti-Terrorist Squad, cited this instant as the moment that marked Imbert as the man for the very top.

Sheila Matthews was still wearing the green floral-print housecoat she had worn when the siege began six days before. Eddie Butler, chosen because he had a hooded anorak, gently steered her out on to the balcony into steady drizzling rain. They manoeuvred past Mrs Matthews's plant-pots to the rail that divided her balcony from that of next door, where two armed policemen waited, guns trained on Butler.

'OK,' said Imbert. 'You can tell him to come back now she's at the railing.' Butler edged back sideways. Nobody moved to grab Mrs Matthews. As she waited she noticed the packet of cigarettes that O'Connell had flung outside. Butler, returning to the others, reported, 'It's all right. The press are here.' It was the insurance the four believed they needed that they were not about to be gunned down.

Only when Butler, hands raised high above his head, was back inside number 22B did the policemen help Mrs Matthews under the railing and into her next-door neighbour's to safety. Their first question understandably baffled poor Mrs Matthews after her unimaginable ordeal. Was her husband 'clean'? Eventually it was explained that the police needed to know whether her husband had been booby-trapped with explosives in any way. He was 'clean', Mrs Matthews confirmed. A WPC bustled her across Balcombe Street to Dorset Square where an ambulance sped her to University College Hospital.

Imbert then kept a long-standing promise conditional upon Mrs Matthews's safe release — the hot meal. A large silver container was lowered down and accepted without demur. There were sausages, Brussels sprouts and croquette potatoes. The men shared the food with Mr Matthews. As they ate, Imbert prepared for more lengthy negotiations and requested a radio black-out. He did not return to the telephone until 3.50 p.m., and then politely enquired, 'If you've finished, why not come out now?' O'Connell agreed.

An unauthorized version quickly spread through the Met that it was only after sampling police canteen food that the terrorists finally agreed to give themselves up.

Part of the reason the siege had gone on for so long was Butler's hope that someone would clear up their safe houses. No one did before the police located them. Their search uncovered more fingerprints — on a copy of the *Evening Standard* at Crouch Hill and on a list of bombing targets at Milton Grove. They belonged to Brian Keenan, the man who had masterminded the entire campaign. He had visited the Unit the previous month.

Keenan was finally arrested in Banbridge, Northern Ireland in March 1979, flown to London and sentenced the following June to 18 years' imprisonment for conspiring to cause explosions.

In Balcombe Street the four Provisionals, described in the *Daily Telegraph* as 'the best team the Provos ever had', went through a final disciplined routine. First they cut up a nylon sheet from the pile of ironing and made themselves makeshift balaclavas. Harry Duggan, the Unit's treasurer, distributed £10 to each man in preparation for the faint possibility that someone might get a chance to make a break for it. They emptied their pockets of car keys and reserve ammunition, laying out their pistols alongside one another on the floor.

'Who's going to come out first?' asked Imbert. It was Eddie Butler, at 4.15 p.m. Crouching marksmen covered every step and, although it was now dark, the floodlights were strong enough to give clear pictures for the long lenses of the outside-broadcast cameras. Hugh Doherty followed a minute later, his hands high above his head.

'Now who's coming next? Mr Matthews? OK. Now, tell Mr Matthews exactly the same. His hands will be above his head. Tell him to keep them there.' Imbert was alert to the idea that the remaining gunmen might yet try and pull a swap. John Matthews was equally alive to the danger of mistaken identity. 'I'm the hostage,' he blurted out as soon as he reached the balcony railing.

Harry Duggan followed at 4.20. Then Peter Imbert had the final telephone conversation with Joe O'Connell.

'OK, Tom. Now you've not left any booby-traps or anything in there have you?'

'No, there's nothing.'

'Now, where are the guns? All on the floor?'

'You know where the curtains are drawn here at the corner, near the TV? They're all just there. OK?'

'OK. Are they loaded or unloaded?'

'Yeah, they're loaded.'

'OK. Don't touch them. Just wait there. I'll tell you when to come. Don't take any notice of anyone except me. OK?'

'OK.'

'OK Tom?'

'All right. Yeah.'
'I'll see you at the station later. OK?'
'See you in the nick.'
'I'll see you in the nick. Don't forget now... '
'I'm leaving the phone down now. It's OK, is it?'
'Yeah, now just a minute before you put it down. Hands above your head and keep them there.'
'Yeah. OK. Right.'

32
'NEVER HEARD
OF THEM'

Eddie Butler on the Guildford Four

Once police had broken down the lounge door of number 22B, Labrador dogs trained to sniff for explosives were sent in first, followed by official photographers and fingerprint men. Within 10 minutes of O'Connell's surrender, the Active Service Unit was rushed to Paddington Green police station less than half a mile away — not for convenience but because it is one of the most secure police stations in London. The men were locked in separate cells.

The public response to the Metropolitan Police's success in bringing the siege to a satisfactory and bloodless conclusion had started with the spontaneous applause of the considerable press corps in Balcombe Street. Telegrams from the Queen and the Prime Minister followed. Detective Inspector Harry Dowswell won the George Medal for pursuing the Provisionals unarmed down Balcombe Street. Thirteen others involved in the chase received £25 each from the Bow Street Magistrates' Court Reward Fund. Commander Roy Habershon, overall head of the Bomb Squad, had a tie designed for all his men involved in the siege. It featured a broken 'Z' in orange on a green background, surrounded by chains. 'Z' was the police code-name for the mysterious 'Michael Wilson'.

Nevill and Imbert waited until the following day before going down to Paddington Green to see who they had caught. They began with Butler, in the matron's room. He talked freely from the outset, giving his family details and the date of his arrival in England — October 10 1974 — as well as the address of the safe house he had shared with Doherty in Crouch Hill and the number in the Active Service Unit — originally six, later reduced to four. Any satisfaction at the co-operative way in which the interrogation was proceeding was abruptly punctured when Nevill asked Butler about his first terrorist operation on the mainland.

'My first job, someone you've already put away for it.'

'Which one?' Neville asked.

'Woolwich.'

'You mean the bomb thrown into the pub, the King's Arms?'

'That's correct.'

'Who were you with on that job?'

'I'm saying what jobs *I'm* on,' Butler insisted.

'Were you in the car?'

'I was out of the car.'

'At the pub?'

'Yes.'

'Did you throw the bomb?'

'No.'

'But you were there when the bomb was thrown?'

'Correct.'

'When you went over there did you know they were going to do a bombing?'

'Yes.'

'Had you been there on a reconnaissance of the pub?'

'I was not.'

'Who made the bomb?'

'I'm not saying.'

'Fair enough. Now you know that Hill and Armstrong have been convicted of the Woolwich bombing. Were you with them?'

'No.'

'You weren't with them?'

'No.'

'I see. Do you know them?'

'Never heard of them,' Butler replied.

'What about the Guildford bombing?'

'Wasn't in London at the time. Wasn't over here at the time.'

The dilemma was laid out clearly from the start. If Butler was telling the truth, there had been a disastrous blunder; it meant that the Woolwich confessions were unreliable and that Hill and Armstrong had been wrongly convicted. Alternatively, Butler could be launching an intricate plot to discredit British justice or to free guilty colleagues. Nevill moved the interview back to the known operations of the Active Service Unit, but he returned to the subject before finishing with Butler for the day.

'Do you know any of the people who were charged with the Guildford and Woolwich bombings?'

'Never heard of them,' Butler repeated. 'Never heard of them until they were up in court.'

Nevill appeared ready to go along with Butler's account that he had bombed Woolwich.

'At the time you did that bombing at the Woolwich public house, were you part of this same ASU?'

'That's right.'

The two Superintendents put the same question to O'Connell and Duggan the next day in their separate cells. (Doherty had not joined the Active Service Unit until well after the Woolwich and Guildford bombings.) O'Connell had hitherto been reasonably co-operative, but greeted this question with total silence. So did Duggan, who had so far refused to give anything more than his rank of volunteer and his name. (This in itself was a breakthrough after his extended use of the alias Michael Wilson. The Irish police found confirmatory fingerprints in Duggan's father's cottage in County Clare and, as a ghoulish postscript, dug up by night a number of local graves in an unsuccessful attempt to unravel the mystery of the bogus burial.)

Nevill, who led the questioning, went back to Butler. Imbert took notes.

'You remember speaking to us about the bombing of the Woolwich pub? As I told you, Hill admitted being one of those responsible. If your team did it, why should he say that?'

'Perhaps Hill had a reason,' Butler replied.

'But why should he say that? He even pointed out the window the bomb was thrown through.'

'He had a reason for it. Our boys were after him, I think.'

'We'll see you about that later.'

Four days later, according to Detective Chief Inspector Munday (a key officer in the arrests at the Maguire household), O'Connell denied that he had been to Woolwich or knew who was responsible. But when Nevill and Imbert put the question to him again, on December 30 in Brixton Prison, O'Connell, after three times insisting he had nothing to say, now started talking.

'Why do you think Hill admitted to this?' Nevill asked.

'Why do I think it?'

'Yes.'

'I don't know.'

'Did he do it?'

'He has been convicted of it, hasn't he?' O'Connell observed.

'But you don't think he did it, do you?'

'Nothing to say on that.'

'Why not? It's done with now. Do you think he had anything to do with it?'

'Do you think any of them did?' countered O'Connell.

'Hill admitted it.'

'Did he?'

'Was it your team?'

'I have nothing to say on it.'

'But you don't think it was Hill and co.'

Nevill's persistence on a point he had ample reason to leave behind, not least because he was getting so little feedback, suddenly made O'Connell realize what had happened.

'One of our team has admitted it, hasn't he?'

'Are you saying that he did it or admitted it?' asked Nevill.

'One of our team has admitted being on it.' O'Connell wanted to get it straight.

Nevill instantly fed O'Connell a name. 'Which one? Eddie?'

'Butler.'

'Did he do it?'

'He has said he had, hasn't he?' O'Connell persisted.

'Was it your team?' Nevill asked again.

If there was a pre-planned conspiracy to take the collective rap for Woolwich, O'Connell seemed strangely reluctant to join in. More than a fortnight had passed since Butler's revelations.

'There's no point in discussing it,' O'Connell said.

'There is a point in discussing it. If Hill and company did not do it and it was down to your team, there is every reason to discuss it.'

'It won't do any good.'

'We are here to get the truth, and if a person didn't do something that's as important to us as if he did. If your team did it there is no point in Hill and company doing time for it.'

'It wouldn't make any difference.'

'Are you trying to shield Hill or Butler or members of your team?'

'I'm not trying to shield Hill,' O'Connell retorted.

'I beg your pardon.'

'They have been looking for them.'

'For what?' Nevill asked.

'For passing information to the Army.'

'Is that why Hill admitted it, to get out of the way?'

'Did he admit it? They knew nothing about it.'

'Hill admitted the Woolwich bomb to both Peter and me. I can assure you of that. Now why would he do that? How would he know the details of it? How would he? Was it your team? Was it? Was it? Was it your team? Were you on it?'

O'Connell gradually relented. 'Our team, not me, four.'

'Four of your team?'

'Yes.'

'And you?'

'Four, me.'

'You.'

'I have nothing to say on it.'

'Are you trying to shield your team or Hill?'

'Not trying to shield anyone.'

'Look, if it wasn't your team then I want no mucking about. If it was, the matter must be reported. We must do something about it.'

'What can you do? They've been convicted of it.'

'That doesn't matter. We have to get the truth. Both Peter and I interviewed Hill and Armstrong and Conlon, and if they admitted it but didn't do it then we want to know. We are after the truth. Will you make a statement to someone independent about it?'

'I will have to speak to the other boys about it first.'

Throughout their custody the men had been kept strictly in solitary confinement — for security and for interrogation purposes.

The next day, New Year's Eve, Nevill questioned the whole team again except for Butler. Duggan now allowed that he had seen Hill and Armstrong's names in the newspapers in connection with the Woolwich bomb, but refused to say anything else. So did Doherty. It was O'Connell who threw in a tantalizing new reference.

'Anything further to say to us about Woolwich?' Nevill asked.

'No.'

'Well, I can only say to you as I said last night we are concerned to get the truth.'

'We wouldn't be prepared to say anything anyway, not unless we spoke to O'Dowd [Brendan Dowd] as well.'

'So if I ask you once again now whether you or your team were involved in the bombing of the King's Arms at Woolwich in November 1974, what is your reply to that?'

'No comment.'

Perhaps Nevill and Imbert concluded that O'Connell and Butler were lying or that they would provide no more information about the Woolwich bombing. At any rate, official records show no further conversations on the subject; no meeting was set up with Dowd; no charges were laid on the basis of the admissions.

Nevertheless, in the light of the two Superintendents' avowed concern for getting to the truth and correcting a possible miscarriage of justice, it is, at the very least, strange that the police informed neither Hill and Armstrong nor their solicitors of the startling new light thrown on their convictions two months earlier. They did, on the other hand, inform the office of the Director of Public Prosecutions, which was so incurious as to take no public action at all.

Certainly, the Balcombe Street men's stated indifference to the fate of the Guildford (and Woolwich) Four was reinforced by their failure to get the information out through their own solicitors. Five months passed before the secret travelled any further. If this was a carefully planned scheme to free the Guildford Four, it was taking a long time to ignite. Or perhaps they simply knew, as O'Connell had cynically observed, that 'It wouldn't make any difference.'

33
TWO OLD GUYS

'I think Dowd was boastfully saying the truth. I think he was pleased to say that there were more actions that he had done — and in cold blood.'

Former police superintendent James Still, 1986

The trial of Brendan Dowd and the North-West ASU in May 1976 could scarcely have provided a greater contrast to the Maguire case. The five defendants spent most of the 10-day hearing at Manchester Crown Court in the cells, after refusing to recognize the court from the outset. The 55 charges connected with the doomed campaign in Manchester and Liverpool cited conspiracy to cause explosions and murder; eight attempted murders; assault and unlawful imprisonment of hostages; and possession of arms, ammunition and explosives. None of the charges against Dowd related to offences in London and the Home Counties.

The five men finally returned from the cells to hear the jury give its verdicts and Mr Justice Cantley describe them as 'dangerous and disgusting'. His name was placed on the next Provisional IRA death list.

Paul Norney smiled at his friends and relatives in the gallery as he was given five life sentences and concurrent prison terms totalling 66 years. Noel Gibson shouted, 'Is that all? Give me more,' as the judge sentenced him to two life sentences and 111 years. Sean Kinsella listened in silence to his punishment of three life sentences and 129 years. Stephen Nordone turned his back on the judge, saying, 'I don't speak to pigs.' He was given three life sentences and 192 years. He struggled and shouted, 'Up the Provos,' as he was taken away. Brendan Dowd stamped his feet in an attempt to drown the judge's words, and when

he attempted to make a political speech he was taken down to
the cells before he could hear his sentence, which was life three
times over and 129 years' imprisonment to run concurrently, for
the 11 charges on which he had been convicted.

After the customary police briefings, the Wednesday-morning
press described Dowd as 'the top terrorist organizer in Britain'.
Yet despite his admissions and a catalogue of forensic and
fingerprint evidence held by the Metropolitan Police Bomb
Squad relating to crimes even graver than those for which he
had just been sentenced, he has never stood trial for them.

In the same month the telephone rang in Alastair Logan's
Guildford office. He had never been satisfied by the verdicts in
the Guildford Four trial, but legal-aid funds had run out upon
conviction and there seemed little prospect of advancing the
defendants' continuing claims of innocence. Gradually, the other
defence solicitors would give up the case, but Logan's persistence
— wholly at his own expense — led him finally to represent
all four.

The caller was Jacqueline Kay, who was connected with the
Northern Ireland Prisoners' Aid Committee, an organization
concerned with the welfare of Republican — principally IRA —
prisoners. Through a solicitor she had heard that Eddie Butler
had made a statement to the Metropolitan Police admitting
that he and others were responsible for the Woolwich
bombing. At a meeting on May 21 with Logan and Paul
Hill's then solicitor, David Melton, Jacqueline Kay suggested
that access to the Balcombe Street men might be arranged
through Frank Maguire, the Independent Republican MP for
Fermanagh and South Tyrone, who was planning to visit them
before their trial.

The matter was delicate. Logan and Melton realized that
they could not interview Butler directly to find out more
about his admissions because, unless they were his appointed
legal representatives, any visit would be supervised by police
officers and Butler might be discouraged from saying anything
that might incriminate himself or his colleagues. Alternatively,

if Frank Maguire were to see all four together, Logan and
Melton supposed, Butler might still remain silent for fear that
his co-defendants would realize that he had made a statement
to the police.

At first sight, Maguire was a strange choice of intermediary.
In Northern Ireland he was better known as a publican, keeper
of Frank's Bar, than as a politician. He had never troubled to
make his maiden speech in the House of Commons. Indeed, in
1979 one of his routine absences from Westminster contributed
to the fall of James Callaghan's Labour Government. But he was
passionately concerned about prison welfare, campaigning as
vociferously for imprisoned Soviet dissidents as for Irish Republicans. He agreed to take a message to Butler and the others,
now held on remand in Wandsworth Prison. The message was
simply that Logan wanted to establish contact; there were no
further details.

Joseph O'Connell wrote to Logan requesting a visit. 'Our
intention was to get solicitors ourselves when our committal
was over and admit it then,' O'Connell told Logan later. 'We had
discussed this. We knew the very time, the day we left, that they
[the Guildford Four] were not responsible for these jobs.' Frank
Maguire's message had pre-empted this strategy, but O'Connell
wanted to hear what Logan had to say.

They met in Wandsworth Prison in June. Since O'Connell had
no solicitor at that time, Logan was able to enter the prison as a
potential legal representative and see him in privileged circumstances — out of earshot of police or prison officers. O'Connell
provided little more information to Logan than he had to the
Bomb Squad. He reiterated that Armstrong and Hill had taken
no part in the Woolwich bombing, but added that neither he
nor any of the others was prepared to make a statement until
another man had been consulted, a man who was now also in
custody and who had played a central part in the bombing of
both Guildford and Woolwich: Brendan Dowd.

Again, the intermediary was Frank Maguire. Logan met
Maguire at Heathrow Airport and drove him to Bristol where

Dowd was being held. Dowd agreed to co-operate, and by October Logan's request had received the necessary high-security clearances and was ready for action. He began with Dowd, now transferred to Albany Prison on the Isle of Wight.

Alastair Logan had to take elaborate precautions against the danger that Dowd's testimony could subsequently be said to have been manipulated, doctored or the result of leading questions. Prison officials supervised the meeting. An official court reporter with a stenograph machine recorded every exchange. Logan himself decided to forgo the role of interviewer; he searched for someone of unimpeachable integrity, unconnected with the case, and settled on James Still, a Metropolitan Police Superintendent recently retired from the Fraud Squad, who was acting as investigator employed by the Senate of the Inns of Court. Still himself took the precaution of undergoing a counsel's briefing on how to avoid the danger of asking leading questions. Both Alastair Logan and James Still were later commended by the Court of Appeal for the scrupulously fair manner in which the prison interviews with Dowd and the Balcombe Street men were conducted.

Dowd did not prove to be a comfortable subject. Still later recalled, 'When I first saw him he was very antagonistic, he was rude to me and, to put it politely, we were almost told to go and take a running jump at ourselves. But after talking to him for some time I think he realized that we were only trying to make an honest attempt at making justice appear to be right and his attitude softened immensely.'

Still immediately told Dowd that anything he said was liable to be handed over to the police and prosecuting authorities. Bearing in mind Dowd's contention that there were members of the Guildford bombing team still uncaptured, his caution about divulging incriminating facts was understandable. 'I wouldn't name names or persons. It is up to these people.'

Dowd refused to give even the sex of his companions or to say whereabouts in London they had been living at the time. He said that the mission had been carried out in a hire-car but refused to specify the model or where he had hired it. 'I wouldn't like to say because you probably would be able to trace it back. The police could trace it back.' He was equally circumspect about the bags in which he claimed the Guildford bombs had been carried: 'Just two bags, two brown satchels. If I actually give you the nature of the bags you probably could trace them back.'

Apart from a break for lunch, the interview lasted continuously from 11.00 a.m. until after 4.00 p.m. From the start Dowd warned against the unreliability of his memory: 'I have been involved in so many bombs and gun battles and what have you, I can't distinguish them.' He had said as much in custody in Manchester when Jim Nevill of the Bomb Squad had come to interview him. Nevertheless, he proceeded to give accounts of the Guildford and Woolwich bombings which, in terms of the level of precise detail, far surpassed the versions supplied by the Guildford Four.

Dowd marked a map of the centre of Guildford with the correct locations of the Horse and Groom, the Seven Stars and their third potential target, The Star. The map showed a multi-storey car-park, of which Dowd gave a strange description: 'Approached from this side [indicating] to get into it. The entrance was underground — a multi-storey car-park — and beside it was another one leading on to the street. There was a foot-bridge connecting the car-park, the two car-parks.'

'Do you remember which level you parked on?'

'I parked on the foot-bridge level. I didn't park on the bottom. I came up one or two. I think it was on the same level as the foot-bridge, I am not sure. Either that one or the one over it.'

This satisfied Still and Logan that Dowd had at the very least been to Guildford at some stage, for there is just such a linked double car-park where Dowd marked it on his map. To enter the multi-storey, which is landscaped alongside a small park and a cliff, the driver has to descend to the bottom tier. The pedestrian exit towards town is via a foot-bridge near the top storey, which joins a conventional, flat, open-air car-park on the top of the cliff. Dowd had accurately described this distinctive arrangement. However, as he had admitted going to Guildford on two reconnaissance trips, the accuracy of his description established nothing definite as to whether he had been there on the night of the bombings.

Dowd claimed to have bombed the Horse and Groom with another person, of unspecified gender, having arrived there 'at about 6.30, 7.00 p.m.' in half-light conditions with rain-clouds. 'I think it was raining, I am not sure. I think it was showers.' Dowd was correct again, according to the meteorological records of October 5 1974.

He completed a second diagram, of the interior of the Horse and Groom on North Street, marking the bus stop just outside. This was a remarkable drawing, as both layout and proportions matched the pub's idiosyncratic single drinking-room with its alcoves, tables and chairs, bench seats and gable end. He wrote 'B' for bomb at the point where the bomb had exploded under the hollowed-out bench seat. Logan and Still were impressed. The only pictorial diagram of the layout of the Horse and Groom had been published at the conclusion of the Guildford Four trial in the *Surrey Daily Advertiser*, hardly a newspaper Dowd would have had access to in HM Prison Strangeways in Manchester.

But even this feat of recall two years later established only that Dowd knew the pub. He could have visited it and specified to someone else where to place the bomb. James Still now pressed for details of the bomb itself. Dowd obliged with detail that underlined the flimsiness of the accounts given by the original defendants.

'Six pounds each. Gelignite, as far as I know. It was Frangex, I think. That is roughly right — I am not sure... There was a Combat pocket-watch. I think it was a Combat, about four-and-a-half-volts bell battery.' The bombs, Dowd continued, had been made in London and primed in the multi-storey car-park.

'Just two wires. Yes, detonator wires... I think they were timed for nine o'clock. When you are using — you can't really gauge them. It can be 10 minutes one way or another... You remove one hand, and the minute-hand was removed. Two wires were attached; one was on to the face of the watch and the second was to the body of the watch. As the hand of the watch comes around, it would touch the pin, drawing-pin, through the face of the watch, wired to. Once it touched it, it would connect the circuit.'

'Can you tell us anything about the drawing-pin?' Still asked.

'No, just a drawing-pin. The sharp end had been removed so it wouldn't penetrate the face of the watch... You make a hole in the glass and you push the pin through the glass to the hole. You must touch the face of the wall and the glass acts as an insulator.'

Everything in the description accorded with the forensic suppositions about the composition of the Guildford bombs except the weight. (The Woolwich scientists had calculated that the explosions had been caused by eight-pound bombs.) The description further fitted bombs made later by the London Active Service Unit that had been found unexploded and had been safely dismantled. Dowd, it was clear, knew how the type of time bomb used at Guildford had been made. He may have made it himself, but there was still no proof that he and not Patrick Armstrong had placed it on October 5. Still and Logan needed information from Dowd that had never been published in the press and never revealed in court — no matter how remote a possibility it was that Dowd could ever have had access to such detail. They needed information that only the real bomber could know and that had never been publicly divulged. Given the necessarily exhaustive nature of press publicity and a four-week trial, it was a tall order.

The questioning concentrated on the customers in the Horse and Groom. Dowd was vague. It was fairly dark in the alcove, he remembered. There were a lot of soldiers in civilian clothes and girls. He thought there was a juke-box and a dart-board. He wasn't sure. He marked his diagram — accurately again — with 'JB' for the juke-box, and suddenly announced, 'There were two old guys with shopping-bags.'

Alastair Logan did not wait for Still's next question. 'In the bar?' he intervened. He knew the case and the documents well enough to be certain there had never, anywhere, been any reference to 'two old guys with shopping-bags'.

'Yes,' replied Dowd. 'Just sitting beside me. Carrier-bags. Must have been waiting for a bus.' He drew two circles marking their position on his diagram. 'Had some large bags of groceries with them. I think they must have been waiting for a bus.'

What Alastair Logan did not know was that the first two customers in the Horse and Groom on the night of the bombing were two men — Leslie Hutton, a 51-year-old labourer, and Arthur Jones, a 59-year-old bookseller. They were near neighbours in the village of Compton and had come into Guildford for some Saturday-afternoon shopping. While they were waiting for their bus in North Street, the Horse and Groom opened up for the evening session. The two men went in, sat down on a bench seat in the alcove and spent a little more than an hour over two rounds of drinks.

Mr Hutton had a Tesco's bag and Mr Jones a Woolworth's bag. Both recalled seeing a youngish couple sitting nearby who were neither military nor market people. Between 6.30 p.m. and 7.00 p.m. the bar was beginning to fill up with soldiers and they left. They made signed statements to this effect to the police in the aftermath of the explosion. Nobody attached any significance to the evidence of Mr Hutton and Mr Jones. Their statements were not produced or referred to in court and they were never called to the witness-stand. Their statements stayed on file with the rest of the unwanted pre-trial depositions on the first floor of Guildford police station. None of the defence solicitors had requested, as they were entitled to, the pre-trial depositions.

How could Dowd have known about them unless he had been in the Horse and Groom as he claimed? If Dowd had been in the Horse and Groom, then — on the police's own calculations — Patrick Armstrong could not have been there. For the police had been adamant that they had traced all the customers of the Horse and Groom except the 'courting couple'. There was no reference to a second missing man. It was either Dowd or Armstrong.

Dowd became more forthcoming about the bomb-container. 'It was brown, probably some sort of plastic, imitation leather. Brown anyway... a shoulder-type bag. You see students, a lot of people, using them... girls, blokes. I suppose you could use them as a handbag as well with a shoulder-strap... There was a flap. I think there was some sort of clasp on the side of it, something like that... Probably a spring clip. I am not really sure. That was just one bag of many as far as I was concerned.'

There had been no forensic evidence at the Old Bailey as to the nature of the bomb-container. According to the original confessions, the bombs had been concealed in oblong cardboard boxes. Alastair Logan made a mental note to make another trawl through the debris from the Horse and Groom.

Dowd recalled setting a rendezvous time of 8.00 p.m. for the other set of bombers to be back at the car-park. This tied in perfectly with the trial estimate of 7.53 p.m. as the likeliest time for the 'courting couple' to have left the bar. He claimed to have been the driver; to have been on probably two reconnaissance missions with the bombing team (Dowd said that as a matter of policy no record had been made or kept and no photographs taken); to have been in overall charge of the operation. He said that a hire-car had been used, rented with forged papers, because Guildford was too far away to take a risk with a stolen car. The car was returned to the hire company. He gave the number of the team as 'probably' four.

When James Still slipped from his exacting standards of not providing gratuitous information and stated that the bombing had been on October 5, Dowd did not take advantage. 'Had it placed in August myself,' he said. When his replies were read back to him, he decided he could not remember what the weather had been like after all.

Much of the afternoon session was devoted to the Woolwich bombing. Dowd's answers were again phrased with the rider that he had been on so many missions and that it had been so long ago that he couldn't be sure of his memory. Nevertheless, he again drew an accurate map and specified correctly which window the bomb had been thrown through.

The King's Arms — 'or was it the King's Head? I'm not sure' — had been chosen because of its proximity to the Royal Artillery Barracks and because they knew it was frequented by soldiers. This time Dowd got the month right: November. Again, there had been unrecorded reconnaissance: 'There was very little, just a couple of trips, couple of nights, different weeks... There were military personnel in the pub.' At one point in the questioning Dowd recalled having gone inside the pub to look. Later he remembered looking through the window. He was sure that the team had comprised four men, two of whom had not been on the Guildford mission.

He gave an exhaustive description of the bomb: '... about eight pounds of explosives, I think, was in it... Safety fuse, what they call blue sump... The sump fuse sets off a commercial detonator which has no wires attached to it. You light a fuse... You have to light it. In the electrical one you use a battery and time.' The fuse, said Dowd, was 'about two and a half inches. That would give you about five seconds, five and a half, six seconds.' He volunteered the additional details that the bomb had contained bolts of the approximate length and width of a fountain-pen and that the whole device had been wrapped in standard half-inch black insulating tape — 'could be black, could be any colour. We had several different rolls' — and carried in a plastic bag. He could not remember any identifying brand-name on the bag.

'On the end of it you put — you tape two matches on the end of it... So when you want to light it, you rub the matchbox across it and it ignites it... safety matches, I think... The point is, after Guildford you couldn't very well go back and plant a bomb somewhere else because they were obviously — the only way you could do it was to throw it. That means it had to be some-where in the city where you could get away quickly. It couldn't be in an isolated area. That was the reason why Woolwich was picked.'

The description of the bomb matched the forensic knowledge of the Woolwich device. It further matched the composition of a throw bomb held by the police which had failed to explode. It matched the known facts about five other London throw bombs from the 18-month campaign of terror. For someone who had not been at Woolwich, Brendan Dowd undoubtedly knew a lot about the Woolwich bomb. It is instructive to compare his account of the device with the account that convicted Paul Hill.

Hill had confessed to looking after a plastic container. 'It contained a yellow-coloured liquid and he [Armstrong] told me not to smell it and not to leave it in a warm place. It was a container like you take camping with a tap on it... He told me to go back to the site and give it a shake, which I did.' In a later statement Hill had described Armstrong allegedly throwing the bomb: 'He then lit the bomb which had a fuse on the top, a small black stub, and it sparked and smoked a bit.'

Verbatim, that was the total sum of information that Paul Hill had offered on the Woolwich bomb. As for the mysterious liquid, Mr Justice Donaldson had acknowledged in his summing-up to the jury, 'Nobody can explain what that yellow-coloured liquid could be, and if it was an explosive you would not have attempted to shake it up and down. You will have to consider whether that gives you any pointer as to whether this statement was accurate or inaccurate.'

Mr Justice Donaldson had, however, seemed powerfully struck by Hill's second description: 'Members of the jury, again you will remember the expert evidence that this was, in the view of the expert, a very accurate description of what that bomb would have looked like when it was being lit and thrown through the window, and he suggested that was not the sort of information that would be available to the general public in any way at all and, indeed, is not the sort of information that anybody without expert knowledge would invent of such an occasion.'

Alternatively, it could be suggested that any member of the public who had seen a few old Westerns at the cinema could have summoned up a similar description. Hill's explanation of his alleged expertise was more succinct: 'They [the police] suggested what I should write down. They just told me how they wanted it written down.'

At any rate, no jury has ever had the opportunity of comparing the relative merits of Dowd's and Hill's descriptions of the Woolwich throw bomb.

The question of whether Brendan Dowd or Paul Hill was the fourth member of the team that bombed Woolwich was to become arguably the most important issue of the whole case. This could not have been immediately apparent to Alastair Logan and James Still. They had secured a remarkably detailed and accurate description of another bomb, but it did not prove that Dowd had been present at the bombing. They pressed on to the night in question.

Dowd admitted stealing the car for the mission. 'I think it was Earl's Court. I am not sure. I think it was Earl's Court, somewhere around there. If you have stolen as many cars as I have stolen, you don't think of just one or two... It was a Cortina. I don't know what they call them — 1962/3, 1963 motor I think — the old box-type, you know... It was blue, dark blue, maroon. Blue or maroon. I am not sure.'

It should now be recalled that Anne Simpson's maroon Cortina had been stolen from outside her house in Ifield Road, Earl's Court, on the evening of the Woolwich bombing. No mention of this car had been made at the original trial. Anne Simpson had not been called. Nor had the policeman who had told Ms Simpson when she reclaimed her vehicle that the police suspected it had been used at the bombing. This matter had remained in police files. The only motor car mentioned in the confessions was in Hill's claim that he had gone to the bombing in the back of a silver-blue sports car. There were, however, a number of sworn statements that alluded to a dark Cortina with four men inside accelerating down Frances Street away from the scene of the King's Arms attack, including the testimony of Mr William Fairs, who gave the car's colour as 'maroon'.

Dowd's recall appeared to be better than he was giving himself credit for. 'We parked down the side of it and I believe that particular night there were some workers outside it digging up a gas meter or something... They had dug up the footpath just in front of the window at the traffic-lights... They didn't try to stop anybody, but I believe they were sitting drinking their tea so they were obviously watching what was happening.' Dowd added that had the road-workers interfered they would have been shot. He further added that he remembered reading something about the gas men in a newspaper in the wake of the bombing. Dowd's frankness disqualified this as potentially unique evidence: no one could rely on information that had appeared in the media. Logan and Still pressed on.

'I was driving so I had just sat in the motor and the others got out,' said Dowd. 'They walked back and just lit the fuse and threw it through the window.'

'Did you see them do that?'

'No, I was pointing away from — sitting with my back to it actually. The car was pointing in the opposite direction... and they just jumped back in the motor and we drove back into the city... I think it was after 10 o'clock.' The bomb had exploded at 10.17 p.m. Again, Dowd's account of where his car had pulled up in relation to other parked cars and his recollection that he had extinguished his headlights matched eyewitness accounts and the known facts.

There was more to come. Dowd suddenly interposed, 'The only incident I can remember is that we went about 200, 250 yards without any lights on. That was the only incident I remember.'

'Was that by design or had you forgotten to switch them on?'

'It was a bit of both but I think it was really, I forgot. I went so fast... I didn't think of it until a motor car coming against me flashed its lights at me... It was coming up from the dock area. I went in that direction down towards the river, and then turned left into the city. I was going down the hill and the car was coming up the hill.'

Unless Dowd had attended the trial — something that has never been remotely suggested — he was not to know that the observant Mr Fairs, who had watched the getaway from his balcony in Frances Street, had told the police about the flashing headlights. It had never been reported from court or anywhere else. Dowd had again provided a piece of information that only someone who had been on the scene could have known.

If Dowd was part of a conspiracy to free Hill and had not been to Woolwich on the night of the bombing, he had digested some highly arcane detail. None of his colleagues ever remembered the business of the flashing lights. Yet Dowd, in due course, would be accused of 'telling a story of events in which he had not taken part and the details of which he had but recently and improperly learned'. It remains impossible to reconcile this official judgment on Dowd's veracity with his exclusive and unanswerable recollection of the flashing headlights.

Finally, Dowd recalled that the team had dumped the car between two and two and a half miles down the road towards central London 'on a back street just up the road... If I had an A-Z... Used a bus. Got a bus back in.' Among the several streets that match this sketchy description is Heald Street, New Cross, where Anne Simpson's maroon Cortina was eventually found. But this information had never left police records.

James Still, the former Metropolitan Police Superintendent brought in as the independent interrogator, was convinced: 'Dowd was undoubtedly quite capable of doing the most diabolical things,' he said later, 'but I was quite satisfied that what he was telling me was the truth and that he had no desire to mislead me in any way. He began to offer details that I was omitting in my questions and I couldn't believe he was inventing them. In my experience I have never met anyone capable of inventing a story in the detail that he gave it to me if they hadn't been concerned with it.'

Dowd twice spontaneously added a further thought of his own: 'I think that the police know that I was there. They didn't charge me because if they had charged me, they would say, "Why did they charge the other people?" They found in the flat in West London in Kensington [the Fairholme Road safe house] — I mean, all the details, same type of equipment was in the flat as they got in Guildford, so they must have known I was involved. I suppose they were satisfied with what they got.

'There are other people inside for something I did. That is something I don't like. Could I put a bit on the end of that? I just want to say, as far as I am concerned these four people convicted for the Guildford, Woolwich pub bombs had no connection whatsoever with me or my colleagues and they are completely innocent of the said offences.'

Still put a less altruistic gloss on Dowd's motives: 'I think Dowd was boastfully saying the truth. I think he was pleased to say that there were more actions that he'd done — and done in cold blood.'

Dowd, number 8662, was returned to the category A high-security wing of Albany Prison. His sustained incarceration in solitary confinement and in the punishment block led to a protest by five other Republican prisoners, which developed into a violent fight with prison warders. As a result, the five men lost between them 10 years of remission. Their treatment prompted a report on the affair by Amnesty International, the Howard League for Penal Reform and the National Council for Civil Liberties.

Alastair Logan caught the Cowes–Southampton ferry and drove back home to Guildford. Presently, he would act in the European Court of Human Rights in some 18 cases alleging inhumane treatment of Republican prisoners in British gaols. For now, he had to ponder the significance of a maroon Cortina and two old guys with shopping-bags.

34
THE BALCOMBE
STREET TRIAL

'Oh, I believed the Balcombe Street gang all the way
through... '

Sir Peter Imbert, quoted in *The Times*, July 12 1988

The Balcombe Street Active Service Unit came to trial at the
Old Bailey on January 24 1977, more than a year after their
capture. The outcome was, understandably, a formality. They
had been caught red-handed in an armed siege; their 'safe'
houses had yielded a cache of weapons and explosives; their
fingerprints were everywhere; and they had freely admitted to
the police a fearful catalogue of terrorist offences. The London
and Home Counties bombing campaign had finally ceased with
their capture, and they offered no evidence in their own defence.
Nevertheless, the two-week trial was to provide a most
revealing insight into the operations of the country's leading
forensic experts, Bomb Squad officers and even the office of the
Director of Public Prosecutions. In a sense, these people found
themselves on trial as much as Joseph O'Connell, Harry Duggan,
Edward Butler and Hugh Doherty.

The security precautions at the Old Bailey were by now
familiar. Alsatian dogs roamed the corridors, and even the
Archbishop of Canterbury, Donald Coggan, was frisked on
an incidental visit to the court. The fact that the judge, Mr
Justice Cantley, had been put on an IRA execution list since
his sentencing of Dowd the previous year did not deter him
from hearing the case. While it could be argued that having
such a personal interest in the matter might have disqualified
him, he reasoned that to submit to such IRA blackmail could,

by extension, mean that other IRA cases would become untriable.

The contentiousness of the Balcombe Street trial began with the empanelling of the jury: it was discovered that the police knew who was on the panel, which raised the possibility of the accompanying danger of 'jury-vetting' by one side of the case. It transpired that no fewer than 10 of the initial jury panel had been affected in some way by the bombing campaign. They were stood down and the defendants proceeded to exercise fully their right to peremptory challenge, each rejecting seven jurors simply on the grounds of appearance and demeanour. This resulted in a jury that included five women and three black people (and, indirectly, in a change in the law later that year, reducing the number of peremptory challenges permitted from seven to three). The jury was to prove a grave disappointment to the police and the prosecution case.

There were 100 indictments — 25 each — against the Active Service Unit, but it was apparent from the outset that the charges were substantially fewer than their actual offences. Indeed, when they had appeared on remand eight months earlier the charge list had totalled 144. The most significant omission lay in the fact that while the original list had included offences dating back to August 1974, the refined list referred to no offence before December 1974. It was wholly understandable that the list should, in the words of the judge, have been 'trimmed down', for almost any single offence would have ensured a full set of life sentences for the Unit, but the revised list included nothing that had occurred before the arrest of the Guildford defendants, despite admissions and evidence available for this period. For some reason the Crown had no desire to link the men in the dock with bombings in Autumn 1974. Certainly, the explosions at Guildford and Woolwich were conspicuously absent from both sets of charges.

O'Connell, Duggan and Butler wasted no time in supplying the missing connection. In the long-standing IRA tradition of refusing to recognize British courts, each refused to plead as the charges were put, but for an additional reason beyond their perception of their offences as political and perpetrated in pursuance of a war. 'I refuse to plead,' said O'Connell, 'because the indictment does not include two charges concerning the Guildford and Woolwich pub bombings. I took part in both, for which innocent people have been convicted.'

His co-defendants adopted the same posture. Curiously, all the national newspaper reporters attending the trial, with the exception of those from the *Guardian*, made no reference to the stated reason behind an otherwise typical IRA refusal to plead. It was, after all, the first public airing of a contended massive miscarriage of justice.

John Mathew QC, leading for the Crown, was instantly decisive in telling the jury that 'Guildford and Woolwich are not a matter for you.' But the two names reverberated throughout the trial. While making no attempt to defend themselves, the Balcombe Street men instructed their counsel to discredit the Crown case against them and to educe evidence that tied them to the Guildford and Woolwich bombings.

The remarkable detail that solicitor Alastair Logan had elicited from his prison interviews was available to the Balcombe Street men's defence team. It enabled them to put awkward questions to prosecution witnesses; questions to which the defence team already had a shrewd idea of the answers.

These tactics bore dramatic fruit when Douglas Higgs took the stand. Higgs was the RARDE principal scientific officer who had been a key forensic witness at the Maguire trial — a civil servant but, above all, an independent scientist with no formal connection with police or prosecution. His office had monitored all the evidence of the IRA bombings in 1974 and 1975. The period of the campaign from Guildford in October 1974 to the night of the seven London bombs in January 1975 was known as Phase One; from Caterham in August 1975 to the Balcombe Street siege in December 1975 was known as Phase Two. In particular, Higgs had personally studied the Phase One throw-bomb attacks of autumn 1974 and had prepared a written analysis for the court:

'I have over 17 years' experience of explosives. Over the period 22.10.74 to 22.12.74 I have examined four incidents involving five devices of which all but one detonated successfully. All of these incidents had one unusual feature in common, compared with all other incidents studied over the previous 12 months, that is, they were either thrown or dropped and detonated almost immediately thereafter. For this reason, and a number of other features which will be outlined, it is suggested that there is a common link connecting them as a series... ' The document itemized the four incidents as the explosions at Brooks's club and the Naval and Military Club; the double bombing of the Talbot Arms where one of the bombs had failed to detonate; and the bomb that had exploded on Edward Heath's first-floor verandah in Wilton Street. Higgs further listed the common features that connected the bombings as a series: all the devices weighed about five pounds; all were packed with a combination of bolts, nails, nuts and washers; all were aimed at windows 'of places where people foregathered'; all had short, non-mechanical fuses; all occurred within a two-month period. The unstated implication was clear — all the bombings had the trademark of a specific unit. They all appeared on the police Incident Chart for the Balcombe Street Unit and one or more of the men had confessed to all of them. Higgs's painstaking trawl through the debris of the explosions and his dismantling of the unexploded bomb were the final seal. His document was dated June 17 1976.

Mr Ian Macdonald, counsel for O'Connell, rose to cross-examine Higgs: 'In view of the common features which Woolwich quite clearly has with those four other incidents that you mention in your statement, Mr Higgs, would you tell us why it was that you omitted any mention of the Woolwich bombing when you were preparing that statement and that correlation?'

'In my original statement the Woolwich one was included but it has subsequently been dealt with elsewhere,' Higgs replied.

'By this particular statement, which I believe was on 17th June last year, Woolwich had already been dealt with.'

So it was established that at some stage Higgs had made a statement that included the King's Arms, Woolwich bombing in a series now being attributed to the Balcombe Street men. Furthermore, he had since taken out the Woolwich reference — an extraordinary development.

Mr Justice Cantley intervened, 'You left it out after Woolwich had been dealt with?'

'Yes, my Lord,' Higgs replied. 'It was in an original statement and, having been dealt with in court, it was left out.' But this was not the truth. Further cross-examination established that the earlier statement in which Higgs had included Woolwich was dated January 26 1976 — after Woolwich had been dealt with. Why, Mr Macdonald pressed, had he included Woolwich in the January statement, when the fact that Woolwich had been dealt with was now being given as the reason for the omission of Woolwich in the present statement?

'That statement in the booklet there is a compilation of all the statements which have been written in connection with this,' Higgs replied. 'This was for my guidance only.'

Unfortunately for Higgs, this was not the truth either. 'That is not quite right, is it, Mr Higgs, because that is a statement which is in exactly the same form as your subsequent statements; it is signed at the bottom of each page by you, isn't it?'

'Yes,' replied Higgs. The two statements were laid out identically. The only differences between the January and June documents were that in the latter statement Douglas Higgs's experience with explosives had graduated from 16 years to 17 years and every reference to the King's Arms, Woolwich had been deleted.

'But you agree, do you, Mr Higgs, that the bombing at the King's Arms public house in Woolwich is linked to the other three bombs?'

'It is linked in philosophy.'

'... All I am asking you, Mr Higgs, is do you agree that Woolwich belonged to that set?'

'It belongs to the set, certainly.'

'And from that, Mr Higgs, you can deduce a number of things... that the same team which did Woolwich did the other throw bombs, that is one conclusion you can draw from your linking up of all the incidents?'

'It is one that can be drawn,' Higgs conceded. But Paul Hill and Patrick Armstrong, who had been convicted of the Woolwich bombing, were securely in custody by the time of the later throw bombs, so it could mean only that Higgs's connections were nonsense (which he strongly denied) or that the Balcombe Street men who had been responsible for the later explosions had also bombed Woolwich, as they were claiming.

Mr Macdonald turned now to the most pressing question of all: 'Well, why did you leave it out? Were you told to take it out?'

'I think I was,' Higgs replied.

'... Mr Higgs, you come to court as a scientist, as an expert, and I take it from that answer that originally you considered Woolwich as part of the throw-bomb series but were told to take it out at a subsequent stage... Well, why did you leave Woolwich out in your second statement, which is produced as part of the depositions in this particular case?'

'I think I have answered that, sir. To the best of my knowledge I was asked to do so, or was advised to do so.'

'Who asked you to do so, or who advised you to do so?'

'Well, this could only have come through the police. We don't take instructions from anyone else.'

'Through the police?'

'I presume so — acting on the advice of counsel.'

The revelation that the police could ask, advise or instruct Government-employed forensic scientists to amend their signed evidence prompted Mr Justice Cantley to join in the cross-examination: 'I cannot follow why you should take something out of an expert witness's statement just because someone has told you to.'

'Well, my Lord, this is perfectly true. I cannot say anything contrary to that... ,' Higgs replied.

'Can you give me any better reason for taking it out than somebody told you to?'

'I think that must be admitted, my Lord.'

Mr Macdonald still wanted to know who had given the instructions. It was hard work. 'Now would you please focus your mind, Mr Higgs, on exactly who it was who came to you, as head of the forensic section, and said, "Will you leave out Woolwich from the throw-bomb series?"'

'I cannot say, sir, offhand.'

'You cannot say?'

'It must have been one of the members of the Bomb Squad on advice, acting on advice from elsewhere.'

'I was wondering if you could do this for me, Mr Higgs. Presumably you have notes which you made about conferences or discussions which you may have had with regard to what you should put in and what you should leave out of your evidence?'

'I have had no conference, sir, regarding what I should put in or what I should not put in in that sense.'

'Is there anywhere in your notes, so far as you are aware, that you have written down who told you to leave out Woolwich?' Finally, Higgs's memory produced a name.

'So far as I can recall it was after a visit to Woolwich [the headquarters of the RARDE] by, I think it was Sergeant Doyle but I couldn't swear to that.'

'Sergeant Doyle?'

'Yes, sir.'

'You mean this gentleman sitting down here?'

'Yes, sir.'

'No one else?'

Higgs's memory lapsed again. 'I cannot recall, sir, if anyone else did come down.'

'So let me understand exactly what you are saying. You are saying that it was on the say-so of Sergeant Doyle of the Bomb Squad that you left out Woolwich?'

'He was presumably acting on advice from counsel.'

Mr Justice Cantley was still at a loss: 'But why you should leave it out because people tell you to I don't quite understand.' He did not, however, pursue the point further. Mr Macdonald was not yet finished with Douglas Higgs, principal scientific officer, but a pressing new question had presented itself. On whose orders had Sergeant Doyle travelled to the RARDE with his instructions?

Detective Chief Superintendent Hucklesby of the Metropolitan Police was recalled to the witness-box. It had been his task to prepare schedules of evidence for the Director of Public Prosecutions' office and for prosecution counsel to help them decide which cases to select for prosecution. He told the court that he had relied upon instructions from Commander Jim Nevill, head of the Bomb Squad, and forensic scientists like Mr Higgs of the RARDE. He had been instructed by Commander Nevill to consider the possible involvement of the Balcombe Street men in the Woolwich bombing (he could not remember about Guildford), a possibility that had been raised by Butler's and O'Connell's having confessed to Woolwich in their early days in custody.

DCS Hucklesby confirmed the existence of a police list of some 60 offences attributed to members of the Balcombe Street ASU. It began with the first unlawful setting-up of an IRA safe house by O'Connell in August 1974 and included a number of bombings in autumn 1974 that had never appeared on any charge sheet: the Victory Club and Army and Navy Club (not to be confused with the Naval and Military Club) bombings of October 11; the Harrow School bomb of October 24; and the King's Arms, Woolwich bomb of November 7. But all these offences had been removed from the police list that was before the court. Mr Richard Harvey, O'Connell's junior counsel, asked, 'At what stage were you asked to leave them out, Mr Hucklesby?'

'This was discussed following the submission of my first major report to the Director of Public Prosecutions at a conference with counsel and —'

'But as an experienced investigating police officer you would accept that in your opinion you had sufficient evidence both from the forensic experts and with the defendants' alleged admissions to prosecute at least some of them for the Woolwich bombing?'

There was a pause of sufficient length for the official stenographer to record the fact before Hucklesby agreed, 'In relation to the Woolwich bombing there was the verbal admission of Butler and some evidence from Mr Higgs of scientific links.'

After Hucklesby had agreed that O'Connell, too, had confessed to Woolwich, Mr Harvey pressed on: 'Mr Hucklesby, I am aware you have done a lot of work in this case which in some respects you must feel has gone to waste, but you must have felt at that stage quite sure in your own mind that you had sufficient evidence to amount to a prosecution on Woolwich?'

'I submitted it to the Director of Public Prosecutions as such, yes.'

An exceptional state of affairs had been laid bare. A combination of freely given confessions and independent forensic evidence had been sufficiently compelling for the Bomb Squad to recommend to the highest prosecuting authority in the land that one or more of the Balcombe Street men should stand trial for Woolwich. Yet, as a result of 'conferences' and 'instructions', far from a prosecution materializing, both the Bomb Squad and the independent explosives expert had seen fit to delete their references to the King's Arms, Woolwich bombing from their court lists as if it had never happened. The most important document of all — Higgs's January 1975 statement linking Woolwich with the throw-bomb series — had not been furnished to the defence in the pre-trial depositions.

By now, the Crown had in its possession the additional confessions of Brendan Dowd and Harry Duggan to Woolwich. This was too many for comfort. More pertinently, it was too many for Paul Hill to be guilty of attending the bombing mission, for all the eyewitnesses had spoken of one car containing, at most, four bombers. Surrey Police, who had been making no public progress on the uncaught bombers whose names they claimed to know, were not involved. The Director of Public Prosecutions was not invited to the Old Bailey to enlighten the court as to why he had ignored the recommendation of the Bomb Squad to prosecute. While everyone agreed that it would have been tiresome and unnecessary to prosecute on every incident, the deaths and injuries at Woolwich made it the biggest crime of the 60 on the original list of incidents (Guildford never having appeared on any public list) and the outstanding candidate to be heard.

An explanation of administrative convenience is hopelessly shoddy in the light of Hill's conviction having been secured in the face of no evidence beyond contested confessions, his defence of alibi and his plea of not guilty, quite apart from the problem posed by there now being available five confessions to a crime committed by only four people. But any other explanation can only be sinister: that the Crown sought to avoid the embarrassing spectacle of the Balcombe Street defendants explaining in full and public detail how they and not Paul Hill had bombed the King's Arms; or, worse still, that by now the Metropolitan Police Bomb Squad, the forensic experts and the Director of Public Prosecutions all knew or suspected that Surrey Police had made an awesome mistake and they were actively covering it up.

Douglas Higgs, at any rate, was unaware of any great moment in his deletion of the Woolwich references. Mr Macdonald had put it to him, 'Yes, but you appreciate, don't you, Mr Higgs, as a scientist, that if you leave out one incident like the Woolwich one, that statement which you then make is going to be quite misleading?'

'No, sir,' came the reply.

Mr Macdonald next turned to Guildford, for which the
Crown now knew that Dowd and O'Connell were claiming
responsibility along with three unnamed persons. Mr Macdonald
was able to establish that even as the Guildford trial had been
proceeding, Douglas Higgs, a witness at the trial, had signed a
statement that linked the two Guildford pub bombings with the
Phase One series of time-bomb attacks. The statement, dated
October 10 1975, had not been produced at the Guildford trial.
Again the defence team had been unaware of its existence. It is
safe to assume that the defendants in the case would have been
extremely interested to know that the bombings they had been
charged with were being linked officially with bombings that had
occurred after their arrest.

The October 1975 document schematically linked eight time
bombs from Phase One: '... the latter [Guildford] incidents are
linked with the remainder by virtue of a nitroglycerine-based
explosive and the identification of many components from a
Smith's pocket-watch at the Seven Stars and fractions of a similar watch bezel from the Horse and Groom... In my opinion, the
extensive use of Smith's pocket-watches, particularly the Combat variety, the use of Ever Ready type 126 batteries, similar
types of adhesive tapes and detonators and, above all, the great
similarity of explosives types are too much of a coincidence to
be other than a reflection of an underlying common source
of supply, information and expertise... The general absence
of certain peculiarities consistently present in other areas of
attack only strengthens my opinion that the incidents considered
herein form a connected set.' Higgs confirmed to Mr Macdonald
that this statement had never been part of a deposition at either
the Guildford trial or the Balcombe Street trial.

The statement proffered by Higgs to the Balcombe Street
trial, dated July 12 1976, reproduced the schematic diagram —
but without Guildford; the list of bombings under review omitted Guildford; and while the conclusion was, verbatim, the same
as that of the earlier statement, there was no longer a single
reference to Guildford in the text. The matter had, of course,

been dealt with but, as in the case of Woolwich, the police had never claimed to have caught the whole team, so on the issues of both scientific integrity and clear justice the omissions were as inexplicable as those relating to Woolwich.

Higgs was followed into the witness-box by Donald Lidstone, another principal scientific officer from the RARDE, who, with 38 years' work with explosives behind him, was even more experienced than his immediate superior, Higgs. He had studied the forensic debris from the Horse and Groom and the time bombs in Phase Two, which included the Caterham Arms bomb. He agreed that the Horse and Groom and the Caterham bombings showed common features in the method and location of placement, the type of explosive, the type of Smith's watch and the timing of detonation, but was reluctant to link them because of the time lapse between them. This contradicted Higgs's evidence. He had linked the Brooks's club explosion (in the same month as Guildford) with the Phase Two bombings. The time lapse had been no problem — and elsewhere Higgs had linked the Guildford and Brooks's club explosions.

Under Ian Macdonald's cross-examination Lidstone now accepted the possibility of a link with Guildford. 'You see, is not the position this, Mr Lidstone,' said Mr Macdonald, 'that if you put the Guildford bombings at the start of Phase One and you have Caterham at the start of Phase Two, you get a striking similarity of pattern on both those phases?'

'Yes, sir... I think the Guildford Horse and Groom could be connected, I won't disassociate myself from that.'

Lidstone had separately come to a conclusion about the Phase Two bombings, more far-reaching than any drawn by Higgs. 'You thought that there was a likelihood that because of those forensic links you found that they were done by the same person or persons?' Mr Macdonald asked. 'Yes, I certainly do,' replied Lidstone. Elsewhere, he described the Phase Two bombings as the work of 'a single cell... a single firm'.

Mr Macdonald moved towards the inevitable conclusion: 'You say Guildford may be linked. If Guildford is linked in the way that you are suggesting that the 15 bombs in the second series are linked, then, on your finding of so many links, that would mean the same person or persons did those bombings, including Guildford, would it not, if you put it in the link?'

'If I put it in the link and if the evidence of handiwork was there as well,' Lidstone conceded.

In the extensive cross-examination that culminated in this point, Mr Justice Cantley had brusquely questioned the issue's relevance: 'So what?' he had asked. Now, following an intervention from John Mathew, QC for the Crown, the judge moved to terminate the line of questioning. '... you need not keep asking the witness about it,' he told Mr Macdonald. 'No,' replied counsel. 'I just thought that there are the two alternatives: either he is right in his evidence and the wrong people have been convicted or, if those people did the bombings which he says are forensically linked, that makes it a likely possibility that they were done by the same person or persons, then there is a lot of doubt about the accuracy of that evidence.'

'I think we have got the point,' the judge concluded. 'I have no doubt the jury will consider it.'

Gerard Conlon, meanwhile, was getting fractured reports of the trial in the high-security wing of Wakefield Prison. On January 31 he wrote home:

> It's the first time I shed a tear in prison. Mum, you'll never know how happy I was to read it and see for the first time since I was arrested that the truth is coming out, now it has been publicly admitted in a court of law that we were not responsible for the charges on which we were convicted. I'm feeling confident about the outcome, everyone must now know that I should be out as the police fitted up the wrong people and it's out in the open now, Mum.

Commander Jim Nevill, head of the Bomb Squad, was asked in court on February 4 why he had not pursued Dowd's and O'Connell's claims to have bombed Guildford. It would have been 'wrong', he explained, because he was not the investigating officer on the case. Separately, he acknowledged that it was at the instigation of the Director of Public Prosecutions that he had sent the instructions to Douglas Higgs to remove the references to Woolwich from his statement.

On February 7 Detective Superintendent Peter Imbert was recalled to the box for questioning about a series of interviews that had not appeared in his main body of evidence — the interviews in which members of the Balcombe Street ASU had confessed to the Woolwich bombing and denied all knowledge of Paul Hill and Patrick Armstrong. Imbert and Commander Jim Nevill of the Bomb Squad were in a unique position, for they alone had heard — and could compare — the respective confessions of both the Guildford Four and the Balcombe Street men. It was Imbert and Nevill who, along with Surrey Police, had shown such scant interest in pressing the Guildford Four for information about the wave of bombings in London apart from those at Guildford and Woolwich.

Mr Lloyd-Eley, QC for Eddie Butler, wanted to know why Imbert and Nevill had not followed up Butler's original admissions about Woolwich, which dated from his first interview in custody after the siege, particularly after Nevill had promised, 'We'll see you about that later.' Imbert replied that they had decided not to follow it up after the final interviews with O'Connell in Brixton Prison: 'Our intention was certainly to ask each one of them but, to put it in common parlance, we drew a blank and we left it on that day.'

'You speak of that as a blank, but so far as Mr Butler was concerned he had made admissions in respect of Woolwich from the very outset?'

'Yes, sir.'

A lengthy wrangle ensued as to whether the present trial was the proper forum in which to discuss the relative merits of the competing claims to have bombed Woolwich. Mr Justice Cantley explained his position: 'I am not the Home Secretary and I am not the Court of Appeal. I do not know whether Hill

and Armstrong have appealed... O'Connell claims the Woolwich
bombing — "I did it" — but I cannot grant him his claim in these
proceedings. If he is right, perhaps there are other proceedings
in which he may substantiate his claim... Butler could be of great
help to him [Hill] if he wishes to go on with his appeal.'

'Most certainly, sir,' replied Detective Superintendent Imbert.

With that, the case for the prosecution closed. All that
remained was for Joseph O'Connell to make an unsworn statement from the dock on behalf of his co-defendants, in preference
to calling any defence witnesses. His insistence on describing the
offences in the context of a state of 'war' and the 'occupation'
of Northern Ireland by the British led to seven objections by
the judge, who told him not to make a 'political speech'.
O'Connell simply ignored Mr Justice Cantley's interruptions
and spoke straight through them, directly at the jury, one of
whom recalls, 'He was absolutely and coldly determined to say
his piece. He stood up in the dock and wouldn't be stopped. He
was very impassioned and emotional about how, in their terms,
they were fighting a war but he was also very controlled, very
intense. He was the cleverest of the lot.' One section passed
without interruption from the judge:

> We have recognized this court to the extent that we have
> instructed our lawyers to draw the attention of the court
> to the fact that four totally innocent people — Carole
> Richardson, Gerard Conlon, Paul Hill and Patrick Armstrong
> — are serving massive sentences for three bombings, two
> in Guildford and one in Woolwich. We and another man
> [Dowd] now sentenced have admitted our part in the
> Woolwich bombing. The Director of Public Prosecutions
> was made aware of these submissions and has chosen to
> do nothing. I wonder if he would still do nothing when he
> is made aware of the new and important evidence which has
> come to light through the cross-examination by our counsel
> during this trial. I will refer to three of those witnesses who
> gave evidence at this trial and whose evidence was also dealt

with in the conviction of those four innocent people... Taking Mr Higgs first, he admitted in this trial that the Woolwich bomb formed part of the series of those bombings with which we are charged; yet when he gave evidence in the earlier Guildford and Woolwich trial he deliberately concealed that the Woolwich bomb was definitely part of a series carried out between October and December 1974 and that people on trial were in custody at the time of some of those bombings. Mr Lidstone in his evidence for this trial tried to make little of the suggestion that the Guildford bombing had been part of the Phase One offences with the excuse — and this appeared to be his only reason — that the Guildford bombing had occurred a long time before the rest. When it was pointed out to him that the time between the Guildford bomb and the Brooks's club bomb which followed Guildford was 17 days, and the Woolwich bomb which followed that was 16 days, and that many of the other incidents with which we are charged had equal time gaps, Lidstone back-tracked and admitted that there was a likely connection. Those two men, Mr Higgs and Mr Lidstone, gave evidence at the Guildford and Woolwich trial which had no place in their true conclusions as scientists; they gave evidence which they must have known was untrue. The evidence which they gave was completely following in line with police lies so as to make the charges stick against those four people. Then we come to Commander Nevill. He said he only wanted to get the truth concerning Guildford and Woolwich in fact when he gave evidence in this trial; yet he has not done. Why? Because Nevill knows that the truth means the end of the road for him and many other senior police officers and because his superiors know it would be a dangerous insight into how corrupt the British establishment really is. This shifty manoeuvring is what we, as Irish Republicans, have come to understand by the words 'British justice'. Time and again in Irish political trials in this country innocent people have been convicted on the flimsiest of evidence, often no more than statements and even 'verbals' from the police. Despite the oft-repeated claim that there is no such thing as a political prisoner in England...

The judge and O'Connell descended into another battle before O'Connell had a brief, final word: 'You continue to interrupt me. As volunteers in the Irish Republican Army we have fought to free our country from its bondage of imperialism, of which this court is an integral part. I have made this statement on behalf of the four of us in the dock.'

With that, O'Connell demanded to be returned to the cells. His colleagues followed. Butler shouted, 'I want to be taken down. I want no part in this farce.' The tension spilled over into an unpleasant exchange between the judge and Mr Richard Harvey, one of O'Connell's barristers. Mr Harvey asked for a copy of O'Connell's speech and the judge replied, 'What do you want it for, as a memento?'

'I regard that remark in rather bad taste,' Mr Harvey retorted, explaining that he wanted it to check against the judge's summing-up. The judge agreed that it was a proper reason, but subsequently refused to supply the jury with a copy.

The jury was out for seven hours and 40 minutes. They returned with unanimous verdicts — but, to the astonishment of everyone in court, some of the verdicts were not guilty. All the defendants were acquitted of crimes involving time bombs and throw bombs from both phases of the campaign: the Putney High Street and Charco Grill bombs of January 1975; the Portman Hotel bomb of October 1975; the Trattoria Fiori bomb of December 1975; and — most tellingly — the Caterham Arms pub bombing of August 1975. All these had been claimed by the forensic experts to belong to a connected series, and there were confessions available (although those of Dowd for the January 1975 bombings were not before the jury).

Alastair Logan, solicitor for the Guildford defendants, had been monitoring the trial: 'Anyone who saw the faces of Nevill and Imbert in court at the time those not guilty verdicts were entered by the jury could not have failed to notice their extreme anger. This manifested itself in an almost uncontrollable outburst by Nevill outside court who demanded to have a copy of the speech from the dock which was made by O'Connell.'

The juror, necessarily anonymous, who has since spoken to the authors about the trial and the verdicts, recalls, 'I remember the police were very shocked by the fact that there were acquittals and, of course, it was quite likely that the Balcombe Street men did do the lot. But what happened was that we were, in a way, rebelling against being railroaded by the court into unanimous verdicts of guilty; as if we were just there to rubber-stamp what the court, the prosecution and the police wanted; as if it was all a foregone conclusion. Some of us got very upset. We thought it was immoral.

'What we did was to look at each charge on its merits. We put each one through a test of whether there was enough confession evidence, or forensic or fingerprint evidence, and if it didn't pass enough of those tests, then we acquitted. Also, we definitely felt that at least some of them were connected with Guildford and Woolwich.'

The Guildford defendants, convicted on confession statements alone, might have wished for a similar rigour from their jury. The Balcombe Street jury were told they were free to go, but all 12 returned for the sentencing.

The defendants, who had remained defiantly in their cells for the jury's verdicts, now returned individually to hear sentence, each flanked by three prison officers. O'Connell ostentatiously turned his back on the judge, placed his arms on the dock-ledge and glared at his guards. Mr Justice Cantley gave him 12 life sentences and additional sentences, to run concurrently, totalling 159 years. He recommended a minimum of 30 years' imprisonment. Eddie Butler stared at the ceiling as he received the same sentence. He left for the cells with a two-fingered 'victory' salute to the public gallery. Harry Duggan, too, received an identical sentence, but heard little of it as he waved his arms and shouted at the judge, 'You can say what you like but I'm not going to listen to you. You would not let me make a statement from the dock so I'm not going to listen to anything you have to say. I intend to go on interrupting you.' Hugh Doherty was sentenced to life 11 times over, with an additional 139 years for his other crimes. He called out, 'Good luck, Mary,' as he was taken down.

The concluding business of the court came at the request of John Mathew, QC for the Crown. The judge formally directed that outstanding charges against O'Connell, Duggan and Butler should not be proceeded with and should be left on file. The list included explosions at Tite Street, Chelsea on November 27 1974; an explosion at the Talbot Arms, Westminster on November 30 1974; and an explosion at the Naval and Military Club on December 11 1974. All were on Douglas Higgs's original lists of the connected series of time bombs and throw bombs in Phase One of the campaign before Guildford and Woolwich were deleted at the behest of the Bomb Squad and the Director of Public Prosecutions.

The jury adjourned for a farewell drink at a nearby pub. Not unnaturally, the conversation reverted to the trial. Unknown to them, a number of plain-clothes policemen were observing, and followed them as they left. Some of the jurors were arrested for suspected complicity in acts of terrorism — on the basis of the pub conversation — and detained for an hour at a police station. Two more were followed into St Paul's underground station: 'The police were running after us down the platform. There was screaming. I was grabbed and abused and the other juror was pressed against the wall of the tube and searched. They did apologize when they realized who we were, but it was a very unpleasant experience. Police emotions were obviously running very high.'

35
THE MAGUIRES
GO TO APPEAL

'I think an injustice was done to all the defendants and
I shall never think otherwise... Perhaps the climate was
wrong at the time.'

Harry Disley, defence solicitor, 1984

In the months that now intervened between the trial of the
Balcombe Street Active Service Unit and the appeal of the
Guildford Four, the application for leave to appeal by the
Maguire household and Guiseppe Conlon was presided over
by Lord Roskill at the Court of Appeal. The Right Honourable
Lord Justice Sir Eustace Wentworth Roskill, then aged 67, is
best remembered now as the author of a 1986 Royal Commission report recommending the abolition of juries in certain
categories of criminal fraud trial. Even in 1977 he enjoyed the
reputation of a profoundly conservative judge among a set of
appeal judges not noted for their liberal tendencies. Sitting with
Lord Justice Waller and Mr Justice Ackner, Lord Roskill heard
the Maguires' application between July 20 and July 29 1977.

Alluding to the Guildford bombing at the start of his
judgment, Lord Roskill said, 'There is no shred of evidence that
any of these applicants was in any way involved in that matter.'
There was no new evidence and the argument centred on what
the defence alleged were misdirections and omissions by Sir
John Donaldson in his summing-up at the end of the original
trial. Now, as then, the focus was principally on the scientific
evidence.

The applicants argued that the conflict between the expert
witnesses meant that the convictions were unsafe, and that

the jury had been misled by the summing-up on a number of important points.

Sir John Donaldson's treatment of the notorious 'exhibit 60' was one example. This was the evidence, produced at the eleventh hour by the principal witness for the defence, John Yallop, that cast doubt on the TLC test for nitroglycerine. Scientists for the Crown had claimed that toluene, the eluent used in tests on swabs of the Maguires' hands, produced results with nitroglycerine that were effectively unique; there was no other substance that could be confused with it. 'Exhibit 60' showed that there was another substance, the explosive PETN, that gave identical results in toluene, and although the doubt this raised was academic in the Maguires' case (since no one was suggesting PETN could have been present), the principle was fundamental to the defence case: the behaviour of nitroglycerine in toluene was not unique. The defence argued that the judge had failed to draw the jury's attention to this issue of principle; but Lord Roskill, recognizing the judge's omission, compounded it by saying, 'He left the point to the jury.' And that was the end of it.

This recognition of the defence argument and total failure to deal with it was to be the hallmark of a judgment that resolved none of the disturbing features of the original trial. About the burden of proof — to take another example — Lord Roskill said, 'If the scientific evidence were cogent enough to justify conviction of itself, nothing more was required. But if the Crown had no other evidence, and that scientific evidence was lacking in the requisite cogency, the verdicts must have been not guilty.' So far so good. He went on to interpret the margin of doubt alluded to by the Crown's witness, Elliott, as follows: 'All the Crown witnesses accepted, as one would expect scientists to accept, that there were in the scientific field unexplored and unknown possibilities.' But he added, 'The Crown has not got to exclude theoretical considerations of that kind before a verdict of guilty can be secured. The test for the jury was whether the Crown's scientific evidence... excluded any other realistic possibility and whether it satisfied the jury beyond all reasonable doubt of the guilt of all or some of the applicants.' In other words, the whole argument of innocence or guilt was reduced once again to the reliability of the test, rather than to the wider issue of whether the Crown had satisfied the jury that the Maguires had handled nitroglycerine.

The sniffer had failed to detect traces of nitroglycerine on Anne's gloves. The Crown had failed to carry out corroborative tests. Some of the results of the initial tests had been contradictory and inconclusive, even within their own terms of reference. But — glaringly — the judgment had been couched in such a way that the jury had never really had to address the mystery of missing evidence, notably the absence of the 'bulk' of explosive, or to consider the shortcomings of the conduct of the tests. Lord Justice Roskill, content to travel the same road as Mr Justice Donaldson before him, failed to discuss these issues to any degree of satisfaction.

Counsel for Pat O'Neill and Sean Smyth argued that their clients had arrived at the house in Third Avenue so late in the evening that there had been no opportunity for them to have participated in any disposal of explosives. The judge had not adequately made this point at the original trial; indeed, he had altogether failed to allude to O'Neill's case except in the most general terms until prompted by counsel for O'Neill to deal with it.

Pat O'Neill, in particular, had a strong case in that he had not reached Third Avenue until seven o'clock in the evening. But where Sir John Donaldson had dealt with the matter by opening the jury's minds to the possibility that explosives had somehow been secreted out of the house under the eyes of watching police when the four men left for the pub and hidden during the 'missing half-hour' before their arrest, Lord Roskill fleshed out the scene — for which there was no evidence whatsoever — until it was almost a certainty: 'There would have been an opportunity extending over about half an hour to have handled explosives, knowing perfectly well what they were doing, between the time when, on the police evidence, they left the house and the time when the police entered the public house.'

There was no evidence that, having entered the pub, they had left it at any time prior to their arrest. No explosives had been found there. And the only evidence of any kind on their activity in the pub was their assertion that they were only just beginning their second round of drinks when the police had come to arrest them. The police recorded the time of their departure from the house at 7.45, but the men insisted that they had left some time after 8.00 — following the phone call from Pat O'Neill's wife, prearranged for eight o'clock. They argued that the 'missing half-hour' in their submission was accounted for by incorrect timing by the police.

Lord Roskill's assertions about the appellants' likely activities in the pub demolished the awkward problem not only of the arrival times of Smyth and O'Neill but also of the absence of the 'bulk' of explosive, which he was satisfied could have been disposed of during the day and at the pub in the evening. For the rest, he was content that the points had been fairly put to the jury and that there was consequently no reason for any of the convictions to be disturbed '... either on the basis of any of them [being] unsafe or unsatisfactory or that the learned judge was guilty of any non-direction or misdirection or that his summing-up was in any way unbalanced'.

Lord Justice Roskill's judgment added nothing of substance to Mr Justice Donaldson's original except to endorse its fallacies and underwrite its conclusions. Leave for any of the Maguire household to appeal against conviction was, unsurprisingly in view of this analysis, refused.

36
NO LURKING DOUBTS: THE GUILDFORD APPEAL

'We need only say that so far as the new evidence is concerned we reject it in all relevant respects. That evidence, therefore, gives rise to no lurking doubts whatever in our minds.'

Lord Justice Roskill

Nobody with a shared interest in the Maguire and Guildford cases could have been encouraged to see that Lord Roskill was to preside at the appeal of the Guildford Four, such had been the resounding manner of his rejection of the Maguire appellants three months earlier.

He was joined by Mr Justice Boreham and by Lord Justice Lawton, who in 1976 had rejected the first Birmingham appeal. The Right Honourable Sir Frederick Horace Lawton in 1987 told the BBC2 programme *Out of Court*, 'I have had 50 years' experience of the administration of justice and I don't think the juries get it all that wrong in the sense of convicting the innocent. They frequently get it wrong in acquitting the guilty.'

On October 10 1977 the three judges made legal history by opening the appeal at the Old Bailey. Their normal venue, the Royal Courts of Justice in the Strand, was not considered to be as secure against terrorist attack as the Central Criminal Courts. In the week before the hearing there had been unsubstantiated press reports of plans for a mass IRA break-out at Wormwood Scrubs, and even before the appeal opened Sir Michael Havers secured an order that no one apart from the lawyers should have any access to either the four appellants or the four members of the Active Service Unit who would give evidence. As usual, intensive precautions surrounded the case, with a prominent show of armed policemen wearing bullet-proof jackets patrolling the environs of the court.

The grounds of appeal were clearly established. Joseph O'Connell, Harry Duggan, Eddie Butler and Brendan Dowd claimed that they, and they alone, had bombed the King's Arms, Woolwich. Dowd claimed that he and a young woman, whom he refused to identify, had bombed the Horse and Groom, Guildford. O'Connell claimed that he and another man and another woman, both of whom he refused to identify, had bombed the Seven Stars, Guildford. Dowd and O'Connell refused to identify their three colleagues on the grounds that they were still at large. All four Balcombe Street men insisted that they had no connection with the Guildford Four and had never heard of them prior to their arrest.

The appellants sought a retrial on the basis of these claims, made in affidavits to Alastair Logan in prison and reiterated from the dock at the Balcombe Street trial. They further invited comparison between the confessions of the Active Service Unit and the contested statements upon which they themselves had been convicted. John Leonard QC, on behalf of the four appellants, had produced a list of 153 discrepancies between those statements. In addition, Carole Richardson sought to have her conviction for Guildford overturned on the basis of the evidence of her original alibi witnesses.

Lord Roskill and his colleagues decided at the outset that they, and not a jury, would appraise the credibility of the dramatic new evidence. This was a momentous decision, which still reverberates, and will be explored in more detail later. For now, it meant that the three judges would adjudicate on the honesty of the ASU. They would not have the benefit of hearing the original witnesses set beside the new evidence. Conversely, no jury would ever have the opportunity of mulling over the new witnesses alongside the old evidence. No forum would hear the whole body of evidence in one piece. The trial was irrevocably split into two halves, a policy that has prompted the condemnation of such eminent jurists as Lord Devlin and Lord Scarman. Interestingly, in his 1987 BBC interview Sir Frederick Lawton underlined, perhaps unwittingly, the dangers inherent in the policy he adopted in 1977. Rejecting the notion that the Court of Appeal made too many mistakes, he argued, 'Approximately eight per cent of appeals against conviction are allowed. Nobody takes the view that judges are infallible. I certainly don't take that view because I know I'm not... You get a "feel" of a case. You decide, "This does sound right or it doesn't sound right." You've got to have this sort of "feeling" in the Court of Appeal because we don't retry cases. We don't see and hear the witnesses. I think it's very largely a matter of experience.' Yet, he added, 'Parliament, rightly or wrongly, and the law of the realm for hundreds of years has said that the jury is the proper tribunal of fact.'

For the Guildford appeal, however, Lords Justice Lawton and Roskill and Mr Justice Boreham were satisfied by cited precedent that it was proper for them to see and hear the new witnesses; that they could constitute the proper tribunal of fact; that they could make a decision as to the credibility of the new witnesses. If judges are as well equipped as juries to perform these functions, it might be argued, then the expensive and tiresome centuries-old requirement of juries might profitably be discarded altogether.

The quality of detail offered by the ASU was, however, so great that their credibility in one crucial area was not even doubted by Sir Michael Havers. After protracted cross-examinations of Butler about Woolwich, he said Butler 'left one in some doubt' but was prepared to accept Butler's presence at the bombing; of Duggan on the subject of Woolwich, Sir Michael said he found the new witness 'convincing'; and of O'Connell on both Guildford and Woolwich, Sir Michael said the account had 'such a ring of truth' that he accepted on behalf of the Crown that 'a great deal of what he says is true'. The evidence — 'by and large' — showed a 'very close personal knowledge' of both bombings. These were, of course, the very attributes that had so impressed Alastair Logan and James Still, the former Metropolitan Police Superintendent. None the less, it was remarkable that the Crown was suddenly declaring itself equally impressed, especially after having taken such apparent pains not to charge the men with the worst two incidents of the entire bombing campaign at the time of the Balcombe Street trial.

Lord Roskill followed suit for the judges, actually exceeding Sir Michael Havers's allowances: 'We are content to assume that O'Connell's story of his presence [at Guildford] and participation may indeed be true and that Dowd may also have taken part... ' They were further 'content to assume' that Butler, Duggan and O'Connell had been present at Woolwich. Considerable credibility had been established. As Lord Roskill said of O'Connell, 'It is difficult to believe that had he not been present on both occasions his knowledge of the detail... could have been wholly invented.'

There was a sting in the tail. Sir Michael argued that the concessions made no difference to the case. In effect, they were all guilty; the team had been twice the size claimed by O'Connell and the others; the Guildford Four had been the 'Second XI'. The Balcombe Street men might be telling the truth about having been present at Guildford and Woolwich, but they were lying in their claim that the Guildford Four had not been present. After all, the prosecution had insisted from the earliest committal proceedings that the Guildford bombing team could have numbered as many as eight. The new evidence, Sir Michael argued, was just an IRA scheme to free colleagues belonging to the same Active Service Unit.

There were numerous problems with this line of argument, most of which were to be glossed over by the Crown, the judges and even the defence. There was no objective, third-party evidence for the notion of an enlarged gang for the bombing of Guildford. No one had identified or counted the bombers. No one knew whether they had travelled to Guildford in one car, two cars or a fleet of coaches. The only basis for the Crown's assertion that the gang had numbered eight was evidence in the defendants' own confessions, which had caused Mullin, McGuinness, Colman and Anne Maguire to be charged with murder at Guildford (and the confessions could not agree on the final tally). But these charges had long since been dropped — admittedly to the chagrin of Surrey Police — because there was not an iota of evidence to support them. Supposing Surrey Police had been correct in charging the extra four — and this is not remotely the authors' contention — then with O'Connell and Dowd also now assumed to be present, the putative gang must be further enlarged to 10. But at the conclusion of the Guildford trial, Surrey Police had gone on record as saying that they knew the identities of two more of the bombers but could not reach them — by implication, that they were safely abroad. This claim could not apply to the four who had been freed; it could not apply to Brendan Dowd, who was in custody; and it could not apply to Joseph O'Connell, who at the time was preparing the micro-switch bomb that killed Professor Gordon Hamilton-Fairley in London's Campden Hill Square. Was the gang now to be enlarged to 12 — or to 15 if Dowd and O'Connell were telling the truth about the extra three they refused to name? Nor had anyone advanced an argument as to why the idea of a team of more than four or five made any sense in the first place.

The appellants had supplied a flimsy and contradictory picture of the cars supposedly used on the Guildford bombing raid: Armstrong had referred to a grey Capri and a light-coloured Ford Anglia; Richardson to a big, creamy-coloured car; Conlon to a dark, four-door saloon; and Hill to a yellow Granada. Dowd had insisted throughout that the Guildford bombing team had fitted into one hired Ford Escort. He had refused to give more details for fear of jeopardizing the current holder of the stolen driving-licence used in the hiring. But now he told Sir Michael Havers that on October 3 or 4 he had hired a white Avenger from the Victoria branch of Swan National car rental in the name of Moffitt. The branch manager was summoned and produced records confirming the hiring of a white Avenger in the name of Moffitt from October 4 to October 10. The rental agreement, bearing the hirer's signature, had been lost, but Swan National produced a rental agreement for a Ford Escort for September 21 to 24, also in the name of Martin Moffitt. The signature was in Dowd's handwriting, but since only a photocopy existed, expert handwriting opinion was not admissible. The dates fitted for the reconnaissance trip Dowd claimed to have made two weeks before the actual bombing.

These details strongly reinforced Dowd's claims with regard to Guildford, but the Crown now sought to establish that Dowd had hired a second car from Swan National — the second car needed to accommodate the enlarged gang. It so happened that a man with an almost identical name — Moffat — had hired a yellow Cortina from September 27 to October 9, a period covering the Guildford bombings. This rental agreement had also gone missing but, again, a Mr R. C. Moffat had made an earlier hiring in September, leaving an address in South Africa and a signature wholly unlike Dowd's. There was nothing in Swan National procedures to prevent someone from hiring two cars simultaneously on the same licence. The Crown now took it as a 'matter of proof' that Dowd had had two cars out at the same time.

This was a prodigious leap. The signature did not match remotely; the surnames were spelled differently; the addresses were different. For Dowd to have simultaneously hired cars under the names of Moffitt and Moffat at the same branch office, he would have to have held two stolen licences with coincidentally similar surnames and been oblivious of the risk of arousing suspicion or detection for hiring under different names. The contention was absurd.

None of this troubled the Crown or the judges. Lord Roskill concluded, 'We feel no doubt that the former car [Moffat's Cortina, hired from September 27 to October 9], which was yellow, was hired by Dowd for the purpose of the Guildford bombings... It will be convenient to mention at this point that in his third statement Hill mentioned a yellow XL Granada as one of the two cars.' There was not a shred of evidence to tie Dowd to Moffat. It was a complete *non sequitur*, yet this was how the existence of the necessary second car for the Guildford bombings was established. Lord Roskill had not found it convenient to mention any of the other cars from the original confessions. It was not until after the end of the appeal that Alastair Logan succeeded in tracing Mr R. C. Moffat in South Africa, who duly confirmed that he had been responsible for both the hirings in the name of Moffat. This proved that the judges were totally wrong in claiming that Dowd had hired the yellow Cortina as the second car. It does not require hindsight to see that they had no grounds to make the initial assumption, let alone be certain of it.

No evidence had been produced to link any of the Guildford Four with any of the London ASU. The safe houses had been scoured for fingerprints and had yielded 18 sets, including those of Joe Gilhooley and Margaret McKearney, but none matched any of the Guildford Four's. This had been confirmed by Commander Jim Nevill of the Bomb Squad at the Balcombe Street trial. The intensive interrogation of the Guildford Four had thrown up no names or links with the Active Service Unit, despite the 50 arrests their confessions had prompted. How could the London ASU have risked using an extra foursome, described with brutal frankness by one of their defence solicitors as 'wallies', and relied upon them to have the nerve to sit on top of primed time bombs and then to give away their own identities in the event of arrest? The ASU's self-discipline with alcohol, while not absolute, was exemplified by their abstinence during the six days of the Balcombe Street siege; the Guildford Four were all steady, even heavy, drinkers. As for drug abuse, the IRA has always regarded it as anathema to the point of dealing with it with strict punishment.

Gerard Conlon wrote home in the middle of the hearing:

Well, Mum, I suppose you want to hear how the appeal is
going? First of all you have got to understand that the three
judges who are doing our appeal are the exact same three
who did Dad's appeal [this was incorrect: only Lord Roskill
was on both cases] and you know what happened to Dad's
appeal don't you? These judges seem to be ultra-friendly
towards the Crown and very icy towards our counsel. They
seem to doubt anything that indicates our innocence, but
they seem to find no bother with what the Crown say. In
fact, you can see that they are bending over backwards to
help them, they are definitely on their side. Mum, on the
evidence given by Joe O'Connell, Brendan O'Dowd, Harry
Duggan and Eddie Butler, we four should be out of prison
because there is no doubt whatsoever that these are the
people who were responsible for the Guildford and Woolwich
bombing, in fact, Mum, the prosecution say that it was true
that they were involved in both bombings but they say we
are connected with them. But they say they can't show or
bring any evidence to connect us with them, so why are
we still in prison? Mum, my counsel told the judges that
when the 'police' (which I call pigs) searched all the flats
that the 'Balcombe Street 4' used they found lots of letters,
documents and other material and nothing they found had
anything relating to us, they also found lots of fingerprints
in the flats used by them but admit none of them were ours.
They have absolutely nothing to show we even knew they
existed, so why are we still in prison? Mum, this is an evil
country...

The defence introduced a further strand of fresh evidence from
John Yallop, Douglas Higgs's predecessor as head — for 12 years
— of the forensic branch at the RARDE, and a key witness at
the trial of the Maguire family. It concerned the container for
the bomb that devastated the Horse and Groom. At the original
trial no one had sought to query the confession statement that
the bomb had been carried in a shoe-box. Brendan Dowd,

however, had recalled that the bomb had been carried in a brown shoulder-bag of a type popular with students, 'probably some sort of plastic, imitation leather'. Yallop had inspected debris at the RARDE: 'I was given the opportunity to look at what I initially thought was all the available exhibits gathered from the scene. I was interested in the item labelled DH7 — primarily broken wood and table legs. There was a piece of brown imitation leather which appeared to have originated from the handle of a bag, slightly wide, a bit like the things you get on shoulder-straps.' The material had embedded itself in the wood with terrific force. Mr Yallop considered, 'In my opinion, these pieces must have derived from something very close indeed and they are certainly consistent with it being the bomb container.'

Understandably, the judges were keen to see item DH7. The defence had expected it to be in court. Sir Michael Havers acknowledged this: 'It should have been and I failed to recognize this.' After some delay, item DH7 was produced from the RARDE's Woolwich headquarters and Mr Yallop confirmed his opinion. However, Mr Yallop had also asked for item DH5 before the trial, and this had not been forthcoming from the RARDE. His interest had been stimulated by written notes by Higgs's colleague, Donald Lidstone, dated January 1975. These referred to 'severely shredded pieces of a vanity bag, a shoe, a lady's holdall and of clothing fabric'.

After the appeal had ended, Alastair Logan gave an account of his attempt to secure the fragment of the bag: 'We went into the office of Mr Higgs at Woolwich Arsenal and asked to see this exhibit. He eventually found the register of exhibits and announced that this particular exhibit, out of all the many, many exhibits that had been held, had been returned to the Surrey Constabulary. Present at that meeting were two exhibits officers from the Surrey Constabulary, and we asked them why it had been returned. They announced that it had been returned in order to return it to its owner. When we asked them whether they had returned it to the owner, they said "no" and stated they had destroyed it. Since I had personally delivered the transcripts of Still's interviews with Dowd and the Balcombe Street men to Detective Superintendent Ronald Underwood of Surrey Police five months previously, I knew they had had ample time to work out for themselves just how important item DH5 had become. I felt they were well aware of its significance. I had the clear impression that Higgs and the detectives were embarrassed that we were asking for it.'

Mr Yallop had further been unsuccessful in his request for a better description of the material until, in June 1977, he obtained a photocopy of Mr Lidstone's 'examination notes' with additional description of the lady's holdall bag: 'Large part of a brown plastic (leather interior) bag which had a large metal zip and plastic loop handle. It [was] badly blown out but not sufficiently to be the bomb-carrier. A piece of similar blown plastic was found, trapped in a split in the leg of the circular table.' Irrespective of the missing exhibit, the former head of the RARDE's forensic branch had now identified a fragment that was consistent, in his opinion, with an imitation-leather shoulder-bag that Dowd, exclusively, had described as the bomb-container used for the Horse and Groom. Donald Lidstone was recalled, and disagreed. In his opinion, the damage to the material was insufficient for it to have been the bomb-container.

The importance to both sides of the case of establishing whether Brendan Dowd had been involved in the bombing of the Horse and Groom was that Surrey Police's painstaking timeplans for every customer who had been in the pub that night had eliminated every customer except for the 'courting couple'. The original trial had established that Patrick Armstrong was the missing man 'kissing and cuddling' at the spot where the bomb had later exploded. Every other man had been identified and ruled out. There was not room for both Dowd and Armstrong, enlarged gang or not.

The appellants' hopeful trump card was Dowd's unprompted recollection in his prison interviews that there had been 'two old men with shopping-bags, waiting for a bus' among the early-evening customers in the Horse and Groom. There had been no reference to them in the original trial, so it was not a detail that Dowd could have picked up from reading newspaper court reports as he sat in prison awaiting his own trial. It was not a detail that Dowd could have been fed by any of the Balcombe Street men, for they had never shared the same prison. It was not a detail that he could have been fed by Patrick Armstrong or any of the Guildford Four. It was certainly not a detail that Armstrong had recalled in his own incriminating confessions. A trawl by the defence through the non-deposition statements, taken by Surrey Police before the trial and never used, had uncovered the evidence of Leslie Hutton and Arthur Jones, whose personal descriptions, whereabouts and timings in the Horse and Groom identified them clearly as the 'two old men' in question. Eight further statements from other customers were produced at the appeal to prove the fact. Short of a miraculous guess, Dowd could not have known about their existence unless he had been present in the pub himself. This time, the Crown were able to offer nothing in rebuttal.

Lord Roskill set the tone of his judgment from the start: 'It is not without some interest, in view of the subsequent history of this case, to observe that while Richardson gave notice of appeal against her various convictions promptly and within time, none of the other three applicants ever sought leave to appeal within time. Their applications for leave to appeal against their various convictions were only made when certain fresh evidence had come to light.' Since counsel had advised that there were no grounds for appeal in the cases of the three male defendants until, precisely, that fresh evidence emerged, it is difficult to imagine how they could have appealed sooner than they did and why Lord Roskill found it of interest. Carole Richardson's promptness (based on the pressing nature of her alibi witnesses) was not, as shall be seen, subsequently held to her advantage either.

The conflicting evidence of Yallop and Lidstone on the handbag fragments was dismissed in a sentence: 'We hope we shall not be thought lacking in respect or courtesy to either of these two gentlemen if we say that we find no help in their evidence which, through no fault of their own, is far too nebulous in character to assist us in solving the crucial problem to which these applications give rise.' The resolution of the conflict, perhaps, was nebulous, but both men had given unequivocal evidence: Yallop that he had found material that could have been the bomb-container described by Dowd; Lidstone that the material could not have been from a bomb-container. Either account may have swayed a jury. Elsewhere, Lord Roskill made passing reference to 'certain allegedly scientific evidence of a Mr Yallop'.

Lord Roskill moved to the question of the credibility of the Balcombe Street men and Dowd and whether they had done the bombings — alone or with the appellants. In particular, he fastened on the Crown's one dispute about the claimed deeds of the ASU. Sir Michael Havers had allowed that O'Connell and Duggan had bombed Woolwich. The judges had allowed that Butler had also been there. But the Crown insisted that Brendan Dowd was lying about his involvement on both the aborted mission on Wednesday November 6 and the actual bombing on Thursday November 7. Sir Michael had claimed that Dowd's lies had 'stuck out like a sore thumb'. If Dowd was lying there was still room for Paul Hill in the car. There was not room for both.

Dowd had made no mention of the aborted Wednesday attempt in his prison interviews. In court, his account of it varied from those of most of his colleagues — including O'Connell who, it was agreed, had been the most convincing of all. O'Connell had even mentioned the use of a green 'Army-style' bush hat, which matched the description of a hat found in the car stolen from Anne Simpson in Earl's Court on the night of the bombing. Ms Simpson's evidence had not materialized at the original trial.

Under cross-examination, Dowd said that the stolen car on the aborted mission was a Ford Cortina. O'Connell, again supported by previously undisclosed evidence on stolen cars, had correctly identified it as a Ford Corsair.

Dowd said that the rendezvous prior to the aborted mission had been in Knightsbridge. The others had specified Sloane Square.

Dowd said that he had not got out of the car at the King's Arms on the first night (Wednesday). O'Connell said that he had — to check with him whether there were sufficient Army personnel in the pub to make it worth bombing.

Dowd said that Wednesday's stolen car had been abandoned in Knightsbridge, close to the rendezvous point. The white Corsair was found in Pimlico, near Vauxhall Bridge.

None of this, it should be recalled, related to the actual bombing mission on Thursday for which Paul Hill had been convicted. Nevertheless, Lord Roskill took Wednesday as his starting point: 'We regard the touchstone by which the credibility of all the new evidence in the relevant respects is to be judged to be that of Dowd... In the witness-box Dowd was a deplorable witness, giving the impression much of the time in this part of his evidence that he was telling a story of events in which he had not taken part and the details of which he had but imperfectly and recently learned. We find it wholly incredible that if Dowd had taken part in the events of the Wednesday night as he alleged... he would not have remembered the details and remembered them much sooner and much more accurately than he was able to do in the witness-box.'

As Dowd's evidence was selected to be the 'touchstone', his mistakes or 'lies' require close scrutiny. He had arrived at the Old Bailey having spent 27 months in custody. For the last 15 months he had been a category A prisoner, and all but seven weeks of that time he had spent in solitary confinement — in isolation units and punishment blocks. Under Rule 43 of the Home Office Prison Rules 1964, which deals with segregation, a prisoner should not be subjected to solitary confinement for more than a month at a time without the approval of the prison's Board of Visitors or the Secretary of State. HM Inspector of Prisons has reported that such confinement can, in effect, be unlimited and be 'psychologically harmful'. Dowd's situation was further complicated by his being on the 'ghost train' — he had experienced eight sudden transfers during this period. The effect on his memory and on his coherence can only be guessed at. He had, on his own admission, been involved in a fearful catalogue of terrorist incidents, quite apart from recces and aborted missions; he had a lot to remember in which one incident could, forgivably, be expected to blend into another with the passage of time. This was the context for his 'deplorable' lies.

Dowd had been uncertain of the Wednesday night aborted mission in his prison interviews with Logan and James Still, yet in the dock he claimed to remember it. He told Sir Michael Havers, 'I did not remember it the first time... I did not remember it then but I have been trying to think and think.' In prison, a year earlier, Dowd had been asked if there had been an aborted mission and had replied, 'No. I'm not sure. There may have been... I think the bomb was made the night before but we could not get a motor... I can't be sure.' The disparity is not disputed; it is explicable by Dowd's having had a year to gather his thoughts and by his lack of certainty, freely acknowledged at the first interview with Logan and Still.

Dowd said that the Wednesday-night car was a Cortina; O'Connell correctly recalled that it was a Corsair. Dowd regularly stole and drove Ford cars for the Unit. They were the easiest models to break into and he had an extensive collection of Ford ignition keys. The two models had similar design and lines, and Dowd had already shown that he rarely distinguished between the two. Upon his arrest in June 1975, Commander Jim Nevill had interrogated him systematically about vehicles used on bombing missions. 'We stole so many,' Dowd had told him. 'They're easy to nick, those old Fords.' On being asked the model, Dowd had repeatedly answered, 'Cortina or Corsair.' A lie or a plausible mistake? Lord Roskill had not been so scrupulous about distinguishing between car models in matching a Granada with a Cortina for the elusive second car at Guildford — on any view, a greater visual mismatch than between a Cortina and a Corsair.

The next 'lie' concerned the rendezvous. Dowd placed it on the south side of Knightsbridge, while O'Connell and Duggan gave it as Sloane Square. As the two locations, linked by Sloane Street, are adjacent and at most half a mile apart, this was hardly a glaring error for an Irishman relatively new to London. Dowd further described the rendezvous pub as being 30 yards from an underground station exit. This neatly matched the pub in Sloane Square described by O'Connell and Duggan.

O'Connell remembered Dowd getting out at Woolwich to double-check the number of soldiers in the King's Arms on the Wednesday night. Dowd denied getting out of the car. Neither Butler nor Duggan was conclusive on the point, so it cannot be said that O'Connell's recollection was more reliable than Dowd's.

Finally, Dowd said the stolen car had been abandoned in Knightsbridge, near the rendezvous pub, in 'roughly the same position as where we parked it originally'. In fact, the stolen car was found in Aylesford Street, Pimlico, a mile from Sloane Square or a mile and a half from Knightsbridge — 'nowhere near', according to Sir Michael Havers. O'Connell specified the point of abandonment as half a mile or a mile after crossing the river at Waterloo or Westminster, which was equally inaccurate. Dowd, conversely, was given no credit for being the only member of the team to specify where the car had been stolen from — 'somewhere around Earl's Court'. It had been taken from Cresswell Gardens, 400 yards from the Earl's Court Road. How Dowd could have known this, unless he had been involved in the Wednesday-night mission, is difficult to understand.

Among the reporters watching the cross-examinations was Peter Chippindale of the *Guardian*, who confirms that Dowd was the weakest of the IRA men: 'He was the last to give evidence and he let it down. He struck me as not all that bright but even his inconsistencies didn't knock much of a hole in the case. They rattled him. But up to that point the performance of the Balcombe Street men was very impressive. There was no impression that they had learned their lines parrot-fashion. Even Dowd, though nervous and wobbly, didn't convey that. All credit to Sir Michael Havers for skill; he did a supreme job in ensnaring Dowd, tugging and pulling at everything he said, making a meal of every tiny point, exaggerating the inconsistencies until something quite small was made to seem large and significant.'

At no stage did the judges invite comparison between Dowd's inconsistencies and the 153 inconsistencies that had studded the confessions of the Guildford Four. At no stage did they invite comparison between Hill's fragmented account of riding to Woolwich in the boot of a silver sports car and the new versions. Instead, Lord Roskill was now ready to flex more of his judicial logic: 'Our conviction that Dowd was lying in relation to the Wednesday night, of course, inevitably casts the gravest doubts as to his veracity regarding the events of the Thursday... If, as we conclude without hesitation, Dowd was not there on either the Wednesday or Thursday nights, it follows not only that Dowd has lied to the court in this respect but that O'Connell, Duggan and Butler have also lied in asserting that he was their companion and was the fourth man on each of those two occasions. We have no hesitation in concluding that each of them has so lied.' That led, in turn, to the 'clear conclusion' that they were all also lying in denying knowledge of Hill and Armstrong with regard to Woolwich.

Now that all four had been established as liars, their claim not to know any of the Guildford Four could be 'wholly rejected as unworthy of credence', so 'the whole of the case in relation to Guildford in so far as it is based upon the new evidence necessarily collapses'. The whole collapse had been set in train by Dowd's alleged lies about the night before the Woolwich bombing. Any difficulty in dealing with what purported to be unique knowledge on Dowd's part about the actual bombings of Woolwich and Guildford was averted by Lord Roskill's reasoning. So, too, was the absence of any evidential link between the ASU and the Guildford Four. Because they were liars, they must have been lying about not knowing the Guildford Four.

Lord Roskill's summing-up of O'Connell encapsulated the problem: 'It is difficult to believe that had he not been present on both occasions his knowledge of the detail... could have been wholly invented. On the other hand he is a man whom any court must long shrink from believing in almost any respect.' He was saying, in effect, that O'Connell was telling the truth but could not be trusted. By that logic, it was pointless to have heard the evidence in the first place: the Guildford Four never stood a chance.

Dowd's exclusive evidence on the actual bombing of Woolwich was quickly ignored or dismissed. For the Thursday, Dowd had correctly specified stealing a 'dark blue or maroon Cortina' — it had been a maroon Cortina (a detail beyond the recall of his colleagues); he alone remembered the detail of driving off from the King's Arms without headlights until being 'flashed' by an oncoming car after 200 yards, as corroborated by the eyewitness account — never before reported — of Mr William Fairs. Lord Roskill disposed of this telling piece of knowledge — 'but, with respect, we can find in this no real support to Dowd's story' — but failed to explain why. Dowd gave a description of how they had reached the place where the car had been abandoned in New Cross: a left turn off the main road, up a short hill, left again, where the car had been parked on the left-hand side of the road, locked, with a block of flats in view. This was an accurate set of directions to the location in Heald Street where the police had found it; but whereas Lord Roskill admitted that he had been impressed by O'Connell's information about stolen cars on the Wednesday and Thursday nights, Dowd's recollections were discounted; he had been established as a 'liar'.

Dowd was further able to locate the nearest bus stop to Heald Street. Ignoring his accurate description, Lord Roskill fastened instead on to one discrepancy about the bus journey — Dowd's claim that the team had changed buses on their way back to central London. None of the others mentioned or recalled this detail. It was enough for Lord Roskill to find 'independent and additional grounds for concluding that he was lying about the Thursday'.

Sir Michael Havers had quite reasonably disposed of the wealth of the knowledge that Dowd had displayed about Guildford by asserting that it could have been picked up on reconnaissance. But the Crown and Sir Michael could not explain away Dowd's recall of the two old men with shopping-bags, waiting for a bus. Lord Roskill dealt with it thus: '... as regards that small detail, that knowledge could easily have been acquired subsequently to the Guildford bombings, having regard to the long interval of time between those events and Dowd's own arrest in July 1975.' Lord Roskill had now launched the theory of a collusion between the Guildford Four — or, more specifically, Armstrong, as the Crown's candidate for the sole 'missing' man from the Horse and Groom — and the Active Service Unit. For the theory to hold up, Armstrong would have had to have told Dowd about the two old men, in a casual conversation or a thorough debriefing, between the bombing and Armstrong's own arrest. The theory did not square with Lord Roskill's other assessment that Dowd had 'but recently' learned his lines; it did not square with the fact that there was still nothing to link Dowd and Armstrong, inside or outside prison; and, above all, it seemed improbable that Armstrong who, if guilty, had failed to establish a competent alibi, should have set in motion an extraordinarily complex and long-term plot to free himself, based on a description of the two old men, at a time when he could not have known that their presence would never be revealed at the original trial.

Dowd's prison movements and spells of solitary confinement were such that he had never been in contact in custody with either the Balcombe Street men or the Guildford Four. There are, of course, ways of passing messages in prison, and the IRA have developed some of the most effective, but neither the Crown nor the judges offered an explanation as to how it could have been done in Dowd's case, bearing in mind the volume of detail he offered; how arcane some of it was; and, especially, how he alone possessed knowledge of it.

Not for the first time, Lord Roskill acknowledged a problem only to dispose of it without explanation: 'We need only say that so far as the new evidence is concerned we reject it in all relevant aspects. That evidence, therefore, gives rise to no lurking doubts whatsoever in our minds. We are sure that there has been a cunning and skilful attempt to deceive the court by putting forward false evidence. O'Connell, Duggan and Butler had ample opportunity whilst awaiting trial to work out how the attempt should be made. Doing so was well within the intellectual capacity of O'Connell. The difficulty lay in finding a substitute for Hill. Dowd was brought in for this purpose. Providing him with his lines could not have been easy as he was not at any material time in the same prison as the others. He did not, or could not, learn his lines properly. This was the reason why the conspiracy failed.'

Apart from unravelling the 'skilful and cunning' conspiracy, the judges had also satisfied themselves that the new evidence contained an exhibit that compounded the guilt of the Guildford Four. This was the undated briefing, known as the 'Dear Joe' letter, from 'Graine', that the police had found in the hastily evacuated safe house in Fairholme Road in February 1975. Lord Roskill found it 'a truly remarkable document... we regard this letter as of great significance'.

What excited their Lordships was a sentence towards the end: 'Get those two Belfast fellows home — clean them up, change them a bit & send them singley [sic] through Glasgow unless you can think of something better.' If the letter had been sent after the bombing of Guildford and Woolwich, Lord Roskill reckoned, this sentence assumed great significance in relation to Hill and Armstrong, 'both of whom come from Belfast'.

Without working out how many young men from Belfast were in England at the time, it is obviously highly circumstantial to link the reference with Hill and Armstrong. O'Connell, who admitted the letter had been addressed to him, insisted that the 'two Belfast fellows' were Ronnie McCartney, now in custody, and a colleague (known as 'Walsh'), still at large, who had been involved in the shoot-out with Hampshire Police at Westridge Road, Southampton on December 23 1974. Lord Roskill rejected this alternative, without explanation, as 'lies'.

There was no detail in the letter that established whether it had been sent before or after the Guildford arrests. O'Connell insisted that it had arrived in January 1975, but this made a nonsense of the reference, as a target, to the 'Cowboy Club — Picadilly [sic] (top serving officers)'. O'Connell and his men, by their own admission, had shot up the Cavalry Club on December 11. If the letter had been sent after that date, the author must surely have known of the attack. But O'Connell insisted that it had been delivered by hand via a courier, so there was no telling how much time had elapsed between its writing and its arrival. The tantalizing 'Dear Joe' letter, in truth, proved nothing.

The judges' remaining act was to reject Carole Richardson's separate appeal application on the grounds of her alibi. Lord Roskill found no reason to diverge from the trial jury's verdict, concluding that the evidence of the alibi witnesses Frank Johnson and Lisa Astin bore 'all the marks of concoction'.

As for the fine timing of the journey from Guildford to Elephant and Castle, Richardson's case was undermined by Lord Roskill's simply getting his facts wrong. First, he put the time of her departure from the Horse and Groom at 6.50 p.m. — earlier than anyone had suggested at the original trial (the best witnesses had said that the 'courting couple' had left at 6.52 or 6.53 p.m., while Sir Michael Havers had been unnecessarily generous in putting the time at 6.55 p.m.). Secondly, Lord Roskill declared her arrival time at the South Bank Polytechnic to have been '8.00 p.m. or thereabouts', despite the fact that the safest time was 7.45 p.m., on the evidence of witnesses accepted by the Crown as reliable, and had accordingly been entered in the grounds of appeal by Richardson's QC.

Lord Roskill had made no more attempt than Mr Justice Donaldson to do the mathematics of the run, but as he had expanded the potential time for the trip by 17 minutes over the time suggested by the available evidence, perhaps it was as well. For good measure, although happily it was immaterial, Lord Roskill was wrong about the time of the Horse and Groom explosion by nearly 30 minutes.

'In the end,' said Lord Roskill, 'we are all of the clear opinion that there are no possible grounds for doubting the justice of any of these four convictions, or for ordering retrials or, in Richardson's case, for quashing her convictions in their entirety. We therefore propose to dispose of all these applications for leave to appeal by refusing them.'

37
DARK AGES

'Mum, we were fitted up something rotten.'

Gerry Conlon, letter to his mother, October 30 1977

After the appeal, the four were sent to separate prisons. None knew even where the others were.

Two days after the appeal had failed, Gerry Conlon wrote to his mother:

Dear Mother,

As you can see I'm now in Manchester Prison and I'm in solitary confinement. I don't know how long I'm likely to be here but let's hope I will be moved soon. I've already put in a petition to be moved to a long-term prison. As you know, Mum, I or the others shouldn't be in prison because we've committed no crime, but while I'm in prison I'm entitled to be at a long-term prison where I can get the same facilities and privileges as any other long-term prisoner. Mum, see who you can about getting me moved, OK? and will you please let my solicitors know where I'm being held, don't forget, Mum, OK?

Mum, I've already wrote two letters to you but they've both been stopped, this letter I'm writing to you now I bought out of my 'wages' so let's hope this one is not stopped as well. Anyway I'm keeping as well as can be expected considering I'm here for something I didn't do, I'm sure you were as sick as I was about the result of the so-called 'appeal' but we never really expected anything else from them, did we Mum? But don't you be worrying Mum it's not over yet...

Mum when you are writing to Dad ask him to write to me as I would like to hear from him, I hope to be moved to him soon. Ask if Paddy Armstrong is back with him and can you find out where Benny is from his mother, OK? and let me know in your next letter to me, don't forget...

Mum, we were fitted up something rotten. Paddy and Paul knew what they were trying to do and say was nothing but lies, anyway we will prove our innocence one day.

Mum, the weather here is very bad, it is either very cold or it's washing down rain, it's true that Manchester is a rainy city, I've often heard people say that. My light in my cell is on all the time, I'm sure they must run up a huge electricity bill, HA HA HA HA.

Mum, is Dad keeping well? He must have been sick about me, but tell him not to worry, as I'm all right. He knows as well as I do that I didn't do what I'm supposed to have done, I can sleep peaceful at night with a clear conscience, can the cops and judges? I wonder if they can...

Mum I will close now, hoping you'll write soon... I've no need to tell you how much I love and miss you Mum. Goodnight and God bless you. Your loving son Gerard.

PS. Mum, don't forget about seeing if you can get me moved otherwise this will be the third out of four Christmases I've been solitary.

For the Guildford Four and those who believed in their innocence the future was bleak. 'It came not as a surprise but as a great sadness,' Alastair Logan remembers. 'I was incredibly depressed and disappointed and felt I had been a party to something dishonest.'

Even before the appeal, Logan had voiced his misgivings privately to Hill's solicitor, David Melton: 'I feel that I have no alternative but to pursue the matter on behalf of Armstrong, because if I do not, no one else will. Status quo is entirely acceptable to the authorities who would be most reluctant to see it disturbed... I feel that I am in a cleft stick. I owe a duty to Armstrong. I firmly believe that he had no connection whatsoever with the Guildford bombing, neither did he have any foreknowledge of it, neither did he know about it afterwards. I believe that he has been convicted [partly]... because his own peculiar physical circumstances at the time of his arrest contributed strongly to his willingness to co-operate with the officers and in turn produce statements which convicted him... I sometimes think it would be easier for everyone if one did not have convictions and principles. I fear that there is a grave risk whatever the outcome of this case and I will be regarded in certain circles as being pro the IRA, which I am not. Many would say that my responsibilities to my family and my business are greater than those to Armstrong, but I fear that the dichotomy is not that easily resolved.'

They had had the strongest new evidence they were ever going to get, but it had not been powerful enough. Now Logan's client, Paddy Armstrong, seemed to be taking it philosophically. 'He said, "You tried your best," and "Where do we go from here?"' But Logan no longer knew.

Paul Hill was taken from the Old Bailey straight to Gartree Prison, Leicestershire. On October 30 he wrote:

> Well Mum, there isn't a lot I feel like saying about all that farce. If you ask me, I'd doubt if they'd believe their own mothers, anyway that's the type of people they are, so what else can I expect from them. I suppose yous will all feel bad about it, but like I said a few months ago, don't be surprised if they don't give us anything. Anyway there it is Mum, nothing I can say hasn't been said before.

Hill, of the four, had had a particularly punishing career in prison. In the first four years alone he had been shunted around 14 times — from Winchester to Brixton to Crumlin Road, Belfast; then back to Wandsworth, Bristol, Albany, Bristol again, Hull, Leicester, Leeds, Long Lartin, Gartree, back to Leicester and once more to Winchester. In seven of these prisons he had served spells of solitary confinement which were sometimes lengthy. He had lost weight and his letters reveal a concern about the effect of the repeated moves and periods of solitary confinement on his mind.

In 1976, Hill and Armstrong had been caught up in the Hull Prison riot in which, for four days in September, prisoners took over three of the four wings of the prison in protest against what they saw as the deteriorating conditions, harsh regime and regular harassment by prison officers there. Hill — who during the occupation had seen his file with its note 'Never to be released' — was one of many who were beaten by prison officers in the punitive aftermath of the riot. He eventually obtained over £1,700 in damages from the Home Office, most of which he gave to his daughter Kara and to his family. The relationship with Gina had broken down and he felt a sense of helpless responsibility at being a father.

At the end of the appeal, Carole Richardson was returned to the 'H' Wing of Durham Prison, the only maximum-security unit in England and Wales for women. In the early sixties, 'H' Wing had been used as a special security and punishment block for male escapees, before being converted to take such offenders as the Great Train Robbers and the Kray twins; the security devices installed for this purpose included dog-runs and electronic surveillance. In official reports instigated by a series of hunger strikes and protests and one major riot, the wing was condemned as claustrophobic and inhumane. By 1971 it had been closed. But in 1974, after a £100,000 face-lift of further security measures, 'H' Wing was reopened to accommodate 36 category A women — though inevitably there are fewer, and the numbers are made up with other female prisoners. 'H' Wing is buried deep inside Durham Prison; through two main gates there is a third gate set in a cage. Visitors face a camera before this gate opens; cameras monitor their progress across a small concrete yard and down four steps to a door. The electronic surveillance is reinforced by men with guard dogs.

It was here, in the latter half of the seventies, that five category A women were imprisoned for IRA offences: Carole Richardson, Anne Maguire, Judith Ward and the Gillespie sisters, Anne and Evelyn, who had been convicted of conspiracy in 1974. Anne Maguire asserts the innocence of all five. The Gillespies considered themselves political prisoners, while Anne Maguire roundly insisted she was nothing of the kind. The three Irish women were drawn together, but the Gillespies, staunch Republicans, regarded Anne as a victim of the British system, pitying her belief that justice could ever derive from it.

The day at Durham began each morning at seven with a wash in cold water and a mandatory stripping of beds and cleaning of cells. Food was prepared in the male wings of the prison and delivered to 'H' Wing by trolley; by the time it arrived it was practically cold. Breakfast — usually porridge and toast — was eaten between 8.00 and 8.20, after which the women were set to work. The Gillespie sisters, in their book *Girseacha i nGeibheann* (translated under the title *Sisters in Cells*), describe the routine with little joy:

> You could either scrub floors or work in the workshop sewing mail-sacks etc. The women were allowed to practise some types of crafts — knitting, plastic-work — and you could take some of this work to the cell with you at night. We used to work from 8.30 a.m. to 11.30 when we had a break. Then we returned to work until 1.00 p.m. We worked rather hard; they kept you at it all the time. And you were paid a 'salary' of course — some 55p a week was our basic when we first arrived at Durham.

> You got your money each Tuesday, when you could buy sweets or postage stamps. We were not allowed chewing-gum — something which was a severe disadvantage to those of us who were giving up smoking — for security reasons. Obviously they still remembered De Valera's old trick in the pre-gum days in Lincoln, and feared that somebody might be able to make moulds of the keys!

Toothpaste and shampoo were legitimate items of expenditure, as were stamps:

> You got one stamp free from the State, but you had to buy the other three if you wished to post the maximum number of letters allowed, four each week. You were also allowed to receive four letters on the basis of 'one in, one out'...
>
> We usually had an exercise period after lunch if the weather was fine. There were no games — just walking about in the yard. But you could talk to other inmates during that period... these sessions did provide an opportunity to catch up on any news that might be abroad in the prison.
>
> Most days in jail were the same — from Monday to Friday at least. One took it 'one day at a time' and looked forward to whatever slight changes in routine there might be at the weekend. That was the time when we had most opportunities to catch up on newspaper reading and to listen to the radio... There were no proper educational facilities in Durham...
>
> The lights were put out about ten each evening. We had been a few years in Durham when somebody got the crazy idea that the lights should not be extinguished completely at night in the case of Category A prisoners. We protested about this to the security people and they made an alternative arrangement that involved checking each hour during the night to make sure that we were still there. Some of the warders checked quietly but others banged the cell doors regularly during the night.
>
> The official position all the time was, of course, that there were no such things as political prisoners or even 'special status' prisoners. And yet the very close supervision they mounted on us hour by hour, day by day, year by year definitely suggested that there was something very 'special' if not also 'political' about us. Certainly, prisoners who claim special status have a tougher time inside — if for no other reason than that an assumption is then made on the part

of the staff that these special-category people are more interested than others in trying to escape. That is one of the explanations — the only one that does not smack of more sinister prejudices at work — of why we were never left more than a month in the same cell during all our years in jail. You would just have got your cell neat and tidy, decked out with a few pictures or other personal touches, when all of a sudden, without warning or apparent reason, you would be ordered to collect your things and get ready for a move to some other cell in another corner of the prison building.

Racism was a further source of harassment, and came from staff and inmates alike. Anne and Evelyn Gillespie describe the fear felt by the Irish prisoners — a category that included Carole Richardson — whenever news broke about a bombing by the IRA:

The night the news about Mountbatten came through we had been knitting in our cell. Carole Richardson was down watching a sports programme on television. She ran up to us, rushed into the cell and closed the door. She was obviously very disturbed. She stood with her back to the door as if she expected an attack and was preparing for a siege. Naturally, we asked her what was wrong. 'You won't believe what they have done!' she said... 'They have just said on television that Lord Mountbatten has been killed.'... It was obviously siege-time... We could hardly believe the news but we were very fearful. There were many former British Army personnel amongst both warders and prisoners... only the tough ones were sent to Durham, as we have stated already... Everybody turned on us again. We were treated just as if we had been outside at the time and had been directly involved in the assassination. Revenge was usually taken on all Irish prisoners in cases like this, including those who had been wrongly convicted in the first place.

No letters survive that reveal Carole Richardson's state of mind in Durham, but an indication of her feelings about the place emerges in uncharacteristic outbursts, such as one in a letter to Lily Hill written from Styal Prison in 1986, four years after her transfer:

> After Durham this place is heaven... I even have a job [here] where I walk around the prison on my own all day. It's still a blessing getting so much fresh air and not through four sets of bars. People here think I'm mad because I love going out in the rain but if they'd seen Durham they'd know why; seeing grass and trees instead of concrete and walls, it's a totally different world. But as long as I remain free in my mind I'll cope with the situation, hard as it often is.

Carole Richardson spent six and a half years in Durham's 'H' Wing, between the ages of 18 and 24; the Gillespies and Anne Maguire eight years; and Judith Ward 13 years. In the summer of 1988 Judith Ward was still there.

Dispersed in their respective prisons, Paddy Armstrong, Gerry Conlon, Paul Hill and Carole Richardson were forgotten by the public, as the Maguire family, Sean Smyth and Pat O'Neill had been forgotten. These were demoralizing years for the prisoners, for their families and for Alastair Logan, because no one at that time was interested in taking up the case. Letters were written and speeches made, but they elicited no response. No journalist saw a story in what had happened. After intensive lobbying of a large number of journalists, Logan persuaded a few lone voices — David Martin in *The Leveller* (December 1977) and Gavin Esler and Chris Mullin in the *New Statesman* (1980; 1982) — for the first time to question the verdicts in the Guildford and Maguire cases. But at that stage no one in the British media or in British politics pursued the matter.

Even visits were difficult, particularly for the three families who had to travel from Belfast. Hill, Conlon and Armstrong were not recognized by the IRA as Republican prisoners and consequently no aid was forthcoming from the Green Cross, which traditionally allocates money to prisoners' families to help fund the costly and difficult journey to England. For Sarah Conlon, who had a husband as well as a son to visit, these journeys were particularly arduous — the more so as time passed and she saw the years in prison and the lack of good medical care telling on Guiseppe's health.

After his conviction, Guiseppe Conlon had been sent to Wormwood Scrubs, where he was given dietary supplements to help him regain the weight he had lost during the trial. The doctor made sure he had warm clothing and he was allocated a job in the tailors' shop where he could sit near the heaters; it earned him a pound a week with which he could buy a little extra food. But in April 1977 he was moved to Wakefield Prison. Almost all his specialist medical care and his dietary supplements — vital to the control of TB — were withdrawn. On one occasion when he had been coughing blood, Guiseppe told his solicitor, the prison medical officer prescribed him Benylin, an inappropriate proprietary cough medicine. Within three months he had lost almost two stone and felt so ill that he had to stop work. This meant he earned no money for food, although Republican prisoners on the wing donated money from their own wages to buy him Complan. His resistance to working either in the dusty tent shop or in the paint shop resulted in his being taken to a cold cell in the segregation unit and fined. As his solicitor at that time, Alastair Logan took a civil action against the Home Office to get an independent medical opinion on his condition.

In January 1978 Conlon was moved back to Wormwood Scrubs where, within five months, Gerry joined him, but the damage to his health in Wakefield was to prove irreparable. In May, Gerry wrote to his mother:

> Dad is not keeping very well. He is now out of the prison hospital and back on the wing. Mum, Dad is only seven stone nine pounds, he looks as if he has just come out of one of Hitler's

concentration camps. Mum he is really looking very ill.

Sarah Conlon knew all too well what was happening. 'At times he knew that he was never going to come out of it. Times that I went on the visits and seeing him coming across these prison yards with two prison officers with Alsatian dogs. And when I enquired, "Why the dogs?", it's in case a prisoner could escape. But my husband could hardly walk to the visiting-room.'

In November 1979 the Home Secretary, William Whitelaw, turned down an application for parole for the third time. Guiseppe became very depressed and on December 31 was admitted to Hammersmith Hospital; the doctor who admitted him described him as 'a breathless, sick man, coughing yellow sputum and blood'. Sarah came over to visit and was allowed to see him every day. His condition began to improve with proper medical care, despite the fact that on January 5 1980, following a rumour that he was going to be 'sprung' from hospital, prison officers moved into the sick room with him.

Then, on January 11, the rumour intensified when a nurse reported hearing prowlers. At 5.30 p.m. Guiseppe was bundled into a wheelchair with a sheet around his shoulders. Sarah, who arrived at the hospital as this was happening, describes the scene as chaos. 'He was surrounded by police who stopped me and asked who I was. I thought Guiseppe had died or something with all the commotion going on in the small ward. I explained who I was and rushed past them and when I went in the drip was away from him, the oxygen was away from him. I was tangled up in the drip and it was a whole turmoil... '

Closely guarded by police and prison staff, he was returned by taxi to Wormwood Scrubs. Sarah, who was allowed to go and see him in the prison hospital, said, 'He barely had a breath.' She asked the priest to try to organize some food for him since he had missed his tea, but when it came — egg and chips — it was stone cold.

On January 18, Guiseppe was moved back to Hammersmith Hospital. This time the corridor outside his room was packed with police and prison officers. Visitors were questioned and searched. It was in these conditions that Gerry was taken to see his father for the last time. He recalls how Guiseppe made him promise not to get himself into trouble by protesting about the circumstances in which — as Guiseppe well knew — he was about to die. A uniformed police officer now sat beside his bed, and there were more stationed on the balcony outside his room. Sister Sarah Clarke, the last visitor to see him alive, describes how he removed the oxygen-mask from his face in order once more to protest his innocence and say to the policeman, 'You should not be here.' No one from his family was with him when, on January 23, he died. His family claim that his death coincided with an order from the Home Office authorizing his release on humanitarian grounds.

Even in death he was to be denied his rights. British Airways workers refused to handle his body for repatriation to Belfast. His solicitor arranged with the Ministry of Defence to have the coffin flown by the RAF from Brize Norton in Oxfordshire to Aldergrove Airport, Belfast, but when the cortège reached Brize Norton the RAF denied all knowledge of it and the coffin had to be returned to London. It was eventually flown by Aer Lingus to Dublin and the Conlon family were faced with a huge bill for the hearse's journey north.

At his funeral on January 29, the family's priest, Father Vincent McKinley — a Canon of St Peter's Procathedral and implacably opposed to the IRA — described Guiseppe Conlon as 'a gentle, kindly soul' who was 'a victim of political expediency, a peace-loving man who shunned violence. He was not a member of any political organization.'

Four days later, Gerry Conlon wrote to his sister:

Ann, you don't have to tell me about how hard it is for Mum, I know, because I feel the same. It's like they have cut a part of me away, I'm just empty inside. Ann, these animals have an awful lot to answer for, they murdered my dad who was an innocent man and I don't care what anyone says, they knew

Dad was innocent just like they know I'm innocent. Ann, it makes you sick the way these hypocrites in this country talk about human rights in the likes of Russia and Chile when they are doing worse here in their own back garden. They scream about dissidents being gaoled in Communist countries for nothing, what about us? And we were not even dissidents. How can they explain or justify what they have done to us, innocent men and women in prison for no crime at all. Ann, when the truth comes out about how we were framed and how my dad was murdered I hope people will finally realize what is happening to innocent people in England.

38
CONFESSIONS

'You may wonder how it is possible to produce quite so detailed a confession if it is not true. You will consider whether there is any other reason, because certainly none has been suggested, for making a confession, other than it was true. There it is.'

Sir John Donaldson, Guildford trial judgment, 1975

Since the only evidence against the Guildford Four was their confessions, Alastair Logan had for a long time been convinced that the only way to unlock the case was to demonstrate that the confessions were nonsense. The problem was how to do this to the satisfaction of a court of law.

His first attempt was during the trial itself. After court on October 8 1975, Armstrong was interviewed by a consultant psychiatrist, Dr Tooley, at Brixton Prison under a truth drug. Armstrong — who says he was conscious throughout — gave a clear account of his early life in Belfast, his activities in Kilburn and his treatment at Guildford police station. It confirmed what he had always said about his innocence of the crime, ill-treatment by the police and his state of mind in custody.

In the summer of 1977, with the certainty that there would be an appeal, Logan subjected Armstrong and his statements to the further scrutiny of psychologists — Barrie Irving of the Tavistock Institute of Human Relations and Professor Lionel Haward of Surrey University.

Haward was a forensic psychologist with many years' experience in the field of confession and the testimony of witnesses. He had used hypnosis principally in the examination of witnesses in many criminal cases, working for both defence and police. It was particularly appropriate that he should interview Armstrong as he had direct experience of examining members of the IRA. In Wakefield Prison on October 1 1977, Haward put Armstrong into a light hypnotic trance. Armstrong remembers it as a curious experience, not unpleasant. The only voice he could hear was Haward's. The interview covered much the same ground as Dr Tooley's had done. In particular, Haward asked Armstrong about the handling and firing of small arms in Belfast — a matter on which he had made detailed admissions in his statements to Guildford police.

'Do you know anything about guns?' Haward asked him now.

'I don't know anything about them at all,' replied Armstrong.

'Have you ever held one?'

'Yes, a small automatic.'

'When?'

'In 1970 or 1971. There were barricades up in the district. They were sniping from the Protestant district. A couple of my friends who were in the IRA showed me two guns they were carrying.'

'Were they loaded?'

'I don't know.'

'Did they show you how the magazine came out?'

'Yes.'

'Did they show you how to cock the gun?'

'No.'

'Did they show you how to fire the gun?'

'If I had to fire it I had to push a small clip at the side, just push it, I am not sure which way.'

'Did you like guns as a child?'

'Yes.'

'When you were older, did you still have an interest in them?'

'No.'

'Do they frighten you?'

'Yes.'

'Have you ever fired one, like at a rifle range?'

'No.'

'I spent some time questioning Armstrong during his hypnotic state regarding the operation of firearms,' Haward wrote in his report. He himself had been an armament instructor in the RAF, so he was well placed to judge Armstrong's knowledge. 'It was quite clear that Armstrong has even less knowledge of small arms than the general public. He says he has been shown an automatic pistol and held one in his hand, but it is clear from his explanation that given such a weapon he would not be able to carry out the necessary actions before it could be fired. Apart from the fact that psychologically Armstrong is not the calibre which would lead to his recruitment by the IRA for any combatant operation, I am of the firm belief that his knowledge of small arms is inconsistent with his having any formal contact whatsoever with the IRA.'

Haward then turned to Armstrong's treatment in police custody. Logan's notes of the interview record several responses that hint at why and how he had come to confess.

'What did you say in your confession statement?' Haward asked.

'They kept asking me questions and I was answering. They said I had done bank robberies in Belfast. Three were writing down on sheets. All were asking questions to me. They were putting words in my mouth and I was agreeing with them.'

'Why?'

'I was scared of them.'

'How did you feel when they described to you the results of the bombing?'

'Sick. I don't believe in that sort of thing.'

'Were there photographs of bodies and people on the walls of the room?'

'No, the photographs were only of the outside of the pubs. There were diagrams with Xs all over them... '

'Why did you agree with them when they put questions to you?'

'They were asking questions and shouting at me. I thought if I said yes I could get it over and done with. I wanted to get them off my back.'

'Did you think about the other men you were mentioning in your statement and what would happen to them?'

'I didn't think too much about the other men.'

'Were you injured from where the police officers hit you?'

'My face was sore and my head was sore. I was shaking and I was very tired. I wanted to get them off my back. Sometimes I fell asleep and they woke me up... '

'Where was the one who hit you?'

'Not very far away.'

'Were you frightened of him?'

'Yes.'

'Where were the others?'

'In a ring around me.'

'What were you doing?'

'I was saying I knew nothing about it. Then I got a dig in the face. I said I knew nothing about it. They were all asking questions at once. They then threatened me, saying what they had seen in the pubs after the bombing about arms and legs being blown off, and that this would happen to me. They called me a fucking lying bastard and pushed me against the wall.'

'Which of all the things that happened to you was the most frightening?'

'The bit about the arms and legs.'

'What happened next?'

'I was sat down in a chair and they kept asking me questions. Officers kept coming in and saying things that others were saying.'

'What else?'

'Dirty Harry [Attwell] kept shouting at me.'

'When you made a statement, what were you thinking about?'

'That it would stop them... '

'At what point was it that you decided to make a statement?'

'When they said they would throw me out of the window and Rowe kicked me on the leg.'

'Why?'

'Because I heard noises outside from the next room and I kept thinking that if they were hitting him what they would do to me. I thought if I give in to them and say what they wanted me to, then it would be OK.'

Interviewed by Yorkshire Television in 1986, Professor Haward commented on his findings: 'Armstrong was maintaining all along that the confession was false and that most of the things he had been saying to the police had been to alleviate his anxiety and escape from what he regarded as an intolerable situation. And under hypnosis he had presented a very consistent picture of this rather inadequate, passive man who'd been caught up in a sort of maelstrom of a situation in which he was quite bewildered and quite bemused by the drugs that he'd had.' He added, with the benefit of hindsight, that the considerable advances in research on false confession since the Guildford trial had indicated 'in virtually every case... that there is a great deal of anxiety, a desire by the person making the confession to escape from the immediate short-term effects of police imprisonment and interrogation quite regardless of the long-term consequences; and I think Armstrong's case fits this pattern almost exactly'.

Barrie Irving, the other psychologist contacted by Logan before the appeal, was also well qualified to examine Armstrong, as he had been involved in overturning the notorious Maxwell Confait convictions, the appeal against which had concluded, so embarrassingly for the Crown, on the very day the Guildford jury were to consider their verdicts.

Confait was a male prostitute who was strangled in April 1972. His home in Lewisham, South London, was simultaneously burned down. Three local boys, Ronnie Leighton, Ahmet Salih and Colin Lattimore, made detailed confessions in police custody as to how they had killed Confait and set light to his house. Their ages were 15, 14 and 18 respectively and they each had a history of 'subnormality'. All had alibis for part of the evening in question, of which Lattimore's was the strongest. There was no evidence against them apart from their confessions, and in court they said they had confessed because they were frightened. The detail had come from the police, they said. All three were found guilty and given long sentences.

In 1974 a second opinion on the time of death revealed that Confait had died at a time for which Lattimore — the self-confessed strangler — had a watertight alibi. Under pressure from a sustained campaign in the media, the wheels of justice ground slowly into action and in October 1975, in the Court of Appeal, Lord Scarman exonerated all three youths. The resulting outcry as to how they could have been convicted in the first place led to an inquiry into the case, led by Sir Henry Fisher. Irving had given evidence to that inquiry, which included proposals for tightening the Judges' Rules on interrogation; its report was eagerly awaited as the Guildford case went to appeal in 1977. (In the event, the Fisher Report was something of a white elephant, acknowledging faults in the system but concluding, with traditional British reluctance to gainsay the decisions of its courts of law, that on the balance of probabilities the boys *had* been involved in the arson and killing. In fact, further new evidence was to come to light in January 1980 which suggested the real identity of Confait's killer. Eight months later, Sir Michael Havers — who was then Attorney General — made a statement that finally cleared the three of all involvement in the crime.)

Irving therefore came to the Guildford case with a particular interest in the phenomenon of confessions in police custody. He did not examine Armstrong in person, but read the principal prosecution statements, Armstrong's proof of evidence and Dr Tooley's report. He analysed the information contained in the material parts of Armstrong's confessions and measured it against the points emphasized by the judge in his summing-up at the trial. His first conclusion was that 'the jury were never presented with a cogent enough view of how confessions which are false come to be made in the absence of intimidation'. They had not been made aware that the effects of the drugs Armstrong had taken, in conjunction with the effects of being kept in custody for some time and interrogated, could have increased his propensity to confess to a crime he had not committed.

Irving pointed out that immediately prior to his arrest, Armstrong had been taking amphetamines and barbiturates in rotation to produce what he called a 'switchback emotional effect'. The pattern had been disrupted by his arrest when he was high on amphetamines. Before his arrest and for the first two days of his detention he had had little or no sleep or food, and this would have made him more vulnerable to the effects of imprisonment and interrogation. During his interrogation he had had no opportunity to see a solicitor. He had been shown to be someone who feared physical violence and tended to be compliant in the face of authority.

His Irish background, his lifestyle, his demeanour and his appearance would have generated neither sympathy nor respect in the police officers dealing with him. For their part, those officers, local to Guildford, had been emotionally involved with what had been a horrific crime; they had felt highly motivated to obtain results and their interrogation of Armstrong had taken place after a considerable period of failure to find those responsible. All these factors, in Irving's view, would have come into play during the interrogation, although whether Armstrong had actually been beaten up or not was largely irrelevant. 'The motivation to confess and the volume of his response to questioning are manifestly symptoms of his withdrawal from amphetamine intoxication. We believe that in combination with lack of sleep and food, withdrawal after the first 24 to 48 hours would have been characterized by paranoia, to the extent that the confession story was not only maintained but refined and embellished.'

Irving's second conclusion related to the detail of the statements Armstrong had made; he was of the opinion that the significance of the detail much vaunted by the judge was largely illusory.

To have made up a long, detailed account of his activities and the activities of others would have been a remarkable feat for Armstrong to have achieved if it had contained a substantial number of verifiable statements. But the feat was considerably diminished if the account only *appeared* to provide information; if others 'unwittingly or consciously' had supplied enough leads for the narrator to build up a convincing but fictional account; and if he had been given time to construct the account and opportunities to add to and alter it later.

Irving observed that most of the statements concerned 'Armstrong's private world' and were therefore not verifiable. There was considerable use of what he called 'pseudo details' about the car and the bomb which could be fitted to a wide range of objects. The detail of the other participants and what Armstrong said they had been doing had to be discounted because it conflicted with their own admissions. This meant that verifiable and critical detail was confined to the geography of Guildford and the pub. Irving noted that Armstrong's identification of the pub had never been properly tested. His knowledge of the geography of Guildford had never been tested — indeed, the possibility of proper testing had been destroyed by his being taken around the town in a police car.

'Interrogation,' Irving continued, '... is a two-way process in which the participants swap information. The interrogator lets the suspect know what he wants to find out, when he is dissatisfied with answers, where he requires extra detail, when he wants to understand connections between statements, what he believes or disbelieves and what his attitudes to the information are... The police statements show that Armstrong was heavily coached by his interrogators. The interrogation situation was such that, if motivated to do so, Armstrong had ample opportunity to construct the outline of a story and then embellish and refine it to comply with the covert instructions from his interrogators. At two critical points this process broke down. Armstrong had to demonstrate a knowledge of Guildford and a knowledge of the pub. Both issues could have been put to the test and yet in both instances information was supplied first by a visit to the scene, second by the wall board [with charts and photographs].'

If the police had left Armstrong in a cell to write or dictate his own account in a single session, it would have been difficult for him to fabricate it. But it had not come about that way. From his experience Irving noted that, in court, information imparted in confession statements is not treated in the same way as other evidence. 'Hearsay, opinion, impression and unverifiable private information of all kinds may be advanced by a suspect as a confession, there being no onus on the prosecution to demonstrate the validity of such statements so long as they add up to admitting the charge.' Armstrong had fallen foul of this practice: his unverifiable statements had been passed off as authentic detail. The police had lacked the 'proper scepticism' to test the validity of whatever detail was verifiable. And they had provided him with a flow of information from their questions and discussion with him. It was, in Irving's view, by no means surprising that he had produced the statements he had.

The question for the defence team was how the experts' opinions could best be used for the appeal. In the event, counsel's advice was that they should not be used. The status of expert evidence, particularly the evidence of psychologists and psychiatrists, has always been viewed with extreme suspicion by the courts and it was not surprising that this particular defence team erred on the side of caution.

But his study of Armstrong's statements had left Barrie Irving with a deep sense of unease. Armstrong, like the other defendants, had alleged that he had not been given adequate periods of rest or meals or the opportunity of a proper sleep in the period prior to making his confessions. 'My conclusion after reading [his statements] was that without corroboration in a case of this kind, one is on very dangerous ground,' Irving told Yorkshire Television in 1986. 'Where there are additional problems about the way in which the interrogation was handled then one is on more difficult ground still, and the raising of those questions in the Armstrong case led me to spend the next 10 years being concerned about the management of interrogation and about confessions.'

The 'dangerous ground' of uncorroborated confessions has long been recognized in many European jurisdictions, and notably in Scotland, where no one can be convicted on the strength of a confession alone. The principle of 'sufficiency of evidence', as it is called, is regarded as an important safeguard against injustice in Scotland. In a note to the authors in 1985, the Scottish Law Lord, Lord Kilbrandon, observed, 'It may be said that statements made by way of admissions, to the police or anyone else, are especially in need of corroboration,' since the fact they are allowed to be heard in court at all 'is itself a relaxation of the rule against hearsay'. The refusal to allow uncorroborated confessions springs from Scots common law, which requires corroboration in all cases. Two confessions to two different officers on two separate occasions would not be sufficient for a conviction, since witnesses cannot corroborate their own evidence and the point at issue is not whether the confessions were made, but whether the facts contained in them are true.

Even British law recognizes that there are dangers associated with confession evidence. As long ago as 1895 the Evidence Act decreed that confessions made to police officers by people in custody are not admissible as evidence. This law does not apply to Britain; it was passed for the British colonies. In England, Wales and Northern Ireland in 1988 uncorroborated confessions may still be used as evidence; it is a matter for the courts to decide. The Emergency Provisions Acts have made it easier for such evidence to be admitted in Northern Ireland, where there has to be evidence of torture or inhuman or degrading treatment in the course of the confession's being obtained (and not just the threat of violence, as in England) before a judge can rule it out.

Recent case law, however, has indicated that confessions are not reliable. In October 1985 an Old Bailey jury considered the case of seven servicemen stationed in Cyprus, accused of spying against the British Government. In custody, all had made detailed confessions. In court, all alleged physical and psychological duress. The jury acquitted them. It was this case, which received a great deal of publicity, that — perhaps more than Confait — alerted public consciousness to the possibility that people, otherwise sound in body and mind may, in oppressive circumstances, confess to crimes of which they are innocent.

Barrie Irving developed his work on Confait and Armstrong in a volume of research on police evidence he undertook for the Royal Commission on Criminal Procedure which followed the Fisher inquiry. He recommended that no suspect should be interrogated when under the influence, or the after-effects, of drugs or alcohol; that no suspect should be denied food, drink or adequate rest; and that no suspect should be denied access to a solicitor. The Police and Criminal Evidence Act 1984, which grew out of the findings of the Royal Commission, incorporated most of Irving's recommendations (though not the recommendation that a solicitor be present at interrogations).

In 1985, when the new law came into practice, it would have been illegal for Armstrong to have been held and questioned under the conditions he had been in 1974. In 1985 the confessions of Carole Richardson, as a minor, would not have been admissible in court. Indeed, it is questionable whether the case would have reached court at all on the strength of its flimsy prosecution evidence. But this was neither here nor there for the Guildford Four: the legislation was not retrospective.

'As far as I was concerned,' Barrie Irving told the authors in 1986, 'by awakening my interest in certain aspects of interrogation practice, [Armstrong] certainly had an effect on my professional life. Small consolation to him, perhaps.'

39
AWAKENINGS

'I think that is what hurts most. Until Gerry Fitt, Merlyn Rees and people like that said they had doubts about our convictions no one really wanted to know. Yet nothing is different now to what it was 10 or 12 years ago. The evidence, or should I say lack of it, is still the same. All that's changed is the people telling it. I don't know. Unfair isn't a strong enough word for what I feel about it all, but I can't think of another one.'

Carole Richardson in a letter to Theresa Smalley,
Styal Prison, September 11 1986

Although he was destined to see none of the benefits, the suffering of Guiseppe Conlon and the wretched circumstances of his death proved to be a turning-point for the two cases. From his sick bed Guiseppe had received some prestigious visitors, among them Gerry (now Lord) Fitt, MP for West Belfast, whose hatred of the IRA was well known; Sir John Biggs-Davison, the Conservative right-wing MP; and Cardinal Basil Hume, Archbishop of Westminster. All of them independently became convinced of his innocence. Thanks to the campaigning of Father Denis Faul and Father Vincent McKinley, powerful influences were gradually being mobilized, though at this stage most of them were mobilized for Guiseppe Conlon alone.

Back in Wormwood Scrubs, his son Gerry waited impatiently for news:

Ann, has Gerry Fitt been in touch with Mum and has he done anything yet? What about Fr Faul, has he been down or has he said anything? Let me know in your next letter. I heard Cardinal O'Fiaich on the radio the other night asking

for Dad's case to be reopened, it's good to know that he's
doing something even if it is over five years too late, the same
applies to Fitt...

Gerry's letters took on a feverish enthusiasm born of new
hope, full of exhortations to his mother, his sisters and his
brother-in-law, Joe McKernan, to undertake fresh campaigns:

Mum, I saw the letter that you had in the *Irish News*, it was
really very very well done, you should do it more often as it
is the only way we can get help.

But the process was painfully slow. The Guiseppe Conlon
case was debated in Parliament on August 4 1980, but nothing
happened. Years passed, and still the voices of a handful of concerned MPs, peers and members of the Roman Catholic Church
in Ireland appeared to be having no effect on the Home Office.
In December 1983, after considering the results of Dr Brian
Caddy's work on the TLC test and his misgivings about the way
it had been used in the Maguire case, the then Parliamentary
Under-Secretary at the Home Office, the young, ambitious Tory
lawyer David Mellor, delivered a further rejection. Replying to
representations made by MPs Sir John Biggs-Davison, Gerry Fitt
and Christopher Price that Guiseppe Conlon should be granted a
posthumous free pardon, he said that all the major points raised
by Dr Caddy had been considered by the jury at the time.

'Assuming, therefore, that the collection procedure [of the
samples from the suspects' hands] was carried out properly
(and Dr Caddy appears to accept that, apart from a minor
discrepancy, it was), we are no nearer to establishing a
convincing innocent explanation for the results of the TLC tests
on Mr Conlon's hands. There is still no evidence that standard
proprietary products can be misidentified as nitroglycerine by
the TLC method, nor has anything emerged to substantiate the
claim that Mr Conlon's hands somehow became accidentally
contaminated. None of the objects in the house, apart from

Mrs Maguire's gloves, proved positive for nitroglycerine and, so far as I am aware, it has never been suggested that Mr Conlon was taking cardiovascular tablets containing nitroglycerine. The question of accidental contact has to be considered with due regard to the fact that the contamination of Mr Conlon's hands, including a strong reaction from his fingernail scrapings, was heavier and more widespread than on all but one of the other suspects'.

'In addition to the scientific issues I have also looked carefully at what Christopher Price and Mr Logan have said about a wider connection between this case and the Balcombe Street siege and the Guildford and Woolwich pub bombings. The claim by the Balcombe Street men that they were responsible for the Guildford and Woolwich bombings was rejected by the Court of Appeal as "a cunning and skilful effort to deceive the court with false evidence". In any event, however, these points seem to bear on why Mr Conlon and his co-defendants came to be charged rather than on the validity of their convictions... The Home Secretary recommends a free pardon only when there are convincing reasons for thinking that a defendant has been wrongly convicted and that he was innocent of any crime. Having considered carefully all the material assembled on Mr Conlon's behalf, I am sorry to have to tell you that I have come to the conclusions that it does not provide grounds for making such a recommendation in his case, or for taking any other action with respect to his conviction.'

The case was no further forward. And yet somehow it refused to go away. The Maguire case, with its vulnerable points — the doubts about Guiseppe Conlon's guilt and the shortcomings of the forensic evidence — provided the media with something of a lever and slowly it began to edge back into the news. The persistence of the prisoners, their families and Alastair Logan was beginning to pay off. David McKittrick wrote about it in the *Belfast Telegraph*. The BBC Northern Ireland programme *Spotlight* had featured Guiseppe Conlon in 1980. On April 18 1983, the BBC's *Panorama* briefly examined the forensic aspects of the Maguire case as part of a programme about the shortcomings of forensic science evidence (a major documentary on Guildford for *Panorama* was at an advanced stage of research, but never materialized). It was not until 1984 that the first networked documentary to consider the Maguire/Conlon case in full was transmitted, by Yorkshire Television on its programme *First Tuesday* ('Aunt Annie's Bomb Factory', ITV, March 6). It was in this programme that Dr Brian Caddy made his most damning analysis of the way in which the TLC test had been performed and used to convict the Maguires.

Almost 10 years had now passed since the arrests, and the Maguires had served their sentences and were soon to be released from prison. Anne Maguire, whose months on bail before the trial had left her with the longest sentence still to serve, was freed from Cookham Wood women's prison on February 22 1985. She came out to a climate of opinion that, at last, was prepared to question the role in which her family had been cast by police, courts and media. Viewers who saw Anne and Paddy with Robert Kee on *Seven Days* (Channel 4, April 20 1985) and with David Frost on *Good Morning Britain* (TVAM, April 28) must have felt unease at the notion of this forthright, apolitical London housewife and mother as the IRA's 'senior armourer', 'evil Aunt Annie' who had presided over bomb-making lessons in her Harlesden kitchen. Anne Maguire's anti-Republican views and quiet insistence on her family's innocence recruited increasing support. Radio Telefis Eireann screened a documentary about the case, covering the same ground as *First Tuesday* but with the considerable benefit of Anne's own participation. The programme had a major impact in Ireland and was shown in an abbreviated form on Channel 4 on May 13 1985.

Four days later Gerry Fitt, who had now been ennobled, introduced a debate on the case in the House of Lords. His impassioned speech was supported by Earl Attlee and Lords Stallard, Annan and Mishcon. Was it true, Fitt asked the

Minister, that a case like this would not now be brought on forensic tests alone; that it would not reach court without evidence of the existence of the 'bulk' of explosive; and that a parallel case against a Palestinian terrorist had been dropped for lack of such evidence even though the TLC test had proved positive? For the Government, Lord Glenarthur confirmed that it is now standard practice to require corroboration of forensic evidence before a case can be brought to court. He was unable to answer Fitt's other two questions, but David Mellor subsequently wrote once more to Lord Fitt to say that there was still not 'sufficient reason' for further action on the part of the Home Secretary.

If the Maguire case, with all the doubts over its forensic evidence and with a strong campaign behind it, was to leave the Government unmoved, what chance could there be for Guildford? Since there had been so little evidence against the four to begin with, there was no material to work on; yet the entire conduct of the case was shot through with obliquity and nonsense. It was with the purpose of questioning some of this that eventually, 11 years after the trial, a television documentary appeared.

'The Guildford Time Bomb' was shown on *First Tuesday* (Yorkshire Television, ITV, July 1 1986). It made no claim to present new evidence. It examined both the lack of evidence and the tight timing on Carole Richardson's alibi, and presented the testimonies of Lisa Astin and Frank Johnson for public scrutiny. It touched on some of the manipulation of evidence by the prosecution at the Balcombe Street trial. James Still, the retired detective who had interviewed Dowd and the Balcombe Street men, spoke of his conviction that, although he abhorred what they stood for, he was convinced they were telling the truth: 'I am satisfied from the detail they gave me that they were the people who committed the offences... what they said couldn't have come from imagination; it had to be from experience.' Barrie Irving, now director of the Police Foundation, and Professor Lionel Haward were interviewed about the problems

of confession evidence and its relation to the case of Paddy
Armstrong. Merlyn Rees was also interviewed. He became
the first ex-Home Secretary publicly to express doubt about
the convictions. Within 24 hours of transmission, the Home
Secretary, Douglas Hurd, announced an internal Home Office
review of the case.

To some British viewers the story probably appeared
incredible. One viewer at least was deeply shaken by it. Carole
Richardson, after seeing a recording, wrote:

> Although I knew all the evidence that was used at the trial
> and the appeal, it still left me shocked that this could have
> been allowed to happen, never mind did. Although I'm living
> through it, it sometimes seems unreal like I'll wake up and
> find it was a terrifying nightmare, but of course I never do.

Eight months previously, the case of the Birmingham bombers
had been reopened following the screening of a *World in
Action* investigation by Chris Mullin and Charles Tremayne
(Granada, ITV, October 28 1985). The awakening interest had
helped to mobilize support for the families of the Birmingham
Six, the Guildford Four and the Maguires and for their
solicitors, who had been struggling over the years to do
what they could. Now the campaign was given further impetus
by the publication of Robert Kee's influential book *Trial and
Error*, which prompted two concerned leading articles in *The
Times* and public announcements, in the form of letters to
that newspaper, by Lord Scarman (October 7 1986), Cardinal
Basil Hume, Archbishop of Westminster (October 13) and Lord
Devlin (October 15).

'Until the recent reforms introduced by the Police and Criminal Evidence Act 1984 there was in our system a dangerously
low level of supervision of the processes of arrest, interrogation
and charge,' Lord Scarman wrote. 'Even today the critical phase,
interrogation, is in reality conducted and supervised only by the
police within a police station.

'The trial and appeal process, which is open and judicial, has shown itself an uncertain instrument for uncovering irregularities, and worse, in the pre-trial process... There is in our pre-trial procedures even today fertile ground for the development of injustice which can, and sometimes does, escape detection during the subsequent trial and appeal process. The Confait case... is a good example; and there would appear to be grounds for querying the justice of the convictions in the Guildford bombing case and in the Maguire explosives case... '

Cardinal Hume's interest in the case had been fired by his meeting Guiseppe Conlon. 'I became absolutely convinced of his innocence and because of that developed profound doubts about the justice of the Maguire convictions... I would strongly urge that in the interests of justice the Home Secretary should exercise the rights available to him under Section 17 of the Criminal Appeal Act 1968 whereby, "if he thinks fit", he can refer such cases back to the Court of Appeal.'

Lord Devlin, one of the most respected authorities in English criminal law, had reasons of his own for disquiet about the convictions and joined his voice to that of the Cardinal. 'Protestations of innocence by prisoners are common enough,' he wrote, 'and support for them by distinguished persons is not unknown. But the total effect must be mountainous before it can command attention.

'Here it is as high as Everest. It has been continuous for years. It has been tested by a number of others besides the Cardinal himself. It is strengthened by all the other considerations mentioned in your leader. It confronts what on paper looks to be a weak case.

'None of this can be admitted and weighed by a court of law. But to do justice in every individual case is sometimes beyond the reach of the law: it is the very thing that in the last resort the royal prerogative is fashioned to attain.'

The pressure on the Home Office continued into the New Year. Two weeks before the announcement of the outcome of the internal reviews, an all-party delegation of MPs and peers met the Home Secretary, and *The Times* ran a third leader (January 8 1987) drawing attention to a judgment by Lord Diplock in 1983, which had ruled that it was not merely new evidence that was needed to reopen a case but 'all questions of fact and law, including "cogent argument"' in circumstances where there was a danger that justice had miscarried.

But neither calls for the exertion of the royal prerogative nor the extremely cogent arguments of this growing number of celebrated protesters were to weigh with Douglas Hurd. On January 20 1987 he announced to the House of Commons that, while he was prepared to refer the Birmingham case to the Court of Appeal, the reviews had yielded no cause for the reopening of Guildford or the Maguire case. 'No new substantive points have been raised,' he told the House. 'The arguments which have been put forward simply repeat or rework those which were aired at trial or on appeal.'

As Cardinal Hume had observed, the Home Secretary can remit a case simply 'if he thinks fit'. Over the years this broad power had been qualified to the point where new evidence or 'considerations of substance' were the prerequisite for a referral. However, in the 27-page memorandum that accompanied his present announcement, the Home Secretary explained that without new evidence or a '*new* consideration of substance' that casts doubt on the safety of the convictions, 'it would not be right' to send the case back to the Court of Appeal. It was not for him to substitute his own judgement for that of the courts on matters that they had already considered; and it would in any case be a futile exercise to remit the case simply on the contention that the courts had got it wrong in the first place.

This reasonable-sounding argument was flawed. The deliberately vague concept of a 'consideration of substance' was a catch-all to retain the Home Secretary's discretion. It had enabled justice to be done in the Confait case, which Roy Jenkins, Home Secretary at the time, had sent back to the court on a 'consideration of substance' — a reassessment of the time of Confait's death. Douglas Hurd's insertion of the word 'new' put a severe limit on the Minister's power. Strictly speaking there had been little 'new' in Confait (as the Crown at that appeal had attempted to argue). But in court Lord Scarman, while accepting that the Confait evidence was not 'new', had overruled the Crown's objection by invoking the original Appeal Act of 1907 which allowed the Home Secretary to remit a case simply if 'the interests of justice' required it.

A correspondence that broke out in the *Guardian* and the *Independent* after the Home Secretary's announcement elicited from David Mellor a concession that it was the 'fresh opinions' of forensic scientists that had reopened the Confait case. Challenged to acknowledge as 'fresh opinion' the reports of Dr Brian Caddy in the Maguire case and a body of psychiatric and psychological evidence on the Guildford confessions, of which the Home Secretary was well aware, the Ministers retreated into silence.

The memorandum in which they argued their case set out each of what it called 'the main grounds on which the Guildford and Woolwich convictions have been challenged'. The first was the sequence of events leading to Hill's arrest. It was in this context that the Home Office now claimed that the security forces had known as early as August 29 1974 that Hill had gone to England 'to carry out bombings' — five clear weeks before the Guildford explosions. The startling implications of this claim, which was entirely new, have been discussed earlier in this book: Hill had signed on the dole in Southampton, lived at the Quex Road hostel and worked on Camden Town building-sites, in all cases using his own name. If he was seriously suspected of being part of an active service unit, there appears to have been a total failure of detection in that he was picked up neither before the offence nor for almost two months after it.

By taking the representations point by point and arguing that each on its own was not a 'consideration of substance', the Home Secretary excluded the basic argument that, when they are taken together, their force is inescapable: the Confait case had provided the Home Secretary with ample precedent for taking an accumulation of such factors into account.

The memorandum took frequent refuge in the argument that because a defence point had been considered by the jury and found wanting, there was no cause to consider it afresh. But in so doing it wholly ignored the fact that the jury at the Guildford trial had not been in possession of the additional evidence of the Balcombe Street men and Dowd, which could be said to cast the original confessions in a new and unreliable light. It made no attempt to review with an independent eye the evidence before the Court of Appeal. In particular, it failed to address the inconsistencies of the judgment, reiterating, for example, that since the judges had examined the evidence of the Balcombe Street men and found Dowd a 'deplorable witness', and since no new 'points of substance' had been raised, there were 'no grounds for any action on the part of the Home Secretary'.

Yet in confining its attention to Dowd's inconsistencies and failures of memory, the memorandum entirely overlooked the *correct* detail he had supplied — detail that supported his claim to have been present to a far greater extent than his errors undermined that claim. The memorandum adopted the same illogical position as the courts, in accepting numerous inconsistencies in the statements of the Guildford Four at the same time as rejecting the Balcombe Street evidence because of the inconsistencies it contained. There were, in any case, far fewer inconsistencies in the Balcombe Street evidence than in that of the Guildford Four.

Elsewhere, the memorandum fudged arguments and displayed a misunderstanding of the issues that appeared almost wilful. Nowhere was this more apparent than in the discussion of the relationship between the Balcombe Street Active Service Unit and the Guildford Four.

'It is argued,' ran the memorandum, 'that the prosecution case rested on proving that the Guildford Four were part of the same IRA unit as the Balcombe Street gang but that they did not succeed in proving any link. The Court of Appeal accepted that members of the Balcombe Street gang could also have been involved in the Guildford and Woolwich bombings. But it is said that this produces more inconsistencies in the story...

'It is not the case that the prosecution had to prove that the Guildford Four and the Balcombe Street Gang were members of the same "active service unit". There is no reason to suppose that only one ASU operated in the South-East in the mid-1970s. Moreover, the Court of Appeal rejected the Balcombe Street men's evidence that they did not know the four.'

The memorandum had completely missed the point. Once the Court of Appeal had accepted that Balcombe Street men had been involved at Guildford and Woolwich, it had become necessary to explain how the Guildford Four could still be guilty, and this the court had signally failed to do. There had been no question of the prosecution's having to prove that both sets of defendants were part of the same active service unit. Since the Home Secretary was presumably not suggesting that two IRA units had bumped into each other coincidentally at Guildford on the night of the bombings, the point at issue — still unanswered — was that the prosecution had to prove that the two groups were part of an enlarged gang for the Guildford operation. The tracing of the genuine Mr Moffat after the appeal demolished the only evidence the Crown had ever advanced that two cars had been hired for Guildford.

It was uncontested that O'Connell and Duggan had gone to Woolwich, and the judges were prepared to accept that Butler had also gone. Furthermore, the court had been able to find no significant detail on which to establish that O'Connell and Dowd had not been telling the truth about Guildford. O'Connell had given such convincing evidence about his activities in the Seven Stars that the Crown had accepted it without even cross-examining him on the subject. Nor had Sir Michael Havers been able to find any way to explain or demolish Dowd's unique recollection of the two old men in the Horse and Groom. All these points were properly matters for the memorandum to consider. It ignored them.

Claims of inconsistencies flowing from the presumption by the appeal judges that members of the London ASU had gone with the four to Guildford were summarily dismissed by the memorandum. 'The only inconsistency which is mentioned is that if Dowd and O'Connell were in the Horse and Groom[1], this left no room for Armstrong. But it is not certain that the police succeeded in tracing everyone who had been in the pub (apart from a courting couple and another man).'

This was an extraordinary assumption: the idea that apart from the 'courting couple' there had been another man — and could indeed have been further characters — in the Horse and Groom who was unaccounted for was entirely new. Throughout trial and appeal, and down the years subsequently, it had never been suggested until January 1987 that the police detection work had been 'uncertain' or that a third person who was unaccounted for had been noticed in the pub. It had never been suggested by the Crown even when the Armstrong and Richardson confessions had inconveniently claimed the presence of another man. This was one of their details that the prosecution had chosen to ignore because it didn't fit the case. If Dowd was in the pub, Armstrong could not have been. The point is unanswerable, and the Home Office appears to have answered it by rewriting history. (There were other inconsistencies, too: first, why was it necessary for so many people to go to Guildford, and how did they get there if there was only one car?; secondly, even if they did all go, there is still a missing woman from the Seven Stars — another terrorist, unnamed and apparently unhunted.)

But the memorandum's most seriously misleading claim was this: 'The suggestion appears to be that the scientific evidence proved that all the bombing incidents originally mentioned were carried out by the same team (i.e. the Balcombe Street Gang). This is not the case. *There was no scientific evidence to*

---

1 The memorandum had wound itself into a knot by suggesting there had been claims of O'Connell's presence in the Horse and Groom. No one had ever suggested that.

link the Balcombe Street Gang with the Guildford and
Woolwich bombings.[1] The only link was some similarity in
the methods used for the Guildford and Woolwich bombings and
certain counts in the indictment against the Balcombe Street
men. It does not follow from this that the same people were
responsible for all the offences mentioned.'

There was, in fact, compelling forensic evidence from the
Government's own scientists to link the Balcombe Street ASU
with the Guildford and Woolwich bombings; the evidence had
been suppressed at the Guildford trial and — as we have
discussed elsewhere — tampered with at the Balcombe Street
trial. The Guildford jury had never heard it. The Appeal Court
should have taken account of it but had failed to do so. A second
link between the two had been established by the discovery at
the Balcombe Street Unit's safe houses of materials identical
to those used in the Guildford and Woolwich bombs. Again,
the Appeal Court judges had not considered it, although they
had seriously considered a spurious link between the mention
of 'Belfast fellows' in the 'Dear Joe' letter (which had also
been found in one of the safe houses) and the fact that
the male defendants in the Guildford case came from
Belfast.

Since the Home Office was defining the 'main grounds' on
which the convictions had been challenged, it was perhaps not
surprising that there were several that were conspicuous by
their absence from the memorandum. In its six-month review of
the case, the Home Office had not found it necessary to contact
any of the solicitors who, over the years, had represented the
Guildford Four — a revealing omission. Apart from the failure
to refer to the crucial question of the manipulation of evidence
by the Crown, critics of the case noted the absence of any
assurance given by the Home Secretary of his satisfaction that
no policeman had been guilty of any impropriety as alleged,
steadily over the years, by the defendants.

1 Authors' italics.

One remarkable omission was the absence of any reference to advances in the field of scientific research on confession evidence in the years since the trial and the appeal, although these had featured strongly in the Yorkshire Television documentary that had prompted the Home Office review. The work of Barrie Irving and its eventual influence on the Police and Criminal Evidence Act, discussed in the previous chapter, had been complemented by that of Dr James MacKeith, a consultant forensic psychiatrist, and Dr Gisli Gudjonsson, a senior lecturer in psychology, working together at the Royal Bethlem and Maudsley Hospitals in South London. MacKeith and Gudjonsson, acknowledged leaders in the field of false confessions, had developed methods of testing the suggestibility of witnesses and the degree to which their evidence could be relied upon; their opinions had been adduced in a great many trials. In the months preceding the Home Secretary's announcement they had been asked to investigate the Guildford case and had begun by interviewing Carole Richardson. Their findings were significant. One might have expected a discussion of them in the Home Office memorandum — both generally and in relation to Richardson in particular.

Indeed, its absence was inexplicable, since their report on her had been commissioned by the Home Office itself.

40
ADVANCES

Interviewer: 'What sort of overall justice do you think they have received?'
Lord Devlin: 'None. Perhaps that's putting it a bit strongly. But either you have justice whole and complete, or you have no justice. You can't have a bit of justice here and a bit of justice there.'

First Tuesday, ITV, March 3 1987

The trail that led the two independent doctors James MacKeith and Gisli Gudjonsson to examine Carole Richardson at Styal Prison had begun with an unexpected phone call on March 30 1984 to her solicitor's clerk at that time, John Avey. The caller was a doctor with the Prison Medical Service, who informed Avey quite bluntly that he believed Ms Richardson to be innocent. Something, said the doctor, must be done. But, in the tradition of the Prison Service's bureaucracy, it took over two years for an examination to be arranged — at the instigation of the defence, but at the request of Styal's senior medical officer and with the approval of the director of the Prison Medical Service.

The interviews took place on April 30 1986 and lasted some five hours. The authorities had given Carole Richardson no warning that she was to be interviewed that day. Nevertheless, 'Miss Richardson was friendly during the interview and testing,' observed Dr Gudjonsson in his report. 'Her account of herself and events surrounding the Guildford bombing was spontaneous and seemed entirely genuine. There were times during the interview when Miss Richardson clearly became upset, for example, cried.'

Of their conversation, Dr MacKeith noted Richardson's claim

to have been struck once by one police officer and twice by another. Further threats had been made, he reported, and she had become 'very distressed, tremulous and frightened of further violence', which had precipitated the hysteria resulting in the interview with the police surgeon, Dr Makos.

'In my opinion,' wrote Dr MacKeith in his report, 'at the time of her arrest Miss Richardson had a vulnerable personality with low self-esteem, poor self-confidence and an undue reliance on the good opinion of others. She was abusing drugs heavily and usually under the influence of them as well as psychologically and possibly physically dependent. Her own account, confirmed to a considerable degree in Dr Makos' statement, indicates that she was in an abnormal state of mind, probably suffering from an acute anxiety state and, by her account, very distressed, frightened and desperate to be relieved of the stress of further interrogation.'

His criticism of the visiting doctor's handling of the interview was severe. Elsewhere in the report he wrote, 'There is no indication that Dr Makos undertook a psychiatric assessment, determined her understanding or perception of her circumstances or generally enquired into matters relevant to the reliability of subsequent statements that she might make... He states that she last took barbiturates on December 2, although Miss Richardson made the unchallenged claim that she took capsules on December 3. He mentions her "admitting to be addicted" to LSD and Tuinal. True dependence on LSD does not occur... He refers for some reason to Miss Richardson's apparently self-incriminating remarks. The WPC [present at their interview] reports what was said differently, although both put what was said in inverted commas, presumably indicating that their account was precisely accurate. Dr Makos does not report trying to clarify what was said, although in fact no bomb was "thrown" in a pub at Guildford. He appears to have taken no interest in Miss Richardson's saying that she had assisted her boyfriend in planting a bomb ("not knowingly") though this raised questions about her capability at the time of forming a criminal intent. Miss Richardson disputes that she made any such admission to him...

'Given Dr Makos' description of her condition, it is, in my opinion, most unlikely that a doctor with appropriate awareness and knowledge would have regarded her as fit for further interrogation and giving of reliable statements without making and recording a careful psychiatric assessment. If one accepts the police evidence about the absence of ill-treatment, as the court did, it is still quite possible that Miss Richardson had the firm understanding that she was unsafe in police custody and so been prone to try to engineer her release from stress by making admissions. Her own account convincingly details her state of mind...

'*I conclude that the statements that resulted in her conviction on the several charges were very probably unreliable.*[1] This opinion does *not* have to rely on accepting Miss Richardson's allegations of police threats, violence or other gross improprieties. It does rely on her specific vulnerable qualities and also her state of mind at the time.'

When he obtained permission from the Home Office in December 1986 to send the reports to Alastair Logan, Dr MacKeith wrote an accompanying letter in which he amplified his conclusion: 'I have profound doubts about whether the statements given [by Carole Richardson to the police] were voluntary and whether the self-incriminating contents were reliable.'

His opinion was reinforced by that of his colleague. Gisli Gudjonsson conducted a series of psychological tests on Carole Richardson. He found her to be of high average intelligence but also unusually suggestible. 'Her suggestibility scores are very high and are twice that expected from her memory and intellectual functioning,' he wrote. '... That is, she yields very readily to subtly leading questions and her answers can be easily altered by pressure. Related to this is her marked tendency towards

1 The emphasis was MacKeith's.

compliance and eagerness to avoid conflict and confrontation with people in authority...

'At the time of the police interviews in 1974 Miss Richardson was undoubtedly a very vulnerable person. It is known that both poor self-esteem and drugs exacerbate suggestibility, and probably also general degree of compliance. For these reasons it is likely that in 1974 Miss Richardson was even more vulnerable to erroneous testimony than she is at present.' Lack of knowledge about the effects of long-term prison sentences on suggestibility and compliance prompted caution in Gudjonsson's conclusions, but he observed that Carole Richardson's suggestibility scores were high in comparison with those of other long-term prisoners. 'Furthermore, bearing in mind the circumstances of the lengthy interrogations and the likelihood that she was exceptionally vulnerable at the time (e.g. low self-esteem, drug withdrawal, highly suggestible), the validity of the confessions made in 1974 must be seriously questioned.'

MacKeith was, in addition, critical of the psychiatric examination carried out before the trial, referring to it as 'deficient' and 'highly unsatisfactory'. 'With the wisdom and privilege of hindsight,' his report concluded, 'and in the light of increased knowledge gained in recent years, I have no doubt that expert testimony could have informed defence counsel and might have been allowed to be presented in court.'

Research carried out in the intervening years was likely to have enhanced the weight of that testimony, for in 1987 the doctors were able to assert, as MacKeith wrote in a letter to Alastair Logan on February 5, that 'among the more than 50 cases of individuals who retracted statements [which they had studied], including some whose acquittals followed after acceptance of our expert evidence, this case ranks among the few in which the individual has been discovered to have several marked and consistent relevant vulnerable characteristics of personality.'

The total absence of comment in the Home Office memorandum on these significant findings has never adequately been explained. 'We do not know if the Minister read our reports,' MacKeith wrote to Logan, 'and, if so, why he has made no reference to them. We do not know whether his advisers are aware that such expert testimony is sometimes accepted in the courts, followed by acquittals.'

That MacKeith and Gudjonsson's reports had been considered in the Home Office review of the case, and dismissed, was acknowledged by the Home Office in a letter to a member of the public dated March 23 1987. The only explanation for the absence of any comment in the Home Office memorandum appeared, lamely, in the *Observer* (March 1 1987): 'The Home Office says the existence of these reports was not revealed because they were not part of the outside submissions made to the Home Secretary.'

Even as the Home Secretary was making his decision not to remit the case to the courts, further matters were coming to light. Anne and Frank Keenan, whose whereabouts had been unknown to the Hill family for some time, declared their willingness to be interviewed. Anne Keenan confirmed that she was still in touch with her friend Yvonne Fox, who had been at the flat in Brecknock Road with Paul Hill on the night of the Woolwich bombing. Mrs Fox, who was British and unrelated to Hill, firmly corroborated the Keenans' evidence that Hill had been at home that night, leaving the flat for a short time to make a phone call to Gina and returning well before the newsflash about the throw-bomb explosion. She had been told to attend court at the original trial, but her evidence had never been heard. If she was to be believed, Paul Hill could not possibly have been part of the bombing team for Woolwich. She was, in effect, a new witness.

The essential mystery surrounding Mrs Fox's evidence was why it had not been heard at the trial. Approaches to Hill's original solicitors, Woodford and Ackroyd of Southampton, had failed to throw light on the matter, Logan being repeatedly told that the files had been destroyed by fire. Interviewed by Yorkshire Television for a second *First Tuesday* documentary,

Mrs Fox was adamant that she had been with Hill at the
Keenans' on the night of the bombing. She remembered the
television programmes they had watched together. 'When I
went in, Frankie [Keenan] was there, Paul was there, Anne
was getting the supper. Paul went out to make a phone call. He
was gone about 20 minutes. When he came back we sat around
talking and watching telly still, and then I left. I got home and
my husband said there'd been a newsflash on the television
about the bombing... I remember that night because of starting
a new job on Monday... I wouldn't be sitting here now if I had
any doubts.'

First Tuesday also interviewed Cardinal Hume about his
reactions to the Home Secretary's announcement. 'I am very
disappointed indeed,' he said, 'because I and many other people
are quite convinced that the Guildford Four are innocent, and
it is a question of British justice... I would say perhaps as much
as justice there is common sense — and I think common sense
dictates that these cases be looked at again.'

The thrust of Yorkshire Television's new programme was to
demonstrate that, despite the Home Secretary's decision, there
was new expert scientific opinion, powerful public concern, a
strand of fresh evidence and — finally — an influential legal
argument as to why the case should not be dismissed.

The legal point was perhaps the strongest of all. As long ago
as 1980, Gerry Conlon, in one of the letters he wrote to bolster
his mother's spirits, had drawn her attention to a chink in the
Home Office armour:

Mum, I'm sure you have either heard on television or read
in the newspapers about Willie Whitelaw releasing two men
from prison last week because he said that there was doubt
about their guilt. Well Mum, I was at the Scrubs with one of
the men for about a year and a half and I got to know him
very well. He was good mates with my dad and I know for a
fact that our case is at least 10 times stronger than his was.
So if Whitelaw is saying that there is doubt in their case and

released them, then we should use their case as a platform for highlighting our own case. Mum can you ask Joe to mention it in his letters, the names of the two men are Michael McMahon and David Cooper. I know Joe should write to Cardinals O'Fiaich and Hume, also Lenihan, and ask Joe to write to Alex Lyon MP, I hear that he would be very interested, also Paul Foot the reporter, don't forget.

The miscarriage of justice in the case of Cooper and McMahon had indeed shaken the legal establishment to its roots, and though its link with Guildford was not immediately clear, there was prescience in Gerry Conlon's excitement.

Cooper, McMahon and a third man, Murphy, had been convicted of murder in 1970 on the uncorroborated evidence of a co-accused — against whom the charges were subsequently dropped. The case, popularly known as the 'Luton post-office murder', had made legal history by going to appeal no less than five times. Murphy's conviction had been quashed, but the convictions of Cooper and McMahon had survived intact, to the deepening concern of a small but eminent body of legal opinion. In May 1978 — after the fourth appeal — Lord Devlin entered the debate when he delivered a lecture at All Souls College, Oxford. In it he criticized the Appeal Court's handling of the Cooper and McMahon case. Among his reasons he listed the fact that the new evidence that had constituted the defence case in the appeals had been heard by judges alone, not by a jury, and had never been heard in one piece. After the failure of yet another appeal, Lord Devlin developed his arguments in his book *The Judge* (1979), and Ludovic Kennedy published a book of his own about the case, *Wicked Beyond Belief* — to which Lord Devlin contributed a legal opinion — and called on the Home Secretary to remit the life sentences of Cooper and McMahon. The book was published on June 26 1980. On July 18 the two men were released from prison.

Despite Gerry Conlon's certainty that his case was 'at least 10 times stronger', the points at stake were abstruse. It was to

be a further six years before Lord Devlin's attention was drawn
to the fact that the legal principles in the Guildford case were
identical to those in the case of Cooper and McMahon. In a paper
written in 1986 he expressed the view that in deciding as to the
credibility of the new evidence of the Balcombe Street men
themselves, rather than referring the case for a retrial so that
the original evidence could be heard alongside the Balcombe
Street evidence, and heard by a jury, the judges had made a
grave mistake.

The precedent for their approach — which in Lord Devlin's
view was a consequence of 'a deep misunderstanding of the
law' — had been set by another murder case, Stafford v. DPP,
in 1974. In that appeal, new circumstantial evidence had been
submitted to the court in the form of written testimonies from
several new witnesses. The question had been whether these
testimonies were enough to turn the scale from guilty to innocent. Instead of asking themselves whether the new evidence
would have influenced a jury, the Court of Appeal judges had
used a new formula: instead of saying that no reasonable jury
could think that it made any difference, they said that they
themselves, the appeal judges, did not think that it made any
difference. Their decision had been upheld by the Lords, who
said that in future it would be optional for a court to follow the
old practice if it wanted to. In other words, the law had got into
a complete muddle.

Lord Devlin said that since then there had been two further
cases in the Court of Appeal in which the court had followed
Stafford and chosen to usurp the function of the jury and decide
for itself the effect of new evidence: the first was the Luton
post-office murder and the second was Guildford. Both these
cases had been presided over by Lord Roskill and yet, ironically,
Lord Roskill himself had earlier delivered an explanation of the
law before Stafford that clearly set out Lord Devlin's very point.

He had said that where fresh evidence was introduced it was
not the job of the Appeal Court to decide whether or not it was
true. The Appeal Court had merely to decide whether or not

the new evidence was capable of being believed by a jury. Once the court had decided that it was, any verdict reached without the benefit of that evidence must be in doubt until the truth or otherwise of the new facts had been established. And the only people who could judge those facts were members of a jury. Lord Roskill went on to say that where it was impracticable to have a retrial before a jury, particularly after a lapse of time, 'it is the plain duty of the court to quash the conviction, not because it is necessarily accepting the truth of what the new evidence has asserted, but because until that truth has been tested, any conviction reached in the absence of that testing is likely to be unsafe or unsatisfactory'.

The evidence of the Balcombe Street men obviously had to be examined with great care. It could have been a concoction by those who had nothing to lose in an attempt to exonerate their 'companions in arms'. The judges had not dismissed the entire testimony as 'incapable of belief'. What they didn't accept was the men's assertion that the Guildford Four had not been at Guildford and Woolwich as well. In Lord Devlin's view, the vital decision as to whether Dowd and the others were telling the truth was a decision that could be made only by a jury. The House of Lords had left the option open for future Courts of Appeal to refer such decisions to a jury, and this was a case where the judges patently should have done so.

'In my opinion,' wrote Lord Devlin, 'the refusal of a new trial violated three fundamental principles of British justice. First, it split the trial arbitrarily into two parts. Over what may be called the first half of the case the jury had deliberated for more than a day before rejecting the defence. Who can say that if the evidence in the first part had been fortified by the second, the jury would inevitably have rejected both?

'Second, it deprived the defendants as to 50 per cent of the trial of their constitutional right to a jury.

'Third, it deprived them of their right of appeal. An appeal requires a review. Judges cannot review their own findings of fact. If judges are going to substitute themselves for the jury at the trial, there must be a second lot of judges for the review.'

Interviewed by Yorkshire Television, Lord Devlin explained, 'Each of these three points constitutes a procedural flaw which should lead by itself to the quashing of the convictions. But it is the middle one — the central one — that is a violation of justice on any basis, however you look at it. I mean, whatever form of procedure, you cannot split a case in half. You can't make the defence deploy half of his witnesses before one tribunal and half of his witnesses before another.'

The new programme, 'A Case That Won't Go Away', was transmitted on March 3 1987 (*First Tuesday*, ITV). On March 4 the Home Secretary agreed to examine the Yvonne Fox evidence. In July, Cardinal Hume led a delegation to Douglas Hurd, which included Lord Devlin, Lord Scarman, two former Home Secretaries — Merlyn Rees and Roy Jenkins — and the author Robert Kee. As well as Yvonne Fox's evidence, they presented new statements from other witnesses who had not given evidence at the original trial, statements that lent weight to the alibis of Hill and Richardson for Guildford.

Eventually, on August 14 1987, Douglas Hurd ordered a police investigation into the new evidence. It would be carried out by Avon and Somerset Police under the leadership of Jim Sharples, Deputy Chief Constable, but its remit was vague. It was not until October 19, at a meeting with an all-party delegation of members of the Irish Parliament, that Hurd further defined its terms. He informed the delegation that the Maguire case would remain closed unless new scientific evidence were to be produced discrediting the forensic tests, but he assured the Irish politicians that he would now be examining 'the whole of the [Guildford] case'. Besides the testimony of Yvonne Fox, he now referred expressly to the reports of MacKeith and Gudjonsson on Carole Richardson and to the legal opinions of Lord Scarman and Lord Devlin.

The *Independent* reported Lord Scarman's reaction to the police inquiry as one of cautious welcome, 'But it is not all we are asking for,' Lord Scarman added. 'The Home Secretary is entitled to take a look at the material, but what we really want is a judicial review.' *The Times* commented that 'the legal opinion from two of the most distinguished Law Lords is the strongest argument yet raised that the 1975 convictions are unsafe or unsatisfactory'.

Before the Home Secretary's opinion of it became known, however, there were to be two set-backs. In January 1988, after a hearing lasting almost a month, the six men convicted of the Birmingham pub bombings once more had their case rejected by the Court of Appeal. The six applied for leave to appeal to the House of Lords, but on April 14 1988 three Law Lords (Lord Keith of Kinkel, Lord Oliver and Lord Griffiths) rejected their application. The point at issue was essentially Lord Devlin's: counsel for the six argued that the Court of Appeal had had no authority to retry the case; its function should have been merely to decide on the relevance and the admissibility of the evidence, leaving the determination of guilt or innocence to a jury. With the Law Lords' decision, the Birmingham case had reached the end of the road as far as the courts were concerned. The news had a crushing effect upon the six men.

The second set-back occurred two months later, on June 16, when an attempt was made to introduce into the Criminal Justice Bill a new clause that would create an independent review body to deal with possible miscarriages of justice. The new tribunal, not all of whose members would be lawyers, would have discretion as to the appropriate handling of each case and wide powers of investigation; it would report directly to the Home Secretary. The idea was no fanciful invention; it adopted one of the recommendations of an all-party select committee on Home Affairs which had reported in 1982 on miscarriages of justice. It reflected the committee's unanimous recognition that there were serious shortcomings both in the Appeal Court system and in the Home Office procedure for examining potential miscarriages — a view the committee had reached after hearing evidence from a number of eminent witnesses. It was no coincidence that the new clause was introduced by the

Conservative MP for Harborough, Sir John Farr, whose constituency took in Gartree Prison, where several of the Birmingham and Guildford men had spent years of their sentences. Much of the ensuing debate was given to discussion of the Birmingham and Guildford cases — 'the greatest contemporary alleged miscarriages of justice and therefore the obvious first candidates for review by an independent review tribunal', according to one contributor, Chris Mullin, now a Labour MP. The vote took place after midnight. Despite all-party support, the new clause was defeated.

41
DISCLOSURES

'I hope that you will find this letter... of some help to Miss
Richardson... '

Dr Kasimir Makos, August 25 1987

Fourteen years after the Guildford and Woolwich bombings,
new evidence and 'fresh opinions' are still coming to light: in
the case of Carole Richardson there have been three further
developments within the last 18 months alone.

In 1987, Maura Kelly, the alibi witness who had failed to
appear in court, came forward and made a fresh statement. In
it she repeated what she had said to Richardson's solicitors in
1975: that Lisa Astin and Carole had spent part of the afternoon
of October 5 1974 at the ABC bakery in England's Lane,
Hampstead, where Maura, who in 1974 was still a schoolgirl, had
a Saturday job. Lisa and Carole had arrived at about 2.30, she
said, had left again and had then returned later in the afternoon,
when they presented her with a little wooden doll, which she had
kept for many years. They had stayed with her until she closed
the shop in the late afternoon and had then departed after a
discussion at the bus stop together. She supplied no precise
time for this. Her testimony did not cover the crucial period of
the bombing, but it corroborated Lisa Astin's evidence that the
friends had been together in North London in the afternoon, and
undermined the claim in some of Armstrong's and Richardson's
confessions that they had spent time in a Guildford Wimpy Bar
waiting for the pubs to open.

Maura Kelly then went on to explain her absence from
court. She said that on February 27 1975, some time after she
had made her original alibi statement to the defence solicitors,

a male and a female officer from Guildford CID had turned up
at a friend's house in Camden Town where she was spending
the afternoon. Maura's mother and sister were in the car with
them. She alleges that the police first said they were searching
for drugs, and poured the contents of a packet of sugar on to
the kitchen work-surface in a perfunctory attempt to find what
they were looking for. Next they informed her that they had
come to question her about the Guildford bombings. Maura and
her mother and sister were driven to Hampstead police station,
where Maura and her mother were taken into an interview
room.

Maura's account of what followed differs from that of the
police. She says they opened by accusing her of sleeping with
Paddy Armstrong. Fifteen-year-old Maura, who had never slept
with anyone, found the charge acutely embarrassing, made, as it
was, in front of her mother. She alleges that the police told her
they could hold her under the Prevention of Terrorism Act for
72 hours.

'The goofy police officer started swearing at me when I kept
telling him that I was not sleeping with Patrick Armstrong and
that I had not been with him on 5 October. I began to get fed
up because they were quite clearly not prepared to believe me
in anything I had to say, and I said to them, "Well, if you want
to put words in my mouth I'll say whatever you like." I know I
was being cheeky. At that, the WPC got up from her chair and
with her open hand slapped me once across the face.'

According to Maura's statement, a row ensued, during which
her sister and a number of Hampstead police officers entered
the room. Maura says she was distraught and crying by this
time. She claims that arrests were threatened. It ended with
Mrs Kelly sweeping her two daughters out of the room and out
of the police station with the words, 'Come on, we're not taking
this.' The police let them go.

The incident may not have amounted to much, but Maura's
statement echoed allegations made by Lisa Astin, who had
also reported being slapped by a WPC when Surrey Police

interviewed her about the alibi. More important, perhaps, was the effect of the incident on Mrs Kelly, who dispatched her daughter to Ireland before the trial. 'I was terrified about appearing in court,' said Maura in 1987, 'and my mum didn't want me to have any more connection with it... A summons came for me to attend court, but I ignored it.'

Had she not been too frightened to appear, the young Maura Kelly would have testified to Richardson's whereabouts for the afternoon. At the other end of the alibi, Frank Johnson did testify for the evening, and has carried the burden ever since. The psychologist Barrie Irving was invited to follow up his original analysis of Armstrong's confessions by considering the position of Johnson and his decision to go to the police.

Early in 1987, in the aftermath of the Home Secretary's decision not to remit the case to the Court of Appeal, Irving interviewed Johnson and tested his evidence against four hypotheses. In the first, Irving assumed Johnson to be a member of or sympathizer with the IRA, closely associated with the bombings, who had attempted to manufacture an alibi for Richardson; in the second, he cast Johnson as an IRA member or sympathizer who had attempted to turn his (genuine) contact with her on October 5 into an alibi; in the third, he reviewed the possibility that the two were friends and the alibi was genuine but Johnson's failure to corroborate times or to survive as a credible witness had brought about the collapse of his evidence. The fourth hypothesis was that Johnson and Richardson had had a date on October 5 at a time that ruled out the possibility of her presence at the Guildford attacks. On volunteering his evidence to the police, Johnson had been systematically intimidated. During interrogation he had withdrawn his account and discredited himself as a witness. According to the fourth hypothesis, he had lived ever since with the trauma of having failed to convince the police and the courts of Richardson's innocence.

In line with the first two hypotheses, as an IRA member or sympathizer Johnson would have had to seek permission to concoct an alibi and the plan would have had to be watertight on corroboration and timing. His alibi had always been vague on time. Had he retracted the story under interrogation he would have been punished for it by the IRA, a consequence that would have been likely to preclude subsequent trips to Ireland. Irving noted that Johnson had continued to travel to Ireland. Despite Johnson's alleged admissions of IRA sympathy, the police never produced evidence to link him with the IRA. His drug use would not have endeared him to the IRA in any case. Irving attached importance to his discovery that the most important model of admiration and respect in Johnson's childhood had been his maternal grandfather, who had been a British soldier stationed at Guildford.

On the matter of timings, Irving observed that Johnson could not have constructed an alibi without knowing exactly what it would have to contain. Thus he would have had to know the timings, yet concern with precise time is largely absent from both his statements. If Johnson sought merely to throw Richardson a lifeline, Irving said he would have expected his subsequent statements on time — once he had learned what timings were actually required of him — to have firmed up in favour of the defence. Yet Johnson is as much in difficulty over the timings now as he was in 1975. His only markers have been linked to incidents: leaving home at twilight; drinking a drink in the Charlie Chaplin; walking to the Poly; and so on. Irving could find no answer to the questions, first, why, if Johnson wanted to push timings into the alibi, did he persist in looking for external corroboration of them rather than insisting on his own memory, and secondly, why, having failed to make the alibi stand up, did he stick so tenaciously to his interest in the case?

In the third hypothesis, 'Frank as the failed but genuine alibi witness', Irving commented on the general excellence of Johnson's memory and on his lack of suggestibility (this had been established independently by Gudjonsson). 'His intention to tell his alibi story, if it was not based on his involvement with the IRA, cannot have other than a moral motivation,' Irving noted.

'He certainly had nothing to gain from it. His dedication to the case has grown with his failure to affect it, again suggesting a moral rather than a practical motivation.'

As noted in the first two hypotheses, Johnson's statements do not contain the kind of information that manufactured statements would have had to provide if they were to have had a chance of success: on the contrary, Johnson has always been uncertain about important details. Moreover, he admitted to Irving that he had become so confused during his interrogation that the confusion lasted long after his release — for more than a year after the trial, he claimed. 'Even now,' Irving wrote, 'Frank reports that he has bouts of confusion during which his view of the case loses the relatively clear outline it has for him at other times.' These bouts of confusion, Irving observed, have been confined to the case; they do not affect other aspects of Johnson's life.

In Irving's view, as a witness Johnson never really had a chance:

The fact that he could identify roughly when events took place on the night in question was never going to have been sufficient for the purposes of this case. For the court to have made a reasonable judgement as to whether Frank's story created sufficient doubt to damage the standard of proof of the prosecution's case irredeemably would have required him to have been handled in his interviews with superlative tact and understanding. He would have had to have been questioned using techniques which psychologists were only just defining as necessary at the time, and were certainly unknown to CID officers. Verbatim records would have had to have been made at every stage. However, the best record available is Frank's own notes made for the solicitor in Newcastle. These were discounted as evidence on the grounds that they were attempts to construct an alibi. They should on the contrary have been treated as contemporaneous notes of Frank's evidence uncontaminated by the effects of police questioning. In fact the process of trying to acquire information from Frank produced an undeniable level of confusion in him which prima facie rendered his evidence as a witness worthless. It can be argued that this is evidence of dangerous mishandling of a witness and prejudicing of the resulting testimony only if it is first accepted that Frank's account is substantially true but lacking in important detail. Had the police treated Frank as a genuine witness for long enough to obtain a full and complete account from him under the best possible circumstances, and had they then treated him as a hostile suspect, the courts could have decided on which account they wished to operate. Unfortunately, the decision to treat Frank as a hostile suspect intervened in the process of his witnessing and destroyed his credibility even though the view of him as a suspect could not in the end be sustained by the police. This is a vital procedural point... : witnesses must not be treated by the police in a manner which will ultimately destroy their value to the courts, otherwise the police are usurping the authority of the courts by corrupting one of the most important resources available — i.e. the witness. Frank's witnessing was a failure, but whether it would have been had he been properly handled is another matter.

But was Johnson's confusion and his collapse as a credible witness the consequence of more than a mere mishandling of the interview? Irving's fourth hypothesis raises the possibility that he might have been systematically intimidated in police custody after the manner described at length in Irving's research for the Royal Commission on Criminal Procedure:

Frank's detailed account alleges a brainwashing approach by a team of officers, using repeated statements running counter to Frank's evidence reinforced by physical violence, threats of violence, threats against his freedom and security and against the well-being of his crippled mother. Were this to be an accurate account, the officers in the case would clearly be liable to long terms of imprisonment. The experience left Frank with moderately severe paranoia, an anxiety state involving cognitive, emotional and gastric symptoms. His experience is parallel to that reported by the US airmen court-martialled after the Korean war for allegedly betraying their country as POWs. Investigation of these cases led US psychiatrists to coin the term 'brainwashing'.

However, it is also the case that Frank's investment in trying to help Richardson, and his failure, could have brought on an attack of paranoia which is responsible for his allegations. A third alternative is that Frank was suffering from an abnormality of mind before the case and his experience since then has exacerbated that problem.

Taking the last argument first, there is no evidence whatever of mental illness in Frank's previous life. He suffered no bad trips on acid, and handled the first part of his interrogation without adverse effects. Neither did Frank suffer from the total experience. His problems after interrogation are highly selective. He was anxious about the case, not about things in general... He has not been adjudged as suffering from mental illness by any professional who has seen him. It is unlikely that serious symptoms such as paranoia would not have been noted before the case.

The explanation that Frank's failure as a witness has caused a subsequent mental breakdown with paranoid delusions about his treatment and interrogation is more plausible. Frank's relationship with his mother suggests a protective, nurturing attitude to women. His failure to help Richardson may have precipitated a crisis really relating to his feelings about his mother. There would then have been an unbearable need to explain failure with subsequent allegations against the police and continued obsessional involvement with the case.

However, this plausible clinical construction does not fit well with the evidence about Frank's life since the case. There have been no marked breakdowns. Frank's relations with his mother remain on an even keel. Frank can discuss his anxieties and confusions and account for that part of them that he believes is rational and the overlaying irrational part which he sees as reaction to his experience. Most telling of all, he has felt better since he has had the opportunity to talk about the case and since the possibility of a retrial or review has increased. This improvement in his mental health would not have happened had the cause of his paranoia and anxiety been some complicated projection of previously existing emotional problems on to his case. We are left therefore with the explanation that his paranoia and anxiety after the trial and his obvious obsession now derive from the things that were done to Frank in custody. Interestingly, Frank is not bitter about his alleged treatment. He has been too anxious about the threats he received in custody and the back-up visits from the police he alleges have occurred since to make any formal complaint.

He is rational and impressively analytic about his plight and the plight of Richardson because of his experience. However, even if the prosecution case breaks on corroboration of Frank's story or even on any other ground, only a confession from one of his interrogators can substantiate Frank's allegations of intimidation...

The third development in Carole Richardson's case struck at the heart of it: the confessions themselves. As part of his continuing investigations, Dr James MacKeith made contact with the police surgeon of whom he had been critical in his original report — Kasimir Makos, who had heard Carole Richardson's first admissions in police custody. The doctor, now retired, had sold his house in Weybridge, Surrey and moved to Belgium, but he responded promptly to MacKeith's letter of introduction, claiming clear recollections of his interview with Carole Richardson. Makos had recently been seen by Avon and Somerset Police as part of the 1987/88 police inquiry into the Guildford bombings, and on discussing this with him — and having conducted his own interview — MacKeith was to write: 'I think it would be interesting to discover what was disclosed by Dr Makos to police when they interviewed him. Unfortunately, the critical significance of the episode from the psychiatric and psychological viewpoint may not have been recognized by the interviewing police officers.' He inferred that the questioning had followed a different line from his own.

The two doctors later met, but the substance of what Makos had to say was contained in his first letter of reply to MacKeith. It threw new light on the events at Addlestone police station on December 4 1974.

Makos had entered the cell at 8.50 in the evening to find Richardson in a state of great agitation, her hair and clothes in disorder, crying and almost throwing herself about. He said she told him she was a drug addict and he formed the opinion that much of her distress was caused by the fact that she had been deprived of drugs since entering police custody. (In his original police statement, it will be remembered, he recorded without comment her claim to be 'addicted' to LSD.)

His letter to MacKeith then makes a startling disclosure, '*In order to calm her and to relieve her mental and physical distress,*' he wrote, '*I administered 50 mgm of Pethidine by intramuscular injection, to which she had agreed.*'[1] This was a revelation. There had never been any record of a Pethidine injection. It was not in Makos's police statement; Richardson's solicitors had never heard of it; and, crucially, it had not emerged in court.

The Pethidine appeared to have a decisive effect. 'Gradually she calmed down,' wrote Makos. 'Her agitation subsided, she ceased crying and after a cigarette smoke she appeared completely calm, composed and very reasonable. It was then she volunteered to confess to me about the bombing incident... '

He began by describing her confession as 'clear, lucid and convincing... She was quite serious about her story but I did

[1] Authors' italics.

not think that at the time she fully appreciated the gravity of
the whole situation.' But his amplification of this line of thought
throws doubt on just how clear and convincing he had really
found it: 'I was, listening to her story, under the impression that
she treated the whole affair [as a] slight prank!... There was
something weird in her confession and I was almost convinced
that she did not realize the meaning of the tragedy nor was she
aware of it.' He returned to the subject later. 'I am still wondering what made her to confess to me at all about this terrible
attack. Was it my sympathetic approach to her in the cell? Was
it the relief she experienced after the Pethidine injection, which
appeared to suit her very well? Or was it just her total confusion
of a drug addict?'

He volunteered the information that 'When I was asked to
see Miss Richardson... the police did not ask me nor suggested
to me that I should obtain any incriminating information in
connection with the bombing of the pub.' Questioned further
by MacKeith, Makos said he had been uncertain how to treat
her confession and whether to report it. He had never before
encountered a prisoner in police custody who had admitted an
offence to him. '*Had it not been for the presence of the
WPC,*' Makos wrote, '*... I probably would not mention
the confession to police in my report.*' When they met,
he gave MacKeith two reasons for this: 'One, that *I wasn't
quite convinced that she was telling something which
had the real meaning*', and the other, '*because I thought
she was playing sort of pranks on everybody.*'[1] His letter
to MacKeith concluded, 'Her confession was so weird that I
was convinced she was playing a brave, juvenile, irresponsible
[game].'

MacKeith found the new information of great significance in
the reconstruction of Richardson's physical and mental state at
the time of her confessions. The critical importance of her disclosures to Dr Makos was not merely that they had been directly

1 Authors' italics.

used at her trial but that they had become the focus of questioning the next day when the police returned to interrogate her. In his report to Alastair Logan, dated June 15 1988, MacKeith wrote, 'Miss Richardson had to contend with the fact that she had made a disclosure within the hearing of a police officer, to a visiting police surgeon. By her account, it was the fact of that disclosure which led, she said, to making more substantial and self-incriminating statements to police the next day.' He added that anybody — and particularly someone suggestible like Carole Richardson — might have found it difficult to explain that the admissions had flowed from an apparently illogical desire to ingratiate herself with a kindly visiting doctor.

Richardson herself has no recollection of receiving any injection — let alone of a potent narcotic like Pethidine — which must raise further questions about her state of mind at the time she was given it. The purpose of Pethidine in this context is as a relaxant. Though it is less strong, its effects are similar to those of morphine, but there is discussion in medical literature of noted side-effects when it is taken in conjunction with amphetamines (such as the speed from which Richardson was withdrawing at the time). It is curious that although Dr Makos's police report records the 200-mg Tuinal capsule he gave her at the end of the interview, neither he nor the WPC made any mention of the Pethidine. According to Dr MacKeith: *'An intravenous injection of Pethidine would certainly have so influenced her mental state, her perceptions, her judgement and her self-control that her disclosures would certainly be regarded as unreliable testimony.'*[1]

MacKeith's concern was that the officers of Avon and Somerset Police might not recognize the full implications for the confessions she had subsequently made: 'If the Home Office instigates further inquiries, I think they would be well advised to ensure that the interview of Dr Makos is informed by questions formulated by a person familiar with the content of our reports,

1 Authors' italics.

and with the way in which her admissions to Dr Makos appear to have had a significant influence on reducing her resistance to making further and more extensive admissions to police the next day and in subsequent interviews.'

On remand at Brixton Prison, Carole Richardson had written to Paddy Armstrong, 'BRITISH JUSTICE... doesn't come into it until the trial.' But in reality it had begun for her earlier than that; at night in a police cell in suburban Surrey the previous December. Here was a 17-year-old girl, alone, suffering the after-effects of a cocktail of drugs and a five-hour interview with three police officers. She was hysterical. A doctor was called. He examined her in the presence of a WPC, diagnosed drug withdrawal and gave her an injection of a further strong drug to make her feel better. Under its influence she told him things that put him in a difficult position. Given her mental state, he might not have taken much notice but for the presence of the 19-year-old policewoman in the cell. Both of them made — conflicting — reports of what Carole Richardson had said, but neither found it necessary to mention the injection. Armed with the doctor's statement, the police resumed their interrogation the next day.

At the trial, the circumstances of this first crucial confession were scarcely touched on. Neither of its witnesses appeared in court. The doctor's statement was read out by a junior barrister, but Mr Justice Donaldson ignored it until prompted by Sir Michael Havers, leading counsel for the Crown, who clearly found it significant. It certainly must have played an influential part in undermining the credibility of Carole Richardson's defence: it was a statement freely given to an independent doctor at a time when she did not appear to be under pressure to make one. Moreover, the defence offered no rebuttal of it. For all its peculiarities, the doctor's evidence was entered unchallenged. At the trial, the Pethidine injection never came to light.

Sir Michael Havers remarked 13 years ago that 'the whole truth' about this case 'will never be known'. That in the summer of 1988 it should suddenly materialize that Carole Richardson's confessions were preceded by a powerful injection of drugs, officially administered, and that such a fact should have been buried for 14 years, makes this a difficult case to close. Indeed, it is hard to understand how any case against Carole Richardson can be maintained at all.

42
A CASE THAT
WON'T GO AWAY

'It always needs immense courage to say, "I'm wrong," and
all possible ways of reopening the case have to be examined
very closely. And I like to think that the anxiety which is
in many people's minds, that they will go on expressing it,
because when there's been a miscarriage of justice, those
cases don't go away.'

Cardinal Basil Hume, *First Tuesday*, ITV, March 3 1987

This book is without an ending. The history of the Guildford
Four and the Maguire household cannot be concluded until
their names have been cleared. The latest new evidence on
Carole Richardson alone raises further profound doubts about
the safety of her conviction. It joins a catalogue of shortcomings
in the Crown case against her and the others — and it is
important to stress all four in the context of the summary
of Carole Richardson's case that follows, for while the injustice
against her can be easily summarized it is no less compelling in
the cases of her co-defendants.

Officially, there is no lurking doubt that she and the others
are guilty. She was found guilty by a jury — but not on forensic
evidence because there was none. Nor was there fingerprint
evidence, exhibit evidence or identification evidence. No witness
picked her out on an identity parade, despite the fact that plenty
of people who had seen and described the 'courting couple'
were given the opportunity of doing so. No one subsequently
identified her in court. There was no evidence to connect her
with the IRA or even with Irish Republicanism.

She had an alibi which she could not at first remember but

which was confirmed by a prosecution witness. Its demolition in court as a concoction involved the hypothesis of a high-speed journey that her solicitor and barrister have always insisted would have been impossible and an alleged suppression of witnesses denounced by her QC as 'dirty tricks'. She has two alibi witnesses who have not retreated from their accounts in 14 years, even though it would have been far easier for them to leave the scarring affair behind.

The only evidence against her remains her own uncorroborated confessions. In Scotland they would not have been deemed admissible; the case against her and her co-defendants would never have reached court. Her confessions were made in conditions that today would rule them invalid on account of her youth and her undergoing a withdrawal from drugs. They were riddled with inconsistencies to the point where the prosecution had to repudiate her claim to have taken part in a second bombing in order for its case against her to survive.

After 12 years during which Richardson continued unswervingly to protest her innocence, the Home Office commissioned tests by a senior psychiatrist whose expertise is recognized by the courts to the extent that acquittals have been obtained in confession cases on the basis of his evidence. He concluded that her confessions were unsafe and not to be relied upon. His report was read by the Home Secretary and passed over without being referred to in the 27-page document on the case that he laid before both Houses of Parliament in 1987.

When four highly experienced Provisional IRA men admitted responsibility for the bombings, to the police and in open court, they were never charged. Crown evidence charting forensic links between the acknowledged activities of these men and the Guildford and Woolwich bombings was removed from the record at the joint behest of the Bomb Squad and the office of the Director of Public Prosecutions. The admissions of the London Active Service Unit were of such quality that they successively convinced a former Superintendent of the Metropolitan Police, the QC for the Crown and three Appeal Court judges of the

men's likely involvement in Guildford and Woolwich. Yet the
same judges rejected them as an IRA plot because of minor
discrepancies in one man's recollections, in spite of the fact that
he had satisfied the prosecution that he was privy to unique,
hitherto unpublished detail about the crimes, detail that had lain
buried in police files.

No jury has ever heard the evidence of those four men
alongside the tattered accounts of Carole Richardson and her
co-defendants. Two Law Lords believe the Appeal Court judges
got their law so wrong that there are three separate grounds for
quashing the convictions. The Home Secretary and the Northern Ireland Secretary of 1974 — the very men who promoted
stringent anti-terrorist measures — have added their concern
to that of a catalogue of names which begins with the Cardinal
Archbishop of Westminster and embraces more than 200 British
MPs; European parliamentarians; American senators; eminent
psychiatrists, psychologists and lawyers; prison officials; senior
intelligence and police sources (none of whom has yet had the
courage publicly to admit concern); and a growing number of
citizens on both sides of the Irish Sea.

If this book serves to confirm Lord Devlin's belief that
there are grounds for concern 'as high as Everest' or, to
put the matter at its lowest, that there is a justifiable lurking
doubt, there must be corrective action. No reputation, either
of an individual or of a national system of justice, can condone
wrongful imprisonment. It has been observed that the Establishment has accumulated a considerable stake in the case; that Sir
Michael Havers rose to become Lord Chancellor; that Sir John
Donaldson is now Master of the Rolls; and that Sir Peter Imbert
is now Commissioner of the Metropolitan Police. All this is — or
should be — irrelevant. So, too, should be the continuing threat
of the IRA, for to trim standards of English justice in the face of
terrorism is self-defeating. Nor should the unpredictable shifts
in Anglo-Irish relations become part of any consideration. While
it is understandable that the Irish Government and judiciary
should be reluctant to hand over wanted suspects to English

justice in the light of this and other cases, no one should expect the British Government to deal in an expedient trade-off.

Sadly it is British justice that is the final hurdle. It has been apparent for years that our system of examining potential miscarriages of justice requires drastic upheaval. It begins with a Home Office that has never, in the memory of Sir David Napley, past president of the Law Society, 'as a result of its own investigations, felt able to recommend a pardon'. It ends with the judicial attitudes embodied by Lord Donaldson and Lord Lawton, who in 1988 have both stated, in effect, that it is more important to worry about guilty defendants going free than innocent ones being sent to prison.

Between these two fixed points it is possible to advocate measures of reform: the improvement of safeguards during the interrogation process; the abolition — called for by Ludovic Kennedy — of the adversarial system of trying a case, in favour of a more objective search for truth; the recognition of the developing science of psychology in relation to false confessions; and the establishment of a tribunal of last resort with the resources to investigate difficult cases and prise them away from the secrecy and reluctance of the Home Office review system. The Law Lords should take the earliest opportunity to restore the law to where it stood for decades, and not allow the Court of Appeal to set itself up as a judge of fact, thereby splitting cases in half and denying appellants the chance to have new evidence heard by a jury. This could easily be done and would sit squarely with the tradition of English criminal law. There is an interesting body of new evidence waiting to be heard in the Guildford case, but there was nothing in the recent Birmingham Six appeal to suggest that the Appeal Court has grown more willing in the intervening years to disturb verdicts. Nevertheless, the Home Secretary enjoys a right to remit the case to the court at any time 'if he thinks fit' — whether or not there is new evidence, whether or not there is 'a consideration of substance' and whether or not the consideration of substance is new.

The case of the Guildford Four has generated concern that will not be mollified by another rebuff from the Court of Appeal or by incomplete Home Office reviews or by unpublished and arbitrary police inquiries. The case should be examined by an independent tribunal with a remit to investigate it in its entirety and hear witnesses old and new. If, at the end of the process, there is a lurking doubt surrounding the guilt of the Guildford Four, the Home Secretary should free them immediately. There is precedent (as in the Confait case, for example) for establishing such a tribunal and there is precedent for the Home Secretary's freeing prisoners without one. The Home Secretary has the option of granting a free pardon — however obnoxious the concept might be to someone who has done nothing to be pardoned. The first step is a matter of political will.

In the meantime, the lives of the four are ticking away. On February 12 1988, Paul Hill, then 33, married a 31-year-old American, Marian Serravalli. They had started corresponding three years previously when she wrote to break the news to him of a friend's death, and after a year she had visited him for the first time in Wormwood Scrubs. The ceremony took place at 9.30 a.m. at Long Lartin Prison, Worcestershire. The small gathering of guests — numbers were limited by Home Office dictum to 15 — was swelled by Special Branch men and prison officers who lined the back of the chapel. The bride had brought her white wedding dress with her from New Jersey. The groom, his dark hair still worn long and swept back from his gaunt face, stood beside her and they exchanged rings.

After the service and the wedding photos, the couple cut the cake. Proceedings were brisk, since Hill had to be back in his cell by 11.45. Bride and family were ushered from the prison to be met by waiting newsmen, most of them from the tabloid press: the *Sun* had announced the event with a front-page headline, 'IRA Pig to Marry'. In the afternoon the wedding reception was allowed to reconvene for a couple of hours. There was neither alcohol nor music, but there were plenty of impassioned speeches. Afterwards bride and groom went their separate ways, their marriage unconsummated.

Hill has been a rebellious prisoner. He has spent an estimated total of almost four years in solitary confinement and has been moved from prison to prison 47 times. (One such move interrupted the wedding plans and set the ceremony back three months.) His weight loss and poor health continue to cause his family serious concern.

Armstrong's medical condition is equally disturbing. At 37 he is unrecognizable as the plump lad with whom Carole Richardson fell in love; his cropped hair has darkened to mid-brown and he is lean and nervous, calmed by anti-depressants. For several years Armstrong was content to work in the gardens at Gartree Prison, where he has long been resident, but this privilege was abruptly terminated on December 10 1987 when a routine prison afternoon was interrupted by the arrival of a helicopter on the sports field. Paddy watched open-mouthed from the potting-shed as one of the most flamboyant escapes in British prison history unfolded before his eyes. In the security-conscious aftermath, however, 'high-risk' category A prisoners like Armstrong were forbidden to work in the gardens. He had to take his turn in the workshop making flip-flops. The change did not suit him. One day in summer 1988 he asked his workshop supervisor to remove him from work since he, Armstrong, sensed that he was about to have a breakdown. His prognosis was correct.

He has not seen his youngest sister since his arrest; she was 14 then; she is now getting on for 30. His mother, Eileen, can afford to make the journey from her condemned flat in the Divis in Belfast once a year if she is lucky. On discovering from television coverage of the case that her son had been taking drugs in 1974, she gave him a clip round the ear in genuine anger.

Armstrong is now a quietly-spoken, thoughtful man who can appreciate the irony of spending his days in Gartree alongside Joseph O'Connell, who was responsible for the bombing of Guildford, and Ronnie McCartney, who has always claimed to be

one of the 'Belfast fellows' alluded to in the 'Dear Joe' letter —
an identity ascribed by the appeal judges to Armstrong himself.
He thinks politically — after his experiences it would be surprising if he did not — yet describes himself as an 'ageing hippy':
Pink Floyd are still his favourite band. He watched the Nelson
Mandela 70th birthday concert on television with delight in June
1988, but with an itch to tell the crowd, 'We're here, too.'

From the day of his conviction it seems that Gerry Conlon
has never stopped fighting. In 1987 he gatecrashed a BBC Radio
team who were making an education programme in Long Lartin
Prison and insisted on proclaiming his innocence. Despite suffering a desperate sense of guilt over his father, he, of the four, has
probably survived prison the best. In 1988, at 34 years old, he
has changed little in physical appearance. He looks healthy and
seems to live on his resilience and his sense of humour. It is still
just possible to recognize the young man whose idea of a good
time used to be to tuck a bottle of vodka under his arm and
prance up the Falls Road doing Rod Stewart imitations with his
mates in the Comanche gang. But to Conlon all that is a long
way away. He claims 800 days in solitary confinement — half as
many as Hill — many of them spent there voluntarily in protest
against prison rulings. He is tolerated by Republican prisoners
but mistrusted — an attitude that dates from 1975 when he
attempted to trade names in return for hoped-for concessions
in the treatment of his father. The names amounted to little,
but the principle still holds. As far as his own case is concerned,
Conlon's outrage at what has happened to him and the others
is undimmed. He is a determined and articulate writer of
letters to campaigners, newspapers and politicians — even to
Mikhail Gorbachov, to whom he offered counter-arguments in
the human-rights debate during the 1988 Moscow summit.

Back home in West Belfast, his mother, Sarah, burns a candle
night and day beside the photographs of her son and her late
husband, Guiseppe. The lives of many of those sentenced in the
Maguire case have been miserably and permanently shattered.
Sarah Conlon would like to retire from her job at the hospital,

but the expense of visiting Gerry in England is prohibitive; she feels she must keep working.

As category A prisoners, Hill, Armstrong and Conlon live a rarefied existence in which their contact with the outside world is even more tenuous than that of other inmates. Their outgoing letters are rationed. They may be visited only in the presence of prison officers, segregated from other prisoners, so they never see a crowd of people from 'outside'. It has been that way for 14 years.

For Carole Richardson, 'recategorized' to B status in 1985, this is not the case. She works in the gardens at Styal Prison, and receives visits alongside the other women in a large, echoing gymnasium. In 1988 she was 31, but there are few changes in her appearance. Her auburn hair is still worn much as it was back home in Kilburn, and she has at last recovered from her allergic reaction to sunlight — legacy of her years in Durham's gloomy 'H' Wing — the treatment for which turned her skin yellow. Her spirit is strong, but it is vulnerable. She veers between irreverent good humour and bleak depression; in the latter frame of mind she recently abandoned an Open University course in child psychology. Unlike the three men, who have retained clear memories of their experiences in 1974 and 1975, Carole Richardson has dealt with hers by blotting many of them out; recollection distresses her.

Her thoughts are for the future — for the children she longs to have and the animals she wants to work with. Her existence was enlivened in 1988 by the arrival at Styal of two goats, six chickens and a kitten. She has retained an ambition to live in the country and work with horses, but the only times she has left prison in recent years have been to make two visits under conditions of high security to Armstrong at Gartree. The one enduring image from the journeys is that of a herd of cows crossing a motorway bridge. The future for Carole and Paddy is unknown. Armstrong speaks vaguely of settling in Austria. Hill looks forward to life in the United States where, thanks to his wife's contacts, he has offers of work. Conlon dreams of travelling the world. But for the moment none of them is going anywhere.

Carole Richardson has been told not to bother applying for parole for at least another six years. Gerry Conlon has a minimum of 16 years still to serve. Paddy Armstrong has a minimum of 21 years still to serve. And Paul Hill faces the rest of his life in prison, unless sickness or extreme old age should intervene. In the light of what is known about their case, such prospects defy contemplation. They are rotting, and with every day that passes English justice is rotting with them.

SELECT BIBLIOGRAPHY

Bishop, Patrick and Mallie, Eamonn, *The Provisional IRA*, Heinemann, 1987.

Coggan, Geoff and Walker, Martin, *Frightened for my Life: An Account of Deaths in British Prisons*, Fontana, 1982.

Coogan, Tim Pat, *The IRA*, Fontana, revised edition 1987.

Flackes, W.D., *Northern Ireland: A Political Directory, 1968-1983*, Ariel, 1987.

Gillespie, Anne and Evelyn, *Sisters in Cells*, Foilseachain Naisiunta Teoranta, 1987.

Haward, Lionel, *Forensic Psychology*, Batsford, 1981.

Huntley, Bob, *Bomb Squad: My War Against the Terrorists*, W. H. Allen, 1977.

Irving, Barrie, *Royal Commission on Criminal Procedure*, CMND 8092, Research Study Numbers 1 & 2, HMSO, 1980.

Kee, Robert, *Trial and Error: The Maguires, the Guildford Pub Bombings and British Justice*, Hamish Hamilton, 1986.

Kelley, Kevin, *The Longest War: Northern Ireland and the IRA*, Zed Books, 1982.

MacLaughlin, Raymond, *Inside an English Jail*, Borderline Publications, 1987.

Mullin, Chris, *Error of Judgement: The Birmingham Bombings*, Chatto & Windus, 1986/Poolbeg Press, 1987.

Stevenson, Prue and Padel, Una, *Insiders: Women's Experience of Prison*, Virago, 1988.

Woffinden, Bob, *Miscarriages of Justice*, Hodder & Stoughton, 1987.

INDEX